LEAVE
NO
ONE
BEHIND

LEAVE NO ONE BEHIND

Time for SPECIFICS *on the* SUSTAINABLE DEVELOPMENT GOALS

Homi Kharas, John W. McArthur, and Izumi Ohno
Editors

BROOKINGS INSTITUTION PRESS
Washington, D.C.

The Brookings Institution is a private nonprofit organization devoted to research, education,
and publication on important issues of domestic and foreign policy. Its principal purpose
is to bring the highest quality independent research and analysis to bear on current and
emerging policy problems. Interpretations or conclusions in Brookings publications
should be understood to be solely those of the authors.

Library of Congress Cataloging-in-Publication data are available.
Library of Congress Control Number: 2019948350
ISBN 978-0-8157-3783-4 (pbk : alk. paper)
ISBN 978-0-8157-3784-1 (ebook)

9 8 7 6 5 4 3 2 1

Typeset in Adobe Garamond Pro

Contents

ON POLITICS

Acknowledgments

This volume is the outcome of a collaborative project between the Brookings Institution and the Japan International Cooperation Agency Research Institute (JICA-RI).

The editors would like to thank the following individuals for their contributions to the authors' workshop: Tamar Manuelyan Atinc, Emily Bove, Mayra Buvinic, David Coady, Shanta Devarajan, Judd Devermont, Tarek Ghani, Margaret Grosh, George Ingram, Paul Isenman, Elizabeth King, Ju-Ho Lee, Robin Lewis, Abdul Malik, Bradley Parks, and Sonia Plaza.

The editors would also like to thank Jennifer Cohen, our outstanding manager of the overall book project, and Cecilia González from the Brookings Institution Press, for providing invaluable editorial support.

Brookings is grateful to JICA-RI for its financial and intellectual support of this project. Brookings recognizes that the value it provides is in its absolute commitment to quality, independence, and impact. Activities supported by its donors reflect this commitment, and the analysis and recommendations contained in this volume are not determined or influenced by any donation. The chapters reflect the views of the authors and not the official position of any specific organization.

LEAVE
NO
ONE
BEHIND

CHAPTER ONE

Getting Specific to Leave No One Behind on Sustainable Development

Homi Kharas, John W. McArthur, and Izumi Ohno

A Compelling Vision

A world free of extreme poverty. Societies that work for everyone. These are the aspirations embedded in the Sustainable Development Goals (SDGs) and the commitment to leave no one behind by 2030. The ambition was formalized in the joint agreement by all 193 United Nations (UN) member states, in September 2015, to pursue the SDGs. In paragraph 4 of the SDG Summit declaration, world leaders agreed:

> As we embark on this great collective journey, we pledge that no one will be left behind. Recognizing that the dignity of the human person is fundamental, we wish to see the Goals and targets met for all nations and peoples and for all segments of society. And we will endeavour to reach the furthest behind first.

In a later part of the same declaration, under Goal 10 for reduced inequalities, world leaders further crystallized their commitment to inclusive societies. In target SDG 10.2, all countries made the pledge to "By 2030, empower and promote the social, economic, and political inclusion of all, irrespective of age,

We would like to thank Lorenz Noe for the empirical updates presented in this chapter.

sex, disability, race, ethnicity, origin, religion, or economic or other status." There is no ambiguity to the promise of sustainable development for all people.

Since 2015, the spirit of "leave no one behind" (LNOB) has garnered increasing traction across a growing number of constituencies. It might not be surprising that UN agencies have prominently adopted the LNOB slogan (e.g., UNDP 2018), but the concept has also started to take hold more broadly. Among national governments, sixteen described detailed LNOB efforts in their SDG voluntary national reviews presented at the UN in 2018.[1] Prominent G-7 economies, such as Canada, Japan, and the United Kingdom, have made their own specific public commitments to leaving no one behind.[2] Leading intergovernmental and nongovernmental organizations outside the UN have also published major LNOB reports (e.g., OECD 2018; Samman and others, 2018) and respective alliances of civil society organizations launched both the Leave No One Behind Partnership in 2016 and the Leave No One Behind Project in 2017. At a more technical level, the Leave No One Behind Data Collaborative focuses on promoting citizen-generated data and an "inclusive data charter." Monash University in Melbourne, Australia, even has its own SDG-focused Leave No One Behind program in partnership with Grameen Australia, teaching social business and entrepreneurship.

Nonetheless, despite the growing resonance around the LNOB phrasing, it is not yet clear the world is implementing relevant policies with corresponding seriousness. For example, estimated numbers of chronically undernourished people have been rising for four years in a row, as of 2018.[3] Aggregate official development assistance to the least developed countries has been declining.[4] Meanwhile, challenges of absolute deprivation and exclusion persist in high-income countries too.[5] And even though the rise of anti-elite political movements in many countries has heightened policy interest in ensuring all societies work for everyone, there are still too few signs of decisive gains in addressing the concerns of people feeling marginalized or left behind.

This edited volume represents an effort to treat LNOB as a serious commitment, with a special emphasis on problems of absolute deprivation and basic needs. Ultimately, LNOB requires clarity on the task at hand—a commitment to supporting specific *people* facing specific *problems* in specific *places*. In this chapter, we provide an overview of the empirical nature of the challenge. We

1. Kindornay (2019).

2. Government of Canada (2018), Government of Japan (2016), UK Department for International Development (2019).

3. FAO and others (2019).

4. OECD (2019)

5. See, for example, figure 11 on OECD country performance in Kharas and others (2018).

then describe key insights generated by each chapter in focusing on many of the specific people, problems, and places that will define whether the world continues to leave large numbers of people behind in 2030.

The Empirical Nature of the Challenge

There is no single answer to the question of "how is the world doing on the SDGs?" The world shows too much variation across too many issues, indicators, and geographies for there to be any simplistic diagnosis of current status. Instead, any effort to leave no one behind needs to begin with an assessment of which people are facing which problems in which places. At a minimum, the scale and geographic distribution of each problem need to be considered.

To that end, a 2018 analysis by Kharas, McArthur, and Rasmussen considers country-level trend assessment of two dozen people-focused SDG indicators with adequate data for analysis. The study estimates the number of people slated to be left behind in each country on relevant SDG targets out to 2030. Here we draw from the same methods to present a summary assessment, in some cases drawing from more recent updates to underlying data sources, including the World Poverty Clock.[6,7] To stress, our emphasis on people-focused economic and social indicators is only meant to drill down on the human dimensions of the LNOB challenge. It is not meant to detract in any way from other important SDG priorities focused on the environment or large-scale issues measured in terms of countries or international aggregates.

In this chapter, we follow the approach first laid out in McArthur and Rasmussen (2018) by distinguishing between two general categories of being left behind. The starkest form is premature death itself, so we group some indicators under a "life and death" category. The second form entails various forms of basic human needs—ranging from income to education to nutrition to equal access to opportunity across genders—that are essential for active and dignity-driven participation in society.

---

6. World Data Lab (2019).

7. Compared to the original results in Kharas, McArthur, and Rasmussen (2018), source data have been updated using more recent data releases from GBD (2017) for violence against women, stunting, wasting, children overweight, and family planning, and from World Bank (2019) for child mortality, primary school completion, pre-primary enrollment, undernourishment, tuberculosis infections, and air pollution. For HIV infections, we also now use World Bank (2019). We exclude indicators for Hepatitis B and malaria infections from this analysis because of substantial revisions to underlying historical country time-series data sources, which prompts uncertainty regarding the robustness of the underlying data estimates.

Life and Death Indicators

Figure 1-1 shows how the world is doing on a cross-section of life-and-death SDG targets, if current trends continue out to the deadline, generally 2030.[8] A complete horizontal bar represents, at the 100 percent level, complete SDG success, meaning the full number of lives saved if all countries register the required rate of progress to meet the relevant target. The lighter shaded portion on the left side of the horizontal bar reflects the share of the target the world is currently on course to achieve. In the top bar, for example, the world is on course to save nearly two-thirds (65 percent) of the relevant number of lives for under-five child mortality. The second bar shows that maternal mortality is only on track to achieve slightly more than one-third (37 percent) of the agreed outcome. On both issues, the world is carrying forward targets that update global ambitions since those included under the predecessor Millennium Development Goals.

The remaining indicators of figure 1-1 are all part of the SDGs' distinctive contributions to the international policy agenda. Target 3.4, for example, aims to reduce premature noncommunicable disease mortality rates by one-third compared to 2015. The world is currently on track to save only 30 percent of the lives required to meet that objective. Recent prospects are even worse for cutting suicide, another part of target 3.4, by the same amount. For traffic deaths, SDG target 3.6 aims at a 50 percent global reduction by 2020. When this objective is applied at the country level, figure 1-1 shows just how little progress the world has so far been on course to make.

Each SDG target embedded in figure 1-1 represents a different type of issue faced by a different range of people. In that regard, figure 1-2 shows the cumulative number of lives at stake on each of the same indicators, from 2019 through to 2030 or corresponding deadline year. "Lives at stake" is defined as the cumulative difference, in each country, between the number of people who will, under current trends, die by 2030, and the number of people who will die if each country achieves the relevant SDG target. When added up, the figure shows that approximately 44 million lives are at stake overall. Nearly two-thirds of these lives—more than 29 million—are estimated as premature deaths due to noncommunicable diseases. The second largest number of lives, at more than 9 million, is composed of children under five. Challenges of suicide, homicide, maternal mortality, and traffic deaths each account for between 1 and 2 million lives at stake.

---

8. In some instances, SDG targets have an earlier deadline, such as the target 3.6 to cut traffic deaths by half by 2020.

Figure 1-1. World Performance on SDG Life-and-Death Targets under Current Trend Out to 2030

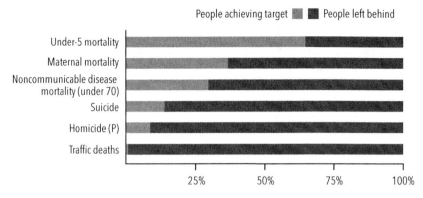

Notes: (P) indicates proxy target used as 50 percent reduction for homicide. Traffic deaths are cumulative 2016 to 2020; maternal mortality applies the global target of 70 deaths per 100,000 live births to each country.

Source: Results update those previously presented in Kharas, McArthur, and Rasmussen (2018). Underlying data are from UN-DESA (2017), UN Statistics Division (2018), World Bank (2019), WHO (2018).

Figure 1-2. Number of Lives at Stake under SDG Life-and-Death Targets—Cumulative 2019–2030

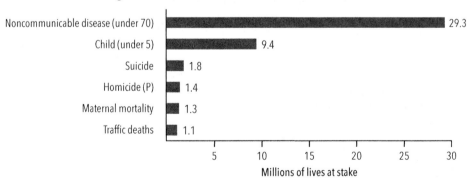

Notes: (P) indicates proxy target used as 50 percent reduction for homicide. Traffic deaths are cumulative over 2019 and 2020; maternal mortality applies the global target of 70 deaths per 100,000 live births to each country.

Source: Results update those previously presented in Kharas, McArthur, and Rasmussen (2018). Underlying data are from UN-DESA (2017), UN Statistics Division (2018), World Bank (2019), WHO (2018).

Basic Needs Indicators

Figure 1-3 presents success ratios corresponding to those in figure 1-1, but now for a range of basic needs indicators. Note that here the number of people left behind is generally estimated only for the final target year, 2030, in order to avoid double-counting. The exception is for HIV infections and tuberculosis infections, which are reported as cumulative gaps from 2016 through 2030. Overall, the estimates in figure 1-3 suggest the world is on course to meet the needs of half the relevant population on only one of the indicators assessed: access to electricity. On the other sixteen indicators, the world is on course to cover less than half the needed ground. Extreme poverty, for example, is on trend to see only 43 percent of the relevant population have their incomes grow above the threshold of US$1.90 per day (in 2011 purchasing power parity dollars). The bottom horizontal bar, for children overweight, shows that the world is actually moving in the wrong direction, since underlying numbers are growing in the vast majority of countries.

Figure 1-4 translates the percentage gaps from figure 1-3 into estimates of the numbers of people grappling with the specific problems reflected by each indicator. For most indicators, the figure again represents a snapshot of the estimated population size still grappling with an issue as of the year 2030. Note that the population reference group differs by indicator, and some individuals might struggle with multiple dimensions of basic needs, so numbers here are not strictly additive or comparable across rows. Sanitation and undernourishment, for example, are measured relative to total population, while children overweight is measured in terms of the much smaller number of children aged two to four years old.

The top bar in figure 1-4 indicates 3.6 billion people suffering from mortality-augmenting air pollution. That number is calculated based on a proxy target of cutting each country's share of people living with air pollution by 50 percent by 2030, so it represents only around half the number of people on trajectory to suffer from the problem that year. The next bar, based on women's representation in government, suggests a gap of nearly 2 billion women and girls still subjected to a lack of equal leadership opportunities in society. This is based on a very coarse assumption that lack of opportunities for women in political leadership reflects a generalized proportionate lack of life opportunities for all women and girls. Meanwhile, an estimated 470 million women aged fifteen to forty-nine will lack access to family planning, and more than 380 million women aged fifteen and older will still be victims of intimate partner violence.

The figure also shows that nearly 2 billion people are on track to be left without sanitation by 2030. More than 650 million people will still be undernourished;

Figure 1-3. World Performance on Basic SDG Needs Targets by 2030, under Current Trends

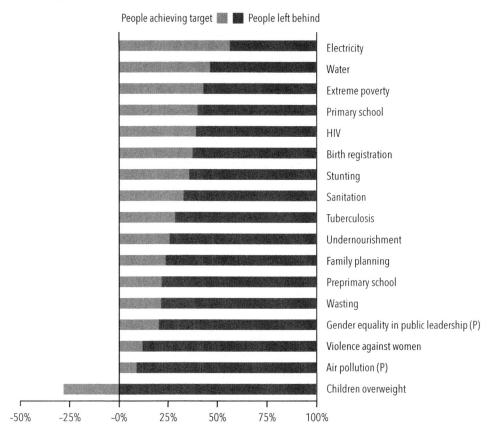

Notes: (P) indicates proxy target used: 50 percent reduction for air pollutions; WHO (2015) target of 90 percent reduction applied to each country for malaria, tuberculosis, and HIV infections; parity for gender representation in public leadership. Figures are for 2030 except HIV and tuberculosis, for which figures are cumulative over 2016 to 2030.

Source: Results update those previously presented in Kharas, McArthur, and Rasmussen (2018). Underlying data are from GBD (2017), UN-DESA (2017), World Bank (2019), World Data Lab (2019).

nearly 600 million people will lack access to drinking water; more than 570 million people will lack access to electricity; and more than 490 million people will still live in extreme income poverty. Meanwhile, unless trends improve, by 2030 more than 10 million people will be newly infected with HIV and more than 54 million with tuberculosis. An estimated 114 million people will not even have had their births registered—a troubling administrative variant of lives not being counted equally.

Figure 1-4. People Left Behind on Basic Needs SDG Targets by 2030, under Current Trends

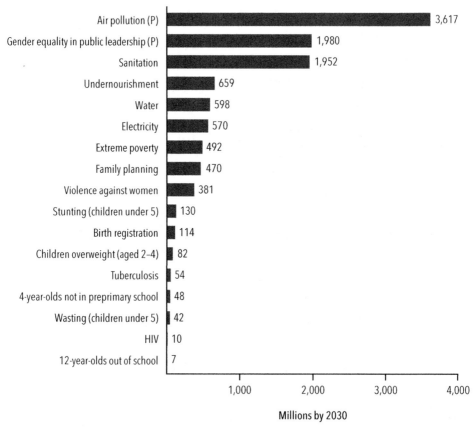

Notes: (P) indicates proxy target used: 50 percent reduction for air pollution; WHO (2015) target of 90 percent reduction applied to each country for malaria, tuberculosis, and HIV infections; parity for gender representation in public leadership. Figures are for 2030 except HIV and tuberculosis, for which figures are cumulative over 2019 to 2030.

Source: Results update those previously presented in Kharas, McArthur, and Rasmussen (2018). Underlying data are from GBD (2017), UN-DESA (2017), World Bank (2019), World Data Lab (2019).

Child-focused indicators show the number of people on trend to be left behind at initial life stages, unless progress accelerates. More than 130 million children under five will be subject to stunting due to poor nutrition and more than 40 million will be subject to wasting. At the same time, more than 80 million children aged two to four will be classified as overweight, highlighting the double-barreled nature of the global nutrition challenge. Meanwhile, more than 48 million four-year-old children will lack access to preprimary education and

7 million twelve-year-olds will not have finished primary school. These age-specific educational gaps can be considered in the context of the 2016 global Education Commission's concern that nearly 900 million children and young adults will not be on track to achieve basic secondary-level skills by 2030.

Where Are People Being Left Behind?

The results presented above highlight the absolute numbers of people who will face the consequences of being left behind on a cross-section of SDG issues. All of these people live somewhere, and there is often considerable geographic concentration to the challenge. On child mortality, for example, three countries—Nigeria, Democratic Republic of Congo, and Pakistan—account for more than half of the lives at stake. On extreme income poverty, five countries—Nigeria, Democratic Republic of Congo, Madagascar, South Sudan, and Mozambique—are on course to be home to more than half of the remaining global challenge in 2030. It is not always the same countries that account for the majority of the global problem on a particular issue, but countries with widespread poverty challenges often face high absolute levels of deprivation on multiple dimensions of people being left behind.

At the same time, many countries facing the deepest problems of people left behind have smaller total populations. These countries might not account for a large share of the global challenge, but their local LNOB task is profound. To that end, Kharas and colleagues presented an approach to identifying the most "severely off-track countries" as a more refined multidimensional method for benchmarking the income-focused concept originally introduced in Gertz and Kharas (2018). By considering a cross section of people-focused SDG indicators anchored in absolute targets—for example eliminating extreme poverty, reducing child mortality rates to no more than 25 deaths per 1,000 live births—it is possible to conduct a synthesis assessment of which countries are facing the deepest challenges across issues.

Such an assessment draws attention to Chad, Central African Republic, South Sudan, Somalia, Democratic Republic of Congo, Papua New Guinea, Guinea-Bissau, Eritrea, Zambia, and Niger as the ten countries with the greatest remaining challenge as of 2030 on absolute measures of deprivation. It is important to note that these countries are all on course to make overall progress between 2015 and 2030, so the situation is far from hopeless, but they are starting in such a challenging position that, even with the progress, large shares of their population are still on course to be left behind. For international partners aiming to fulfill the SDG commitment to leave no one behind, a careful balance of efforts is required to support both the countries with large absolute numbers of people being left behind and the countries with large proportionate shares of people being left behind.

Crucially, the challenges of people being left behind are not, by any stretch, exclusive to low-income countries. No OECD country is yet fully on track to ensure no one is left behind across the SDGs (Kharas and others, 2018). Even high-income countries—for example, Canada, with its reputation for strong public institutions—still face gaps in access to basic services like clean drinking water, including for indigenous people, and is not yet on track for any SDG indicators of gender equality (Biggs and McArthur, 2018). More broadly, most countries still face significant challenges of relative domestic poverty and food insecurity, in addition to problems like universal achievement of basic learning outcomes. And almost all countries need to grapple with problems like obesity, violence against women, and people being subjected to air pollution. Every society faces its own form of imperatives in order to leave no one behind.

Ideas for a Way Forward

In line with this volume's emphasis on getting specific on LNOB, a cross section of distinguished researchers and practitioners have contributed twelve separate chapters focusing on a range of pertinent challenges. No two chapters take the same exact approach, which reflects the diversity of topics, backgrounds, and perspectives involved in this collective analysis. It is important to note that the contributions do not pretend to address all dimensions of the LNOB imperative. Rather they represent a group of insightful voices aiming to treat LNOB as a serious objective. To that end, we have organized the contributions under three respective headings: those focused on specific people; those focused on specific problems; and those focused on specific places. This is followed by a final chapter on the political economy of power.

Specific People

Chapter 2 focuses on people left behind because of gender inequality, with emphasis on the most vulnerable women and girls—especially those who lack skills, opportunities, and a sense of self-efficacy. According to Hilary Mathews and Michelle Nunn, SDG 5—for gender equality—has an explicit focus on structural change, as expressed in targets for nondiscrimination in political institutions; addressing employment barriers, such as in unpaid care; and eliminating gendered forms of social control, including harmful traditional practices and violence against women. Gender dimensions also cut across all sixteen of the other SDGs. The authors are leaders at CARE, the prominent nongovernmental organization with several decades of experience in development and humanitarian work. Based on the organization's operational insights, the authors argue that policymakers and aid practitioners have tended to misinterpret the problem of gender inequality and, as a result, have been applying solutions that fall short of what is needed. They propose two levels of action. The first level falls within the existing paradigm of international assistance: tackling the data gaps that hinder our understanding of what even works where and for whom. The second level focuses on structural changes that strengthen and diversify local, national, and international coalitions for gender equality. This ultimately requires transforming traditional power dynamics, leading the authors to call for an explicitly feminist approach to international development.

Chapter 3 focuses on the "ultra-poor," a subset of the people living in extreme poverty who are defined by both severe material destitution and psychological despair. Lindsay Coates and Scott MacMillan suggest scalable, evidence-based solutions that can break the trap of ultra-poverty, drawing from a growing body of evidence on the "graduation approach" that their own organization, BRAC, has piloted in Bangladesh and other countries. A development organization founded and based in Bangladesh, BRAC is known for running adaptive, hands-on programs on a massive scale. To tackle ultra-poor people's complex and heterogeneous needs, the graduation approach emphasizes a sequence of interventions tailored to each culture, context, and population. In focusing on social protection, livelihood promotion, financial inclusion, and social empowerment at the same time, the approach includes a focus on nonmaterial factors like activating people's sense of self-worth and injecting well-founded hope and optimism into their lives. The authors stress the need to strengthen evidence on how well different approaches address ultra-poverty while also arguing for the need to think beyond purely economic support strategies, such as unconditional cash transfers or universal basic income. Based on growing evidence on the "science of hope," Coates and MacMillan believe development agencies that espouse a belief in LNOB need to deepen their understanding of, and investments in, tackling the special human attributes of ultra-poverty.

Among the world's poorest people, a majority are smallholder farmers, most of whom produce staple food crops that are consumed on-farm or sold in nearby markets, often with little formality. For these households, one important way to boost incomes is to become part of formal value chains linking food suppliers, distributors, retailers, and customers. In chapter 4, Jane Nelson describes how inclusive business models and alliances can support smallholders to become more commercially viable in this regard. For smallholders, the obstacles to value chain connections tend to be multifaceted, so—although data remain too scarce on the current reach of inclusive business models—success typically requires public sector, private sector, and civil society actors to collaborate in a systemic manner. There are many practical challenges to implementing multi-stakeholder strategies in cooperation with farmers themselves, but individual interventions, such as contract farming, savings groups, and producer collectives, have all demonstrated evidence of a considerable positive impact. For the hundreds of millions of smallholder households still struggling to convert their farms into sustainable enterprises, governments, companies, and nongovernmental actors all have a role to play.

Migrants and refugees form an entirely different category of people at risk of being left behind. In chapter 5, Dany Bahar and Meagan Dooley document the rapid recent rise in refugees worldwide, from about 15 million in 2005 to over 25 million today. They note that over 85 percent of refugees are hosted in developing countries, which frequently struggle to provide support and services to these guests while also dealing with the needs of their own vulnerable populations. Often the barriers faced by refugees also affect all migrants, a much larger population (migrants comprise 3.3 percent of the world's population, an estimated 266 million people). Despite common rhetoric to the contrary, Bahar and Dooley argue the cross-border movement of people is a significant long-term positive for those who move, as well as for both the host and the sending countries. They recommend increased action to integrate migrants and refugees into inbound labor markets by providing work permits, freedom of movement, and job-matching programs. Migration's benefits can also be increased through policies that facilitate entrepreneurship, an activity in which migrants tend to engage in higher proportions than natives. At the same time, the authors stress the importance of investing in infrastructure and public services in communities experiencing fast and large influxes of refugees. Based on the reviewed evidence, the chapter argues for human mobility to be viewed not as a risk but as an opportunity for expanding growth and human capital accumulation.

Specific Problems

In considering the component problems of LNOB, one of the most salient aspects of the 2030 SDG time horizon will be quickly evolving industry skill requirements around the globe, alongside rapid population growth in many low-income countries with weak national education systems. In that context, Rebecca Winthrop and Lauren Ziegler focus on a crucial dual educational component of the LNOB challenge in chapter 6. First, millions of children who are excluded from formal education systems still require basic access. Second, education systems themselves need to ensure all participating young people are empowered with quality twenty-first-century skills that are relevant to the world they will enter upon graduation. Winthrop and Ziegler argue that the double task can only be addressed if policymakers shift mindsets. Instead of the traditional step-wise thought process of promoting access first, then quality, then relevance, education systems need an innovation-based "leapfrog" mindset of promoting access, quality, and relevance all at once. The core of a leapfrog pathway is to transform teaching and learning to be more student-centered while also transforming the recognition of learning to be more individualized. In many contexts, leapfrogging can be further scaled up by diversifying the people and places that foster learning and by leveraging data and technology to provide continuous feedback on the quality of teaching and learning. Despite the enormity of the challenge, a cross section of practical examples from some of the world's most remote and marginalized communities show the broader viability of leapfrogging.

As another crucial element of fostering both human capital and well-being, health is a precondition for achieving economic, social, and environmental dimensions of sustainable development. It is also a universal human right. In chapter 7, Krishna D. Rao, Saeda Makimoto, Michael A. Peters, Gabriel Leung, Gerald Bloom, and Yasushi Katsuma focus on the challenge of achieving universal health coverage (UHC) for vulnerable and marginalized populations who are at risk of poor health and healthcare disparities, with inadequate financial protection. After discussing the intersectionality between different forms of vulnerability in relation to health, the authors analyze the existing disparities in service coverage and financial hardships faced by vulnerable populations. They then propose policy options to address such UHC gaps. The authors suggest progressive universalism as a key principle to achieving UHC, by first targeting the health needs and financial protection of the most vulnerable populations, including migrants. At the same time, operationalizing this principle requires better information on vulnerable populations; health systems oriented toward primary healthcare while ensuring quality of care; strong linkages with secondary and tertiary care levels; adequate financing for health; and the adoption of innovative technologies. Development partners can play an important role in providing necessary financial resources, creating networks for knowledge exchange, and promoting the scaling up of innovations, including new technologies to make affordable, quality health services accessible to the neediest people.

Chapter 8 addresses the challenge of narrowing the gender gap in financial inclusion, based on the analysis of cross-country data drawn from the World Bank's Global Findex Database and rural Philippines survey data collected by the Japan International Cooperation Agency (JICA) Research Institute. Authors Eiji Yamada, Erica Paula Sioson, Enerelt Murakami, and Akira Murata point out that access to affordable and useful financial services is one of the basic requirements that help people to secure their economic stability and healthy life. But overall recent global progress in financial inclusion, measured by formal and mobile money account ownership, has not automatically improved the gender gap in access. Some countries—such as Bangladesh, Pakistan, and Nigeria—face even worsening disparities. The authors conduct an in-depth analysis of the Philippines as a case study of relevant issues. This reveals considerable heterogeneity of gender-equitable financial inclusion across the country and also within municipalities. Based on JICA's project experiences and broader findings in relevant literature, the authors suggest possible measures to address demand- and supply-side barriers to equity, ranging from material to social constraints. Given the diversity of situations present within and across countries, the authors further recommend mutual policy-learning efforts spanning both developed and developing countries.

In broader debates around financing the SDGs, there is much discussion about the role of domestic resource mobilization as a source of funding for various LNOB policies and programs. In chapter 9, Nora Lustig, Jon Jellema, and Valentina Martinez examine how viable this might be in practice. They ask a seemingly simple question: could one eradicate poverty by reallocating all subsidies to the poor and then filling the remaining income gap with tax-financed transfers? At least for nine sub-Saharan African countries in the authors' sample, the answer is a resounding no across nearly all the scenarios they consider, based on a variety of different poverty lines and technical approaches. To understand the constraints, the intuition follows not from theory but from a close examination of what is practical. Lustig and colleagues start by acknowledging that subsidies largely go to the relatively well-off (think petrol subsidies that only go to those rich enough to own cars), but in low- and lower-middle income countries they are generally too small to make a material dent in country-wide poverty even if redistributed to the poor. That leaves taxes as a funding source for transfers, but it turns out that most tax systems rely heavily on consumption taxes. So when taxes are raised in order to finance transfers, prices go up and the poor are hurt. The net impact, then, depends on whether the poor are hurt more by the price increases than they benefit from the transfers. The authors find that in most of their scenarios, exploring interventions like universal or targeted income supplements, the tax levels required to make a substantial dent in poverty in low- and lower-middle income countries are simply too high to be feasible within the sample of modern market-oriented economies. They therefore caution against getting too excited by the idea of tax mobilization as a source of funding anti-poverty programs.

Specific Places

The book's final section focuses on topics pertinent to the geography of LNOB. In chapter 10, Jennifer Cohen, Raj M. Desai, and Homi Kharas stress that for too many people living in poverty the place where they are born determines their life opportunities. In the development community's common discourse, "place" has usually implied "country," but there is growing recognition that many low-income countries have their own regions of relative prosperity while many middle-income countries have regions of poverty. This understanding has been deepened by new data sets that make use of satellite-based imagery and can be used to define problems at a more granular level than the country. In their chapter, Cohen and colleagues look at the world's 3,609 subnational districts and provinces and ask what income levels are likely to be in these areas in 2030, if recent trends persist. Areas below a 2030 average income threshold of $4,900 per capita (in 2011 purchasing power parity terms) are dubbed "poverty hotspots," meaning places where there are likely to be substantial concentrations of extreme poverty in 2030. The authors then consider whether there are policy levers that can accelerate growth in these places, and find several candidates—investment in human capital, investment in physical connectivity, investment in resilience to environmental and conflict-related shocks, and national policies to improve governance. For each of these policy levers, the authors provide examples of how governments have actually used spatial targeting to good effect. At the same time, Cohen and colleagues note that, for at least one major multilateral institution, aid does not seem to have been prioritized toward poverty hotspots. They call for greater use of spatial information and targeting to accelerate growth and poverty reduction where it is needed most.

Among the varying geographies confronting the LNOB challenge, the fraction of people living in extreme poverty in fragile states is growing steadily and projected to reach at least 50 percent by 2030. This is a result of both the difficulties in reducing poverty in fragile states and the rapid fall in poverty in non-fragile states. Addressing the fragile state-based concentration of poverty is, therefore, at the heart of the LNOB agenda. As Landry Signé outlines in chapter 11, this requires addressing fragility itself, which is not an easy problem to solve, since many countries' fragility has persisted for decades and little foreign investment flows inward to these places. Conflict, low-level violence, gender inequality, low domestic resource mobilization, limited aid, poor governance, weak connectivity, and low human capital complicate any interventions. Signé nonetheless offers some practical ideas for making progress. First, he unpacks fragility and suggests what kind of interventions should be prioritized in individual country contexts to bridge the gap between policy goals and implementation outcomes.

Second, he emphasizes two approaches that offer promise: support for private business and a greater focus on cities. On the private sector side, Signé points not just to the job creating benefits of private investments, but also to the role of sound business practices, especially in resource extraction, and the much broader feelings of inclusion that a vibrant private sector can bring. He also emphasizes the need to tackle fragility at the local level, especially in cities where levels of violence are high. At this level, transparency and accountability are critical elements of improved governance.

Tony Pipa and Caroline Conroy further stress the importance of cities in chapter 12. In the SDG framework, municipal issues were given prominence through Goal 11 for sustainable cities and communities. But as Pipa and Conroy explain, Goal 11 on its own is not enough to tackle the urban LNOB challenge. The world's fastest growing cities are in low-income countries grappling with intense poverty problems, and too little is known about how many extremely poor people even live in these urban areas. National governments at all income levels have a particular responsibility to ensure "no city is left behind" in national SDG processes, including in their voluntary national reviews presented at the UN. At the same time, urban governments often form the frontlines confronting the daily societal realities spanning all seventeen SDGs, even if they typically only have direct jurisdiction and administrative capacities to take on a subset of the challenges. Bridging this gap forms a pivotal task for LNOB. Fortunately, a growing number of cities of varying income levels are undertaking "voluntary local reviews" to demonstrate their strategies to advance the SDGs. Local governments are commonly finding it most useful to boil the seventeen goals down to their three-part essence of integrating economic, social, and environmental problem-solving. In this respect, many local leaders are pioneering some of the most innovative approaches to SDG implementation. Pipa and Conroy argue that they can only succeed at scale through support from both national policymakers above and engaged community members below.

The Political Economy of Power

All of the preceding insights and recommendations—whom to target, on what issues, and in which places—will not be of much use if, in the final analysis, power imbalances within countries prevent effective implementation. In this volume's final chapter, Paul O'Brien argues that people are not being "left behind" so much as "pushed behind." Addressing this challenge, he argues, requires a discussion about power—what it means, who holds it or doesn't, and how it might be redistributed. According to O'Brien, historical theories of power, from Hobbes to Foucault, discussed power exclusively as a finite relationship (if one person holds it, another cannot). Around the turn of this century, feminist and development thinkers opened up an analysis of power as ability that is not so zero sum (power as ability can be grown in one person without another person losing out). While O'Brien believes that feminist thinking on power has been transformative for development practice, he also argues that not enough attention has been given to relative power. For the SDGs to succeed, he argues that zero sum relational power over economic resources and political choice must not only be redistributed away from those who have too much, but also can and should be held by those left behind. O'Brien lays out two proposals for doing so. First, political power should be redistributed away from autocrats who suppress political freedoms and oppress those frontline human rights defenders of the SDGs. When this happens, relational (democratic) power will return to active citizens. Second, economic power should be redistributed away from the extreme wealthy and shared more broadly by more people on an increasingly stressed planet. Feminism, O'Brien concludes, can take us beyond the false choice between amplifying power as ability and redistributing zero sum relational power. He closes by calling on us to understand power in both its forms—as a relationship and as ability—as they manifest in the world, in our organizations, and in ourselves.

Conclusion

This volume's dozen distinct contributions draw attention to the broad range of issues that underpin the LNOB challenge, while not professing to form anything like a comprehensive review of the problems that need to be addressed to shift LNOB from slogan to specifics. A number of chapters draw attention to the intersectionality through which some individuals confront multiple LNOB issues at once—for example, a migrant woman in a fragile poverty hotspot with weak systems for health and education. A call for specificity on LNOB should not generate faulty policy segmentation. A human being can be left behind for many reasons.

Many of the chapters also draw attention to data gaps. Whether considering issues of gender, geography, poverty, or even financial inclusion, the world needs better information to understand exactly who is getting left behind, where, and why. National governments need to prioritize these issues in their SDG voluntary national reviews to the United Nations. They could usefully all commit to present, by the end of 2020, their own domestic estimates of who is getting left behind on each issue in each community.

The calendar for bringing LNOB to life is crucial. At the time of writing, in mid-2019, it is not yet clear whether any country in the world has yet internalized the relevant practical questions for action. With little more than a decade remaining to deliver on the 2030 SDG promise, governments and international partners need to implement much more comprehensive approaches to targeted, outcome-oriented, and innovation-based policies and budgets. As many of the chapters in this volume demonstrate, the challenges are significant. But they are not insurmountable. For the SDGs, if the world acts quickly, there is still time to help the many millions of specific people facing specific problems in specific places. There is still time to ensure societies work for everyone.

References

Biggs, Margaret and John W. McArthur, "A Canadian North Star: Crafting an Advanced Economy Approach to the Sustainable Development Goals," in *From Summits to Solutions: Innovations in Implementing the Sustainable Development Goals,* edited by R. M. Desai, H. Kato, H. Kharas, and J. W. McArthur (Brookings, 2018), 265–301.

FAO, and others. 2019. *The State of Food Security and Nutrition in the World 2019: Safeguarding Against Economic Slowdowns and Downturns* (Rome: FAO).

Gertz, Geoffrey and Homi Kharas. 2018. "Leave No Country Behind: Ending Poverty in the Toughest Places," Brookings Global Economy and Development Working Paper 110, February.

Global Burden of Diseases (GBD) 2017 SDG Collaborators, "Measuring Progress from 1990 to 2017 and Projecting Attainment to 2030 of the Health-Related Sustainable Development Goals for 195 Countries and Territories: A Systematic Analysis for the Global Burden of Disease Study 2017," *Lancet,* vol. 392, no. 10159 (November 10, 2018), 2091–138.

Government of Canada. 2018. "The 2030 Agenda for Sustainable Development," (https://international.gc.ca/world-monde/issues_development-enjeux_developpement/priorities-priorites/agenda-programme.aspx?lang=eng).

Government of Japan. 2016. "Sustainable Development Goals (SDGs) Implementation Guiding Principles," Sustainable Development Goal Promotion Headquarters, Prime Minister's Office. (http://www.kantei.go.jp/jp/singi/sdgs/dai2/siryou1e.pdf).

International Civil Society Centre. 2019. "Leave No One Behind" (https://icscentre.org/our-work/leave-no-one-behind/).

International Commission on Financing Global Education Opportunity. 2016. *The Learning Generation: Investing in Education for a Changing World.* Report.

Kharas, Homi, John W. McArthur, and Krista Rasmussen. 2018. "How Many People Will the World Leave Behind? Assessing Current Trajectories on the Sustainable Development Goals," Brookings Global Economy and Development Working Paper 123, September.

Kindornay, Shannon. 2019. *Progressing National SDG Implementation: An Independent Assessment of the Voluntary National Review Reports Submitted to the United Nations High-level Political Forum in 2018* (Ottawa: Canadian Council for International Co-operation).

OECD. 2018. *Development Cooperation Report 2018: Joining Forces to Leave No One Behind.*

———. 2019. "Development Aid Drops in 2018, Especially to Neediest Countries," Development Assistance Committee, April 10, 2019 (https://www.oecd.org/dac/financing-sustainable-development/development-finance-data/ODA-2018-detailed-summary.pdf).

Samman, Emma, and others. 2018. *SDG Progress: Fragility, Crisis and Leaving No One Behind*, Overseas Development Institute and International Rescue Committee September.

UK Department for International Development, "Leaving No One Behind: Our Promise," Policy Paper, updated March 6, 2019 (https://www.gov.uk/government/publications/leaving-no-one-behind-our-promise/leaving-no-one-behind-our-promise).

United Nations Development Program (UNDP). 2018. "What Does It Mean to Leave No One Behind?" UNDP discussion paper and framework for implementation. July.

United Nations Population Division, Department of Economic and Social Affairs (UN-DESA), *World Population Prospects: The 2017 Revision.*

United Nations Statistics Division. 2018. "SDG Indicators Global Database" (https://unstats.un.org/sdgs/indicators/database/).

World Bank. 2019. "World Development Indicators Database" (https://databank.worldbank.org/data/source/world-development-indicators).

World Data Lab. 2019. World Poverty Clock [data file] (http://worldpoverty.io/).

World Health Organization. 2018. "Global Health Observatory Data Repository: Premature NCD Deaths (Under Age 70), Data by Country" (http://apps.who.int/gho/data/node.main.A862).

PART I
People

CHAPTER TWO

Women on the Move
Can We Achieve Gender Equality by 2030?

Hilary Mathews and Michelle Nunn

Introduction

When the 193 United Nations member states signed on to the Sustainable Development Goals (SDGs) in 2015, they established gender equality as both a stand-alone goal and a central tenet to achieving an inclusive and sustainable development agenda by 2030. Most policymakers would agree that aspiring to gender equality is not controversial as an *ideal*.[1] The prospect of actually arriving at that ideal within fifteen years, however, requires profound, coherent and concurrent change in politics, economics, and society. From this perspective, the adoption of SDG 5 was radically hopeful.

Consider the story of Salamatou, a Nigerien woman forced at age thirteen to marry a sixty-year-old man. She had four children by age twenty and could not read or write. Salamatou's life changed when she joined a savings group that provided solidarity with other women and resources to start her own business. She left her husband, educated her younger children, and helped to create more than 175 savings groups for three thousand people. Yet for every woman like Salamatou, there are many more who face lack of economic opportunity, discrimination, and violence without any support. Will the global community fulfill its commitments to ensure these women and girls are not left behind but instead can realize their own potential?

---

1. Gender equality is a globally accepted norm insofar as it is enshrined in the Convention on the Elimination of All Forms of Discrimination Against Women and the Beijing Platform for Action.

A quarter of the way to 2030, the UN's assessment is that "while some forms of discrimination against women and girls are diminishing, gender inequality continues to hold women back and deprives them of basic rights and opportunities."[2] A recent survey of gender equality advocates shows that most of them believe progress on gender equality is stagnating, and a 2018 Brookings Institution poll revealed that only 29 percent of policymakers ranked gender equality (SDG 5) as one of the top six sustainable development goals.[3] The OECD cautions: "Donors are failing to implement effectively a twin-track approach and should increase support for dedicated programs with gender equality and women's empowerment as a principal objective to respond to commitments in the Agenda 2030 for Sustainable Development."[4] And the World Economic Forum forecasts it will take the world 108 more years to achieve gender parity.[5]

Worse yet, instead of prioritizing gender equality, social and political forces in many parts of the world are actively conspiring to hold women and girls back. A 2017 research report commissioned by Mama Cash and Urgent Action Fund[6] concluded that efforts by the state to constrain civil space are increasing—and disproportionately affecting feminist groups. Progressive activists are not alone in registering their alarm at the prospect of rights rolled back; a group of more than thirty women leaders and former heads of state published an open letter in *The Guardian* in February 2019, warning, "As women increasingly occupy meaningful spaces in local, national, and international political structures, and in socioeconomic, scientific, and sustainable development debates, and as we engage through civil society in many campaigns, we see now, close to a quarter of a century after Beijing, more movements gaining traction that seek to halt the gains made and erode the rights won by women."[7]

While this view is dim, there have been some bright spots for gender equality. The #MeToo movement has shed more light on sexual violence—one of the most devastating and highly stigmatized forms of gender inequality. Several major policy changes at global and national levels are poised to create a fairer environment for women and girls. And the business case for investing in women has never been stronger, supported by global, regional, and sector-specific evidence showing the economic gains from increased female employment and more

2. United Nations Sustainable Development Goals. Goal 5 (https://sustainabledevelopment. un.org/SDG5).

3. Equal Measures 2030 (2018), 2, and Custer (2018).

4. OECD (2018a).

5. World Economic Forum (2017).

6. Bishop (2017).

7. Kate Lyons, "Rise of the 'Strongman': Dozens of Female World Leaders Warn Women's Rights Being Eroded," *Guardian*, February 28, 2019.

diverse workforces.[8] These advances counter pessimistic narratives that gender inequality is too intractable a problem to be solved, or an issue too few people care about. But why have we not made more progress—especially for the most vulnerable women and girls? And what can be done to make good on the 2030 commitment to leave no one behind?

Using examples from CARE's own work and drawing on our experience in the development and humanitarian sectors, we argue that policymakers and implementers have tended to misinterpret the problem of gender inequality, and as a result have been applying solutions that fall short of what is needed. Bias and lack of data have inhibited our focus on those most in need, and we have not yet realized the opportunity to come together as an effective and diverse coalition for gender equality. Ultimately, what is needed is a dramatic shift in our collective sense of accountability that would enable us to bring the right stakeholders together to tackle the roots of inequality and focus on the right people. This will require transforming traditional power dynamics and amplifying the voices and the solutions of the most marginalized; it requires a feminist approach to international development.

Why Are We Not Solving the Root Problem?

We are nowhere near "critical mass" in terms of the necessary political energy or investments to achieve SDG 5 or the gender dimensions of other goals by 2030. But the challenge is not only that we need *more*—more funding for evidence-based interventions, more voices engaged in innovative problem-solving, more power devolved to women's rights organizations and women themselves. Sustainably addressing gender disparities requires adaptable solutions that are fit for the complexity of the problem. In too many places, resources are underutilized and the root causes of gender inequality are obscured as policymakers and implementers are lured by silver-bullet solutions that are not capable (on their own) of delivering transformational and sustainable change. When we allow this to happen, we get off track, solving for relevant but less systemic problems.

Development practitioners often focus on approaches to expand the agency of individual women and girls. Examples include building women's and girls' skills and self-confidence through trainings on literacy, entrepreneurship, negotiation, and legal rights; and resource transfers targeted to female beneficiaries, such as cash, school uniforms, or mobile phones. These kinds of interventions support profound and necessary improvements in women's and girls' lives. In many cases, the outcomes they deliver—healthier, better educated, or more

8. OECD (2018b), World Economic Forum (2017).

productive women and girls—can have ripple effects that affect communities and institutions. However, individual capacity improvements do not necessarily lead directly and inevitably to increases in gender equality. Moreover, there are examples of unintended consequences from such approaches. This is not to say that women in poverty should not have more assets, or that the prospect of back-lash should deter efforts to empower women and girls. Rather, these examples underscore the need to promote gender equality and concurrently mitigate risk by engaging with the complexity of social ecosystems, which include changes in individuals. At CARE, we know this from our own experience.

More than ten years ago, the findings from CARE's Strategic Impact Inquiry on Gender Equality showed that across more than four hundred of the organiza-tion's programs, 60 percent of women-focused projects were targeting women's own capabilities. The study determined that these individual-level approaches generated impacts that were useful but short-term, limited in scale, and ulti-mately reversible. CARE identified major opportunity costs in the ways we were addressing gender inequality, stemming in part from a lack of sophistication about the very nature of that injustice:

> On one side, we see a clear aptitude to work at the scale of 9 million women in a single project, fostering changes in women's knowledge, income, skills, participation, decision-making in households and com-munities, health-seeking behaviors, and literacy. On the other, we see the failure to guide those changes to their strategic potential due to weak understanding of gender, power, and the political economic context. . . . Our research demonstrates a widespread tendency in CARE to call "empowerment" (or "gender equity") any activity which is intended to benefit women.[9]

These sobering findings led to a new era of gender equality programming within CARE based on the adoption of CARE's Gender Equality Framework, which recognizes that gender (in)equality is created through the interplay of individual agency, relations, and structural factors. The Gender Equality Frame-work is depicted in figure 2-1.

The organization also redoubled efforts to support staff capacity building and accountability systems to deliver more robust gender equality outcomes. While these have been positive developments, we are constantly pushing our-selves to deliver sufficiently transformative gender interventions, which not only take account of gendered conditions but also seek to change the very rules and

9. Mosedale (2005) and Martinez (2006).

Figure 2-1. CARE's Gender Equality Framework

BUILD AGENCY
Building consciousness, confidence, self-esteem and aspirations (non-formal sphere) and knowledge, skills and capabilities (formal sphere).

CHANGE RELATIONS
The power relations through which people live their lives through intimate relations and social networks (non-formal sphere) and group membership and activism, and citizen and market negotiations (formal sphere).

TRANSFORM STRUCTURES
Discriminatory social norms, customs, values and exclusionary practices (non-formal sphere) and laws, policies, procedures and services (formal sphere).

Source: CARE International, 2018a.

systems that enable them to persist. It bears asking why we, and so many others, are tempted to solve a complex, systems-level problem like gender inequality with discrete, individual-level solutions. We see four overarching reasons for this tendency:

It Is Easy to Confuse Ends and Means

Gender inequality is not caused by shortcomings within women and girls, though it is manifest when women and girls lack skills, opportunities, and a sense of self-efficacy as compared to their male counterparts. It is a common mistake to conflate ends with means and causes with consequences. The success of efforts to address gender inequality must be assessed through their impacts on the women and girls who overwhelmingly bear the burden of that injustice. And similarly, the pathways to gender equality must critically engage and amplify the voices of women and girls. But achieving gender equality is not possible with an *exclusive* focus on women and girls; after all, gender equality is a social ideal that necessarily involves people of all genders and changes in the institutions that govern human opportunities, rights, and behavior.[10] It is well understood among both feminists and mainstream development practitioners that the achievement of gender equality is dependent on structural change. In fact, this was a demand well met in the articulation of SDG 5—which, unlike the MDGs, has an explicit

---

10. This brief article focuses on men and boys and women and girls; however, CARE International's 2018 Gender Equality Policy recognizes that gender is non-binary.

focus on structural change, expressed in targets focused on nondiscrimination in political institutions, elimination of gendered forms of social control such as harmful traditional practices and violence against women, and addressing such barriers to employment as unpaid care. Nevertheless, the idea persists that targeting women and girls with individual-level interventions is sufficient in itself to contribute to greater gender equality. And this error has profound practical implications. Focusing on women's and girls' capabilities without addressing the relationships and systems that shape their opportunities makes them less likely to deliver sustainable results. The good news is, as box 2-1 illustrates, that with deliberate intent, many interventions that might otherwise focus only on individual skills-building or improved sectoral outcomes can contribute to gender-related social change.

The Political Nature of Gender Can Be Uncomfortable

Individual-level solutions are attractive in part because they tend to be technical in nature and relatively apolitical. Addressing gender dynamics at the family, community, and institutional levels is inescapably about adjusting power relations and can be uncomfortable or untenable for policymakers, politicians, and implementers whose viability may be threatened by wading into potentially controversial social issues. One of the obvious implications of this fact is that governments, international nongovernmental organizations (INGOs), and other actors wary of the political nature of structural change are not capable of being, and should not be, the principal enablers of gender equality, though they can be critical partners. Feminist thinkers have noted the risks of technocratic approaches that are incapable of the activism that would challenge power holders while at the same time drawing power and funding away from underfunded women's movements.[11] On the other hand, Weldon and Htun's extraordinary work analyzing data from more than seventy countries showed that it was feminist activists who were the "most important and consistent factor driving policy change" to address violence against women.[12] The upshot is that traditional development actors may have access to important capacities and funding, but it is women's movements that have the intention and the orientation to deliver transformative change. Until traditional development actors acknowledge the value of women's rights actors and partner with them effectively, we will continue to see interventions that are useful and even innovative, but fall short of the political ambition of realizing universal gender equality.

11. Arutyunova and Clark (2013), Cornwall (2014).
12. Weldon and Htun (2013).

Box 2-1. The Transformative Potential of VSLAs

CARE's Village Savings and Loan Association (VSLA) platform reaches some of the poorest communities in the world. These are self-help groups of fifteen to twenty-five members who come together to buy shares, lend to one another, grow businesses, access insurance, and build up savings to invest in things like education, housing, agriculture, small businesses, and health services. Participation in VSLAs has been proven to increase women's savings, knowledge of basic financial principles and entrepreneurship, and contribute to household resilience to economic shocks, food security, and improved health and nutritional outcomes. With deliberate efforts to account for the interpersonal, social, and structural context of women in a particular community, VSLAs have further potential to contribute to gender equality. These "VSLA+" models include contextualized approaches to address women's workloads and the burden of care, engage men and boys in ensuring equitable intra-household relationships, reduce the risks of gender-based violence, and develop women's social capital and group political consciousness for collective action.

Source: CARE 2017 (working paper)

We Prefer What We Can Count

It is easier to count workshops delivered, number of women and girls trained, and percent changes in knowledge and attitudes than it is to assess shifts in policy implementation, social norms, or domestic workloads—and the complex interplay between these phenomena. When policymakers and practitioners invest in what is easier to measure, we create false proxies for gender equality and fail to follow through on the systemic work needed for broad-based change.

Accountability should be the foundation of any development effort. But what does accountability look like in practice, and how do we establish the proof and the accompanying narrative of what is effective for gender equality, as for any development outcome? The more complex a goal the harder it can be to identify and measure the manifestations of change, and the longer we may have to wait to see impact. This is not to argue that it is impossible to evaluate progress toward gender equality or that we should not try—indeed, there are many strong examples of measures, indexes, and approaches that suggest that the state of the art in measuring gender equality is evolving. Research from the Evidence-Based Measures for Research on Gender Equality (EMERGE) project led by the University of California at San Diego and tools such as the Women's Empowerment in Agriculture Index are cases in point. Evaluators have demonstrated ways to constructively engage with the "messy complexity" that is inherently a part of social change, but this is often methodologically difficult and resource-intensive work.[13]

If we are attached (as we should be) to the idea that we need to demonstrate progress, and we have limited resources (money, time, or human capacity), in many cases we are incentivized to either (1) skew our choice of measures toward false proxies that are not actually suited to assess a phenomenon as complex as gender equality, or (2) opt for simpler interventions with easily quantified outcomes that are ultimately insufficient to address gender inequality. It is easy to say that we should not fall for such perverse incentives, but in practice this happens all the time. We need to establish systems to effectively counter this tendency while we continue to develop improved practices for measuring gender outcomes, especially at the level of relations and structures.

The Imperative to Scale Can Be Tricky

The ambition to "leave no one behind" requires massively scaling up the reach and impact of efforts to empower *all* women and girls. That global urgency has not consistently translated into meaningful country-level action, however, and lackluster efforts are one reason why we see insufficient progress on gender equality. Even where there is the will to demonstrate progress, governments and partners must grapple with a number of complex and sometimes conflicting imperatives raised by the mandate to scale. The challenge is summed up in this Brookings publication:

> An important finding from the case studies is that the more comprehensive and multifaceted a program is in terms of the developmental problem that is being addressed and in terms of the range of interventions that are covered, the more difficult it is to systematically and effectively focus on scaling up . . .[14]

This is completely logical, and yet gender inequality is arguably one of the most complex and multifaceted development challenges imaginable. So, what to do? Much like our affinity for easily quantified inputs and outcomes, development actors are attracted to approaches that can be easily replicated and aggregated to affect larger numbers of people. But we've just argued that the simplest, individual-level, apolitical interventions are necessary but not sufficient

13. With regard to "messy complexity," see Agnes Quisumbing, "Data Can Be Sexist. Here's How IFPRI Is Fixing that Problem," *IFPRI Blog*, February 20, 2019.

14. Begovic, Linn, and Vrbensky (2017).

to contribute to profound systemic change. So we find ourselves lodged between the rightful demand to create impact on a society-wide scale and the reality that the easiest interventions to scale may be unable to catalyze necessary structural change. To get ourselves out of this quandary, we have to move away from a project mindset that would equate scaling with larger unit numbers of the same intervention, to a paradigm that recognizes that as we aim for society-wide impact, we have to adopt altogether different approaches. In other words, societal change is not just individual or community change on a larger scale; it is a qualitatively different objective with unique requirements. The CARE framework in figure 2-2 highlights these distinctions.

From left to right, the first three building blocks at individual, group, and community levels are drawn from the CARE Gender Equality Framework and are more typical of project-level interventions (with most interventions in the development sector focused on the skills-building aspects of individual agency). The fourth domain, social change at scale, requires a shift in tactics in support of movement actors who are best placed to leverage the positive momentum and progress achieved at the other levels for widespread action and change. Even within more traditional project-based approaches, however, it is possible to embed strategies that are supportive of the political consciousness (within individuals) and solidarity (within groups) that are foundational for movement-based

Figure 2-2. CARE's Continuum of Collective Action for Gender Equality

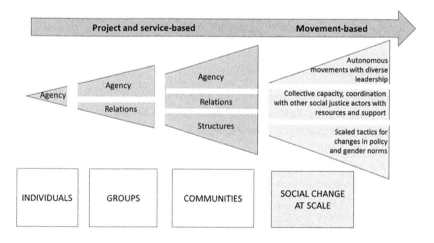

Source: Adapted from a CARE Internal Working Paper written by Bartel, 2017.

action. Such strategies need to be carefully considered and paired with risk mitigation measures to counter potential backlash. While the arrow suggests an overall direction from left to right, the diagram is not intended to suggest a linear "to-from" process. The most appropriate entry points for intervention, the strategies for developing each building block, and the ideal mix and sequencing among them varies based on the local context and is likely to change over time. This reinforces the importance of gender and power analysis in a given context, willingness to set long-term goals while pursuing feasible changes in the short-to-medium run, and a commitment to adaptive management.

Why Are We Not Focused on the Right People?

As changemakers become more clear-eyed about the root causes of gender equality and intentional about the multilevel, transformational approaches that are necessary to "solve" such a complex problem, a corollary question emerges: at global, national, and local levels, which groups of people are the rightful beneficiaries of efforts to hasten the realization of gender equality? The SDG agenda requires that we consider which people are most likely to be left behind by development efforts, including those who suffer the most from gender discrimination. From the most macro lens, the answer is women and girls, but this is an insufficiently specific starting point for effective intervention, as women and girls are not a monolithic group. Moreover, focusing broadly on "women and girls" not only results in blind spots about *which* women and girls, but also overlooks the potential vulnerabilities of some men and boys as well as people who do not fit into binary gender categories. We note that three shortcomings hamper our ability to serve those most affected by gender inequalities:

We Do Not Know Which Women and Girls

The SDG mandate is to empower *all* women and girls. But there is no doubt that some women and girls are much more likely to be left behind, and efforts to address gender inequality must explicitly target them. This requires the tools and the intention to understand who these women and girls are, and the multiple dimensions of their vulnerability in very specific contexts. This is hardly a new concept in development, but we have been surprisingly bad at moving from theory to practice.

Intersectionality is the understanding that gender inequality overlaps or intersects with other forms of vulnerability to compound the disadvantage experienced by the most marginalized groups. The dimensions of vulnerability that should be considered in an intersectional analysis are dictated by context, but typically include issues like age, income, ethnicity, religion, sexual orientation, and (dis)ability. While intersectionality is a concept that comes from feminist theory,[15] it is one that is widely understood in development circles, even if not referred to in the same terms. In addition to seeking the stories of individual women and girls, we have to be able to generate and analyze data across place and time to identify typologies of vulnerability, as box 2-2 highlights. This is the basis both for designing effective interventions and for assessing progress. Yet currently there is not enough reliable data to fulfill the global monitoring requirements of the vast majority of SDG targets, much less to generate sophisticated intersectional analyses that would help identify those most likely to be left behind in a given country, region, or community.[16] While data gaps exist across the SDGs, commentators from Melinda Gates to Caroline Criado Perez have noted that data can be sexist, and the lack of data on women and girls in particular suggests that policymakers simply do not prioritize their needs or experience.[17]

> For many of the SDG targets and indicators, information is not yet disaggregated by sex, there is no intention to disaggregate by sex, or there are data gaps that prevent us from measuring key issues, which hamper our ability to understand today's gender differences and the direction of travel for the well-being of girls and women. Indeed, gender bias is often ingrained in the way that we measure—or fail to measure—aspects of a person's life.[18]

In sum, we frequently have no idea which women and girls are most vulnerable, or even if gender discrepancies are at play for some key outcomes. This suggests a critical need to step up efforts to collect and analyze gender data and enable women's rights and other social justice actors to utilize this information to hold governments and other actors accountable for leaving no one behind.

We Focus Only on Women and Girls

It is necessary to acknowledge that women and girls will be the prime beneficiaries of gender equality efforts, not only because the international community has made a commitment to them as a group continuously left behind, but also because this commitment is constantly under threat. Part of the debate about

15. Crenshaw (1989).
16. UN Women (2018).
17. Criado-Perez (2019), Bill and Melinda Gates, "We Didn't See This Coming," Gates Notes. February 12, 2019.
18. Equal Measures (2018).

Box 2-2. Why Intersectional Analysis Matters

Intersecting social and income-based factors can lead to vastly different profiles of vulnerability across women and girls, even within the same country. For example, in Nigeria, women and girls from the poorest households are nearly five times as likely to be married before the age of eighteen as those from the richest households. In the United States of America, the share of black and Native American women who live in poverty is twice as high as the share of white women. And in Nepal, poor women and Madhesi Dalit women are two to three times more likely than the average Nepali woman to report that being a woman is a disadvantage. The availability, analysis, and use of multidimensional gender data is critical so that policymakers can institute targeted efforts to reach the women and girls being left behind, and so that rights advocates can hold them accountable for doing so.

Sources: UN Women (2018) and the Asia Foundation (2019)

male engagement for gender equality stems from legitimate concern that men and boys might co-opt these efforts, diminishing the possibilities for systemic change and undermining the voices of women and girls. The backlash to the #MeToo movement is one example in which some have attempted to disproportionally shift public focus to the specter of false accusations against men rather than the more systemic problem of sexual violence experienced by women. This co-option can also manifest in the erosion of limited resources to address the priorities of women and girls in order to accommodate strategies to work with men and boys.[19] This is why SDG 5 calls for the empowerment of all women and girls—to ensure that the mandate for gender equality is unmistakably female-centered.

Yet gender equality is also relevant for men and boys, not only because they may be allies to or detractors from the equality agenda, but also because their lives are governed by gendered norms and opportunities.[20] Given the tension between possible subversion and the requirements for holistic social change, there is little consensus among development and assistance practitioners about when and how to engage men and boys in the promotion of gender equality. The International Center for Research on Women succinctly captures this tension: "The primary challenge embedded in this work is how to engage men and boys effectively without instrumentalizing them as a pathway to women's empowerment on the one hand, or marginalizing women and girls in gender equity work on the other."[21] Achieving this balance requires program approaches that are practical but also

19. CARE International (2016).
20. An exclusive focus on women and girls may also cause us to overlook the vulnerability of people who do not fit into a binary gender framework.
21. Glinski and others (2018).

political, grounded in larger structural realities. Gender-synchronized programming is a promising approach that attempts to address these needs by enabling exploration of the experiences of individual men and boys while situating those within a larger framework that holds men accountable to gender equitable progress that benefits all people.

We Get Stuck in the Humanitarian/Development Divide

Despite the universality of the SDGs, the international community tends to focus on development contexts and neglect the possibilities for advancement in emergencies or fragile states. This is perhaps especially true when considering gender equality, since it is not typically considered a "basic human need" and is therefore a secondary consideration, if a consideration at all, in humanitarian responses. Radhika Coomaraswamy, former Special Rapporteur of the UN Secretary-General on Violence against Women, wrote in her review of the implementation of UN Security Council Resolution 1325, "In spite of the repeated call to bridge the distance between development and humanitarian actors, none of the 169 individual targets contained in the seventeen sustainable development goals addresses the specific needs of women and girls—or civilians generally—in conflict zones."[22] Thinking about humanitarian versus development scenarios can lead to the assumption that transformative change is impossible across crisis situations. This misconception results in missed opportunities to address gender dimensions of vulnerability for some of the world's most marginalized people.[23]

The impact of crises on people's lives, experiences, and material conditions differs based on their gender and sexuality. And in many cases gender inequality is an underlying cause of vulnerability in crisis. Our activities during a humanitarian response can increase and reinforce, or reduce, existing inequalities. Many humanitarian actors have experience delivering gendered and intersectional analyses that enable the adaptation of crisis response along a continuum from gender sensitive to transformative, depending on the context. Such adaptations might mitigate gendered risks, increase equitable access to and benefits from services and interventions, or support strategic opportunities to promote gender equality given changing gender norms and relations in crisis.

For example, CARE's rapid gender analysis in Mozambique, in the aftermath of Cyclone Idai, revealed heightened safety concerns within transit camps among widows, adolescent girls, and persons with mobility issues, at the same time that

---

22. Sen (2018).

23. If current trends persist, more than 80 percent percent of the world's poorest populations will live in these fragile contexts by 2030. Kharas and Rogerson (2017).

a lack of systemic collection of sex, age, gender, and disability disaggregated data among humanitarian responders was inhibiting efforts to identify whether cross-sectoral responses were meeting the needs of these at-risk groups.[24] Surfacing this contradiction led to clear recommendations for improved monitoring and evaluation practice to reduce protection risks and increase accountability to vulnerable groups.

In Yemen, joint research by Oxfam, CARE, and GenCap showed how the conflict was upending traditional gender roles and causing backlash against women in the form of gender-based violence (GBV). At the same time, it also presented opportunities for the renegotiation of gender roles and relations within families and communities, as survival had become contingent upon new ways of dividing labor, care, and decisionmaking.[25] As a result, CARE became much more deliberate about GBV prevention programming, as well as including women and girls in income generation and "cash for work" opportunities.

Addressing gender equality within humanitarian response is not only a question of instituting appropriate programmatic approaches, however; it also means enabling women (and girls, when appropriate) to lead at local, regional, and international levels (box 2-3). This is relevant to staffing within international humanitarian organizations but, more important, implies increased funding and support for local women's organizations. While INGOs and donors have increasingly endorsed the localization agenda and some (notably Canada, Sweden, and France) are applying a feminist lens to humanitarian assistance, we are far from realizing either of these ambitions.[26] Both frameworks—localization and feminism—require significant power shifts as well as fundamental changes to the modalities of assistance. Until we better enable these priorities, women and girls in crisis—and especially the most vulnerable subgroups—will continue to be left behind.

Where Do We Go from Here?

The SDGs set out two propositions that are at once radical and inspiring: the first, that we should commit ourselves to the profoundly political project of realizing a gender equitable world by 2030; and the second, that we should bring about that world by focusing on those with the least amount of power, so that no one is left behind. While the word "feminist" does not feature in the SDG

24. Haneef and Tembe (2019).
25. Gressmann (2016).
26. 2016. "The Grand Bargain—A Shared Commitment to Better Serve People in Need," and Thompson and Clement (2019).

Box 2-3. Six Contributions of Local Women Responders

Collaboration with women-led groups, organizations, and networks is often assumed to take place when a crisis is over and development work starts. CARE's research in Malawi and Vanuatu showed how women responders contribute to a more contextualized and effective humanitarian response overall. The six core contributions of women responders include:

1. The *access* women responders may have, permitting them not only to act as first responders but also support more marginalized populations.

2. The contextual *understanding* women responders bring to the needs and realities of different groups, of how to engage with key stakeholders and of how to respond creatively to barriers.

3. Their ability to use social capital and networks to *reach* other women.

4. Their ability to provide a space for and *raise women's voices* and support women's *leadership.*

5. Their ability to offer *solidarity* to other women and girls in day-to-day spaces and activism.

6. Their ability to make interventions gender-*transformative* and potentially more *sustainable.*

Source: CARE International 2018(b)

Agenda, the core elements of that agenda are broadly aligned with what we might consider a feminist approach to international development—namely, recognition of the centrality of gender and other intersecting forms of identity-based marginalization in determining who risks being "left behind"; critical awareness of power relations with an intent to transform them; and accountability to the voices and solutions of the disenfranchised.

Given the implicit feminism of the SDGs, the challenge for international actors committed to gender equality is not to define a new way forward, but to be accountable to that already progressive framework. Doubling down on our commitment to gender equality is especially urgent given the increasing threats to women's rights and shrinking civic space. Our brief review in this chapter suggests two levels of action that would enable us to recommit to accountable progress on gender equality, especially for the women and girls most likely to be excluded from the benefits of change. The first level of action is more easily tackled within the existing paradigm of international assistance and focuses on addressing the conceptual and data-related challenges that hinder our ability to better understand what works where and for whom. The second level of action requires aid actors to take an honest look at ourselves to assess whether the current incentive structures and normative frameworks that shape our practices and accountabilities enable us to do what is required to contribute to gender equality by 2030.

With these two levels of action in mind, we offer the following four recommendations:

First, international actors should invest in improved "gender data" and measurement systems for gender equality, with a focus on how this information translates into power and action. Improving intersectional approaches to data collection, analysis, and use is key to targeting the most vulnerable women and girls with relevant and effective interventions. Multidimensional gender data needs to be collected and used across all sectors, and particularly where such data is lacking, as in fragile contexts and domains such as public finance and rural development. Partnering with local, women-led organizations to leverage their knowledge of marginalized women and girls across the continuum of development and humanitarian contexts, and supporting women's rights groups to interpret and use gender data to inform evidence-based advocacy for gender-equitable practices, services, policies, and laws, is critically important and currently underfunded.

Second, policymakers and practitioners must adopt approaches to promoting gender equality that recognize the complexity of social change. This requires long-term planning while instituting feasible, short- and medium-term changes based on clearly elaborated assumptions that are tested along the way. Gender markers, well-developed theories of change, feedback and consultation with program participants, and appropriate measurement and evaluation for course correction are essential tools on this path. Aiming for social change at scale also implies supporting collective action for gender equality and building learning and evidence around gender-synchronized approaches.

Third, we recommend strengthening and diversifying international, national, and local coalitions for gender equality. Donors and implementers should dramatically increase assistance to women-focused and feminist organizations and networks through flexible funding modalities that are sustainable, predictable, and grounded in partnership rather than paternalism. Government actors can accelerate progress toward gender equality by providing funding and convening opportunities for cross-sectoral planning, data sharing, and accountability to gender equality outcomes. And private sector actors should be encouraged through both business and moral arguments to consider how gender equality is vital to the achievement of their own goals.

Last, we urge development and assistance actors to build a culture of self-reflection and transparency—in which we forthrightly address the power dynamics at global, national, local, and institutional levels that affect which women and girls are left behind and shape our own behavior and accountabilities as a sector.[27] Practically speaking, this means embedding gender-transformative policies and practices within development institutions; acknowledging the tensions and complexities between the demands to sustain our own organizations and the imperative to shift power to local actors; and inviting women's rights activists to hold aid actors accountable by publicly sharing our program data with them and including them as critical partners in strategy development and evaluation efforts.

We still have more than a decade to reach our goals for 2030. The complexities and slow pace of change toward gender equity can be disheartening; however, women across the globe are on the move. Every day, through our work at CARE, we see determination and a sense of possibility reflected even in the depths of some of the most protracted crises in the world—from Afghanistan to West Bank Gaza. Our obligation is to make sure that the women and girls who face seemingly insurmountable odds because of their gender and where they were born, their social class, or the color of their skin are not "left behind" by discriminatory institutions. Everyone should enjoy the benefits of social and economic progress. We must tap into and unleash individual passion as an engine for collective action, remove obstacles in the paths of women and girls, and hold the powerful—including ourselves—accountable for commitments to gender equality. Will we achieve gender equality by 2030? That future is not written, but radical hope and concerted action is the only option worth considering.

References

Arutyunova, A., and C. Clark, 2013. "Watering the Leaves, Starving the Roots: The Status of Financing for Women's Rights Organizing and Gender Equality." Association for Women's Rights in Development.

Asia Foundation. 2019. "A Survey of the Nepali People 2018."

Begovic, M., J. Linn, and R. Vrbensky. 2017. "Scaling Up the Impact of Development Interventions: Lessons from a Review of UNDP Country Programs," Working Paper 101(Brookings).

Bishop, K. 2017. "Women and Trans-Led Organizations Respond to Closing Space for Civil Society." Mama Cash, Urgent Action Fund. July.

CARE International. 2016. "Engaging Men and Boys for Gender Equality Series: Man in the Mirror—Reflections on Men and Boys." Brief 3.

———. 2018a. "Gender Equality and Women's Voice: Guidance Note."

27. As Paul O'Brien writes in this same anthology, ". . . we may have to take some of the attention we have been putting toward better understanding those being 'left behind,' and marshal our efforts to ask, 'being left behind by whom?'"

———. 2018b. "Women Responders: Placing Local Action at the Center of Humanitarian Protection Programming."

Cornwall, A. 2014. "Women's Empowerment: What Works and Why?" UNU-WIDER.

Crenshaw, C. 1989. "Demarginalizing the Intersection of Race and Sex: A Black Feminist Critique of Antidiscrimination Doctrine, Feminist Theory, and Antiracist Politics." University of Chicago Legal Forum. 140: 139–67.

Criado-Perez, C. 2019. "Invisible Women: Exposing Data Bias in a World Designed for Men."

Custer, S., and others. 2018. *Listening to Leaders 2018: Is Development Cooperation Tuned-In or Tone-Deaf?* Williamsburg, Va.: AidData at William & Mary.

Equal Measures 2030. 2018. "Data Driving Change: Introducing the EM2030 SDG Gender Index: Executive Summary." July.

Glinski, A., and others. 2018. "Gender Equity and Male Engagement: It Only Works when Everyone Plays." Washington: ICRW.

Gressmann, W. 2016. "From the Ground Up: Gender and Conflict Analysis in Yemen."

Haneef C. and Tembe M. 2019. "CARE Rapid Gender Analysis: Cyclone Idai Response, Sofala Province Mozambique."

Kharas, H. and A. Rogerson. 2017. "Global Development Trends and Challenges: Horizon 2025 Revisited." London: Overseas Development Institute.

Martinez, E. 2006. *Synthesis Report Phase 2: CARE International Strategic Impact Inquiry on Women's Empowerment.*

Mosedale, S. 2005. "CARE Strategic Impact Inquiry on Women's Empowerment."

OECD. 2018a. "Aid to Gender Equality and Women's Empowerment: An Overview."

———. 2018b. "Is the Last Mile the Longest? Economic Gains from Gender Equality in Nordic Countries."

Sen, G. 2018. "The SDG and Feminist Movement Building." UN Women.

Thompson, L. and R. Clement. 2019. "Defining Feminist Foreign Policy." Washington: ICRW.

UN Women. 2018. "Turning Promises into Action: Gender Equality in the 2030 Agenda for Sustainable Development."

Weldon, S. and M. Htun, "Feminist Mobilization and Progressive Policy Change: Why Governments Take Action to Combat Violence against Women," *Gender & Development*, vol. 21, no. 2 (2013), 231–47.

World Economic Forum. 2017. *The Global Gender Gap Report 2017.*

———. 2018. *The Global Gender Gap Report 2018.*

CHAPTER THREE

Breaking Out of the Poverty Trap

Lindsay Coates and Scott MacMillan

Introduction

In 2018, one of us visited a rural village in Bangladesh to speak to participants in a "graduation program," a term used to describe programs designed to break the poverty trap with a boost of multiple, sequenced interventions. When we asked one woman what the program had changed for her, she brought out a piece of paper inviting her to a village event. Before she went through the program, her neighbors barely knew she existed, she said. Now she was a member of the community, invited to people's homes and weddings. One hears echoes of this sentiment from participants in similar graduation programs worldwide. Such stories illustrate just one of the many cruel aspects of ultra-poverty: those afflicted by it tend to be invisible—to neighbors, distant policymakers, and nearly everyone in between.

The ultra-poor need to stop being invisible to policymakers. We need to pay closer attention to the poorest and the unique set of challenges they face, for without a better understanding of the lived reality of ultra-poverty, we will fail to live up to the promise of "leaving no one behind." Without programs tailored for people in these circumstances, the extreme poverty rate will become increasingly hard to budge. We are already starting to see this reflected in global poverty data. For decades, the global extreme poverty rate, defined as the portion of humanity living below the equivalent of $1.90 per day, fell rapidly, from 36 percent in 1990 to 10 percent in 2015. Earlier in this decade, optimism took hold

With special thanks to Emily Coppel and Isabel Whisson.

that we may even remove extreme poverty from the face of the earth.[1] The World Bank has interpreted "eradication" as less than 3 percent, but optimism is now waning that we will reach even that milestone by 2030. The World Bank's own 2018 Poverty and Prosperity report offers a stark warning: "To reach our goal of bringing extreme poverty below 3 percent by 2030, the world's poorest countries must grow at a rate that far surpasses their historical experience."[2] Another report projects that climate change and forced displacement will cause another 100 million people to fall into extreme poverty by 2030.[3] Even if 4 percent of the world's population remains below the threshold in 2030, this will be an estimated 340 million people, more than the current population of the United States—hardly a footnote or a rounding error.[4] This is unacceptable from a moral, rights-based standpoint. It is also an inefficient use of global human potential, creating less opportunity and progress for us all. Breaking the poverty trap so that hundreds of millions can become productive economic citizens is both an ethical imperative and sound economic policy.

This chapter seeks to advance an understanding of the microeconomic and psychological reality of what it means to be ultra-poor, while pointing to an emerging set of scalable, science-based solutions that can break the trap. "The poor" are not a homogenous group, and even the term "extreme poor" is often used to lump together people facing very different circumstances. Using the graduation approach pioneered by BRAC as one example, this chapter will highlight ways to tackle ultra-poverty through the emerging "science of hope," which posits that when coupled with skills and material support, an injection of well-founded hope and optimism into the lives of the ultra-poor can break the poverty trap. A growing body of evidence suggests that programs activating people's sense of self-worth lead to improvements in employment, earnings, mental health, political awareness, and women's influence in the household. There is also growing evidence to suggest that when it comes to ultra-poverty, purely economic boosts, including relatively quick fixes such as unconditional cash transfers or universal basic income, can fail to break the trap, while more holistic changes make the crucial difference.

1. Lowrey (2013).
2. World Bank (2018).
3. Hallegatte and others (2016).
4. Also concerning is that the majority of progress against extreme poverty in recent decades came from East Asia and the Pacific region, with much of it tied to China's rise. This will not necessarily carry over into other regions. In sub-Saharan Africa, absolute numbers of the extreme poor are actually growing, from 278 million in 1990 to 413 million in 2015. See World Bank, 2018, "Poverty and Shared Prosperity 2018—Piecing Together the Poverty Puzzle."

What Is Ultra-Poverty?

Ultra-poverty is hard to define. The commonly accepted extreme poverty income threshold is currently $1.90 per day, and the ultra-poor tend to live on less than that. At levels that low, income- and consumption-based definitions stop being meaningful. Those who work closely with the ultra-poor observe that their suffering has a distinctive character, even compared to people just slightly better off. We define ultra-poverty as a sub-segment of extreme poverty characterized by material destitution and psychological despair so severe that mainstream development assistance and market-led solutions make no dent in it. It is among the clearest examples of a poverty trap: a self-reinforcing state of physical, material, and psychological deprivation seemingly immune to most interventions designed to boost people's income and well-being.

A useful lens through which to view ultra-poverty is economist Amartya Sen's definition of poverty as a "deprivation of basic capabilities," including the freedoms and choices that most of us take for granted, specifically "the substantive freedoms [a person] enjoys to lead the kind of life he or she has reason to value. In this perspective, poverty must be seen as the deprivation of basic capabilities rather than merely as lowness of incomes, which is the standard criterion of identification of poverty."[5] Based on qualitative reports from development workers and researchers, a functional understanding of what ultra-poverty looks like has emerged, and it tracks closely with Sen's definition.[6] Far beyond simply having low incomes, the ultra-poor are bereft of any semblance of those substantive freedoms.

Figures vary as to how many people fall into this category, as the data is spotty and the definition remains loose, but the number likely remains in the hundreds of millions. According to a 2007 report from International Food Policy Research Institute based on 2004 data, about 162 million people lived in ultra-poverty, which was defined at the time as living on less than 50 cents a day, in 1993 purchasing power parity (PPP) dollars, with an additional 323 million living in "medial poverty," defined as living on between 50 and 75 cents a day.[7] According to a more recent estimate from 2017, 736 million people live in extreme poverty—that is, below $1.90 per day in 2011 PPP terms—and of these, more than half, or around 394 million people, are living in ultra-poverty.[8]

5. Sen (1999).

6. See "Impact Pathways: Stories from People Behind the Numbers," from Akhter U. Ahmed and others, "The Impact of Asset Transfer on Livelihoods of the Ultra Poor in Bangladesh," Research Monograph Series No. 39, BRAC Research and Evaluation Division, April 2009, (http://ebrary.ifpri.org/utils/getfile/collection/p15738coll2/id/125248/filename/125249.pdf)

7. Ahmed and others (2007).

8. Reed and others (2017).

All poverty arises from a complex set of interrelated causes, often tied to failures in politics and governance along with systematic marginalization of minorities, migrants, and—almost universally across cultures—women. For those at the very bottom, addressing the problem requires highly adapted approaches that account for the unique characteristics of ultra-poverty in each region or even community. The indicators of ultra-poverty are multi-modal: the Global State of Ultra-Poverty, which numbered the population of global ultra-poor at 394 million, defines ultra-poverty using the Multidimensional Poverty Index, a measure that uses methods developed by Sabina Alkire and James Foster of the Oxford Poverty and Human Development Initiative.[9] The method assesses poverty across multiple indicators, including education, electricity, sanitation, and access to drinking water.[10]

It is challenging to promote common approaches to such complex, multifaceted problems, each with their own set of contextual realities. Worse yet, access to existing support programs—whether provided by government or civil society—is spotty across regions, which is again tied to discrimination as well as political and social marginalization. In some places, promoting access to a local government vaccination program might help solve a critical health need; in other places, such a program might not even exist for anyone.

Despite the uneven progress and complexity of the diagnosis in any given context, interest in addressing ultra-poverty—and the capacity to do so—is growing among governments and global development institutions. The Partnership for Economic Inclusion (PEI), which is housed at the World Bank and advocates for accelerated innovation and scaling of the graduation approach,[11] gives a snapshot of progress in its 2018 State of the Sector report.[12] Governments from thirty-four countries are now engaged in graduation (sometimes also referred to as "productive inclusion"), double the number from 2016, reaching an estimated 14 million people.

The Power of Hope

What creates a poverty trap? Development practice and a growing body of evidence suggest the ultra-poor may often be caught in a self-perpetuating trap of

---

9. Ibid.

10. Ibid. See Oxford Poverty and Human Development Initiative, "Global Multidimensional Poverty Index," (https://ophi.org.uk/multidimensional-poverty-index/).

11. PEI is the successor to the Graduating the Poor Initiative, previously housed at Consultative Group to Assist the Poor (CGAP), which oversaw the first series of global graduation pilots to test the effectiveness of the model.

12. Arevolo, Kaffenberger, and de Montesquiou (2018).

hopelessness, which sustains itself based on a person's inability to imagine that a better world is possible.[13] The trap of hopelessness likely arises in part from cognitive overload. The poor have many choices, and as unfashionable as it may sound, in many cases they have too many choices. They can walk several miles for their child's booster immunization, or they can work that day. The choice is entirely theirs. The stress of being poor—including the uncertainty of paid labor, of not knowing where your next meal will come from, and the constantly looming threat of health shocks—is compounded by the necessity of making a multitude of important decisions like these every single day.

Sendhil Mullainathan, an economist, and Eldar Shafir, a psychologist, explore the phenomenon of the "bandwidth tax," which depletes one's finite cognitive resources.[14] The authors cite studies on parenting: Air traffic controllers, on a busy day at work, when they have to make hundreds of potentially life-or-death decisions, tend to be worse parents that evening, compared to less busy days; the children of people on food stamps behave worse at school at the end of the month, when the family's food stamps are running out, suggesting that parents' daily worries trickle down to their children, affecting their faculty for self-control.[15] Mullainathan and Shafir call this the "present-day cognitive load of making ends meet," and it is especially acute for those living in ultra-poverty.

Some might object that it is overly paternalistic to ascribe people's suffering to hopelessness, as though all that is needed is a shift in mindset. This would be a misunderstanding of the nature of both the problem and the solution. In fact, many of the freedoms we take for granted actually result from what Esther Duflo calls a "subtle paternalism." For instance, people in richer countries usually do not have to worry about boiling their water before drinking it, because the state has decided it is better for them to have treated water coming from their faucets.[16] Far from infringing on Sen's "substantive freedoms," this actually gives us more freedom to pursue other sources of satisfaction and meaning, for it removes a source of stress from our lives and allows us to apply our cognitive resources elsewhere. For most people struggling with ultra-poverty, even modest goals such as owning chickens are out of reach—and known to be out of reach—without a material boost.

13. Abhijit Banerjee and Esther Duflo cite evidence to suggest that, much like nutrition, psychological factors have physiological and material consequences. In many cases, when incomes rise for the very poor, food expenditure rises roughly proportionally to overall consumption. If the poverty trap were caused by undernutrition only, hungry people would have invested most of their new income in food, so they could work more and earn more money. See "Poor Economics," Public Affairs, 2011, 22–28.

14. Mullainathan and Shafir (2013).

15. Ibid., 155–57.

16. Duflo (2012).

We are not suggesting that psychological factors like stress, hopelessness, or the bandwidth tax are the sole factors keeping people in ultra-poverty. Hope and confidence alone will not buy you chickens; in many cases, people's pessimism is entirely warranted. But we have little doubt these psychological factors are at work and too often ignored. The question is whether a material boost alone would break the trap and thus shift the psychology, or whether psychology remains a barrier unto itself. We posit, based largely on qualitative observations of how people break the poverty trap, that in most cases of ultra-poverty, even if material conditions change through a sudden positive shock (such as a one-time income boost or transfer of assets), the psychological factors remain an obstacle. There is not yet overwhelming evidence for or against this hypothesis. It is one that can and needs to be empirically tested, as we will soon discuss.

Graduation: A Case Study in the Science of Hope

The graduation approach has gained recognition over the past five years as one of the most rigorously tested interventions in international development. Broadly speaking, it is a sequenced set of services tailored to the culture, context, and population of the ultra-poor, designed to give a one-time boost to break the poverty trap. These interventions generally include livelihood training, transfers of cash and productive assets, and encouragement of savings, all facilitated through in-person coaching. They focus on the needs of the household as a whole, with women usually as the primary program participants. When adapting graduation globally, BRAC applies a framework approach to ensure that programs meet four goals: social protection, livelihood promotion, financial inclusion, and social empowerment. For details of the graduation methodology used by BRAC in Bangladesh, the largest and longest-running such program in the world, see box 3-1.

The role of the coach is key, for this is how these programs build hope. Each participant is assigned a caseworker or coach tasked with conducting regular individual check-ins, typically at the participant's home. In addition, the coach meets regularly with small groups of participants who live in the same village or neighborhood. In the group setting, participants learn from and receive encouragement from one another. These recurring touchpoints remind the participant that change is possible and support will be available along the way. The entire program is notably time-bound, usually running for about two years, during which a person living in dire poverty can be expected to transform his or her life, "graduating" onto the economic ladder—at least to the bottom rung of it—where he or she will enjoy a degree of control and independence, often for the first time in his or her life. Emphasis is on the participants to lead their own

Box 3-1. An Overview of BRAC's Ultra-Poor Graduation Program

BRAC's Ultra-Poor Graduation (UPG) program (formerly called Targeting the Ultra-Poor) is the first and largest such program in the world. Launched in Bangladesh in 2002, the program has reached 1.9 million households, or more than 7 million people, as of 2019.

The process of participant selection begins with a rigorous period of targeting, including community meetings to identify the poorest people in the area. Program staff follow up with door-to-door visits, using questionnaires to help verify who qualifies.

Participants are trained in certain self-employment skills–how to take care of a cow or small shop, for instance–and in a one-time transfer, they are given a productive asset, such as livestock, agricultural inputs, or goods for small trade.

In the program's earlier phases, participants were given limited consumption support in the form of cash and food to offset the opportunity cost of not engaging in menial wage labor or begging while they learned new livelihoods. Recognizing the improving poverty environment in Bangladesh, this provision has since been replaced with a "savings match," whereby BRAC matches money participants put aside, which helps build a habit of saving. Participants also receive financial training, including saving for the future, budgeting, and using credit to help sustain or grow their micro-enterprises.

Program staff make sure participants' children are going to school, have balanced diets, are not at risk of child marriage, and ensure the household has access to healthcare, clean water, and a latrine. The program also mobilizes the community to help oversee aspects of the program, provide support where needed, and integrate the ultra-poor into local life, in part by setting up village development committees, which include local elites.

The graduation rate of participants–that is, the percentage that leaves a rigorously defined category of ultra-poverty based on a set of predefined indicators and takes up more sustainable livelihoods–usually exceeds 95 percent.

progress, with the knowledge that at the end of the two-year period, they will be on their own. If this progress stalls, the caseworker will be there to help.

To be sure, the "graduated" ultra-poor are still poor, but they have secured stable incomes for their families and are finally in a position where their hard work actually gains traction. They have broken free from the poverty trap, because the program has addressed the multifaceted nature of that trap, whereby any one of a multitude of factors—including lack of skills, low assets and capital, ill health and poor nutrition, battered confidence and hopelessness—could have weighed them down and prevented them from breaking free.

BRAC's original graduation program emerged from the organization's recognition of its own failure to reach the poorest in Bangladesh, where the organization was founded in 1972. By the late 1990s, BRAC had grown to become a well-established microfinance provider in Bangladesh, offering credit services and training throughout the country. Staff recognized that although many women—for the microfinance program was exclusive to women—were using small loans to grow and expand their businesses, a substantial population was so marginalized they failed to benefit from microfinance or any other mainstream development programs that BRAC offered.

Research and adaptation are central to the BRAC approach. Launched in 2002, the Ultra-Poor Graduation (UPG) program evolved as it encountered unforeseen challenges, its staff tweaking it to account for the changing poverty context in Bangladesh. This was often in response to studies and evaluations conducted by BRAC's independent research unit, which has published twenty-five working papers since 2004, each examining a cultural nuance, challenge, or component of the program in depth. Topics have included how to effectively find and target participants, how to leverage relationships and engage with village elders to facilitate social inclusion, and whether credit combined with grants can address ultra-poverty in a more sustainable manner than grants alone.[17]

By 2007, qualitative and quasi-experimental studies suggested the two-year program was having a profound and long-lasting impact. Scholars from the London School of Economics began a randomized controlled trial (RCT), covering about eight thousand women in just over fourteen hundred villages. A working paper released in 2013 found significant gains versus a control group, including a 38 percent increase in income and "large and sustained impacts on the occupational choices and economic lives of the eligible poor."[18] Most notably, participants' gains had persisted after four years, or two years after they had stopped receiving direct support, suggesting the program had indeed broken the poverty trap. The program also saw gains in self-reported happiness, value of assets, a reduction of anxiety, and other non-economic indicators of improved well-being. Since then, several follow-up surveys using the same baseline have found that participants continue to gain ground, even seven years after entering the program.[19] Additional follow-up studies are underway.

Following early indications of the effectiveness of BRAC's graduation program in Bangladesh, interest grew in knowing whether the BRAC results could be replicated in other geographic and cultural contexts. Starting in 2006, the

---

17. Noor and others, "Stories of Targeting: Process Documentation of Selecting the Ultra Poor for CFPR/TUP Programme," CFPR-TUP Working Paper Series No. 1, BRAC Research and Evaluation Division, April 2004 (https://research.brac.net/new/publications/documentation); Naomi Hossain and Imran Matin, "Engaging Elite Support for the Ultra-Poor," *Development in Practice*, November 2007; Jinnat Ara and others, "Walking on Two Legs: Credit Plus Grant Approach to Poverty Reduction," CFPR-TUP Working Paper Series No. 25, BRAC Research and Evaluation Division (http://research.brac.net/new/staff/ultrappor).

18. Bandiera and others (2013).

19. Bandiera and others, "Labor Markets and Poverty in Village Economies," *Quarterly Journal of Economics*, vol. 132, no. 2 (May 2017), 811–70; Balboni and others, "Transforming the Economic Lives of the Ultra-Poor," Growth Brief, International Growth Centre, December 2015.

Figure 3-1. BRAC's 2007 Targeting the Ultra-Poor Graduation Program

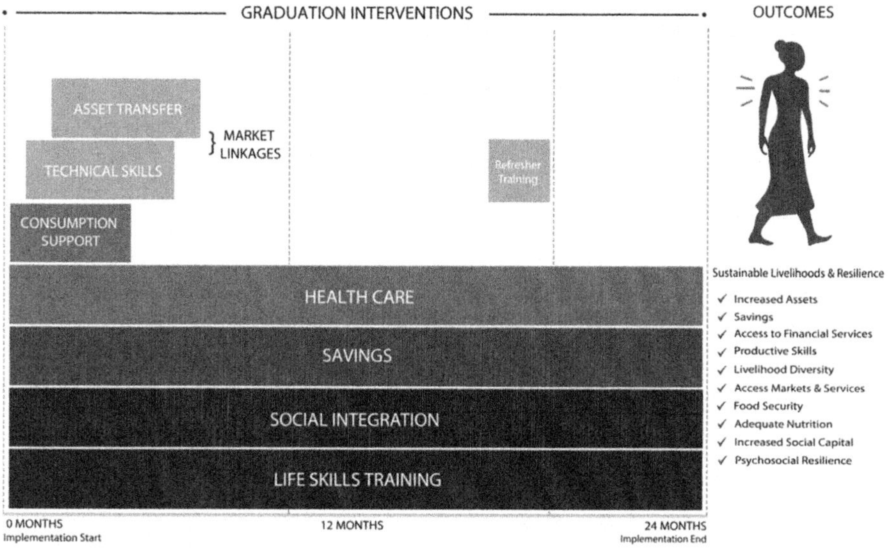

GRADUATION INTERVENTIONS   OUTCOMES

ASSET TRANSFER

} MARKET
  LINKAGES

TECHNICAL SKILLS

CONSUMPTION
SUPPORT

Refresher
Training

HEALTH CARE

SAVINGS

SOCIAL INTEGRATION

LIFE SKILLS TRAINING

Sustainable Livelihoods & Resilience

✓ Increased Assets
✓ Savings
✓ Access to Financial Services
✓ Productive Skills
✓ Livelihood Diversity
✓ Access Markets & Services
✓ Food Security
✓ Adequate Nutrition
✓ Increased Social Capital
✓ Psychosocial Resilience

0 MONTHS   12 MONTHS   24 MONTHS
Implementation Start   Implementation End

Source: Credit: Amplifier Strategies

Consultative Group to Assist the Poor (CGAP) and Ford Foundation collaborated to lead a set of pilots in eight countries, testing adaptations of BRAC's approach (box 3-2). The process culminated in 2015, when a group of researchers published the combined results from RCTs covering more than ten thousand households in six of those countries, comparing participants' results to that of a control group one year after graduating from the program. The results were impressive across the board: income and revenues were significantly higher in the treatment group in every country, and household consumption was significantly higher in all countries except one, Honduras.[20] The question of whether graduation could be a globally adaptable solution to extreme poverty was answered with a resounding yes. Graduation began gaining prominence in development circles, sparking a wave of investment in close to a hundred programs worldwide since the findings were released.

Comparing Graduation to Unconditional Cash Transfers

As the graduation approach has gained traction, another category of interventions, unconditional cash transfers (UCTs), has caught the attention of donors

20. Banerjee and others (2015).

Box 3-2. Evidence Shows the Graduation Approach to Be a Globally Adaptable Solution to Extreme Poverty

Between 2006 and 2014, the Ford Foundation, Consultative Group to Assist the Poor, and several international and local partners tested and adapted the graduation approach in ten pilot programs in eight countries. Randomized controlled trials were conducted in six of the sites—in Ethiopia, Ghana, Honduras, India, Pakistan, and Peru.

Each program ran for two years, with the evaluations assessing results at the end of the program and one year after its completion. Program adaptations in each country were designed to take into account local market forces, barriers to economic activity facing the ultra-poor in each context, existing social protection programming with which to link participants, program eligibility criteria, and graduation indicators specific to the community.

The studies found that every group of economic outcomes improved significantly relative to the comparison group, both immediately after the program ended and a year later. Graduation households' consumption increased 16.4 percent in Ethiopia, 13.6 percent in India, and 10.2 percent in Pakistan, with similar improvements observed in savings, asset holdings, and food security. Impacts also extended to psychosocial well-being. In Ethiopia, Ghana, Honduras, India, and Peru, improvements in self-reported happiness and stress remained positive a year after the end of the program. Women also became more likely to be politically active and reported having greater input in household financial decisions. Most notably, the results were largely consistent across multiple contexts and partners, signaling that ultra-poor households faced similar constraints across diverse contexts, which graduation was largely effective at addressing.[a]

a. Abdul Latif Jameel Policy Action Lab. 2015. "Building Stable Livelihoods for the Ultra-Poor," Policy Bulletin, September.

and development agencies by recording strong gains with equally robust (albeit shorter-term) randomized impact evaluations. These programs are establishing the idea of cash benchmarking, testing the hypothesis that everything delivered during the course of a development intervention—be it training, technology, assets, education, health, or social support—might be better off delivered to participants as cash. If the intervention does not outperform cash along desired impact indicators, it should be scrapped in favor of UCTs—so the thinking goes. Compared to graduation programs, UCT programs can be politically appealing for governments, since a UCT program typically makes less effort to identify participants, a cost-saving measure that also avoids hard choices about whom to include. Many UCT programs use simple targeting criteria, such as whether a potential participant has a thatched or a metal roof.[21] This absence of robust

---

21. This was one of the methods initially used by GiveDirectly, one of the UCT pioneers. More recently, the organization began targeting entire villages using national poverty data, then enrolling all households in a single village, akin to a universal basic income plan.

targeting makes it more difficult to meaningfully compare UCT programs with highly targeted graduation programs, since the two approaches may have heterogeneous results for different groups, based on participants' initial level of poverty or other baseline characteristics.

Perhaps the most well-known UCT studies are the ones on the GiveDirectly program in Kenya.[22] The initial results showed broad, positive changes from unconditional cash transfers after nine months, including increased consumption and savings, investments in livestock and durable assets (mainly metal roofs), and increases in revenue from agriculture and business activities. Other studies of unconditional or near-unconditional cash transfers have also yielded initial positive results. The Ugandan government's Youth Opportunities Program in northern Uganda tested the effect of giving large, near-unconditional cash grants (participants were merely required to state how much of the grant they would invest in training) to thousands of unemployed youth, with grant sums worth twice their average annual income. Recipients invested the grants mainly in vocational skills training, and after four years, business assets were 57 percent higher than a control group, work hours 17 percent higher, and earnings 38 percent higher.[23] Cash transfers have led to improvements in non-economic indicators in other contexts, such as early marriage and teenage pregnancy, as in a 2011 study comparing conditional and unconditional cash transfers in Malawi.[24]

Newer evidence suggests these gains may fade over time, however. A follow-up on the Malawi study showed that the short-term benefits of monthly cash transfers largely evaporated after two years.[25] The three-year results from the GiveDirectly Kenya program, released in 2018, have led to multiple interpretations, including one that suggests the gains from cash had dissipated at the three-year mark. Though the results are subject to debate, there is even some evidence that the transfers had negative spillover effects, in the sense of having actually caused harm to non-recipients in the same village. The authors concluded that "cash transfers result in sustained increases in assets," but that "long-term impacts on

---

22. Johannes Haushofer and Jeremy Shapiro, "The Short-Term Impact of Unconditional Cash Transfers to the Poor: Experimental Evidence from Kenya," *Quarterly Journal of Economics*, vol. 131, no. 4 (November 2016); Johannes Haushofer and Jeremy Shapiro, "Household Response to Income Changes: Evidence from an Unconditional Cash Transfer Program in Kenya," Princeton University, November 2013 (www.princeton.edu/~joha/publications/Haushofer_Shapiro_UCT_2013.pdf); Johannes Haushofer and Jeremy Shapiro, "The Long-Term Impact of Unconditional Cash Transfers: Experimental Evidence from Kenya," January 2018 (http://jeremypshapiro.com/papers/Haushofer_Shapiro_UCT2_2018-01-30_paper_only.pdf).

23. Blattman, Fiala, and Martinez (2014).

24. Baird and others, "Cash or Condition? Evidence from a Cash Transfer Experiment," *Quarterly Journal of Economics*, vol. 126, no. 4, November 2011, 1709–53.

25. Baird, McIntosh, and Özler (2016).

other dimensions, and potential spillover effects, remain to be substantiated by future work."[26] The nine-year impact of the above-cited Youth Opportunities Program in Uganda was even more lackluster. While researchers found the program had strong economic effects for at least the first four years, after nine years, the control group and treatment groups had converged, reducing the long-term impact to zero.[27]

Despite the attention both graduation and unconditional cash transfers have received, few studies have directly compared graduation and unconditional cash transfer programs in the same setting.[28] There are currently less than a handful of current and ongoing studies that do compare cash and graduation, and while they have produced notable results, none has produced generalizable evidence of cost-effectiveness.[29] This is a salient gap in the development literature, for such studies would measure the relative cost-effectiveness of two of the most successful approaches to poverty reduction. It would also allow one to make bolder claims about which approaches work best for whom, based on heterogeneous baseline characteristics of a given population. While we are advocates for the graduation approach, we are open to empirical evidence that may show that, for certain populations, UCTs could be a more cost-effective solution. As the authors of the GiveDirectly RCT argued: "What is needed now, in our view, are studies that compare the effect of cash transfers to those of other interventions that have been shown to be effective in improving outcomes in developing countries. For instance, are UCTs more or less effective than ultra-poor graduation programs . . . and on what dimensions?"[30]

26. Haushofer and Shapiro (2018).

27. Blattman, Fiala, and Martinez (2014).

28. A 2016 meta-analysis attempted a cost-effectiveness comparison of forty-eight programs in three categories (UCTs, graduation, and generic livelihood programs). Based on available evidence, the paper called the graduation approach "the clearest path forward to reduce extreme poverty in a sustainable manner," with the caveat that additional direct comparisons were needed. See Munshi Sulaiman and others, "Eliminating Extreme Poverty: Comparing the Cost-Effectiveness of Livelihood, Cash Transfer, and Graduation Approaches," CGAP and IPA, December 2016.

29. A study published in December 2016 made a direct comparison of a BRAC graduation program in South Sudan and a similarly expensive unconditional cash-transfer program. The study found "evidence of positive consumption effects from both treatments, but a persistent wealth effect only from [graduation]." See Reajul Chowdhury and others, "Valuing Assets Provided to Low-Income Households in South Sudan," University of California, Riverside, December 2016 (https://economics.ucr.edu/pacdev/pacdev-papers/valuing_assets_provided.pdf).

30. Haushofer and Shapiro (2018).

Taking Graduation to Scale

Donors and development agencies need to reevaluate how they think about investing in and delivering complex, multidimensional implementations at scale. The graduation community has proven that complex programs for the ultra-poor can be adapted successfully. Leading implementers such as BRAC offer technical assistance to governments and others looking to implement such programs.[31] While global partnerships such as the Partnership for Economic Inclusion housed at the World Bank encourage the uptake and scaling of graduation programs by client governments, additional high-level guidance would spur much-needed action. One model could be the set of norms and standards developed by the World Food Program, World Bank, and other actors, on how to develop and implement effective school-feeding programs.[32]

Without additional funding, we risk leaving the ultra-poor behind and falling short of the extreme poverty eradication goals. There is a tendency among donors to favor relatively simple, high-impact interventions, whose results are easier to replicate and scale. Bed net distribution, vaccination, and cash transfer programs (both conditional and unconditional) have gained popularity, partly for these reasons. But the complex nature of the poverty trap necessitates multifaceted programs. While graduation is sometimes seen as too costly to scale, the long-term cost-benefit analysis works in its favor. Most of the major studies on graduation include cost-benefit analyses showing gains that outlast the period of direct support, making it likely that a single upfront investment is a more effective way of helping the poor than many smaller payments over time.[33]

BRAC's success in Bangladesh can largely be credited to the sustained funding it received for over a decade, which enabled years of iteration and adaptation to address the complexity of challenges facing the ultra-poor. This included large sums of unrestricted funding from the UK and Australian aid agencies as part of a Strategic Partnership Arrangement.[34] The sustained financing mechanism provided BRAC with uniquely flexible capital, akin to what Acumen calls "patient capital."[35] BRAC's success with the program also challenges the notion that civil

31. BRAC assisted many of the earlier graduation adaptations and, as of 2019, is offering technical assistance to ongoing non-BRAC graduation programs in Kenya, the Philippines, Egypt, Lesotho, Rwanda, and Egypt.

32. Bundy and others (2009).

33. Banerjee and others (2015); Bandiera and others (2013). The Bangladesh RCT estimated a benefit/cost ratio of 3.2, assuming economic benefits persist for 20 years with a discount rate of 5 percent.

34. BRAC/DFID/AusAID Strategic Partnership Agreement (SPA)—Terms of Engagement, (2012).

35. See Acumen, "Patient Capital" (https://acumen.org/about/patient-capital/).

society organizations cannot be effective agents of scale. In fact, a 2019 report from the UK's public foreign aid watchdog cited BRAC's graduation program as one of the "best buys in development."[36] While such arrangements have gone out of favor with many donors, the success of graduation is a validation of the argument for sustained, flexible investments in organizations that are committed to learning and iterating.

When governments can be convinced of the value in this, they often provide the best mechanism to reach large numbers of the ultra-poor. Many of the largest graduation-style programs (outside Bangladesh) are operated by governments. Many build on existing government services, improving the effectiveness and reach of investments governments are already making in cash transfers, financial services, livelihoods, or healthcare. Thus, governments may already have many parts in place, which means the development of graduation programs can consist of a coordination or deepening of existing measures, rather than having to start from scratch. Ongoing pilots in the Philippines, Rwanda, and Kenya link participants to existing social assistance programs such as job readiness training and subsidized health insurance.

New funds for graduation may also be available through innovative financing mechanisms. Development impact bonds (DIBs) are well suited to highly measurable and evidence-based approaches like graduation. In 2018, a development impact bond, worth $5.28 million and funded by the U.S. and U.K. aid agencies along with private donors, enabled Village Enterprise to reach twelve thousand ultra-poor households in Kenya and Uganda. As long as participants make progress based on pre-agreed indicators as measured by an external evaluator, payment is unlocked and private funders receive back the capital they put in.[37] Like the "patient capital" model, the implementer is judged by the results they achieve, not how closely they follow a method pre-agreed with the funder. This should create incentives for iteration and adaptation to contexts, which is key to successful graduation programming. Moreover, with DIBs, governments can be the "outcome payer," increasing government ownership of interventions to support ultra-poor citizens while delegating implementation.

Conclusion

Policymakers need to understand the complex needs and unique set of challenges faced by the poorest segments of the human population. If we are to live

---

36. Independent Commission for Aid Impact, "DFID's Partnerships with Civil Society Organizations: A Performance Review," April 2019 (https://icai.independent.gov.uk/html-report/csos).

37. See Village Enterprise, "The Village Enterprise Development Impact Bond," (https://villageenterprise.org/our-impact/development-impact-bond/).

up to the promise of leaving no one behind—if we are to truly invest in human capital, such that humanity's untapped resources of talent and ingenuity are harnessed for global growth and the common good—we must start by better understanding the special character of ultra-poverty and why it is qualitatively different from other forms of poverty. Part of the reason is nonmaterial factors such as stress, hopelessness, and in the words of Mullainathan and Shafir, the constant "present-day cognitive load of making ends meet," which bears down like a weight too great to lift. Poverty is, at heart, a deprivation of one's capacity to be fully human—to dream, to plan, to arrange one's imagination to see a better future. The graduation approach offers a way out.

The challenge now is to mobilize donors and the development community to provide resources to scale up such programs so we can finally eradicate extreme poverty from the face of the earth. Admittedly, in the words of BRAC's founder, Sir Fazle Hasan Abed, "asking policymakers to invest in optimism and self-worth may sound like a vague, soft-hearted appeal."[38] It is anything but that, thanks to the emerging science of hope. When combined with the right amount of material support, an injection of hope and self-esteem can break the poverty trap for millions.

References

Abdul Latif Jameel. 2015. "Building Stable Livelihoods for the Ultra-Poor." Poverty Action Lab, Policy Bulletin.

Abed, Fazle H. 2018. "Building Human Capital Means Investing in the Science of Hope," Thomson Reuters Foundation, October 17 (http://news.trust.org/item/20181017120852-ak1io/).

Acumen. n.d. "Patient Capital." (https://acumen.org/about/patient-capital/).

Ahmed, Akhter U., and others. 2007. "The World's Most Deprived: Characteristics and Causes of Extreme Poverty and Hunger." 2020 Discussion Paper 43, International Food Policy Research Institute (www.ifpri.org/publication/worlds-most-deprived).

Ahmed, Akhter U., and others. 2009. "The Impact of Asset Transfer on Livelihoods of the Ultra Poor in Bangladesh," Research Monograph Series No. 39, BRAC Research and Evaluation Division (http://ebrary.ifpri.org/utils/getfile/collection/p15738coll2/id/125248/filename/125249.pdf).

Ara, Jinnat, and others. 2018. "Walking on Two Legs: Credit Plus Grant Approach to Poverty Reduction," CFPR-TUP Working Paper Series No. 25, BRAC Research and Evaluation Division (http://research.brac.net/new/staff/ultrappor).

Arevolo, Ines, Michelle Kaffenberger, and Aude de Montesquiou. 2018. *2018 State of the Sector—Synthesis Report.* Partnership for Economic Inclusion, 26.

---

38. Fazle Hasan Abed, "Building Human Capital Means Investing in the Science of Hope," Thomson Reuters Foundation, October 17, 2018 (http://news.trust.org/item/20181017120852-ak1io/).

Baird, Sarah, Craig McIntosh, and Berk Özler. 2016. "When the Money Runs Out: Evaluating the Longer-Term Impacts of Two-Year Cash Transfer Program." University of California, San Diego (http://gps.ucsd.edu/_files/faculty/mcintosh/mcintosh_research_SIHR.pdf).

Balboni, Clare, and others. 2015. "Transforming the Economic Lives of the Ultra-Poor." Growth Brief, FIRMS, International Growth Centre, 4.

Bandiera, Oriana, and others. 2013. "Can Basic Entrepreneurship Transform the Economic Lives of the Poor?" Working Paper, International Growth Centre (www.theigc.org/wp-content/uploads/2014/09/Bandiera-Et-Al-2013-Working-Paper.pdf).

————. 2017. "Labor Markets and Poverty in Village Economies," *Quarterly Journal of Economics*, vol. 132, no. 2 (May 2017), 811–70.

Banerjee, Abhijit, and others. 2015. "A Multi-faceted Program Causes Lasting Progress for the Very Poor: Evidence from Six Countries," *Science*, vol. 348, no. 6236,1260799-3.

Banerjee, Abhijit, and Esther Duflo. 2011. *Poor Economics: A Radical Rethinking of the Way to Fight Global Poverty* (Philadelphia: Public Affairs).

Blattman, Christopher, Nathan Fiala, and Sebastian Martinez. 2014. "Generating Skilled Self-Employment in Developing Countries: Experimental Evidence from Uganda." *Quarterly Journal of Economics*, vol. 129, no. 2, 697–752.

Bundy, Donald, and others, "Rethinking School Feeding: Social Safety Nets, Child Development, and the Education Sector," World Food Program and the World Bank, 2009.

BRAC/DFID/AusAID Strategic Partnership Agreement (SPA)—Terms of Engagement. 2012. (https://dfat.gov.au/about-us/publications/Documents/brac-spa-terms-engagement.pdf).

Chowdhury, Reajul, and others. 2016. "Valuing Assets Provided to Low-Income Households in South Sudan." University of California, Riverside. (https://economics.ucr.edu/pacdev/pacdev-papers/valuing_assets_provided.pdf).

Duflo, Esther. 2012. "Human Values and the Design of the Fight Against Poverty." Tanner Lectures (draft). (https://www.povertyactionlab.org/sites/default/files/documents/TannerLectures_EstherDuflo_draft.pdf).

The Economist. 2013. "Poverty: Not Always with Us" (www.economist.com/briefing/2013/06/01/not-always-with-us).

Hallegatte, Stephane, and others. 2016. "Shock Waves—Managing the Impacts of Climate Change on Poverty." *Climate Change and Development Series* (Washington, D.C.: World Bank).

Haushofer, Johannes, and Jeremy Shapiro. 2013. "Household Response to Income Changes: Evidence from an Unconditional Cash Transfer Program in Kenya." Princeton University (www.poverty-action.org/sites/default/files/publications/Haushofer_Shapiro_UCT_2013.pdf).

————. 2016. "The Short-Term Impact of Unconditional Cash Transfers to the Poor: Experimental Evidence from Kenya." *The Quarterly Journal of Economics*, vol. 131, no. 4, 1973–2042.

————. 2018. "The Long-Term Impact of Unconditional Cash Transfers: Experimental Evidence from Kenya" (https://jeremypshapiro.appspot.com/papers/Haushofer_Shapiro_UCT2_2018-01-30_paper_only.pdf).

Hossain, Naomi, and Imran Matin. 2007. "Engaging Elite Support for the Ultra-Poor," *Development in Practice,* vol. 17, no. 3 (June), 3.

Kristof, Nicholas, "The Power of Hope Is Real," *New York Times*, May 21, 2015 (www.nytimes.com/2015/05/21/opinion/nicholas-kristof-the-power-of-hope-is-real.html).

Lipton, Michael. 1986. "Seasonality and Ultra-Poverty." *IDS Bulletin 17.3* (https://michaellipton.files.wordpress.com/2012/02/seasonalityandultrapoverty1986.pdf).

Lowrey, Annie, "Is It Crazy to Think We Can Eradicate Poverty?" *New York Times*, May 5, 2013 (www.nytimes.com/2013/05/05/magazine/is-it-crazy-to-think-we-can-eradicate-poverty.html).

Mullainathan, Sendhil, and Eldar Shafir. 2013. *Scarcity: Why Having Too Little Means So Much* (New York: Times Books).

Noor, Marufia, and others. 2004. "Stories of Targeting: Process Documentation of Selecting the Ultra Poor for CFPR/TUP Programme," CFPR-TUP Working Paper Series No. 1, BRAC Research and Evaluation Division (https://research.brac.net/new/publications/documentation).

Oxford Poverty and Human Development Initiative. n.d. "Global Multidimensional Poverty Index" (https://ophi.org.uk/multidimensional-poverty-index/).

Sulaiman, Munshi, and Farzana Misha. 2016. "Comparative Cost-Benefit Analysis of Programs for the Ultra-Poor in Bangladesh." Copenhagen Consensus Center (www.copenhagenconsensus.com/sites/default/files/sulaiman_misha_ultrapoor.pdf).

Sulaiman, Munshi, and others. 2016. "Eliminating Extreme Poverty: Comparing the Cost-effectiveness of Livelihood, Cash Transfer, and Graduation Approaches." Washington, D.C.: CGAP.

Raza, Wameq A., and Ellen Van de Poel. 2016. "Impact and Spillover Effects of an Asset Transfer Program on Malnutrition: Evidence from a Randomized Control Trial in Bangladesh." Working Paper.

Reed, Larry, and others. 2017. *The Global State of Ultra-Poverty 2017—A Global Analysis of the Greatest Opportunities to End Ultra-Poverty by 2030*. Uplift and the RESULTS Educational Fund (www.ultra-poverty.org/assets/downloads/gsup-2017-report.pdf).

Sen, Amartya. 1999. *Development as Freedom* (New York: Random House).

Sturla, Kate, Neil Buddy Shah, and Jeff McManus. 2018. "The Great DIB-ate: Measurement for Development Impact Bonds." Stanford Social Innovation Review (https://ssir.org/articles/entry/the_great_dib_ate_measurement_for_development_impact_bonds).

United Nations. 2013. *A New Global Partnership—Eradicate Poverty and Transform Economies Through Sustainable Development* (https://www.post2015hlp.org/the-report/).

Village Enterprise. n.d. "The Village Enterprise Development Impact Bond" (https://villageenterprise.org/our-impact/development-impact-bond/).

World Bank. 2012. *World Development Report 2012: Gender Equality and Development* (Washington, D.C.: World Bank), 5.

———. 2013. *World Development Report 2013: Jobs.* (Washington, D.C.: World Bank), 15.

———. 2018. "Poverty and Shared Prosperity 2018—Piecing Together the Poverty Puzzle." (Washington, D.C.: World Bank), xi.

CHAPTER FOUR

No Smallholder Farmer Left Behind

Jane Nelson

E fforts to improve the prosperity and resilience of smallholder farmers and rural households represent one of the greatest challenges and opportunities for achieving the goal of "no one left behind." The estimated 500 million smallholder farmers in developing countries are among the world's poorest and most vulnerable people.[1] The 2019 Global Food Policy report estimates that, "globally, 80 percent of the extreme poor (living on less than $1.90 per day) and 75 percent of the moderately poor (living on $1.90 to $3.20 per day) live in rural areas."[2] Most of these people work in agriculture.[3]

This chapter focuses on the potential of inclusive business models and large-scale alliances as solutions for reaching more smallholder farm households and enabling them to integrate into formal markets. It illustrates some of the key obstacles these farmers need to overcome to become more productive, prosperous, and resilient and how collaborative, market-driven approaches can help address these challenges. The chapter concludes with some key lessons learned on implementing these solutions and recommendations for increasing their systemic impact.

1. Food and Agriculture Organization of the United Nations (FAO), *Smallholder and Family Farmers,* Fact Sheet (Rome: FAO, 2012). The FAO defines smallholder and family farmers as those working on up to ten hectares.

2. International Food Policy Research Institute (IFPRI), *2019 Global Food Policy Report* (IFPRI, 2019). Poverty lines are calculated using 2011 PPP dollars; A. Castaneda and others, "A New Profile of the Global Poor," *World Development* 101 (2018): 250–67.

3. World Bank Group, *Ending Poverty and Hunger by 2030: An Agenda for the Global Food System,* 2nd ed. (World Bank Group, 2015).

It is important to note at the outset that the majority of smallholder farmers, especially in Sub-Saharan Africa and Asia, currently lack the capacity, incentives, or proximity to integrate effectively into formal markets and corporate value chains. Targeting public sector research, assistance, incentives, and investments to the poorest rural households and regions will remain essential to enabling hundreds of millions of people to grow out of poverty.[4] Even those farmers who are integrated into the supply chains of large-scale agricultural enterprises as customers and suppliers do not always earn a living income, especially on a sustained and reliable basis. Research by the Consultative Group to Assist the Poorest (CGAP) and the Farmer Income Lab, estimates that about 200 million smallholders are producing food as part of formal supply chains.[5] Many of these farmers remain in extreme poverty or risk falling back into poverty as a result of climate-related or economic shocks. As such, there is a dual challenge of raising the productivity and capabilities of some 300 million smallholder farmers to enable them to access markets and to benefit from doing so, while at the same time continuing to raise and sustain the incomes and livelihoods of some 200 million smallholders who are already participating in formal markets and value chains. Public sector leadership and engagement is essential to addressing both of these challenges, alongside the evolution of market-led approaches and new types of public-private partnership.

Defining Inclusive Business Models and Large-Scale Alliances

Inclusive business models and large-scale alliances offer untapped potential for smallholder farmers to become small business enterprises. Such models and alliances can integrate smallholder farmers who are already producing, or have the potential to produce, food and other cash crops into local, national, and global supply chains and markets.

What are inclusive business models? The International Finance Corporation (IFC) provides a useful definition: "a business that provides goods, services and livelihoods on a commercially viable basis, either at scale or scalable, to people living at the base of the economic pyramid, making them part of the value chain of

---

4. John W. McArthur, "Agriculture's Role in Ending Extreme Poverty," in *The Last Mile in Ending Extreme Poverty*, edited by Laurence Chandy, Hiroshi Kato, and Homi Kharas (Brookings Institution Press, 2015): 175–218.

5. Robert Peck Christen and Jamie Anderson, *Segmentation of Smallholder Households: Meeting the Range of Financial Needs in Agricultural Families*. CGAP Focus Note, no. 85 (April 2013); and Farmer Income Lab, *What Works to Increase Smallholder Farmers' Income? A Landscape Review*, Working Draft for Discussion, Commissioned by Mars Incorporated and completed by Dalberg and Wageningen University and Research, 2018.

companies' core business as suppliers, distributors, retailers or customers."[6] Some definitions also include employment. These approaches are sometimes referred to as the base of the pyramid business models or as creating shared value models.[7]

The concept and practice of inclusive business models gathered momentum in the 1990s and early 2000s. They evolved in parallel with increased private sector investment in developing countries and the growing recognition in the development community that market-based solutions and non-state actors have an important role to play in efforts to eradicate poverty. Some corporations in agribusiness, financial services, information and communications technology, healthcare, housing, energy, mining, infrastructure, and tourism also started to recognize the business benefits and potential development impact of implementing inclusive business models.

Agriculture has been a major sector of focus in this emerging field of practice. Examples range across the food value chain. They include inclusive business models that provide affordable and accessible inputs to smallholder farmers, such as seeds, fertilizers, equipment, advisory services, financial products, and market information aimed at improving risk management, raising yields and productivity, and linking to income-generating markets. They also include investments in off-farm enterprises along the food value chain, such as small warehousing, processing, distribution, and retail businesses, as well as interventions to deliver essential goods and services to rural communities, such as health services, education, clean water and sanitation, energy, and physical and digital infrastructure.[8]

Inclusive business models are established to overcome a variety of market failures and governance gaps that impede the integration of smallholder farmers into formal value chains or their access to essential goods and services. These obstacles are usually complex and interdependent, so effective implementation often requires a multistakeholder group of actors delivering multidimensional interventions with aligned incentives. This is the case at the level of many project-level interventions and individual inclusive business models that work with a specific group of farmers. Collaboration is even more important in driving the

6. IEG | World Bank Group, *IFC's Experience with Inclusive Business: An Assessment of IFC's Role, Outcomes, and Potential Scenarios, An Independent Evaluation* (March 9, 2018).

7. C. K. Prahalad, *The Fortune at the Bottom of the Pyramid: Eradicating Poverty Through Profits* (Wharton School Publishing, 2016); Michael Porter and Mark Kramer, "Creating Shared Value: How to Reinvent Capitalism—And Unleash a Wave of Innovation and Growth," *Harvard Business Review* (January 2011).

8. Jane Nelson, *Expanding Opportunity and Access: Approaches that Harness Markets and the Private Sector to Create Business Value and Development Impact* (Harvard Kennedy School Corporate Social Responsibility Initiative, 2010); BMZ, Federal Ministry for Economic Cooperation and Development, *Growing Business with Smallholders: A Guide to Inclusive Business* (Bonn: GIZ, November 2012).

type of change needed at a system level to achieve greater scale and impact in empowering millions of smallholder farmers.

System-level or large-scale alliances are composed of a larger number of companies, government bodies, and other development actors, often numbering in the hundreds, collaborating to drive change across entire commodity value chains, agricultural corridors, landscapes, and regions, or at a global level.[9] These alliances do not replace the need for specific inclusive business models and programmatic interventions. Rather, they aim to enable such interventions to have an impact beyond what any one of them could achieve alone. They are usually established to achieve one or more of the following objectives: mobilizing financial and other resources; leveraging breakthrough technologies; developing and spreading norms and standards; improving and coordinating research, data collection, and analysis; and advocating for policy reforms and behavior change.

Examples include the Alliance for a Green Revolution in Africa, the New Vision for Agriculture, the Farm to Market Alliance, the Global Alliance for Improved Nutrition, the Food and Land Use Coalition, CGIAR (the world's largest agricultural innovation network), and the Council on Smallholder Agricultural Finance. There are also commodity-focused platforms, such as the World Cocoa Foundation, the Better Cotton Initiative, the Ethical Tea Partnership, and the Global Aquaculture Alliance. Certain industry-led platforms are also starting to drive collective commitments by their member companies to support smallholder farmers and rural enterprises. They include the Consumer Goods Forum, the Sustainable Agriculture Initiative Platform, and GSMA, the latter of which represents the interests of mobile operators globally.

Helping Smallholder Farmers Overcome Obstacles

Inclusive business models and large-scale alliances can help overcome a variety of operational, financial, social, environmental, and policy challenges that prevent smallholder farmers from becoming more prosperous and resilient small enterprises. On rare occasions, commercial solutions for farmers in extreme poverty are viable on their own from the outset. In many cases, they need to be combined with more traditional donor-supported development interventions and humanitarian assistance. In others, impact investing or blended finance from both public and private sectors is necessary to catalyze and scale market-based solutions.

9. Jane Nelson, *Partnerships for Sustainable Development: Collective Action by Business, Governments and Civil Society to Achieve Scale and Transform Market,* Business and Sustainable Development Commission (Harvard Kennedy School Corporate Responsibility Initiative, 2017); Christina Gradl and Beth Jenkins, *Tackling Barriers to Scale: From Inclusive Business Models to Inclusive Ecosystems* (Harvard Kennedy School Corporate Responsibility Initiative, 2011).

What obstacles need to be overcome to enable smallholder farmers to prosper? While there are substantial differences across geographies, commodities, and income levels, there are a number of similar obstacles for most small farm businesses to overcome at every stage of the agricultural value chain.

Improving Access to Productive Resources and Market Integration

Many smallholders lack access to reliable and affordable financing, technologies, information, or other agricultural inputs and advisory services, all of which are essential to managing farm-level risk and improving productivity and quality. Together with price uncertainty, the lack of access to reliable market information and infrastructure, from storage facilities to transportation, limits smallholders' bargaining power and their links to local and global market opportunities. Inclusive business models, especially those that incorporate innovative digital and life science technologies, can play a valuable role in overcoming some of these production and income-generation challenges.

The majority of agricultural inclusive business models focus on improving farm-level performance and market integration. These models range from corporate-led initiatives by input providers, consumer goods companies, traders, and financial, digital, and infrastructure companies to market-led initiatives convened by development finance institutions (DFI). Examples of the latter include the IFC's Inclusive Business Models unit and the International Fund for Agricultural Development's (IFAD) program on Producer Public-Private Partnerships (4Ps) in agricultural value chains, as well as the agri-focused initiatives of most bilateral development finance agencies.

In addition to creating more jobs, efficient and inclusive agricultural supply chains can help lower consumer prices, thereby raising real incomes of poor people in both rural and urban areas while, at the same time, raising relative prices received by farmers, providing them additional income as well as incentives to enhance productivity and to diversify.[10] The case for engagement is, therefore, substantial. The World Bank, for example, estimates that growth originating in agriculture is two to four times more effective at reducing poverty than growth originating in other sectors.[11] It makes the case that, "Raising the returns to labor in agriculture and in jobs in the food system, including in agribusiness, can significantly contribute to shared prosperity."[12]

---

10. World Bank Group, *Ending Poverty and Hunger by 2030: An Agenda for the Global Food System*, 2nd ed. (2015).

11. Ibid.

12. Ibid.

Improving Access to Basic Services, Food Security, and Nutrition

In addition to lacking on-farm productive inputs and income-generating market access opportunities, many smallholder farm households lack affordable access to basic goods and services essential for poverty alleviation, such as nutritious foods, education, clean water and sanitation, energy, and healthcare. For example, despite the fact that smallholder farmers produce some of the major commodities consumed in the world and up to 80 percent of the food supply in Asia and Sub-Saharan Africa, they are among the most undernourished and food insecure populations, making up half of the world's hungry people.[13] In addition, these farmers are often excluded from social safety nets, insurance schemes, cash transfer programs, technologies, and other interventions that can help rural communities survive crises and improve resilience in the face of conflict and climate related or economic shocks. Overcoming these obstacles usually requires combining inclusive business models and market-driven approaches with humanitarian assistance and donor or philanthropic support.

The World Food Programme's (WFP) public-private partnerships offer examples of aligning and sequencing humanitarian and market-led approaches. In addition to its ongoing mandate to deliver food assistance in emergencies, WFP is working systematically with vulnerable rural communities to improve nutrition, income-generating opportunities, and longer-term resilience. WFP's Food Assistance for Assets and its Rural Resilience Initiative with Oxfam America are examples. The organization has also made a commitment to source more of its staple food requirements for responding to humanitarian emergencies from local smallholder farmers in the regions where it is operating. It is doing so by working in partnership with private-sector enterprises and donors to build inclusive business models, such as Purchase for Progress and the Farm to Market Alliance.

Similar combinations of humanitarian and market-led approaches can be found in the delivery of healthcare, water, energy, and a range of financial services. In the case of access to essential drugs and vaccines, for example, some pharmaceutical companies, both global and local, are developing inclusive business models or impact investing initiatives to help address "last mile" rural health challenges. Many are doing so in partnership with information technology and digital companies; large footprint investors such as agribusiness and energy and mining companies; donors; and public and private research institutes.

13. IFPRI. *2019 Global Food Policy Report* (2019); See also: Shenggen Fan, "Small Farmers Can Help Meet Sustainable Development and Climate Goals—But They Need Our Support," IFPRI (April 11, 2016), www.ifpri.org/blog/small-farmers-can-help-meet-sustainable-development -and-climate-goals-they-need-our-support.

Addressing Climate Change and Environmental Health Challenges

Climate change is placing substantial pressure on other drivers of rural poverty. Data is currently limited on the percentage of GHG emissions accounted for by smallholder farmers.[14] There is no doubt, however, that these farmers are among the world's most vulnerable populations when it comes to adapting to the negative impacts of climate change. The 2016 Global Food Policy report summarizes this multidimensional challenge: "Climate change exacerbates the production challenges faced by smallholders and increases the likelihood of agricultural and income losses, pests and diseases, and asset depletion. For example, yields of staple crops grown by smallholders, such as maize, rice, and wheat, are expected to decline in the coming years as a result of climate change."[15]

A growing number of inclusive business models and large-scale alliances are focused on supporting climate-smart agriculture and access to insurance, sustainable infrastructure, and other services to improve the climate risk management, mitigation, and adaptation capabilities of smallholder farmers and rural communities.[16] Policy reforms and government-led efforts to place prices on carbon, water, and other ecosystem services also will be essential alongside publicly funded social safety nets, infrastructure investments, and cash transfers.

In addition to climate change, many smallholder farmers face a variety of challenges that degrade both the environment and human health while also threatening livelihoods and resilience. They include indoor air pollution, unsafe use of chemicals, soil degradation, loss of biodiversity, and high exposure to neglected tropical diseases. These challenges are further exacerbated by limited health and environmental literacy and lack of access to basic health and environmental management tools. Environmental NGOs and intergovernmental institutions, such as the International Union for Conservation of Nature (IUCN), the United Nations Environment Programme (UNEP), the Nature Conservancy, the World Wildlife Fund (WWF), and the World Resources Institute are starting to work with corporations and development NGOs, such as CARE and Oxfam, to develop partnerships and inclusive business models that focus on tackling environmental health challenges within the broader context of farmer livelihoods.

14. CGIAR, *Better Methods to Measure the Emissions of Small Scale Farming,* CGIAR Research Program on Climate Change, Agriculture and Food Security, Research in Action Factsheet (2013).

15. IFPRI, *2016 Global Food Policy Report* (2016).

16. Simon Winter, Maaike Bijker, and Melissa Carson, *The Role of Multi-Stakeholder Initiatives in Promoting the Resilience of Smallholder Agriculture to Climate Change in Africa* (Harvard Kennedy School Corporate Responsibility Initiative and Dalberg Research, 2017).

Tackling Gender Inequality

It will be impossible to eradicate poverty and achieve food security without empowering women farmers. Estimates vary, but according to the World Bank, women represent some 40 percent of the agricultural labor force in Sub-Saharan Africa, and in some countries their contributions exceed 50 percent.[17] The contribution of rural women to poverty eradication and food security is likely to be higher if one includes their work within households, food processing, and kitchen gardens or homestead plots, which are often not counted as agriculture, as well as their off-farm income-generating activities.[18] Yet, due to a variety of social and economic obstacles, women farmers produce yields of 20 to 30 percent less than men.[19]

Tackling gender inequality in rural communities can lead to higher productivity and income generation, better nutrition, and more household income spent on education and health. The World Bank estimates, for example, that if women farmers had the same access as men to resources such as credit, inputs, technology, and knowledge, they could achieve gender parity in farm yields and potentially reduce the number of hungry people by about 12 percent to 17 percent.[20]

Concerted efforts are required to make women's empowerment an explicit goal of inclusive business models. Research by the Asian Development Bank focused on rural and urban inclusive business models in Asia and Latin America found that in more than 100 examples studied, only thirteen explicitly aimed to empower women and ten identified implicit benefits for women in describing their mission.[21] Much more needs to be done to improve rights and opportunities for rural women across the food value chain, from women as agricultural producers and workers to consumers of basic services.

Unilever provides one example of an integrated effort to achieve women's empowerment. In 2014, the company made an explicit commitment through the Enhancing Livelihoods pillar of its Sustainable Living Plan to empower 5 million women by 2020 through a combination of fairness in the workplace, providing economic opportunities, and building inclusive business models.[22] The company

17. World Bank Group, "Help Women Farmers 'Get to Equal,'" Brief (April 18, 2017), www .worldbank.org/en/topic/agriculture/brief/women-farmers-getting-to-equal.

18. Cheryl Doss, Ruth Meinzen-Dick, Agnes Quisumbing, and Sophie Theis, "Women in Agriculture: Four Myths," *Global Food Security* 16 (2018): 69–74.

19. World Bank Group, *Ending Poverty and Hunger by 2030: An Agenda for the Global Food System*, 2nd ed. (2015).

20. Ibid.

21. Asian Development Bank, *How Inclusive is Inclusive Business for Women? Examples from Asia and Latin America,* (2016): 10.

22. Unilever, *Opportunities for Women: Challenging Harmful Social Norms and Gender Stereotypes to Unlock Women's Potential,* (March 2017).

does not stipulate how many of these women live in low-income rural communities in developing countries, but states, "In 2016, we enabled over 800,000 women to access initiatives aiming to develop their skills and expand their opportunities in our extended agricultural supply chain."[23] The company has also committed to develop a set of global land rights principles, which, among other goals, will aim to enhance women's land rights.

A second example is the Livelihoods Fund for Family Farming (L3F) established in 2015 by Mars Incorporated and Danone and joined by nine companies since. Their goal is to help 200,000 smallholder farmers convert to climate-smart sustainable farming practices, increase yields and incomes, and improve livelihoods and women's economic empowerment, positively impacting 2 million people in rural communities over the next decade.[24] DFIs, such as the IFC, and international NGOs, such as CARE and World Vision, are also starting to work with companies to explicitly integrate gender equality into agricultural inclusive business models and impact investing initiatives.

Improving Children's Rights

The figures are stark when it comes to the well-being of many children in low-income farming communities. The combination of high levels of child labor, lack of access to education, and hazardous working conditions can result in human rights abuses and the undermining of future opportunity for millions of children. The International Labour Organization (ILO) estimates that the majority of child labor, approximately 60 percent, occurs in agriculture, including farming, fishing, aquaculture, forestry, and livestock. This adds up to nearly 100 million girls and boys.[25] Meanwhile, in 2018, the FAO found that, "after years of steady decline, child labor in agriculture has started to rise again in recent years driven in part by an increase in conflicts and climate-induced disasters."[26]

Tackling the challenge of child labor calls mainly for humanitarian interventions and policy reforms, although inclusive business models that place a high priority on respecting human rights are an important part of the solution. A number of the world's leading agribusiness and consumer goods companies, for example, are working to integrate the corporate responsibility to respect human

23. Ibid.

24. Livelihood Funds, "Livelihoods Fund for Family Farming," www.livelihoods.eu/l3f/.

25. ILO, "Child Labor in Agriculture," https://www.ilo.org/ipec/areas/Agriculture/lang--en/index.htm; See also: ILO, *Accelerating Action against Child Labour,* Global Report under the Follow-Up to the ILO Declaration on Fundamental Principles and Rights at Work 2010 (2010).

26. FAO, *"Child Labor in Agriculture Is On the Rise, Driven by Conflict and Disasters"* (June 12, 2018), www.fao.org/news/story/en/item/1140078/icode/.

rights, including efforts to tackle child labor, into their inclusive business models, based on the UN Guiding Principles on Business and Human Rights.[27]

Advocating for Policy Reforms to Support Smallholder Farming

In too many cases, national policies, regulations, and fiscal incentives create barriers to smallholder prosperity and resilience. This ranges from a lack of government prioritization for agriculture and land tenure reform to public subsidies and financing mechanisms that explicitly favor large farms over small, urban consumers over rural, environmentally unsound farming practices over climate-smart and resource-efficient ones, and infrastructure investments in industrial sectors over infrastructure for food production, storage, market access, processing, and distribution. Although official development assistance for agriculture has more than doubled in real terms since the early 2000s, recent levels still represent less than half the amount invested in agriculture in the mid-1980s.[28]

As the 2016 Global Food Policy report states, "Although smallholder agriculture is often recognized as a vital sector for development, it has rarely enjoyed the policy and institutional support necessary to allow smallholders and rural economies to thrive."[29] More than any other change, policy reforms and improved public governance and accountability at both the national and local levels will be essential to achieving the goal of "no smallholder farmer left behind." Large companies, industry associations, NGOs, and multistakeholder alliances can play a collective role in advocating for and supporting food policy reform, both in donor and developing country partner governments. They can also help governments improve agricultural delivery models, data collection, and data analysis.

In summary, interventions and investments to improve the productivity, incomes, and resilience of smallholder farmers require diverse groups of actors working systematically together to address multidimensional and interdependent challenges. There is also the need to work simultaneously at the household, on-farm, off-farm, local, national, and global levels.[30] While inclusive business models and

27. United Nations Human Rights Office of the High Commissioner, *Guiding Principles on Business and Human Rights: Implementing the United Nations "Protect, Respect and Remedy" Framework* (New York and Geneva: United Nations, 2011).

28. Based on data taken from OECD Development Assistance Committee Creditor Reporting System online database (https://stats.oecd.org/), and from John W. McArthur, "Agriculture's Role in Ending Extreme Poverty," in *The Last Mile in Ending Extreme Poverty,* edited by Laurence Chandy, Hiroshi Kato, and Homi Kharas (Brookings Institution Press, 2015): 175–218.

29. IFPRI, *2016 Global Food Policy Report* (IFPRI, 2016).

30. Farmer Income Lab, *What Works to Increase Smallholder Farmers' Income? A Landscape Review,* Working Draft for Discussion, Commissioned by Mars Incorporated and completed by Dalberg and Wageningen University and Research, 2018.

large-scale alliances can address only some of the obstacles faced by smallholders, they can play a vital role alongside public sector policy reforms and investments and, where, needed humanitarian assistance.

Implementing and Evaluating Inclusive Business Models

How widespread are inclusive business models today? There are hundreds of examples of multinational companies, domestic companies, NGOs, and DFIs working together on inclusive business models or participating in alliances to support smallholder farmers. Unfortunately, however, there is no comprehensive mapping or rigorous data on the number of companies implementing such models or the total number of smallholder farmers being reached. Nor is there reliable and comparative data on improvements in farmer incomes and livelihoods as a result of being integrated into inclusive business models.

More refined analysis and research are required in each of these areas, but the broad direction for public and private sector engagement is clear. As outlined earlier in this chapter, a combination of market-driven inclusive business models supported by policy reforms and incentives is required to improve the incomes and livelihoods of the estimated 200 million smallholder farmers who already participate in formal markets and value chains. At the same time, public policies and government- or donor-led programs are required to enable about 300 million additional smallholder farmers to access markets and to benefit from such access. Public sector leadership is essential, but the need to engage many more companies, impact investors, social enterprises, and other partners in building inclusive business models and value chains is also clear.

Key Actors in Building Inclusive Business Models

The majority of inclusive business models that focus on smallholder farmers involve formal partnerships and informal interaction between the following groups of actors, a growing number of which are using digital platforms to lower transactions costs, increase efficiencies, and improve the quality of risk management, program delivery, and evaluation:

- *Farmers' organizations and aggregators:* Farmer cooperatives, producer collectives, smallholder representative bodies, and women's organizations.

- *Input providers:* Local enterprises, ag-tech entrepreneurs, or large companies providing a variety of inputs such as seeds, fertilizers, irrigation, tractors and other equipment, energy, data analysis, training, and advice.

- *Off-takers and customers:* Large farms that manage smallholder out-grower schemes, local traders and trading companies, multinational food and beverage companies, and a wide variety of local processing, distribution, and retail enterprises.

- *Financial services providers:* Microfinance institutions, local banks, and insurance companies and digital financial technology platforms.

- *NGOs and research institutes:* Development and environmental NGOs and local or international research partners, who often play valuable roles in program design, implementation, farmer outreach, and evaluation.

- *Development finance institutions:* Most multilateral and bilateral DFIs have established market-based programs focused on addressing smallholder and rural poverty. These programs invest in, provide loans to, or partner with other actors in the value chain, including both agribusiness companies and financial intermediaries.

- *Donors and foundations:* Some level of grant funding is often required to address market failures or deliver essential goods and services, such as healthcare, education, clean water, and sanitation. These may not be direct inputs to increase farm yields and incomes but can have a substantial impact on tackling rural poverty, especially for women.

An emerging group of companies is developing and scaling breakthrough technologies, which have a vital role to play as drivers of inclusive business models. They range from digital and life science start-ups to large, established science-based corporations. Many are implementing technology solutions that can be applied directly by farmers themselves, such as the use of drought, flood, and pest resistant seeds, e-extension services, precision agriculture, weather-linked insurance, digitally enabled marketplaces, and shared mechanization services.

Others are applying technologies such as satellite-enabled remote sensing and spatial mapping, combined with Big Data, machine learning, and predictive analytics to dramatically improve data collection and analysis.[31] This can range from mapping crop yields, weather patterns, and water insecurity to disease surveillance and population health patterns. Such information can, in turn, provide an evidence base for better decisionmaking and resource allocation, in both the public and private sector.

31. Jennifer L. Cohen and Homi Kharas, "Using Big Data and Artificial Intelligence to Accelerate Global Development" (November 15, 2018). This report is part of "A Blueprint for the Future of AI," a series from the Brookings Institution that analyzes the new challenges and potential policy solutions introduced by artificial intelligence and other emerging technologies, www.brookings.edu/research/using-big-data-and-artificial-intelligence-to-accelerate-global-development/.

The World Economic Forum (WEF) has identified twelve breakthrough tech-nology innovations that offer potential for making food systems more inclusive, efficient, nutritious, and sustainable. Most of these require inclusive business models and large-scale alliances to be implemented and scaled.[32] WEF argues that the following technologies in particular could help smallholder farmers improve yields and income by 1 percent to 7 percent: mobile service delivery; big data and advanced analytics; microbiome technologies; gene-editing for multi-trait seed improvements; off-grid energy generation and storage; and biological crop-based protection and micronutrients for soil management.[33] If applied with complementary financing, advisory, and market information services, their impact on yields and income is likely to be higher.

Often underpinning successful inclusive business models are intermediary organizations, system integrators, or systems leaders that are able to cultivate a shared vision for change, coordinate and align incentives, and enable mutual accountability for performance among diverse actors.[34]

At the level of specific inclusive models, intermediary organizations include agri-based social enterprises such as IDH Sustainable Trade, TechnoServe, Root Capital, and Hello Tractor that combine agricultural, development, and business expertise to coordinate different actors and facilitate effective linkages between individual companies and smallholder farmers or producer organizations.

One illustrative example is Project Nurture, a partnership between the Coca-Cola Company, the Bill & Melinda Gates Foundation, and TechnoServe that integrated more than 50,000 smallholder farmers in Kenya and Uganda, a third of them women, into the company's mango fruit value chain. Over a period of five years, the partners needed to engage with and coordinate at least forty other public and private entities to develop and implement the initiative.[35]

As outlined earlier in this chapter, at a broader system level, large-scale alli-ances serve as intermediaries and system integrators. They are being established as platforms for coordinating hundreds of different actors and inventions across entire value chains, agriculture corridors, landscapes, and regions, and at a global level. The goal of such platforms is to achieve greater scale and systemic impact than any inclusive business model can achieve alone.

The Alliance for a Green Revolution in Africa (AGRA) offers an illustrative

32. World Economic Forum, *Innovation with a Purpose: The Role of Technology Innovation in Accelerating Food Systems Transformation*, Report Prepared in Collaboration with McKinsey & Company (January 2018).

33. Ibid.

34. Jane Nelson and Beth Jenkins, *Tackling Global Challenges: Lessons in System Leadership from the World Economic Forum's New Vision for Agriculture Initiative* (Harvard Kennedy School Corpo-rate Responsibility Initiative, 2016).

35. Beth Jenkins and Lorin Fries, *Project Nurture: Partnering for Business Opportunity and Devel-opment Impact* (Harvard Kennedy School Corporate Responsibility Initiative, 2012).

example. AGRA receives funding support from more than twenty public and private sector organizations and is working with governments in eleven African countries to help coordinate hundreds of other partners that are enabling or engaging directly with African smallholder farmers. Its current goal is to increase the incomes and improve food security for 9 million farm households by 2021 through direct interventions and investments with farmers. In addition, it aims to contribute to increasing the incomes and improving food security of another 21 million farm households by the same year through collective efforts to strengthen key market systems and improve policy frameworks, state capabilities, and public-private financing mechanisms. Helping to build and strengthen a variety of inclusive business models and value chains is one element of AGRA's approach.[36]

Assessing the Development Impact of Inclusive Business Models

There is emerging evidence on the development impact of inclusive business models and some of the interventions that are most effective in raising farmer incomes. Two recent studies are worthy of note. One is an evaluation of the IFC's experience with inclusive business models, published by the World Bank's Independent Evaluation Group (IEG) in 2018.[37] While recognizing the challenges of data collection and analysis, IEG concluded that across all sectors, including agriculture, "Notably, no trade-off between profitability and inclusion objectives is apparent in available evidence."[38]

However, the evaluation found less evidence of environmental and social benefits: "The performance of inclusive agribusiness projects is also comparable with that of other IFC agribusiness projects, except for their environmental and social (E&S) ratings, which are weaker, mostly owing to challenges involving land issues and waste processing unrelated to the inclusive nature of their business models."[39] This finding suggests the need for combining policy reforms with inclusive business models and the need for a "whole value chain" approach, from farm to market to processing and distribution. The evaluation concluded: "Factors affecting the success of inclusive agribusiness projects include adequacy of managerial decisions, regulatory action or inaction by the government,

---

36. Alliance for a Green Revolution in Africa, "AGRA: Growing Africa's Agriculture." Corporate profile, https://agra.org/wp-content/uploads/2018/10/AGRA-Corporate-Profile.pdf.

37. Independent Evaluation Group (IEG), *IFC's Experience with Inclusive Business An Assessment of IFC's Role, Outcomes, and Potential Scenarios*, IEG Meso Evaluation (World Bank Group: March 30, 2018).

38. Ibid.

39. Ibid.

fluctuations in global commodity prices, and adverse changes in country conditions."[40] In short, even well-managed and commercially viable inclusive business models require appropriate policies and government support to sustain improved incomes and deliver broader social and environmental benefits for farmers.

The second study was commissioned by Mars Incorporated for the Farmer Income Lab and conducted by Wageningen University and Dalberg. It reviewed publicly available evidence to assess the question: "What are the most effective actions that lead buyers can take to enable smallholder farmers in global supply chains to meaningfully increase their incomes?"[41] The authors identified sixteen types of intervention, mostly at the farm level, that have been widely considered to be effective and, hence, widely adopted; implemented for five or more years, thereby generating evidence over time; and subject to substantial research on their effect on income. They scanned 564 sources representing 1,652 underlying individual studies, including meta-studies.[42] The sixteen interventions were assessed for their income impact, scale, durability over time, and gender inclusion of female and male farmers.

Key findings of the analysis are summarized in table 4-1, which categorizes the interventions based on their income effects. Three types of intervention stood out for their ability to increase farmer incomes at 50 percent or more at scale: poverty graduation schemes, out-grower schemes and contract farming, and climate change adaptation programs.

As described in chapter 3 of this volume, poverty graduation schemes are initiatives that provide a bundle of services, offered in sequence, designed to "graduate" farmers from direct support to meet their basic needs to the types of support that enable them to increase productivity and independently earn a consistent income. These schemes "typically include a combination of social assistance (for example, cash transfers, health services), financial services, skills training, seed capital or access to employment and mentoring."[43] Out-grower schemes and contract farming provide farmers with access to buyers to sell a specified quantity of a commodity at a future date, and sometimes at a guaranteed price. They often include the provision of technical assistance and financial support. Climate-smart business models deliver a combination of financial tools, training, and inputs, such as climate-resilient seeds, to help smallholders adapt to and build resilience to address the negative impact of climate change.

---

40. Ibid.

41. Farmer Income Lab, *What Works to Increase Smallholder Farmers' Income? A Landscape Review,* Working Draft for Discussion Commissioned by Mars Incorporated and completed by Dalberg and Wageningen University and Research (2018).

42. Ibid.

43. Ibid.

In addition to identifying and assessing specific interventions, the authors found four critical cross-cutting success factors in the most successful case studies reviewed: bundling services; connecting deeply with farmers; customizing interventions; and partnering with governments, civil society actors, and peers.

In summary, while the sixteen interventions identified in the research offer useful guidance on the types of investments and business models that have potential for raising farmer incomes, they are usually not sufficient on their own. Even the most successful of these achieved 50 to 100 percent improvements in income, when it is estimated that a 200 to 300 percent improvement would be required in many cases to achieve a living income. In 2019, the Farmer Income Lab commissioned additional research to identify a set of more systemic case studies that have demonstrated income improvements of 200 percent or more.

Lessons Learned and Recommendations for Scaling Impact

Inclusive business models and the broader alliances that often evolve to support and scale them are by no means a panacea. Nor are they substitutes for public sector spending in rural communities or for national and global policy reforms aimed at making food systems more inclusive, sustainable, efficient, and nutritious. Yet, they offer an important set of options for helping to increase smallholder incomes and resilience.

Inclusive business models and alliances are not easy to implement or sustain. They require working closely with smallholder farmers to make sure initiatives are demand-driven and that risk burdens are more equally shared and market power dynamics addressed.[44] They usually involve high transaction costs, alignment of incentives among diverse participants, and long-term commitments. They require delivering short-term results while simultaneously investing in systemic solutions that may take many years to evolve.

Despite these challenges, a growing number of collaborative efforts demonstrate potential. Almost all effective inclusive business models and large-scale alliances to improve the productivity, prosperity, and resilience of smallholder farmers share common building blocks. These include strengthening legal rights and security of land tenure; bundling financial and nonfinancial services and technologies at the farm level based on close consultation with and capacity building of farmers; improving access to essential services such as health, education, energy, clean water, and sanitation; promoting women's empowerment; protecting children's rights and supporting youth development; facilitating farmers'

---

44. Oxfam, *A Living Income for Small-Scale Farmers: Tackling Unequal Risks and Market Power* (Oxfam Discussion Papers, November 2018).

Table 4-1. Analysis of Interventions

Category of Intervention	Description of Evidence	Relevant Interventions
Category 1 **High income impact demonstrated at scale**	Evidence demonstrates income increases of 50%+ can be achieved for large numbers of farmers (5,000+).	Poverty graduation schemes Out-grower schemes/contract farming Climate change adaptation
Category 2 **Medium income impact at scale with demonstrated impact on income enabling factors**	Evidence demonstrates 10% to 50% improvement in income across 5,000+ farmers, as well as strong performance of proxy indicators, such as production or empowerment.	Savings-led groups Access to finance Producer collectives
Category 3 **Interventions with mixed evidence of impact across the selected criteria**	Evidence demonstrates 10% to 50% improvement. While these interventions may not be able to deliver greater than 50% increases consistently, they can deliver positive results in specific contexts.	Agro-corridors Productivity enhancement Land tenure security Market information systems Crop insurance Farmer field schools
Category 4 **Medium income impact with demonstrated limited impact on income enabling factors**	Evidence demonstrates 10% to 50% increases and limited change in other income enabling factors such as empowerment.	Certification Post-harvest loss prevention
Category 5 **Interventions that did not show significant income increases**	Evidence demonstrates these interventions deliver income improvement of less than 10%, though they are highly scalable and could be part of a broader approach.	Pricing arrangements Input subsidies

Source: Adapted from Farmer Income Lab, "What Works to Increase Smallholder Farmers' Income? A Landscape Review," Working Draft for Discussion, 2018.

ability to organize and aggregate; improving the transparency and accountability of public expenditures; and investing in better data collection and analysis.

Beyond specific programmatic interventions, there are seven broader contextual lessons that actors involved in inclusive business models and large-scale alliances need to consider as key principles for achieving scale and systemic impact:

Align development and humanitarian interventions. Given the need to both increase smallholder farmer incomes and decrease their vulnerability to economic and climate-related shocks and conflict, development and humanitarian actors must work more cooperatively in rural communities. This cooperation is essential to achieve flexible sequencing or graduation along the spectrum of humanitarian needs and market-based solutions as well as better coordination and responsiveness during periods of emergency and protracted crisis. Inclusive business models rarely reach the poorest and most vulnerable smallholder farmers. Serving these farmers requires publicly financed services and infrastructure alongside donor funding and humanitarian assistance.

Strengthen the links between agriculture, health, and nutrition initiatives. Given that many smallholder farmers are among the most malnourished and hungry people in the world, better alignment between the agriculture and nutrition communities is essential. Sustainable Development Goal 2 (SDG 2) is one of the first global commitments to explicitly combine agriculture and nutrition in its goal to "end hunger, achieve food security and improved nutrition and promote sustainable agriculture." It offers a useful set of targets and indicators for joint action.

Link agricultural, environmental, and climate investments. Increased efforts are needed to improve coordination and joint funding between agricultural, environmental, and climate change organizations and mechanisms. In addition to tackling specific challenges, such as water scarcity, soil degradation, and biodiversity, there is a need for systemic landscape approaches to improve the ability of smallholder farmers to adapt to climate change and to strengthen the resilience of rural communities more broadly. This calls for a combination of public and private investments, from weather-linked insurance and incentives for farmers to implement climate-smart practices to cash transfers, grants, and public infrastructure funding.

Build linkages between on- and off-farm opportunities and rural and urban areas. On-farm and off-farm interventions must be addressed more holistically to provide farming households with greater flexibility to move between jobs and different types of income-generating activities, depending on the time of the year and farming cycle or during emergencies. Linked to this is the need for better coordination between rural and urban development interventions. UNDP administrator Achim Steiner and the International Food Policy Research Institute's (IFPRI) director general Shenggen Fan comment: "Although agricultural production is critical to rural economies, rural revitalization goes far beyond agriculture. It includes the development of non-farm opportunities and it makes cutting-edge technology and innovation the linchpins of rural economic growth. . . . One essential driver of rural revitalization is *rurbanomics,* an approach that emphasizes the linkages between rural and urban economies."[45]

Combine disruptive new technologies with scaling older technologies that work. There can be no doubt that today's disruptive technologies and the convergence between them, from digital platforms to advances in life sciences and material sciences, offer some of the greatest untapped potential to transform the productivity, incomes, and resilience of smallholder farmers. One crucial challenge is to improve digital access for farmers. According to analysis by the Global System for Mobile Communications (GSMA), "the vast majority of the 1.2 billion people worldwide not covered by a broadband capable network live in rural areas."[46] There is also a need to combine disruptive new technologies with tried and tested technologies, such as drip irrigation, crop diversification and intercropping, integrated pest management, zero tillage, and residue retention.

Invest holistically in institutional, digital, and physical infrastructure. Increased public investment, combined with blended financing mechanisms and market-based delivery models, will be essential to increase rural access to reliable and affordable infrastructure, from roads and food storage facilities to clean water and energy infrastructure to broadband networks. In addition, initiatives to scale-up physical and digital infrastructure must integrate or be closely coordinated with investments in social and institutional infrastructure. This includes more efficient and accountable public sector institutions, such as rural utilities and extension services,

---

45. Achim Steiner and Shenggen Fan, "A Global Rural Crisis: Rural Revitalization is the Solution" (IFPRI: March 27, 2019). Drawn from Achim Steiner and Shenggen Fan, "Rural Revitalization: Tapping into New Opportunities," in *2019 Global Food Policy Report* (IFPRI, 2019).

46. GSMA, *Enabling Rural Coverage: Regulatory and Policy Recommendations to Foster Mobile Broadband Coverage in Developing Countries* (London: GSM Association, 2018). See also: World Bank Group, *Future of Food: Harnessing Digital Technologies to Improve Food System Outcomes* (World Bank Group, April 2019); FAO, *Tackling Poverty and Hunger through Digital Innovation* (Rome: FAO, August 2018).

as well as more inclusive and accountable community and market organizations, such as farmer cooperatives, producer collectives, and women's groups.

Leverage public and private research institutes. National and global research institutes need to take concerted action to undertake joint projects, share data and findings, and advocate for public funding to support more integrated approaches to agriculture, food security, and rural development. CGIAR, for example, has transformed itself from a network of agronomy-focused public research institutions to a network of public and private partners that are taking a more system-level approach to integrate research on food security, health, the environment, climate change, and prosperity. Other public and private research institutes have the potential to follow this more collaborative and systemic approach.

Conclusion

The underlying drivers of smallholder poverty, exclusion, and vulnerability are not only multidimensional but also interdependent. Effective solutions have to match this complexity with interventions that are equally multidimensional and interdependent. Efforts to "leave no one behind" cannot succeed without a concerted and collaborative effort to "leave no smallholder farmer behind." There is everything to play for. As Bill Gates has argued, "Helping the poorest smallholder farmers grow more crops and get them to market is the world's single most powerful lever for reducing hunger and poverty."[47]

For smallholder farmers, encouraging examples are starting to emerge of collaborative approaches and system level leadership. They include inclusive business models, blending financing mechanisms, and large-scale alliances among companies, governments, research institutes, and NGOs to bridge policy gaps, address market failures, support research and development, and test innovations that have the potential to scale. These collaborative efforts are still too few, too slow, and too small in terms of impact, but they demonstrate what is possible and provide a clear direction for joint action. If they can be scaled and replicated, they have the potential to improve the prosperity and resilience of millions of smallholder farmers and the rural communities in which they live.

47. Bill Gates, World Food Prize Speech, Des Moines, IA (October 15, 2009).

CHAPTER FIVE

No Refugees and Migrants Left Behind

Dany Bahar and Meagan Dooley

hree and a half out of every thousand people in the world today is a refugee—an individual who has fled their country of origin due to conflict or persecution.[1] The United Nations High Commissioner for Refugees (UNHCR) estimates that 25.4 million people were in refugee and refugee-like situations in 2018, the highest number seen since World War II (figure 5-1).

Enshrined in the 1951 United Nations Refugee Convention and 1967 Refugee Protocol (henceforth collectively referred to as the 1951 Convention), a global governance system exists to provide protections to refugees, who by nature of fleeing are no longer entitled to the rights and protections provided by their home countries. However, these international standards are not always enforced or implemented, which often leaves refugees in vulnerable situations. While the 1951 Convention highlights a series of steps states should take to promote refugee integration, it does not require any action beyond non-refoulement: forcibly sending refugees back to their countries of origin.[2] Without any enforcement mechanism, states have come up with creative ways to avoid obligations that come with refugee status, such as, for example, Turkey's move to classify asylum seekers as "temporary guests" instead of refugees.[3]

Even once they reach—and even settle in—a country of asylum, many refugees remain vulnerable, as domestic policies toward refugees vary widely. While some countries grant refugees full rights to healthcare and education services,

---

1. UNHCR (2018a).
2. Siegfried (2016).
3. Kirisci (2014).

Figure 5-1. Total Stock and Population Share of Refugees, 1990-2017

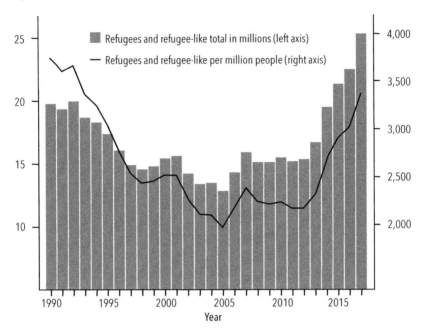

Source: UNHCR Population Statistics

others restrict access, leaving the bulk of care provision to nongovernmental organizations (NGOs).[4] Sometimes these restrictions are a matter of public sector capacity: while Jordan initially gave Syrian refugees free access to primary care facilities, the healthcare system quickly became overwhelmed, and in 2014 they began requiring refugees to pay at non-insured Jordanian rates.[5] However, other times there may be outright discrimination. For example, Bangladesh does not allow Rohingya refugees to enroll in public schools, and has recently cracked down on illegal enrollment in the Cox's Bazar region.[6] In addition to explicit barriers, two-thirds of refugees live in countries where the official language is different from their mother tongue, which limits their ability to utilize health and education services.[7] These barriers result in real losses in human capital; refugee children are five times as likely to be out of school, with only 50 percent enrolled in primary school and less than 25 percent enrolled in secondary.[8] These access

4. WHO Eastern Mediterranean Region (2018).
5. Nielsen (2017).
6. Human Rights Watch (2019).
7. UNICEF (2017).
8. UNHCR (2016).

barriers may be particularly detrimental for women and girls, who face a higher risk of sexual and gender-based violence (SGBV) during displacement and are more likely to be pulled out of school in response to financial hardship.[9] Refugee populations may also face difficulties integrating into the labor market in host countries, which limits their ability to become self-sufficient. While the 1951 Convention pushes for unfettered access to wage and self-employment, many countries deny refugees formal labor market access.[10] Even where participation is allowed, permit fees, mobility restrictions, and discrimination may limit employment options. Thus, many refugees, especially women, remain relegated to the informal sector, lacking protections and formal redress mechanisms for exploitation and harassment.[11]

On top of this, a lack of documentation can exacerbate the above vulnerabilities. While many asylum seekers enter the country and register with the national authorities and UNHCR to receive official refugee status, some remain undocumented. In fact, many refugees flee without formal identification such as birth certificates, marriage licenses, and passports.[12] Without proper documentation, access to humanitarian aid, education, health, and social services may be limited. In order to register a birth in Jordan, for instance, parents must provide proof of marriage, which means many refugee children remain unregistered and unable to attend school.[13] Women are particularly affected, as undocumented women face an increased risk of SGBV, workplace exploitation, and forced marriage.[14] Without documentation, refugees live in limbo—unable to return home due to safety concerns, yet vulnerable to harassment and deportation in their new countries.

With a lack of coordinated global response to the current refugee crises, refugees and asylum seekers are critically in danger of being "left behind"—or, more aptly, "left out" of the 2030 development agenda.

Refugees, Migrants, and the 2030 Agenda

The current debate around refugees has largely taken place in developed countries. Yet it is important to remember that low- and middle-income countries host 85 percent of the world's refugees; indeed, sub-Saharan Africa alone hosts

9. Pittaway and Bartolomei (2018).
10. Wirth and others (2014).
11. Wirth and others (2014); IOM (2013).
12. IHRD and NRC (2016).
13. Ibid.
14. Anani (2013); Bartolomei and others (2003).

26 percent of them.[15] Developing nations are thus trying to balance their own development priorities with acute humanitarian needs. Indeed, the poor in these countries are often hardly better off than the refugee populations themselves, which can exacerbate feelings of resentment. An inclusive "no one left behind" agenda requires that refugees and vulnerable host community members alike receive adequate support to access social services and integrate into the community.

While refugees are uniquely vulnerable, the larger global migrant population also faces many of the same hardships and uncertainty. As of 2018, the World Bank Global Knowledge Partnership on Migration and Development estimates that there were 266 million people living in a country other than where they were born.[16] In fact, migration itself is a very old phenomenon, much older than international trade or capital flows. Scientists believe that the first massive migration of modern humans happened between 60,000 and 80,000 years ago.[17] In spite of this long tradition of human mobility, accepting migrants and refugees has always been controversial, and countries have never fully opened their borders to people in the same way they have opened them to goods and capital flows. In recent decades, during the peak of globalization, other global flows have grown at a much faster pace than migration. Export flows, for example, have grown considerably over the past 25 years, accounting for less than 20 percent of global GDP in 1990 to over 30 percent in 2015. During the same period, however, the global population share of migrants has stagnated at around 3.3 percent (see figure 5-2).

While global conversations around refugees and migrants remain distinct, the lines between migrant, asylum seeker, and refugee are increasingly blurred. The 1951 Convention spells out a rather narrow definition for refugee—one who fears persecution due to their race, religion, nationality, social group, or political affiliation. This limited definition leaves many out, including those fleeing widespread unrest, famine, economic collapse, and natural disaster (including outcomes from climate change). Many who fall into this wider migrant category are also vulnerable and face difficulties integrating into their new countries, despite the fact that they migrated "willingly." Thus, a discussion about potential policies to ensure that refugees are not left behind remains incomplete without framing the issue within the larger migration debate. Migration was notably included in the Sustainable Development Goals (SDGs). SDG 8—inclusive growth and employment—calls for expanded labor protections to cover vulnerable migrant

---

15. UNHCR (2018a); UNHCR (2019b).
16. KNOMAD (2019).
17. Gugliotta (2008).

Figure 5-2. Trade to GDP Ratio vs. Migrant Population Share

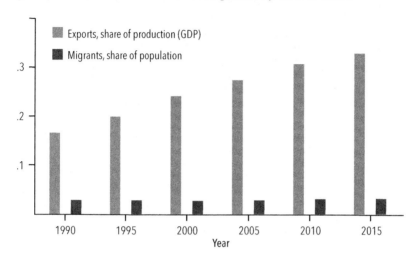

Source: World Development Indicators
Note: Exports data is reported for 2014

workers, especially women (target 8.8).[18] SDG 10—reduced inequalities—highlights the need for orderly, safe, and regularized migration policies, measured by the share of recruitment costs borne by employees (target 10.7). It also calls for the reduction of remittance fees to less than 3 percent by 2030 (target 10.C). SDG 17—partnerships for the goals—includes remittance flows as a critical element of future development financing (target 17.3).

The inclusion of migration in the SDGs is an acknowledgment that migration is a fact of life; despite increasingly isolationist rhetoric from the West, it is unlikely to stop any time soon. While the SDGs were an important starting point for the global conversation around migration, there is much room for improvement. The targets primarily relate to remittance and recruitment costs, and make no mention of undocumented migrants, asylum seekers, and refugees. Yet progress on a number of goals for the population as a whole depends upon the inclusion of migrants and refugees. For instance, in order to end global poverty (SDG 1), vulnerable refugees and migrants, who often come to their host countries with few assets and social networks, should have access to social safety nets until they become self-sufficient. Similarly, in order to achieve quality health outcomes (SDG 3) and education for all (SDG 4), refugees and migrants should be given access to public health and education systems. Formal labor market access

18. IAEG-SDG (2016), Annex IV.

and worker protections must extend to migrants and refugees in order to achieve full, productive employment (SDG 8). True gender equality (SDG 5) means that refugee women—who face overlapping vulnerabilities due to their gender, nationality, and socioeconomic status—have access to the inputs, knowledge, and assets they need to reach their full potential. Alongside efforts to combat the root causes of climate change (SDG 13), the international community should also invest in mitigation and resiliency strategies to address the growing threat of human displacement due to increasing natural disasters.

But beyond the fact that the SDGs should be more inclusive of migrants and refugees who are in danger of being left behind, there is another important, perhaps larger, aspect to consider when thinking about migrants and the 2030 development agenda. Refugees and migrants, we claim, are perhaps the missing piece that could help sending and receiving countries alike achieve lasting sustainable growth, enabling progress on a whole range of development goals. As poverty becomes increasingly concentrated in fragile and conflict-affected regions, finding ways to encourage resiliency and recovery efforts will be a core component of a global poverty agenda that seeks to "leave no one behind." Refugees represent an underutilized resource in this effort, a key conduit between more fragile countries of origin and host countries. Integrating and creating opportunities for migrants and refugees to succeed in their new countries is not only the right thing to do but is smart policy—what we call a "win-win-win" formula for sustainable growth.[19] First, such policies are a win for migrants and refugees, for it allows them to begin to rebuild their lives, earn better wages, and invest in their own human capital. Second, it is a win for receiving communities, which gain productive workers who contribute to the tax base, start businesses, and foster connections with diverse markets. Third, greater integration also creates wins for sending countries due to remittance flows, diaspora business connections, and knowledge diffusion. Eventually, some migrants and refugees may return to their countries of origin, bringing with them the skills and assets gained in their host countries during displacement. There is a core role for public policy in helping to bring about these ends.

Potential Gains from International Refugee and Migration Flows

The rhetoric surrounding international refugee and migration policies has become increasingly polarized over the last decade, especially in developed nations. The global recession exacerbated feelings of economic and social dislocation for the working and middle class in many countries, caused by globalization, the changing nature of work, shifting demographics, and increased strain on post–World

19. Bahar (2018).

War II era social welfare systems.[20] Tapping into these real and perceived feelings of loss, politicians on the far right have increasingly combined populist economic policies with nativist worldviews, using immigrants and refugees as scapegoats for changing economic realities.[21] Refugees—and migrants, more broadly—are painted as a drain on national resources; they place increased pressure on public services, are dependent on welfare programs, and compete for increasingly scarce jobs.[22]

While it is important to acknowledge the political realities that shape the debates around refugees and migrants, it is also important to put these debates in context. Only 1 percent of all refugees are resettled in a third country like the United States or Germany; most remain in their initial country of asylum, typically a neighboring country in the region.[23] Nationalist rhetoric has largely focused on these highly visible 1 percent, ignoring the fact that the bulk of the hosting responsibility, and hence integration challenges, rests on developing countries. Furthermore, the global discourse has belabored the costs of integration, but rarely discussed the potential gains. Taking a nuanced view—holding the real and perceived political costs of integration in tension with the gains—is an important first step in reshaping the global policy debate around refugee and migrant integration.

Occupational Upgrading

A growing body of evidence suggests that, on average, an influx of immigrants into the labor market has little to no aggregate effect on natives' wages and employment.[24] The extent to which migrants and refugees affect the wages of natives is a function of whether the foreigners are complements to or substitutes for native workers. If they are substitutes, we would expect to see downward pressure on native wages due to increased competition for a limited supply of jobs (at least until the capital stock is replenished), in line with the basic economic model. If migrants and refugees are complementary to the local labor force, bringing new skills and knowledge, then their presence could result in an increase in natives' wages. Among economists, there is wide consensus that complementarity of skills is more likely among skilled workers.[25] At the same time, there is less of a consensus on the degree of substitution between unskilled

20. Papademetriou and others (2018); Bernstein and DuBois (2018).

21. Polakow-Suransky (2017).

22. Nezer (2013); GAO (2012); Singer and Wilson (2006).

23. UNHCR (2019a).

24. National Academies of Sciences, Engineering, and Medicine (2017); Kerr and Kerr (2011); Clemens and Hunt (2019).

25. See Docquier and Rapoport (2007) for a review of this literature.

migrants and natives.[26] While there is no definitive answer to this question, most of the evidence suggests that low-skilled immigration does have, at most, a very small, temporary negative effect on the wages and employment of unskilled native workers and previous waves of immigrants.[27]

But recent evidence suggests that inflows of unskilled migrants into an economy could benefit unskilled native workers in the medium-to-long run. In particular, evidence suggests that natives often respond to an influx of unskilled migrants and refugees into the labor market by upgrading their skills and moving up the occupational ladder. A study of the sudden inflow of refugees, 40 percent of whom did not have high school degrees, to Denmark from 1991 to 2008 found that the entry of unskilled workers into the labor force resulted in upward occupational mobility for natives, away from manually intensive tasks toward more complex jobs.[28] As a result, salaries increased without evidence of worker displacement. Low-skilled immigrants and refugees often fill labor shortages or jobs that natives are less likely to perform, such as manual labor–intensive occupations.[29] This allows for greater task specialization, encouraging natives to shift to more skill-intensive occupations with higher pay.[30] By filling labor shortages, migrants can make both individuals and businesses more productive, stimulating economic and job growth. Migrants make up an important part of the workforce in many fundamental occupations that support high-skilled workers—such as home health aides, construction workers, cooks, and truck drivers—which are among the fastest-growing occupations in the United States in the next decade.[31] Increased migrant and refugee participation in reproductive labor occupations, such as caregiving and domestic work, lowers the cost of these services, which has allowed more high-skilled native women to join the labor force.[32]

Entrepreneurship and Job Creation

Migrants contribute to the local economy not only as laborers, but as business owners and entrepreneurs. Migrants engage in entrepreneurship at much higher rates than natives; in the United States, for example, migrants make up 15 percent of the population yet represent 25 percent of entrepreneurs.[33] This is not all

26. See Clemens and Hunt (2019) for a review of this literature.
27. Ottaviano and Peri (2012); Orrenius and Zavodny (2007); National Academies of Sciences (2017).
28. Foged and Peri (2016).
29. Clemens and others (2018); Clemens (2013).
30. Peri (2012).
31. U.S. Bureau of Labor Statistics (2016); Prchal Svajlenka (2017).
32. Peri (2013); Furtado and Hock (2010).
33. Kerr and Kerr (2016).

that surprising, as migration may preselect individuals with more entrepreneurial tendencies. The act of moving to a new country, even when relocation is forced, as in the case of refugees, involves great risk. Migrants and refugees may be able to parlay this risk-taking behavior into the business sphere by starting new ventures, an inherently risky undertaking.[34] In Turkey, for example, Syrian refugees started 6,033 formal companies between 2011 and 2017, accounting for 39 percent of new foreign-owned firms in the country in 2016.[35] When migrants create new businesses, they also create jobs, becoming employers in their communities. Remember that it is small firms that are the engines of job growth (in the United States, for example, small firms account for two-thirds of new job creation each year[36]). Migrants and refugees may also expand consumer demand for certain goods and services, which could lead to increased demand for labor, and hence job creation, in these sectors.[37]

Trade, Investment, and Remittance Flows

Migrants and refugees can also play a fundamental role in fostering international trade and investment. Since migrants and refugees have knowledge of the business environment in both sending and receiving countries, they can act as mediators between businesspeople in both places, lowering transaction costs.[38] This fact is exemplified by the crucial role that Vietnamese refugees played in establishing trade and investment networks between the United States and Vietnam. U.S. states that randomly received more Vietnamese refugees in the 1970s are larger exporters of goods and services to Vietnam today than states who received fewer refugees.[39] These diaspora connections can greatly benefit countries of origin as well. For example, Taiwanese immigrants working in the U.S. tech sector were able to partner with venture capital firms to spur entrepreneurial development in their home country. Due to their knowledge of the Taiwanese economy, firm history, and government regulations, these high-skilled immigrants helped venture capitalists invest in local firms with the most promise.[40] For developing countries overcoming conflict, in particular, this flow of investment could be a key enabler of economic recovery.

Perhaps the most important way sending countries benefit from out-migration

34. Borjas (1987); Zucker and Darby (2007); Honig and others (2010).
35. Ucak and others (2017).
36. U.S. Bureau of Labor Statistics (2018).
37. Ruhs and Vargas-Silva (2018).
38. Kapur and McHale (2005).
39. Parsons and Vezina (2018).
40. Saxenian and Sabel (2009).

is through remittance flows. Remittances—money that migrants send back home to friends and family—can act as a powerful poverty-reduction device, allowing those left behind to share in the economic benefits of increased labor productivity and significantly increase their consumption. Remittances are no longer a trivial part of global financing flows; remittances to low- and middle-income countries reached US$529 billion in 2018, and are projected to surpass foreign direct investment in 2019.[41] This will likely be an increasingly powerful force for growth in the future.

Knowledge Diffusion

In addition to financial flows, migrants and refugees can play a significant role in transferring technologies and knowledge across borders. This knowledge diffusion works both ways—migrants and refugees can bring new ideas and products from their countries of origin to their new countries, or they can share new technology and innovation learned abroad with their home countries. This two-way transfer contributes to more competitive and diversified economies in both places.[42] An illustrative example of this phenomenon is Franschoek Valley, South Africa. Today, Franschoek is known for its high-quality wineries, which produce a significant share of all South African wine exports. The town was founded by French Huguenot refugees, who settled there in the seventeenth century after being expelled from France. These refugees brought their knowledge of French winemaking with them, and used it to turn the valley into the first-class wine exporter that it is today, competing in global markets with wineries from all over the world. Consistent with this finding, our ongoing research shows that the nations that emerged from the former Yugoslavia benefited enormously from the knowledge and experiences gained by Bosnian, Croatian, and Serbian refugees who were temporarily resettled in Germany during the 1990s.[43] These countries have experienced high export growth in sectors where more refugees worked during displacement, specifically knowledge-intensive sectors where workers gained analytical and managerial skills. This is consistent with growing evidence about the importance of management in increasing firm-level productivity in developing countries.[44]

41. KNOMAD (2019).
42. Bahar and Rapoport (2018).
43. Bahar and others (2018).
44. Bloom and others (2010); Bloom and Reenen (2010); Bender and others (2018).

Maximizing Gains and Mitigating Costs of International Refugee and Migration Flows

While there are real fiscal and political costs associated with greater refugee and migrant integration, there are also enormous gains to be had for sending and receiving countries alike. But failure to integrate—whether due to explicit barriers to health, education, employment, and documentation services, or implicit barriers such as discrimination and xenophobia—limits the realization of these economic gains, and risks leaving refugees and migrants behind. Migration is a fact of life, unlikely to decrease in coming years. It is thus in the interest of the international community to find ways to help refugees and migrants integrate into their local economy and community, in order to take advantage of the economic gains that come with international migration flows and ensure that refugees and migrants have the tools they need to live with agency and dignity.

In order to realize these gains, public policy measures are often required to deal with regulation or market failures that hinder the successful integration of refugee and migrant workers. In the section that follows, we highlight a series of steps host nations can take to maximize the gains and mitigate the costs of international refugee and migration flows.

Formal Labor Market Access

First, at the risk of stating the obvious, refugees and migrants must be granted formal rights to stay and access labor market opportunities in their host countries in order to reap the economic gains discussed above. Formal labor market access allows refugees and migrants to be employed, create businesses, and employ other workers, without fear of retribution for working illegally in the informal economy. Formalization also gives refugees and migrants a sense of stability, allowing them to invest in themselves and in their receiving communities. Research shows that the faster refugees are able to integrate into the economy and access labor market opportunities, the more successful they will be in the long run.[45]

A key first step in this effort is streamlining access and lowering entrance barriers to formal work authorization. Ideally, all refugees would be granted formal labor market access without the need for a permit, as permitting systems can deter the most vulnerable—especially those who lack formal documentation—from applying.[46] When a permit system is in place, however, work access should

---

45. Marbach and others (2017); Bakker and others (2014).
46. Clemens and others (2018).

not be tied to a specific employer, which can lead to exploitation.[47] Additionally, permits should be free, as associated costs are either the responsibility of the employer, which can limit incentives to hire refugees, or borne by the refugees themselves, which can be cost-prohibitive. These issues are important not only for refugees, but for migrants as well. Many low-skilled migrant workers find overseas employment through recruitment firms, which often charge exorbitant rates, paid back by migrants as a share of their yearly income.[48] In addition, visas may be tied to specific employers, leaving migrants, especially women, at greater risk of exploitation, harassment, and even human trafficking.[49] Granting migrants and refugees formal labor market access offers them a form of workplace protection, giving them greater bargaining power they can use to advocate for better salaries and working conditions.

However, it is important to note that granting formal labor market access to refugees and migrants may have less of an impact in places with a large informal labor market. Refugees and migrants already have access to these informal employment opportunities, so formal sector access will not lead to wide-scale labor market adjustments.[50] There is a greater risk of refugee/migrant and native substitutability when workers are concentrated and competing for low-skilled jobs in the informal market. Additionally, a large informal sector limits the impact that formalization would have on the direct expansion of the tax base, as refugee and migrant businesses will likely stay in the informal sector. Despite these caveats, granting formal access can still yield economy-wide benefits. Even if only a few migrants and refugees are able to find formal employment opportunities, formalization can still potentially improve working conditions in the informal sector, since migrants now have the option to seek work elsewhere if abuses occur.[51]

Freedom of Movement

In addition to formal labor market access, successful integration is contingent upon refugees and migrants having the right to freedom of movement. While most refugees live in urban and semi-urban areas among host communities, 35 percent remain in camps, which limits their interactions with the broader economy.[52] Employment opportunities are scarce in the informal camp economy,

47. Buffoni and others (2017); MMC (2017).
48. KNOMAD (2019).
49. IOM (2013).
50. Clemens and others (2018).
51. Ibid.
52. UNHCR (2018b).

which can reduce the incentive to invest in education and skills development.[53] This limited economic integration hurts not only refugees, but natives as well: as consumers, refugees only buy from refugee-owned camp businesses, and as employers, they only hire refugee workers.[54] In order to realize the full gains of economic integration, refugees should be allowed to move and work outside of camp boundaries.

Even outside of camp settings, refugee freedom of movement may be limited. Both Turkey and Switzerland implemented internal redistribution schemes in recent years, assigning refugees to a sub-national region to relieve pressure on border areas.[55] Refugees only have access to public services in their assigned city, and lose access to benefits if they leave without permission. While this has mitigated some of the negative effects of increased public service demand, there are often few employment prospects and a lack of affordable housing in assigned cities. This forces many refugees to choose between moving to a larger city with better work opportunities and losing access to health and education services.[56] Place-based entitlements disincentivize refugees from responding to regional variation in economic opportunities, which prolongs their dependence on public assistance programs. Giving refugees the right to freedom of movement, and delinking assistance from place of residence, increases the likelihood of integration into the formal economy, which could expand opportunities for refugees and natives alike.

Active Labor Market Programs to Improve Matching

In order to facilitate economic integration and employment, many development actors have invested in livelihood and job training programs for refugees. However, a review of existing program evaluations suggests that refugee livelihood initiatives have largely failed.[57] Most programs have focused on supply-side interventions, without paying much attention to market demand. For example, female refugees in Uganda received NGO support to start handicraft enterprises, but most had a difficult time sustaining the business, due to limited demand for nonessential goods.[58] Demand-side programming has been dominated by cash-for-work programs, largely criticized for disrupting local labor markets. In acknowledgment of this failure, both the multilateral and NGO community

---

53. Clemens and others (2018); Alix-Garcia and others (2017).
54. Betts and others (2018); Clemens and others (2018).
55. UNHCR (n.d.); Gesley (2016).
56. Kirisci (2017); Leghtas and Hollingsworth (2017).
57. Jacobsen and Fratzke (2016).
58. Easton-Calabria (2016).

have refocused their attention on market systems development, looking at market demand and supply chain networks to see what sectors might be best suited for refugee firm entry.[59] Thus far, these efforts have been fairly small-scale, but represent promising areas for further study and investment.

Additionally, programs that help refugees verify skills, degrees, or certifications earned in their countries of origin can improve labor market integration and matching. A lack of credential recognition may act as a formal or informal barrier to employment. Due to country-specific regulations, a foreign license may not be seen as equivalent to a domestic license. Foreign credentials may also be implicitly viewed as less rigorous due to a lack of information on the part of the employer. In order to address this constraint, most OECD countries have a formal process for foreign skill/degree assessment and recognition for migrants.[60] Immigrants that receive recognition are more likely to be employed in higher-paying jobs, as opposed to menial jobs for which they are overqualified. However, few immigrants take advantage of this service: only 38 percent of migrants with tertiary education applied for degree recognition in 2017.[61] Efforts to streamline bureaucratic hurdles and recognize nonformal and on-the-job learning might enhance service usefulness. Similar recognition systems are being adapted to verify refugee skills and education. World Education Services, for example, piloted a qualification assessment for Syrian refugees in Canada to help reconstruct their academic histories and offer equivalent credentials when documentation was missing.[62] The EU likewise is developing a "qualifications passport" to assess refugee higher education credentials.[63] Both Denmark and Finland have used skills assessments as a means of assigning resettlement locations, placing refugees in cities with business opportunities that match their skill sets.[64] While further study is needed to assess the long-term impact of these interventions and their scalability, verification systems could help refugees and migrants signal their value-add to potential employers or investors, indicating they have the training and experience necessary to succeed.

59. UNHCR and ILO (2018); EMMA (2019).
60. OECD (2017).
61. Ibid.
62. World Education Services (2018).
63. Council of Europe (2018).
64. Danish Ministry of Education (2019); Finland Ministry of Employment and the Economy (2015).

Voluntary Relocation to Reduce Pressure on Local Infrastructure

When refugees and migrants enter a new country, they tend to cluster around ports of entry, large cities, and areas with preexisting migrant communities. This concentration can exacerbate the risk of short-term negative labor market outcomes for natives, due to increased competition over scarce jobs and additional, rapid-onset demand for limited public goods such as infrastructure and services. Voluntary relocation could help relieve short-term pressure on local infrastructure caused by sudden refugee and migrant inflows, improving outcomes for newcomers and natives alike.

In fact, a study looking at the effectiveness of integration policies for refugees in Germany following World War II found that low mobility likely hindered refugee labor market success.[65] Thus, increased refugee movement within the country could have improved labor market outcomes. Since migrants and refugees tend to be more mobile due to fewer locational ties than natives, voluntary relocation is a feasible policy solution to alleviate some of the strain on frontline areas. As a result, some scholars have suggested implementing an incentive-based system to promote voluntary internal relocation to places with lower migrant density, where more opportunities could exist.

Many have argued for some form of tradeable cross-country refugee quotas that resemble carbon-taxing schemes, based on ideas grounded in mechanism design theory.[66] Under such a proposal, an international organization such as UNHCR would allocate refugee resettlement quotas by country, based on an agreed-upon set of criteria such as population and market size. Countries would then be allowed to trade quotas on an open marketplace. Such a system could also take refugee and country preferences into account, allowing refugees to rank potential destination locations and countries to prioritize specific refugee demographic profiles (for example, giving preference to women and children).[67]

This scheme could also be adapted to a national level to help disperse newcomers across sub-national boundaries, based on criteria such as employment opportunities, school capacity, and housing affordability. The Immigration Policy Lab out of Stanford University has proposed using an algorithmic matching program as an internal redistribution tool.[68] The program uses historical data on refugee resettlement outcomes and estimates the likelihood that a refugee will find work in a given location based on their demographic profile. It then assigns

---

65. Falck and others (2012).
66. Fernandez-Huertas Moraga and Rapoport (2015).
67. Jones and Teytelboym (2017); Andersson and others (2018); van Basshuysen (2017).
68. Bansak and others (2018).

the refugee to the location where they have the best chance of finding employment. This fall, Switzerland began piloting algorithmic matching to assign asylum seekers to cantons, replacing their previous random assignment scheme.[69] A similar machine-learning placement program, Annie, is currently being piloted by the Hebrew Immigrant Aid Society (HIAS) in the United States.[70]

Given that refugees were forcibly displaced from their home countries, any such relocation scheme must be voluntary in nature, but could include some form of incentive payment to encourage and subsidize relocation. Since many refugees have often lost most of their assets and savings during displacement, even a modest payment could make a large difference in an individual or family's decision to move. Evidence on how to properly design such incentives, though, is still thin. In Bangladesh, Innovations for Poverty Action achieved some initial success providing a monetary incentive to families to help lower the cost of migratory travel, though the program did not see similar gains at scale.[71]

Investing in Host Communities

Relocation aside, additional public investment in infrastructure and public services can help mitigate the costs associated with rapid population inflows. International support is critical in this effort, particularly in countries with limited fiscal capacity. These investments would benefit both refugees/migrants and natives in the long run. Yet there is a major gap in the development financing architecture to respond to these needs.[72] The World Bank established a US$2 billion lending fund in 2017 to help low-income refugee-hosting countries invest in projects that support both host communities and refugees, such as basic services, infrastructure, and livelihoods initiatives.[73] But this fund is likely inadequate for the scale of financing needed to respond to long-term, structural changes in host communities. In response, host nations have taken matters into their own hands. The Jordanian government requires that 30 percent of all donor funds go toward projects that benefit vulnerable Jordanian populations.[74] The Colombian government recently announced US$229 million in credit lines for infrastructure, public service, and capital investments in highly affected refugee-hosting regions.[75] Failing to invest in host nations is shortsighted, for without support, the very

69. Stanford University (2018).
70. Calamur (2019).
71. Levy and Sri Raman (2018).
72. Charles and others (2018).
73. World Bank (2018).
74. 3RP (2019).
75. Agencia EFE (2019).

conflicts they are sheltering refugees from may spill over into their own borders. Furthermore, without investing in the native population alongside the refugee community, social tensions between natives and refugees may spark domestic unrest, instability, and potential violence.

It is important to note that official development assistance is not the only means of mobilizing additional financing for hosting regions. Interesting new work around diaspora bonds suggests that there may be innovative ways to harness diaspora networks and existing remittance flows to fund future entrepreneurship and development opportunities.[76] Reducing remittance fees is a key piece of this puzzle. If remittance fees, the cost of sending money home, measured as a percent of the amount transmitted, fell from their current level of 7 percent to the SDG target of 3 percent, an additional US$23 billion would have reached low- and middle-income countries in 2018.[77] This is a core policy area for the international community to address.

Access to Credit to Foster Small Business Creation

Besides investment in infrastructure and public goods, there is a key role for private capital to help jump-start resiliency and recovery efforts in refugee-hosting communities. In order to experience some of the larger gains of refugee and migrant integration, such as firm development and job creation, entrepreneurs must have access to capital. Yet access to capital is often constrained in many host countries. Refugees and migrants may be restricted from opening a bank account or applying for a loan, due to outright legal discrimination or lack of documentation.[78] Where permissions do exist, they still may lack access to adequate financing because they appear to be a riskier investment, or they lack the necessary collateral or credit history to obtain a loan.[79] Indeed, refugee business owners in Turkey and South Africa reported that limited access to start-up capital was a major impediment to firm growth.[80] There is a clear role for public-private partnerships here. Funds, originating either from foreign aid or private sources, can be delivered through formal financial entities to expand financial inclusion and encourage service usage.[81] Local governments and development actors can provide risk guarantees to national banks that give loans to

76. Kayode-Anglade and Spio-Garbrah (2012); Ketkar and Ratha (2009); Famoroti (2018).
77. KNOMAD (2019).
78. Pistelli (2017).
79. OECD (2011); Blanchflower (2009); Albareto and Mistrulli (2011).
80. Ucak and others (2017); Crush and others (2017).
81. El-Zoghbi and others (2017).

refugee and migrant entrepreneurs.[82] Over a hundred countries have some form of partial credit guarantees for small and medium-size enterprises, which could be expanded to include refugee entrepreneurs.[83] UNHCR and the Swedish government are currently working to establish a risk guarantee facility for financial service providers who grant loans to refugees and vulnerable host populations. Initial four-year pilots in Jordan and Uganda are currently underway, implemented by the Grameen Foundation.[84]

Forming Skills Before Migration Occurs

Such public-private partnerships can extend beyond financing to employment. While skilled migration raises the risk of a "brain drain" in developing countries, public-private partnerships can help link skill formation and skilled migration in a way that is mutually beneficial for both sending and receiving countries. Under a bilateral Global Skill Partnership (coined by Clemens 2015), workers in a skilled profession such as nursing would be trained in their country of origin, where the cost of training is much lower. A private employer in a destination country would pay for training for migrants, and subsidize the cost for non-migrants. Some of the trainees would then immigrate to the destination country and work for the employer, paying off the cost of the training for themselves and their host country counterparts with a portion of their wages. The destination country gains the skilled workers they need at a fraction of the cost. The migrant makes much higher wages then they would have at home, well offsetting the cost of the training. The origin country gains skilled, qualified nurses at little cost, who help strengthen the national healthcare system, creating spillover benefits for the whole population. Such programs also create incentives for human capital accumulation in the sending country, offering the potential for future migration and higher wages to those who accumulate the necessary skills.

Similar bilateral agreements have been tried in the past with mixed results.[85] However, this past record highlights key design features that are critical for success. Employers need to be involved in program design to ensure training matches the skills needed for on-the-job success. Programs should recognize migrants' past training and employment experiences. In a partnership between Finland and the Philippines, for example, applicants with a nursing degree from a Filipino university only need to complete one additional year of training in Finland,

---

82. Chehade and others (2017).
83. Douette and others (2012).
84. Inclusive Finance Network Luxembourg (2019).
85. See Clemens (2015) for a thorough review.

rather than two.[86] Though a variety of funding arrangements exist, none should place an undue burden on the migrants themselves. A German-Tunisian program, for example, failed because while the employers covered the costs of the training, students had to take out loans to cover room and board once they reached Germany.[87] Finally, such arrangements only work if they expand the supply of skilled workers in sending countries. In some small island countries, skills partnerships could create labor shortages at home if the majority of skilled workers chose to migrate. Thus, such partnerships should be context-specific, designed with input from sending and receiving countries.

Such innovative policies do require initial cooperation and investment, but can quickly become profitable and self-sustaining, helping both sending and receiving countries experience the gains (and mitigate the risks) of international migration. While such partnerships are a more natural fit for regularized migration flows between a stable developing and developed country, there might be ways to expand these arrangements to include asylum-seekers and refugees. Perhaps as a component of a larger cross-country refugee relocation scheme, private sector partners who are interested in hiring refugees could fund training programs in borderline hosting countries for refugees and natives, with an agreement to sponsor relocation and employment for a set number of refugees in a third country. Such a partnership would reward borderline countries for hosting refugees by subsidizing training for natives, while also relieving some of the long-run integration challenges through resettlement sponsorship.

Shared Global Agenda

Encouragingly, the international community has achieved some progress in pushing for a new global agenda around refugees and migrants. The Global Compacts on Migration (GCM) and Refugees (GCR) are an attempt by UN member states to present a coordinated response to the current migratory crises, balancing the need for a safe and regularized process for migrants and refugees while also upholding state sovereignty. The GCR acknowledges that developing nations have borne the brunt of the refugee crisis, and so, developed nations must share in the financial burden to alleviate pressure.[88] Additionally, the GCM affirms that as a core component of any immigration reform effort, the international community must help developing countries address the conditions that

86. Wildau (2011).
87. Clemens (2015).
88. UN (2018a).

cause migrants to emigrate in the first place.[89] The compacts create a structure for information sharing between host nations and migrants/refugees, establishing a more transparent system where people are able to make informed choices about movement ex ante.[90] Building on the international consensus that came out of the SDGs, the GCM and GCR represent a key step forward in reframing the global narrative around forced and voluntary migration.

Conclusion

In an increasingly interconnected world, greater human mobility should be viewed as an opportunity rather than a risk, a vehicle for expanding growth, trade, and human capital accumulation. Migrants and refugees bring skills, knowledge, innovation, and networks to their host nations, a core engine for economic growth. Yet to date, they represent a largely underutilized resource. In fact, refugees and migrants risk being left behind, as they are neither protected by the laws of their countries of origin nor entitled to rights in their new countries. In order to capitalize on the opportunity migrants and refugees present, countries need to create enabling environments that provide stability and predictability, giving newcomers the security to invest in their own human capital, businesses, and communities. States should grant migrants and refugees the right to work, freedom of movement, and protections under the law. In addition, the international community should help host nations invest in public services and infrastructure in highly affected regions, and help expand refugee access to financial services. Public-private partnerships can help facilitate skills training and employment in ways that benefit both sending and receiving countries, migrants and non-migrants alike. A common international framework, such as that spelled out under the GCR and the GCM, can help to ensure that migrant and refugee rights and protections are not location-dependent, but informed by a larger consensus about the rights of forced and voluntary migrants. This suite of enabling policies represents a win-win-win formula, creating opportunities for migrants/refugees, host nations, and countries of origin to reap the gains from international migration flows.

Naturally, as with any other change that affects the economy, integrating refugees and migrants into the labor force might result in some people being worse off in the short term, even when the aggregate gains are positive. But that speaks to the need for investment in social safety nets and robust retaining programs to protect workers who might be substitutes for migrants, as opposed to rejecting

89. UN (2018b).
90. Bahar (2019).

refugees and migrants outright. The global dialogue around migrants and refugees has become clouded in recent years, but it is important to remember that global migration is not a new phenomenon. Though there are some short-term risks, overall refugees and migrants represent untapped potential: if properly integrated into their local community and the global economy and given the right protections and support, refugees can be an asset—not a burden—for all countries involved. Therefore, integrating and protecting refugees is not only morally right, but also the smart thing to do to ensure that no one is left behind.

References

3RP. 2019. *Regional Strategic Overview 2019/2020.* Amman, Jordan: UNHCR and UNDP.

Agencia EFE, "Gobierno Colombiano Invertirá 229 Milliones Dólares en Frontera con Venezuela," *La Vanguarida*, April 14, 2019.

Albareto, Giorgio and Paolo Mistrulli. 2011. "Bridging the Gap Between Migrants and the Banking System." Bank of Italy Working Paper 794.

Alix-Garcia, Jennifer, Erhan Artuc, and Onder Haruf, *The Economics of Hosting Refugees: A Host Community Perspective from Turkana* (Washington: World Bank, 2017).

Anani, Ghida, "Dimensions of Gender-Based Violence against Syrian Refugees in Lebanon," *Forced Migration Review*, no. 44 (2013), 75–78.

Andersson, Tommy, Lars Ehlers, and Alessandro Martinello. 2018. "Dynamic Refugee Matching." Lund University Department of Economics Working Paper 2018, 7.

Bahar, Dany, "Why Accepting Refugees Is a Win-Win-Win Formula," *Brookings Institution Up Front Blog*, June 19, 2018.

———, "A Wall Can't Fix What Global Migration and Refugee Compacts Can," *Brookings Institution Up Front Blog*, January 10, 2019.

Bahar, Dany and Hillel Rapoport, "Migration, Knowledge Diffusion and the Comparative Advantage of Nations," *Economic Journal*, vol. 128, no. 612 (2018), 273–305.

Bahar, Dany, Andreas Hauptmann, Cem Ozguzel, and Hillel Rapoport. 2018. "Let Their Knowledge Flow: The Effect of Returning Refugees on Export Performance in the Former Yugoslavia." CESifo Working Paper 7371.

Bakker, Linda, Jaco Dagevos, and Godfried Engbersen, "The Importance of Resources and Security in the Socioeconomic Integration of Refugees. A Study on the Impact of Length of Stay in Asylum Accommodation and Residence Status on Socioeconomic Integration for the Four Largest Refugee Groups in the Netherlands," *Journal of International Migration and Integration*, vol. 15, no. 3 (2014), 431–48.

Bansak, Kirk, and others, "Improving Refugee Integration Through Data-Driven Algorithmic Assignment," *Science*, vol. 359, no. 6373 (2018), 325–29.

Bartolomei, Linda, Eileen Pittaway, and Emma Elizabeth Pittaway. "Who Am I? Identity and Citizenship in Kakuma Refugee Camp in Northern Kenya, *Development*, vol. 46, no. 3 (2003), 87–93.

Bender, Stefan, and others, "Management Practices, Workforce Selection and Productivity," *Journal of Labor Economics*, vol. 6, no. S1 (2018), 371–409.

Bernstein, Hamutal and Nicole DuBois. 2018. *Bringing Evidence to the Refugee Integration Debate.* Urban Institute Research Report.

Betts, Alexander, Naohiko Omata, and Olivier Sterck. 2018. *Refugee Economies in Kenya.* University of Oxford Refugee Studies Centre.

Blanchflower, David, "Minority Self-Employment in the United States and the Impact of Affirmative Action Programs," *Annals of Finance*, vol. 5, no. 3 (2009), 361–96.

Bloom, Nicholas and John Van Reenen, "Why Do Management Practices Differ across Firms and Countries?" *Journal of Economic Perspectives*, vol. 24, no.1 (2010), 203–24.

Bloom, Nicholas, and others, "Why Do Firms in Developing Countries Have Low Productivity?" *American Economic Review*, vol. 100, no. 2 (2010), 619–23.

Borjas, George, "Self-Selection and the Earnings of Immigrants," *American Economic Review*, vol. 77, no. 4 (1987), 531–53.

Buffoni, Laura, Maha Kattaa, and Zeina El Khalil. 2017. *Periodic Analysis of Syrian Workers in Jordan.* Geneva, Switzerland and Washington: ILO, World Bank, and UNHCR.

Calamur, Krishnadev, "How Technology Could Revolutionize Refugee Resettlement," *The Atlantic*, April 26, 2019.

Charles, Sarah, and others. 2018. "Five Ways to Improve the World Bank Funding for Refugees and Hosts in Low-Income Countries and Why These Dedicated Resources Matter More than Ever." Center for Global Development Policy Note, November.

Chehade, Nadine, Antoine Navarro, and Danielle Sobol. 2017. "Remittances and Financial Inclusion: A Demand-Side Analysis of Low-Income Jordanians and Syrian Refugees in Jordan." CGAP Working Paper.

Clemens, Michael A. 2013. "International Harvest: A Case Study of How Foreign Workers Help American Farms Grow Crops—and the Economy." New York, New York and Washington: Partnership for a New American Economy and Center for Global Development.

———. "Global Skill Partnerships: A Proposal for Technical Training in a Mobile World," *IZA Journal of Labor Policy*, vol. 4, no. 2 (2015).

Clemens, Michael A. and Jennifer Hunt, "The Labor Market Effects of Refugee Waves: Reconciling Conflicting Results," *ILR Review*, vol. 72, no. 4 (2019), 818–57.

Clemens, Michael A., Cindy Huang, and Jimmy Graham. 2018. "The Economic and Fiscal Effects of Granting Refugees Formal Labor Market Access." Center for Global Development Working Paper 496.

Council of Europe. 2018. "European Qualifications Passport for Refugees" (www.coe. int/education/recognition-of-refugees-qualifications).

Crush, Jonathan, and others. 2017. "Refugee Entrepreneurial Economies in Urban South Africa." SAMP Migration Policy Series 76.

Danish Ministry of Education. 2019. "My Skills and Qualifications File" (www. minkompetencemappe.dk).

Docquier, Frederic and Hillel Rapoport. 2007. "Skilled Migration: The Perspective of Developing Countries." IZA Discussion Paper Series 2873.

Douette, Andre, Dominique Lesaffre, and Roland Siebeke, *SME's Credit Guarantee Schemes in Developing and Emerging Economies: Reflections, Setting-Up Principles, Quality Standards* (Bonn, Germany: GIZ, 2012).

Easton-Calabria, Evan. 2016. "Refugees Asked to Fish for Themselves: The Role of Livelihoods Trainings for Kampala's Ruban Refugees." University of Oxford Refugee Studies Centre Research Paper 277.

El-Zoghbi, Mayada, and others. 2017. "The Role of Financial Services in Humanitarian Crises." Access to Finance Forum 12.

EMMA. 2019. "About Emma" (www.emma-toolkit.org).

Falck, Oliver, Stephan Heblich, and Susanne Link, "Forced Migration and the Effects of an Integration Policy in Post-WWII Germany," *BE Journal of Economic Analysis & Policy*, vol. 12, no. 1 (2012).

Famoroti, Michael, "Foresight Africa Viewpoint—Debt by Diaspora: Ties that Bond," *Brookings Institution Africa in Focus Blog*, January 24, 2018.

Fernandez-Huertas Moraga, Jesus and Hillel Rapoport, "Tradable Refugee-Admission Quotas and EU Asylum Policy," *CESifo Economic Studies*, vol. 61, no. 3–4 (2015), 638–72.

Finland Ministry of Employment and the Economy. "Action Plan on Integration to Take Account of Increasing Immigration." Press Release, November 27, 2015.

Foged, Mette and Giovanni Peri. "Immigrants' Effect on Native Workers: New Analysis on Longitudinal Data," *American Economic Journal: Applied Economics*, vol. 8, no. 2 (2016), 1–34.

Furtado, Delia and Heinrich Hock, "Low Skilled Immigration and Work-Fertility Tradeoffs among High Skilled U.S. Natives," *American Economic Review*, vol. 100, no. 2 (2010), 224–28.

GAO. 2012. *Refugee Resettlement: Greater Consultation with Community Stakeholders Could Strengthen Program*. Washington: GAO.

Gesley, Jenny. 2016. "Refugee Law and Policy: Switzerland." *Library of Congress*, March.

Gugliotta, Guy, "The Great Human Migration," *Smithsonian Magazine*, July 2008.

Honig, Benson, Israel Drori, and Barbara Carmichael, *Transnational and Immigrant Entrepreneurship in a Globalized World* (University of Toronto Press, 2010).

Human Rights Watch. "Bangladesh: Rohingya Refugee Students Expelled." Press Release, April 1, 2019.

[IAEG-SDG] Inter-Agency and Expert Group on SDG Indicators. 2016. *Report of the Inter-Agency and Expert Group on Sustainable Development Goal Indicators*. New York: UN, Annex IV.

[IHRD and NRC] International Human Rights Clinic at Harvard Law School and Norwegian Refugee Council. 2016. *Securing Status: Syrian Refugees and the Documentation of Legal Status, Identity and Family Relationships in Jordan*. Boston, Mass. and Oslo, Norway: IHRD and NRC.

Inclusive Finance Network Luxembourg. "Access to Financial Services for Refugees in Jordan and Uganda." Press Release, March 12, 2019.

IOM. 2013. "Tacking Action against Violence and Discrimination Affecting Migrant Women and Girls." IOM Factsheet.

Jacobsen, Karen and Susan Fratzke, *Building Livelihood Opportunities for Refugee Populations: Lessons from Past Practice* (Washington: Migration Policy Institute, 2016).

Jones, Will and Alexander Teytelboym, "Matching Systems for Refugees," *Journal on Migration and Human Security*, vol. 5, no. 3 (2017), 667–81.

Kapur, Devesh and John McHale. 2005. *Give Us Your Best and Brightest: The Global Hunt for Talent and Its Impact on the Developing World*. Washington: Center for Global Development.

Kayode-Anglade, Seliatou and Nana Spio-Garbrah. 2012. "Diaspora Bonds: Some Lessons for African Countries." AfDB Africa Economic Brief, vol. 3, no. 13.

Kerr, Sari Pekkala and William R. Kerr. 2011. "Economic Impacts of Immigration: A Survey." Finnish Economic Papers, Finnish Economic Association vol. 24, no. 1, 1–32.

———. 2016. "Immigrant Entrepreneurship." National Bureau of Economic Research Working Paper 22385.

Ketkar, Suhas and Dilip Ratha, "New Paths to Funding," Finance and Development, vol. 46, no. 2 (2009).

Kirisci, Kemal. 2014. Syrian Refugees and Turkey's Challenges: Going Beyond Hospitality. Washington: Brookings.

———. "Don't Forget Non-Syrian Refugees in Turkey," Brookings Institution Order from Chaos Blog, June 22, 2017.

[KNOMAD] World Bank Global Knowledge Partnership on Migration and Development. 2019. Migration and Remittances: Recent Developments and Outlook. Washington: World Bank.

Leghtas, Izza and Ann Hollingsworth. 2017. I Am Only Looking for My Rights: Legal Employment Still Inaccessible for Refugees in Turkey. Washington: Refugees International.

Levy, Karen and Varna Sri Raman, "Why (and When) We Test at Scale: No Lean Season and the Quest for Impact," Evidence Action, November 19, 2018.

Marbach, Moritz, Jens Hainmueller, and Dominik Hangartner. 2017. "The Long-Term Impact of Employment Bans on the Economic Integration of Refugees." Immigration Policy Lab Working Paper 17-03.

[MMC] Mixed Migration Centre. 2017. Decent Work for Whom? Economic Integration of Refugees and Other Foreign Nationals in the Middle East. Geneva, Switzerland: MMC.

National Academies of Sciences, Engineering, and Medicine. 2017. The Economic and Fiscal Consequences of Immigration. Washington: The National Academies Press.

Nezer, Melanie. 2013. Resettlement at Risk: Meeting Emerging Challenges to Refugee Resettlement in Local Communities. Washington: Hebrew Immigrant Aid Society.

Nielsen. 2017. Health Access and Utilization Survey: Access to Health Services in Jordan Among Refugees from Other Nationalities. Geneva, Switzerland: UNHCR.

OECD. 2011. International Migration Outlook 2011. Paris, France: OECD Publishing.

———. 2017. Making Integration Work: Assessment and Recognition of Foreign Qualifications. Paris, France: OECD Publishing.

Orrenius, Pia M. and Madeline Zavodny, "Does Immigration Affect Wages? A Look at Occupation-Level Evidence," Labour Economics, vol. 14, no. 5 (2007), 757–73.

Ottaviano, Gianmarco I. P. and Giovanni Peri, "Rethinking the Effect of Immigration on Wages," Journal of the European Economic Association, vol. 10, no. 1 (2012), 152–97.

Papademetriou, Demetrios G., Natalia Banulescu-Bogdan, and Kate Hooper. 2018. The Future of Migration Policy in a Volatile Political Landscape. Washington: Migration Policy Institute.

Parsons, Christopher and Pierre-Louis Vezina, "Migrant Networks and Trade: The Vietnamese Boat People as a Natural Experiment," Economic Journal, vol. 128, no. 612 (2018), 210–34.

Peri, Giovanni, "The Effect of Immigration on Productivity: Evidence from U.S. States," Review of Economics and Statistics, vol. 94, no. 1 (2012), 348–58.

————, "The Economic Benefits of Immigration," *Berkeley Review of Latin American Studies*, Fall 2013, 14–19.

Pistelli, Micol. 2017. "Removing Barriers to Expand Access to Finance for Refugees." FinDev Gateway, March.

Pittaway, Eileen and Linda Bartolomei. 2018. "From Rhetoric to Reality: Achieving Gender Equality for Refugee Women and Girls." World Refugee Council Research Paper 3, August.

Polakow-Suransky, Sasha, *Go Back Where You Came From: The Backlash Against Immigration and the Rate of Western Democracy* (New York: Nation Books, 2017).

Prchal Svajlenka, Nicole. 2017. "Immigrant Workers are Important to Filling Growing Occupations." Center for American Progress, May.

Ruhs, Martin and Carolos Vargas-Silva. 2018. "The Labour Market Effects of Immigration." The Migration Observatory Briefing.

Saxenian, AnnaLee and Charles Sabel, "Roepke Lecture in Economic Geography Venture Capital in the 'Periphery': The New Argonauts, Global Search, and Local Institution Building," *Economic Geography*, vol. 84, no. 4 (2009), 379–94.

Siegfried, Kristy, "Time to Reform the Way We Protect Refugees?" *New Humanitarian*, May 9, 2016.

Singer, Audrey and Jill H. Wilson, *From 'Here' to 'There': Refugee Resettlement in Metropolitan America* (Brookings, 2006).

Stanford University, "Switzerland Launches Program to Test AI for Refugee Integration," *Phys.org*, May 30, 2018.

UN. 2018a. *Report of the United Nations High Commissioner for Refugees—Part II Global Compact on Refugees.* UN General Assembly Official Records 73rd Session, Supplement No. 12.

————. 2018b. *Global Compact for Safe, Orderly and Regular Migration.* New York: UN.

U.S. Bureau of Labor Statistics. 2016. "Fastest Growing Occupations." Occupational Outlook Handbook.

————. 2018. "Annual Gross Job Gains and Gross Jobs Losses by Age and Average Size of Establishment." Business Employment Dynamics Data.

Ucak, Selen, Jennifer P. Holt, and Kavya Raman. 2017. *Another Side to the Story: A Market Assessment of Syrian SMEs in Turkey.* New York: Building Markets.

UNHCR and ILO. 2018. *SAIM: A Systematic Approach to Inclusive Markets for Refugees and Host Communities: A UNHCR-ILO Programme.* Geneva, Switzerland: UNHCR and ILO.

UNHCR. 2016. *Missing Out: Refugee Education in Crisis.* Geneva, Switzerland: UNHCR.

————. 2018a. "Figures at a Glance" (www.unhcr.org/figures-at-a-glance).

————. 2018b. *Global Trends: Forced Displacement in 2017.* Geneva, Switzerland: UNHCR.

————. 2019a. "Resettlement" (www.unhcr.org/resettlement).

————. 2019b. "Where We Work: Africa" (www.unhcr.org/africa).

————. n.d. *The Practice of "Satellite Cities" in Turkey.* Geneva, Switzerland: UNHCR.

UNICEF. 2017. *Education Uprooted.* New York: UNICEF.

van Basshuysen, Philippe, "Towards a Fair Distribution Mechanism for Asylum," *Games* vol. 8, no. 4 (2017).

WHO Eastern Mediterranean Region. 2018. *Health of Refugees and Migrants: Situation Analysis and Practices in Addressing the Health Needs of Refugees and Migrants.* Geneva, Switzerland: WHO.

Wildau, Bjarne, "Filipino Nurses Receive Their Finnish Nursing Degrees," *ScandAsia. com*, June 2, 2011.

Wirth, Anna, Cara Defilippis, and Jessica Therkelsen. 2014. *Global Refugee Work Rights Report*. Oakland, Calif.: Asylum Access.

World Bank. 2018. "IDA18 Regional Sub-Window for Refugees and Host Communities" (ida.worldbank.org/replenishments/ida-18replenishments/ ida18-regional-sub-window-for-refugees-host-communities).

World Education Services. 2018. *A Way Forward for Refugees: Findings from the WES Pilot Project*. Toronto, Canada: World Education Services.

Zucker, Lynne G. and Michael R. Darby. 2007. "Star Scientists, Innovation and Regional and National Immigration." National Bureau of Economic Research Working Paper 13547.

PART II
Problems

CHAPTER SIX

Leapfrogging to Ensure No Child Is Left Without Access to a Twenty-First Century Education

Rebecca Winthrop and Lauren Ziegler

M any people agree that education plays a crucial role in helping address a range of burning problems around the globe. Those worried about how to constructively harness the talents of the world's youth, with four in ten people being under the age of twenty-five, globally, argue that an essential piece is providing them the needed training and skills to actively and positively contribute to society through employment and civic engagement.[1] Concerns over rapid technological progress, especially the increasing automation of tasks among both blue collar and white collar jobs, leads many business leaders, policymakers, and pundits to call for a doubling down in education and skills development to help both the young and old adjust to this changing world. Education is also often emphasized as a crucial part of the solution to growing income inequality within nations and seen as a solution to a range of other social ills.[2]

But the real question is, what type of education can contribute to reducing inequality? Should communities and jurisdictions looking to harness the power of education to address inequality focus first and foremost on getting all children through the school door? Once this is accomplished, should they turn their focus

---

1. World Bank, "Atlas of Sustainable Development Goals" (http://datatopics.worldbank.org/sdgatlas/).
2. Reeves (2017).

to improving schoolchildren's acquisition of central academic knowledge and skills, such as literacy and numeracy? Then, finally, once this is well established, should they turn their attention to ensuring that students develop higher-order thinking skills especially relevant to the world of work such as problem-solving and digital literacy? Indeed, this has, by and large, been the approach used around the globe and across time for developing universal schooling systems that are intended to serve all young people, not just children of the elite.

The problem with this approach is that there is a high degree of risk that it will maintain a different kind of inequality in the long term. Focusing on a "back to basics" education for the children who are furthest behind, often the poorest children living in the poorest countries, alongside a twenty-first century education for those children who have mastered the basics—often the richest children in the richest countries—will move the goalposts for both groups but maintain the gaps.

Take the case of Madagascar versus Finland, which exemplifies how education policy is playing out around the globe. In Madagascar, only 42 percent of children have completed primary school, and just 28 percent of in-school children of primary age are proficient in reading.[3] The government's education sector plan is heavily focused on helping young people enroll and stay in school and on improving students' academic learning, especially in basic literacy and numeracy. As only 20 percent of teachers in the country have received professional training, significant government effort will be needed to train teachers and place them in rural and hard-to-reach communities.[4]

Meanwhile, in Finland, often heralded as one of the best education systems in the world, with top scores in the international skills assessment of fifteen-year-olds, educators are taking seriously the prospects of educating children for a changing world.[5] They are not content to rest on their laurels as one of the consistently top-scoring systems; instead, the government is ushering in reforms that seek to prepare students for a fast-paced, boundary-bending, technology-enabled world. Recent reforms require schools to increase the teaching of multidisciplinary themes, such as urbanization or the environment, allowing students to draw on the range of traditional school subjects to solve problems rather than keep knowledge development compartmentalized as the organizing principle of learning.

What will happen to the students entering school in Madagascar twenty years from now? Will they stand any hope of developing the broad range of skills that Finnish students will likely have by then? Skills such as collaborative problem-solving or using technology not only to consume information but to

---

3. UNESCO, "World Inequality Database on Education" (www.education-inequalities.org).
4. World Bank (2018, 11).
5. OECD, "Program for International Student Assessment" (http://www.oecd.org/pisa/).

create solutions, all essential competencies to thrive in a world where automation is on the rise. Or, despite improved access to schools and mastery of literacy and numeracy, will they again be woefully left behind, missing crucial skills they need to thrive?

This challenge frames the focus of this chapter. What new education strategies and approaches are needed to truly help level the playing field and make sure the poorest children in all societies are not left behind? Any country that wants to ensure its workforce has capabilities needed to manage a changing world will need to adopt an education system that emphasizes skills such as critical thinking, digital literacy, and collaboration, no matter how difficult that may seem.

We argue that it is possible to close gaps in education, or to "leapfrog" educational progress, so all children, whether in Madagascar or Finland, experience a twenty-first century education that will deliver on the promise of schooling for improving the range of social ills societies face. In this chapter, we draw on our existing work, *Leapfrogging Inequality: How Remaking Education Can Help Young People Thrive*, to discuss the why, where, and how of leapfrogging in education so no child is left behind.[6] We begin by discussing the state of global education inequality in section one and outlining what children and where are the furthest behind. In the second section, "Why We Need to Leapfrog: A Hundred-Year Education Gap in Twenty-First Century Education," we present arguments for why the current stepwise approach of ensuring access, quality, and relevance is not working, and why we need to embrace new mental models for rapidly accelerating—in other words, leapfrogging—education progress. In the third section, "How to Leapfrog: Harnessing Innovation that Reaches Those Left Behind," we discuss in depth how to leapfrog in education, including providing a clear definition of the concept as well as a map outlining the main education approaches that can deliver access, quality, and relevance all at once and ultimately close educational gaps faster than current approaches allow for. In the final section, we offer recommendations to the global community on how to elevate the leapfrog mindset and approach as a standard way of thinking about educational development.

The Global Education Challenge: Twenty-First Century Education for Too Few

If the education community continues to use current approaches, by 2030, the target date for achieving the UN Sustainable Development Goals (SDGs), 884 million children and youth—more than half of all school-age children in

---

6. Winthrop, Barton, and McGivney (2018).

the world—will not be on track to achieve basic secondary-level skills across a breadth of competencies, including literacy, numeracy, problem-solving, and critical thinking.[7] This is, indeed, an urgent and global problem. Children and young people not well-served by today's education systems comprise various demographics and groups, yet the greatest predictor of whether a child will have access to a quality twenty-first century education is based on income level both between and within countries. In low-income countries, nine out of every ten young people are projected to be left behind by 2030—meaning they will not achieve basic secondary-level skills—compared to five out of ten young people in middle-income countries and three out of ten in high-income countries.[8]

These deep disparities highlight that in most countries around the world, schools serve some children well and others poorly. This inequality is a multidimensional problem involving access—getting students through the school doors; quality—ensuring students master central academic competencies; and relevance—providing an education that meets the demands of the twenty-first century.

Out-of-school children face multiple barriers to access, including the intersecting disadvantages of poverty, gender, and location. In the world's poorest families, children are not sent to school because they need to provide either labor or income to support their families. And while many countries have eliminated school fees, poor families often have prohibitive indirect costs for materials such as uniforms and books.[9] Girls, conflict-affected children, and children with disabilities often face additional barriers to schooling, particularly in low-income contexts.[10]

Approximately 263 million children and youth between the ages of six and seventeen are out of school today, a number that has remained almost the same for the past decade.[11] Of these children, 64 million are of primary school age, with more than half living in sub-Saharan Africa, and 199 million are of lower and upper secondary school age.[12] An estimated 50 percent of all out-of-school children of primary age reside in conflict-affected countries.[13]

When we look at access to education through a country lens, we find that countries with the lowest primary school completion rates are South Sudan,

---

7. Education Commission (2016, 13).

8. UNESCO (2015, 13–14).

9. Bentaouet, Kattan, and Burnett (2004).

10. Hindman (2009, 4); UNESCO Institute for Statistics and UNICEF (2015); Wodon and others (2017).

11. UNESCO Institute for Statistics (UIS) (2018, 1).

12. Ibid. (7).

13. UNESCO Institute for Statistics and UNICEF (2015, 11).

Chad, Niger, Guinea-Bissau, and Burkina Faso.[14] However, the countries with some of the poorest-performing education systems often have relatively small populations. So—while it is crucial to find ways to address their needs—if we are to meet SDG 4, the global community will also need to focus on those countries that have the largest total number of children not accessing quality education. Research from Brookings colleagues Homi Kharas, John McArthur, and Krista Rasmussen estimates that if recent trends continue, by 2030 half of all children who do not complete primary school will come from just five countries: Ethiopia, Uganda, Pakistan, Sudan, and Mozambique (see figure 6-1).[15]

However, getting children through the school door is only the first step. All too often, children are not mastering basic academic content while in school. Economist Lant Pritchett has documented the flat "learning achievement profile" of students in several countries: for every year spent in school, the amount that students have learned in subjects like literacy, numeracy, and science barely increases.[16] Here again, income level often plays a role in whether a student achieves basic proficiency. In poorer countries, such as India, Bangladesh, Kenya, Pakistan, and Tanzania, assessments show that 50 percent or more children finish their primary schooling unable to read simple texts or solve basic math problems.[17] Even in a developed country like the United States, the gap between rich and poor students on the secondary-school mathematics proficiency examination under the PISA is the largest in the world—nearly 40 percentage points.[18]

Lack of quality education can be due to numerous factors. To begin with, there are simply not enough teachers for all of the world's children. In fact, UNESCO estimates 69 million new teachers will be needed to reach SDG 4, which includes replacement for attrition and recruitment of new teachers to bring class sizes down to 40 students or less.[19] Teachers in the poorest countries are often teaching classes of 60 or more students at a time, with 10 students for every book and rarely enough room for all children to have a place to sit.[20] A Ugandan education official recently expressed his frustration to us that class sizes in his district are closer to 120 students.[21] In many African countries, students average

---

14. UNESCO, "World Inequality Database on Education" (www.education-inequalities.org).

15. Kharas, McArthur, and Rasmussen (2018, 18).

16. Pritchett (2013, 14).

17. Ibid.

18. UNESCO, "World Inequality Database on Education" (www.education-inequalities.org).

19. UNESCO Institute for Statistics (2016).

20. Benbow, Mizrachi, Oliver, and Said-Moshiro (2007); Results for Development Institute (2016).

21. Personal communication with Amos Opaman, Uganda National Examinations Board, April 17, 2019.

Figure 6-1. Number of Children Who Do Not Complete Primary School

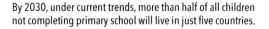

By 2030, under current trends, more than half of all children
not completing primary school will live in just five countries.

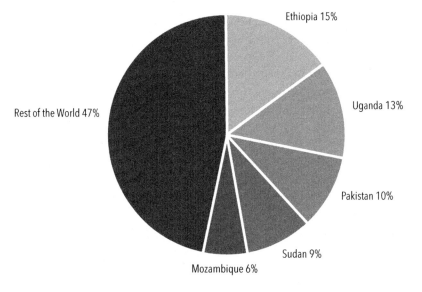

Note: Due to insufficient data, Nigeria was not included in the analysis.

just under three hours of instruction each day.[22] And, too often, poorer countries spend a disproportionate amount on wealthier and better-off students. UNICEF estimates that low-income countries spend on average 46 percent of total public education resources on the most educated 10 percent of students, largely due to the higher per capita costs of secondary and post-secondary education that the more advantaged students attend, relative to the cost of primary school.[23]

In addition to a lack of access and poor quality, the final way education systems leave children and youth behind is through lack of relevancy. Education is relevant if the content, competencies, and skills young people learn connect with and help prepare them for the world they will enter after school completion. Relevant education systems recognize that technology is changing the way we live our lives and the skills we need to thrive. Research from the OECD finds that 50 to 70 percent of a worker's tasks may become automated due to advances in technology, and hence require different skill sets from employees.[24] For example,

22. Bold and others (2017).
23. UNICEF (2015, 58).
24. Arntz, Gregory, and Zierahn (2016).

the World Economic Forum finds that in South Africa, core job skills across all industries are shifting, and skills like flexibility, knowledge of information and communications technology, and emotional intelligence are increasingly desirable.[25]

Developing these types of competencies requires not only connecting the class lessons with the daily lived experiences of students and their communities but also different teaching approaches. Young people need, for example, to practice being flexible or working together with others to solve problems, all of which entail a more experiential form of learning than is typically experienced by students.[26] Practicing applying math, science, and history concepts to collectively solve a problem in their community is one way to ensure education is relevant. Indeed, evidence shows that today, most students in most countries are in schools that have only a limited use of these types of student-centered learning approaches. In Ethiopia, for example, one study found that student-centered activities account for only 11 percent of class time.[27] A similar study in Cambodia found that 61 percent of class time is devoted to direct student instruction and only 15 percent is used for student-led work.[28] Even in the developed world, teachers rely heavily on teacher-led instruction. In all education systems across the OECD countries, for example, students report using memorization more frequently than learning strategies that involve making connections and finding new ways to solve a problem.[29]

In light of the changing demands of work and also citizenship, relevant education systems recognize that students need opportunities to put their subject knowledge, from literacy and numeracy to science and art, into practice in their communities. A focus on developing the breadth of skills and competencies needed to thrive in a fast-changing world ensures that young people will be able to adjust to rapidly shifting demands in work and life.

Why We Need to Leapfrog: A Hundred-Year Education Gap in Twenty-First Century Education

The prevailing education mindset of attending first to access, then to quality, and finally to relevance will prevent us from helping young people in Madagascar catch up with those in Finland and ultimately from ensuring no child or youth is left behind. We need to find new ways to advance education, characterized by

25. World Economic Forum (2017).
26. Sawyer (2014).
27. Frost and Little (2014).
28. Benveniste, Marshall, and Araujo (2008).
29. Echazarra and others (2016).

new mental models that will facilitate rapid acceleration of progress. In other words, we need approaches that can leapfrog progress. There are four main arguments for why these types of new approaches are needed.

First, the current pace of change is simply too slow. For example, on many education measures there is a shocking "hundred-year gap" between the poorest and most wealthy students.[30] In our past work *Why Wait 100 Years: Bridging the Global Gap in Education*, we show that with current education approaches it would take approximately a hundred years for girls and boys in poor countries to catch up to the education levels of children in rich countries. This gap will likely only grow bigger when looking at the ability of students to master twenty-first century skills.

The slow pace of change is just as evident between poor and rich communities within countries and regions. For example, given the current projected growth in completion rates in sub-Saharan Africa, boys in the top wealth quintile are expected to achieve secondary school completion by 2041; however, girls in the lowest wealth quintile will need 70 additional years until 100 percent of them reach that milestone.[31] Extensive studies of educational inequality in the United States also highlight the alarming slowness of efforts to close the gap in achievement scores, social and emotional skills, and college completion between high- and low-income students.[32] At current rates, it will take another 60 to 110 years to close the gaps in the academic and behavioral competencies between high- and low-income children entering kindergarten in the United States today.[33]

Second, we know that the prevailing incrementalist approach to change will not be enough to close the vast education gaps. In a careful review of what types of approaches are needed to meet the education SDG, the 2016 International Commission on Financing Global Education Opportunity (Education Commission) argues that progress can be made by improving the efficiency of the existing education system with evidence-based and inclusion-oriented policies. But it also strongly argues that without harnessing new models we will never succeed. "Education systems must innovate and change rather than just replicate past success," especially because of the evolving nature of skills that young people need and because many countries are "hitting the limits" of what their education systems can achieve through incremental approaches.[34]

Third, scholars of innovation theory argue that breaking free from dominant logic—namely, entrenched patterns of thought and action—and the resulting

---

30. Winthrop and McGivney (2016).
31. UNESCO (2014).
32. Murnane and Duncan (2011).
33. Reardon and Portilla (2016).
34. Education Commission (2016, 16).

tendency to act in accord with past decisions, also known as path dependence, can be one of the biggest barriers to harnessing new approaches.[35] True educational innovation and change requires a break from the dominant stepwise logic of progress. Ever since the concept of universal schooling for all citizens arose in Prussia in the mid-1700s, national systems of education have been guided by a mindset that educational development should follow a stepwise approach of first expanding access, then attending to academic quality, and last, pursuing relevance. This stepwise approach was how schooling systems took hold and developed across Europe and North America over the past two hundred years. It also is what has characterized the development of education systems in the latter half of the twentieth century throughout much of the global south.

As a recent example, the Millennium Development Goals focused first and foremost on access to schooling for girls and boys. Only in the last ten years, as the global community gained more comparable data on student proficiency, have global education decisionmakers begun to focus more seriously on quality, or on how much—and in many cases, how little—children are learning on essential academic subjects such as literacy and numeracy. Achieving the sort of learning that students across the world both need and deserve requires an entirely new mental model of innovation-based leapfrogging.

Fourth, and perhaps most important, while many actors in the global education community may argue that the idea of embracing new models so all young people can get a twenty-first century education is simply too difficult or unrealistic, there is a strong demand from national governments to do just that. In a survey by our Brookings colleagues Esther Care and Helyn Kim, of 152 countries' education policies and implementation plans, the vast majority, 73 percent, articulate a vision and objective that sets forth clear goals around helping all young people develop both strong academic skills as well as the twenty-first century skills needed to thrive in the future. The problem, however, is that very few countries have an understanding of how to accomplish this goal. Only 17 percent of countries surveyed have a detailed and clear plan on how to implement reforms that would provide this type of well-rounded education for every child.[36] There is an urgent need to provide education decisionmakers with new, practical approaches that could help them begin to envision what leapfrogging in education could look like. Providing this guidance is essential if the global community is to truly respond to the demand coming from countries around the world.

---

35. Prahalad and Bettis (1986).
36. Care and Kim (2018).

How to Leapfrog: Harnessing Innovation that Reaches Those Left Behind

While there is a compelling case for why we need to embrace a leapfrog approach in education, the question still remains on how exactly this should be done. We turn now to three questions in an attempt to develop a clear picture of leapfrogging: What is the definition of leapfrogging in the education sector? What does a leapfrog approach to education look like? Is leapfrogging in education possible in the here and now?

What Is the Definition of Leapfrogging in the Education Sector?

Leapfrogging, often described as the ability to jump ahead or make rapid and nonlinear progress, is not well defined in the education sector. Sometimes, in the business literature, it is associated with innovation that disrupts existing paradigms rather than sustains them in a different form.[37] More frequently, leapfrogging is used colloquially to describe examples of rapid change. For example, the term "leapfrogging" often appears in relation to telecommunications sector in the developing world, where certain nations have been able to bypass whole phases of infrastructure and institution-building that other countries had to experience. Many African countries, for example, never systematically invested in laying telephone lines, yet today access to mobile phone service on the continent has grown so rapidly that in many cases communities are more likely to be connected to the outside world via mobile phone service than to have access to electricity or running water.[38]

For the education sector, we define leapfrogging as any practice, whether new or old, that can improve access, quality, and relevance at the same time, closing gaps much faster than the current rate of change. There are two important distinctions for how we use the term "leapfrogging" in education compared to its use in other sectors, such as telecommunications. First and foremost, it is essential to be clear on the type of education you wish to leapfrog toward, as the objective of education varies widely by constituency. For us, leapfrogging focuses on generating dramatic acceleration in progress toward providing all young people with the breadth of skills and competencies they need to thrive in the twenty-first century.

37. See, for example, Christensen, Horn, and Johnson (2008); Keeley (2013); and Voelpel, Leibold, and Tekie (2004). In academic literature more broadly, "leapfrogging" as a term is used to describe widely different concepts across diverse disciplines, from patterns of urban development to improvements in hospital performance to descriptions of voting patterns. There is no clear definition that cuts across disciplines. See, for example, "Look Before You Leap," *Economist*, August 6, 2016; and Sommer (2013).

38. Winthrop (2016).

Second, leapfrogging does not necessarily mean throwing out the legacy infrastructure of education systems (e.g., schools) but rather building on it to obtain greater results. Leapfrogging harnesses innovation to help education systems go further than their traditional limits. This is distinctly different from sectors such as telecommunications, where the old approach of laying copper wire for connectivity has given way to cell phone towers altogether. Hence, although leapfrogging often connotes skipping steps to advance along a particular path, we do not stick narrowly to this idea. We take inspiration from the overarching concept that rapid and nonlinear progress can be made without following the usual path, perhaps skipping steps but also possibly ending up in a new place.

What Does a Leapfrog Approach to Education Look Like?

The goal of leapfrogging is to move from pursuing educational development in the traditionally sequential process of access then quality then relevance (figure 6-2) to pursuing access, quality, and relevance all at the same time. How, one might ask, can this be done, especially for those who are the furthest behind? After more than three years of research, including a review of the existing literature, conducting over a hundred interviews, and analyzing almost three thousand education innovations from 166 countries, we developed a "leapfrog pathway" (figure 6-3), which provides a map for leapfrogging in education while recognizing context and leaving room for ongoing growth.

There are four elements to our leapfrog pathway. The first two are essential for transformation. The latter two accelerate the scale-up of leapfrog approaches to reach those furthest behind, but may not be essential in every context. They are each briefly described below.

Essential Elements of Educational Leapfrogging

1. *Transforming teaching and learning to be more student-centered.* This implies children having education experiences that include not only teachers' direct instruction on key subjects, something necessary for students to remember and understand important concepts, but also experiences where teachers let students lead, allowing them to make judgments, evaluate, and create new work, experiences that are essential in helping develop the twenty-first century skills young people need.

2. *Transforming recognition of learning to be more individualized.* This implies that when students' learning is assessed, teachers are tracking progress against a variety of measures from academic mastery to ability to work with others to solve problems. It also means students are allowed to progress

onto more difficult material once a skill is developed rather than when the grade is completed, and given the opportunity to demonstrate competence directly to employers rather than rely so heavily on diplomas from educational institutions—in other words, approaches that increasingly recognize individual differences in students' learning and skills.

Figure 6-2. Traditional Pathway for Education Progress: Access, then Quality, then Relevance

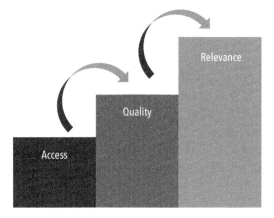

Figure 6-3. The Leapfrog Pathway: How to Pursue Access, Quality, and Relevance at the Same Time

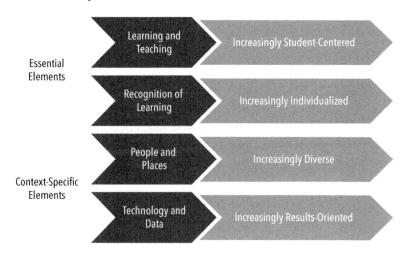

Context-Specific Accelerators for Educational Leapfrogging

3. *Transforming the people and places where learning takes place to be more diverse.* This means that, in addition to learning from licensed teachers in the classroom, young people are engaging in learning from community leaders and professionals, frequently in interactions outside of school—including, for example, working on projects with civil society advocates or business leaders, or engaging in discussions with doctors or sanitation workers or scientists. Experiences that harness a range of human and physical resources outside the classroom walls can be especially powerful in contexts where trained teachers are in short supply but may not be needed to develop twenty-first century skills in all contexts.

4. *Transforming the use of technology and data to deliver better results.* This means that the effective use of technology and data will, for example, provide continuous feedback and information on the quality of the teaching and learning experience in a way that allows adults and children engaged in education activities to modify and adapt their work. It also means that these powerful tools will be harnessed to modify and redefine what is possible—for example, connecting students in remote towns to scientists in urban areas, rather than just replacing existing analog functions (e.g., multiplication worksheets on tablets versus on paper).

Is Leapfrogging in Education Possible in the Here and Now?

Even if the discussion of leapfrogging in education is convincing in theory, the question still remains as to whether it is actually feasible in practice in the communities that need it most. In our study of education innovations around the globe, we found that leapfrogging through innovation is indeed possible. To us, innovations are any ideas or technologies that reflect a break from previous practice, often new in a particular context, even if not new to the world. We found many education innovations that served marginalized communities utilizing leapfrog approaches, although by no means did all innovations have leapfrog potential.

A selection of examples below illustrates the potential of innovation to help education leapfrog. These innovations represent a mix of programs, policies, and types of schools. While many of them have developed on the margins of education systems, they demonstrate what is possible even in some of the hardest to reach areas of the world.

Colombia

Through its Literacy Education and Math Labs program (LEMA), the non-profit Literacy4All has reached almost 1 million young learners across four continents with simple board games that improve literacy and numeracy. At its core, LEMA is about teaching language systems—including the language of mathematics—through exploration, collaboration, and risk-taking. The concept originated in rural communities in Colombia as an intervention to teach literacy to adults and quickly expanded to schoolchildren around the world due to its fun and simple nature. LEMA games are low-tech and made from local materials and follow tried and tested approaches to learning. The games can take place during the school day in small-group sessions, as well as after school with the help of community members called learning coaches. Literacy4All provides training to learning coaches and teachers on how to model the games. Impact studies in the Dominican Republic show that over the course of one year, first-grade LEMA students improved their scores on a literacy assessment by 50 percentage points, ending the school year at a third-grade reading level. The games also help instill in students twenty-first century skills, like critical thinking.[39] LEMA transforms the teaching and learning experience by using gaming principles, actively engaging students, and relying heavily on diverse people and places where the learning experience can take place. Where there are limited numbers of trained teachers, community members can be supported to be learning facilitators, and the game often engages multiple generations in the community.

South Africa

Since 1999, the program Go for Gold has served disadvantaged youth in South Africa through its four-phase "education-to-employment" program. It is a successful example of diversifying the people and places where students learn, combining both traditional classroom and workplace experiences that create opportunities for students to engage in experiential learning and for potential employers to directly assess their abilities. Companies, particularly in the construction industry, are eager to participate, as they struggle to fill vacant jobs, especially for positions such as project foreman and engineer. Students involved in the program come from impoverished regions where dropout rates are high and unemployment rates even higher. The program begins in a student's last two years of high school, when students complete after-school coursework in math, science, technology, and life skills and receive mentoring from employees in Go for Gold partner companies. In phase two, students secure a paid yearlong internship with a partner company; and in year three, if companies believe the

---

39. Winthrop, Barton, and McGivney (2018, 64–66); Literacy4All (www.literacy4all.org).

student has potential to be a good employee, go on to receive tertiary studies on scholarship from the company. The program ends with students receiving a technical degree and a job offer in hand, usually with the company where they interned, as companies have already invested in the student and have had a chance to see their work. Go for Gold stands as a unique model of authentically verifying learning. Instead of simply choosing candidates based on credentials such as post-secondary degrees—rough proxies for student skills and competencies at best—employers can evaluate learners directly in their future workplaces. More than 80 percent of Go for Gold's four hundred participants achieved a bachelor's pass on the secondary leaving exam—the score required to attend college. This stands in stark contrast to the 27 percent of South African youth who obtain such a result nationally. More promising yet, 80 percent of participants completed tertiary studies on time, and all secured full-time employment following graduation.[40]

Tanzania

Camfed, a large international nonprofit focused on girls' education in sub-Saharan Africa, has a Learner Guide Program that is an example of diversifying who teaches poor and rural girls. It also provides an innovative pathway for the ministry of education to recruit and certify more female teachers, which are desperately needed in hard-to-serve areas. In this program, Camfed trains recent graduates of secondary school to serve as mentors and peer teachers in rural African schools. These young women, known as learner guides, return to their rural schools no longer as students but to deliver a curriculum on self-awareness, resilience, and well-being to local learners and to provide tutoring and mentorship support. Upon completion of the twelve- to eighteen-month program, learner guides receive access to low-risk, interest-free loans and qualify for fast-track teacher certifications. So far, 5,425 learner guides have served more than 300,000 students across 1,643 schools in Tanzania and three other sub-Saharan African countries. An independent evaluation found that 91 percent of surveyed participants in Tanzania and Zimbabwe reported that the learner guide program positively affected their attitude toward school. Additionally, academic outcomes improved greatly. Program evaluations "have shown that in Tanzania, literacy test scores among marginalized girls reached by Camfed showed more than double the rate of learning than among girls in comparison schools—and in maths nearly five times the rate."[41]

---

40. Winthrop, Barton, and McGivney (2018, 57–58); Go for Gold (http://goforgold.org.za/).

41. Winthrop, Barton, and McGivney (2018, 70); Campaign for Female Education (https://camfed.org/our-impact/learner-guide-program/).

South Sudan

South Sudan's ministry of education partnered with the nonprofit War Child to design and deliver its primary education distance-learning curriculum to young people in some of the most difficult-to-reach communities. This program, called Can't Wait to Learn, uses gaming technology to deliver literacy and numeracy skills to children in conflict-affected regions, and can be facilitated by diverse members of the community, including but not limited to trained teachers. The games are delivered via offline tablets at informal learning centers for out-of-school children, as well as in formal schools with the support of either a community facilitator or a teacher. Solar-powered charging stations ensure the tablets can always be in use, even in conflict-affected environments. Young people are learning both essential academic skills and ways to manipulate digital technology. The low-cost innovation has now spread to Jordan, Lebanon, and Uganda. A study of the innovation in South Sudan showed that children are learning from the game, particularly those furthest behind.[42]

India

Mindspark is an adaptive learning platform developed by a private company and currently operating in seventy public schools in the low-income state of Rajasthan, serving over twelve thousand students and expanding across India and the United States. This technology uses machine learning to help students master essential academic competencies on their own. The product has been used in a range of contexts in India, including after school in study centers with students from low-income communities. In a randomized control trial study by the Abdul Latif Jameel Poverty Action Lab (J-PAL), researchers found that students who attended Mindspark centers for over four and a half months improved their math and Hindi scores by 0.36 and 0.22 standard deviations, respectively. In practical terms, this means that Mindspark students improved their test scores more than twice as fast as students who did not participate. This is an example of technology redefining what is possible for communities that lack high-quality schooling and instruction.

Brazil

One of the few examples of system-wide leapfrogging comes from one of the remotest parts of the globe, the Amazon jungle. The Amazonas Media Center for Education was created by the state ministry of education to provide formal secondary education to rural communities in Brazil's Amazon region, where access traditionally was limited. This government-led innovation enables teachers in

42. War Child (https://warchildholland.org/projects/cant-wait-to-learn).

the region to support each other, simplifying the roles each plays while also providing students access to expert knowledge. The top teachers in the state are designated as "lecturing" teachers and are based in the region's capital, providing lessons via a two-way video satellite uplink from a media center in the capital. Lecturing teachers broadcast to a thousand small classrooms around the state, where students are supported by "mentoring" teachers, who assist young people in navigating their homework, class discussions, classroom management, and other intra- and interpersonal support. Crucially, the lessons are all adapted to the local realities of rural children, allowing for natural connections between the lessons studied in class and the ways in which they experience their natural and social environment. Students are learning, many who never had access before, as evidenced by their performance on national exams. This creative use of technology, transforming teachers' roles, and envisioning a different teaching and learning experience have all helped truly leapfrog education so that some of the children who have been the furthest behind have opportunities to access high-quality education that is relevant to their lives.

Recommendations

This chapter aims to share insights that can inspire action-oriented governments, civil society organizations, educators, philanthropic investors, and members of the business community to consider the serious prospect of rapid, nonlinear educational progress and to reflect on what more needs to be done to make leapfrogging in education a reality. There is no reason that the children and youth of Madagascar cannot develop the competencies and skills that their counterparts in Finland are learning, or that those young people left behind in any country could not access the type of twenty-first century education they so deserve.

We argue that the following three recommendations are essential if the idea of leapfrogging in education is to move into scaled-up practice for those who need it most:

1. *Leaders must adopt a leapfrog mindset.* Above all else, apex political leaders—from heads of state and government to ministers of finance and education and the global organizations that support them—must all believe leapfrogging is possible. The very act of articulating a new vision of education progress—one that harnesses innovation to achieve improved education access, quality, and relevance for the most marginalized communities—will help drive the types of changes that are needed to provide all children a twenty-first century education. Governments are the ultimate duty-bearer of children's right to education, and the direction on how to achieve quality

and relevant education for all must first and foremost come from presidents and prime ministers. Breaking from the dominant logic of stepwise educational development will be difficult, but by articulating a clear vision of education leapfrogging and requesting consistent and thoughtful discussion among relevant ministers on how to leapfrog, top political leaders can certainly inculcate a mindset shift.

2. *A leapfrog lab must be established to help ministries of education use new education policy design approaches.* Each jurisdiction must find what innovative approaches are effective in their context and for the particular needs of their students. To achieve this, the process of designing education policies and their corresponding implementation plans in most contexts must be opened up to include the perspectives of new actors from technologists to sociologists to local teacher organizations to business communities to research groups and human-centered design organizations. Education decisionmakers and their teams need exposure to the range of different models that are possible and that help transform teaching and learning. One way of executing this is for the global community to establish a mechanism that pulls together existing leapfrog-related evidence, actors, and guidance from diverse disciplines that would provide ongoing advising to ministries of education. This virtual "leapfrog lab" would connect and build off existing organizations with similar interests to develop a space for creative and iterative design workshops with a range of stakeholders and unlikely thought partners at the beginning of the policy design progress.

3. *The global community must develop actionable evidence on scaling-up leapfrog approaches.* There is an urgent need to develop evidence that can be easily used by education decisionmakers to guide them on how to design and implement leapfrog approaches that scale. Currently most efforts, including our own, have focused on identifying and highlighting innovations and, in our case, putting forward a conceptual framework that identifies which innovations have the potential to leapfrog. But this is just the beginning. There is a need for the range of actors invested in developing evidence and public goods—from data sets to analytical tools—to look seriously at what they can do to advance understanding of approaches that provide access to quality and relevant education for all children, especially those in the hardest-to-reach communities.

Leaving No One Behind

At all levels of economic development, the leapfrog pathway to education is designed to address access, quality, and relevance at once, rather than following a slow, sequential approach. By making teaching and learning more student-centered and the recognition of learning more individualized, innovations can leapfrog progress in education much faster than the status quo. In addition, diversifying people and places and using results-oriented technology and data can support further transformation. In examining the current state of global education innovations through our catalog, we learned that the education innovations community is energetic, diverse, and widespread. Children from poor and wealthy families alike are participating in new approaches that are changing, with impressive results, how schooling is delivered, what is taught, and how teaching is done. Ultimately, this richness of education innovations holds promise for leapfrogging education that helps to address global education inequality.

Innovators, policymakers, and funders must work together to take the next steps that will make leapfrogging a reality to ensure that all children have access to a quality twenty-first century education. The world needs to set its sights on bringing promising practices to scale in diverse communities, starting first with the most marginalized. The international community can create an enabling environment that accelerates progress in education and ensures a generation of young people is not left behind.

References

Arntz, Melanie, Terry Gregory, and Ulrich Zierahn. 2016. "The Risk of Automation for Jobs in OECD Countries: A Comparative Analysis." OECD Social, Employment and Migration Working Papers, No. 189. OECD Publishing.

Benbow, Jane, and others. 2007. "Large Class Sizes in the Developing World: What Do We Know and What Can We Do?" American Institutes for Research under the EQIP1 LWA (http:// pdf.usaid.gov/pdf_docs/Pnadk328.pdf).

Bentaouet Kattan, Raja and Nicholas Burnett. 2004. *User Fees in Primary Education*. World Bank.

Benveniste, Luis, Jeffrey Marshall, and Caridad M. Araujo. 2008. *Teaching in Cambodia*. World Bank (https://openknowledge.worldbank.org/handle/10986/8073).

Bold, Tessa, and others. 2017. "What Do Teachers Know and Do? Evidence from Primary Schools in Africa." World Bank Policy Research Working Paper 7956. World Bank.

Care, Esther and Helyn Kim. 2018. "Assessment of Twenty-First-Century Skills: The Issue of Authenticity," in *Assessment and Teaching of Twenty-First Century Skills:*

Research and Applications, edited by E. Care, P. Griffin, and M. Wilson (Cham, Germany: Springer).

Christensen, Clayton M., Michael B. Horn, and Curtis W. Johnson. 2008. *Disrupting Class: How Disruptive Innovation Will Change the Way the World Learns* (New York: McGraw-Hill).

Echazarra, Alfonso, and others. 2016. "How Teachers Teach and Students Learn: Successful Strategies for School." OECD Education Working Paper No. 130. OECD (doi:10.1787/5jm29kpt0xxx-en).

Education Commission [International Commission on Financing Global Education Opportunity]. 2016. *The Learning Generation: Investing in Education for a Changing World* (http://report.educationcommission.org/report).

Frost, Melanie and Angela W. Little. 2014. "Children's Learning Practices in Ethiopia: Observations from Primary School Classes," *Oxford Review of Education*, vol. 40, no. 1: 91–111 (doi.org/10.1080/03054985.2013.873526).

Hindman, Hugh D. 2009. *The World of Child Labor: An Historical and Regional Survey* (New York: M. E. Sharpe).

Keeley, Larry. 2013. *Ten Types of Innovation: The Discipline of Building Breakthroughs* (New York: John Wiley & Sons).

Kharas, Homi, John W. McArthur, and Krista Rasmussen. 2018. "How Many People Will the World Leave Behind?: Assessing Current Trajectories on the Sustainable Development Goals." Brookings Institution Global Economy & Development Working Paper 123.

Murnane, Richard J. and Greg J. Duncan. 2011. *Whither Opportunity? Rising Inequality, Schools, and Children's Life Chances*. Russell Sage Foundation.

Prahalad, C. K. and Richard A. Bettis. 1986. "The Dominant Logic: A New Linkage between Diversity and Performance." *Strategic Management Journal*, vol. 7, no. 6: 485–501 (doi:10.1002/smj.4250070602).

Pritchett, Lant. 2013. *The Rebirth of Education: Schooling Ain't Learning.* Center for Global Development.

Reardon, Sean F. and Ximena A. Portilla. 2016. "Recent Trends in Income, Racial, and Ethnic School Readiness Gaps at Kindergarten Entry." *AERA Open*, vol. 2, no. 3: 12 (doi:10.1177/2332858416657343).

Reeves, Richard. 2017. *Dream Hoarders: How the American Upper Middle Class Is Leaving Everyone Else in the Dust, Why That Is a Problem, and What to Do About It.* (Washington: Brookings).

Results for Development Institute (R4D) and International Education Partners Ltd. 2016. *Global Book Fund Feasibility Study: Final Report.* R4D (https://r4d.org/wp-content/uploads/R4D-IEP_GBF_Full-Report_-web.pdf).

Sawyer, Keith. 2014. "Conclusion. The Future of Learning: Grounding Educational Innovation in the Learning Sciences," in *The Cambridge Handbook of the Learning Sciences*, 2nd ed., edited by Keith Sawyer (Cambridge University Press), pp. 726–46.

Sommer, Simon. 2013. "Commentary: Leapfrogging as a Principle for Research on Children and Youth in Majority World Settings." *Journal of Research on Adolescence*, vol. 23, no. 1: 187–88 (doi:10.1111/j.1532-7795.2012.00835.x).

UNESCO. "World Inequality Database on Education" (www.education-inequalities. org).

———. 2015. *Global Education Monitoring Report: Education 2030: Equity and Quality with a Lifelong Learning Perspective.* UNESCO.

————. 2014. "Teaching and Learning: Achieving Quality for All." *Education for All Global Monitoring Report.* UNESCO.

UNESCO Institute for Statistics. 2016. *The World Needs Almost 69 Million New Teachers to Reach the 2030 Education Goals.* UIS Fact Sheet No. 39. UIS.

————. 2018. *One in Five Children, Adolescents and Youth is Out of School.* UIS Fact Sheet No. 48. UIS.

UNESCO Institute for Statistics and UNICEF. 2015. *Fixing the Broken Promise of Education for All: Findings from the Global Initiative on Out-of-School Children.* UNICEF (https://www.unicef.org/publications/index_78718.html).

UNICEF. 2015. *The Investment Case for Education and Equity.* UNICEF (https://www.unicef.org/publications/index_78727.html).

Voelpel, Sven, Marius Leibold, and Eden B. Tekie. 2004. "The Wheel of Business Model Reinvention: How to Reshape Your Business Model to Leapfrog Competitors." *Journal of Change Management,* vol. 4, no. 3: 259–76 (doi:10.1080/14 69701042000212669).

Winthrop, Rebecca. 2016. "How Can We 'Leapfrog' Educational Outcomes?" *Stanford Social Innovation Review.* November 7 (https://ssir.org/articles/entry/how_can_we_leapfrog_educational_outcomes).

Winthrop, Rebecca, Adam Barton, and Eileen McGivney. 2018. *Leapfrogging Inequality: Remaking Education to Help Young People Thrive* (Washington: Brookings).

Winthrop, Rebecca and Eileen McGivney. 2016. *Why Wait 100 Years? Bridging the Gap in Global Education* (Washington: Brookings).

Wodon, Quentin, and others. 2017. *Economic Impacts of Child Marriage: Global Synthesis Report.* World Bank.

World Bank. 2018. *Madagascar Basic Education Support Project.* World Bank. (http://documents.worldbank.org/curated/en/517281522548048451/pdf/Madagascar-PAD-P160442-2018-03-12-638pm-03122018.pdf).

World Economic Forum. 2017. *The Future of Jobs and Skills in Africa.* World Economic Forum (http://www3.weforum.org/docs/WEF_EGW_ FOJ_Africa.pdf).

CHAPTER SEVEN

Vulnerable Populations and Universal Health Coverage

Krishna D. Rao, Saeda Makimoto, Michael Peters,
Gabriel M. Leung, Gerald Bloom, and Yasushi Katsuma

Introduction

Health is now recognized as a driver of economic development. Healthy people are more productive, have higher average incomes, spend less on healthcare, and create savings that are an important source of economic investment. Health, particularly in the early years of life, also contributes to other forms of human capital, such as cognitive ability and higher educational achievement. The importance of health in human capital and economic development makes investment in health critical. In recognition of this, in 2015, the UN General Assembly adopted the 2030 Agenda for Sustainable Development; health is the focal point of Sustainable Development Goal 3 (SDG 3): "To ensure healthy lives and promote well-being for all at all ages." Because the determinants of health include factors beyond coverage of health services, achieving SDG 3 will depend on progress in poverty reduction, education, nutrition, gender equality, clean water, sanitation, and transportation, among others. The UN resolution on SDGs exhorts countries to "achieve universal health coverage (UHC) and access to quality healthcare. No one must be left behind." This places UHC as the central target that underpins the achievement of improved health under the current development agenda.

Countries aspiring to UHC aim for all members of their population to be able to obtain the health services they need without experiencing financial hardship. UHC is built on three pillars—increasing coverage of services so that everyone has access to needed healthcare, improving quality of services, and ensuring that using health services does not put patients at risk of financial hardship.[1] At its core, UHC means nondiscrimination; policies that exclude certain individuals or groups are inconsistent with the goals of UHC.[2] A growing number of countries are formalizing their political commitments to UHC by establishing a legal mandate for universal access to health services and products in their national laws. Since 2013, at least seventy-three countries have passed legislation on UHC.[3] Yet much remains to be done.

These international declarations and the formulation of national strategies for making progress toward UHC would appear to reconfirm the universal right to health. In practice, however, substantial inequalities persist. Numerous studies on health disparities have affirmed the inverse care law, which states that those with the greatest health needs receive the least healthcare services.[4] This is due, in part, to deficiencies in the formulation and implementation of strategies for health system development. But it also reflects patterns of social and economic inequality and the inability of politically weak and vulnerable groups to ensure that their rights and entitlements are honored by governments and other stakeholders. Strategies for reducing inequalities in access to healthcare need to address the social and political factors that influence the performance of health systems.[5]

Vulnerable populations are a bellwether for the success of UHC policies. One of the biggest challenges to achieving UHC is to find ways to reach vulnerable populations—those who are at risk of poor health and healthcare disparities—with limited health resources. Vulnerable groups have adverse health outcomes compared to others, as they live in hard-to-reach places; are excluded from services because of gender, age, ethnicity, or other characteristics; and may not participate in health programs because they lack awareness of their entitlements, or because of their own beliefs, or due to financial constraints or the legality of their status. In many cases, they are excluded from the formal and informal processes that influence the performance of the health system and its direction of development. Making vulnerable populations a focus of UHC strategies is not without its pitfalls. Attention to vulnerable groups can be politically problematic, because it can be viewed as favoring certain groups over others and because it challenges dominant political arrangements.

This chapter seeks to understand the experience of vulnerable populations in the era of UHC. It begins by discussing how vulnerable populations are defined,

1. World Health Organization (2019a).
2. Ooms and Hammonds (2015).
3. World Health Organization (2019b).
4. Hart (1971).
5. Bloom (2019).

and the intersectionality between different vulnerabilities in relation to health. It then provides a selective review of studies documenting the extent to which vulnerable populations have service coverage and financial protection. The last section is devoted to offering policy options for achieving UHC without vulnerable groups left behind. This chapter argues that progressive universalism is a useful principle to guide a country's UHC strategies. It advocates a bottom-up approach to direct resources to the neediest in society first. In doing so, attention of government action and policy are focused on vulnerable populations.

Vulnerabilities, Vulnerable Populations, and Their Health

The last century has witnessed remarkable improvements in global health. Today, people live an average of thirty-eight years longer than a century ago.[6, 7] Over the last three decades, the number of children who die before reaching the age of five has been reduced by nearly two-thirds.[8] Despite these remarkable overall gains, there are certain regions of the world, especially sub-Saharan Africa and parts of Asia, that have not equally benefited from these global trends. Even in countries that have achieved high levels of average health, there are population subgroups that experience health outcomes far below the national average. People in both of these contexts experience one or more vulnerabilities that constrain their ability to live long, healthy lives.

The Many Dimensions of Vulnerability

There are a number of approaches to defining who is vulnerable. National governments and development agencies have traditionally conflated vulnerability and poverty. An individual is considered poor if their income level is below some established threshold or by their relative position in the income distribution. Here vulnerability arises from limited economic means and command over the material goods (e.g., food, housing) required for a basic standard of living. Several other attributes are also used for classifying people as vulnerable. Depending on the context, gender, race, social position, age, disability status, sexual orientation, ethnicity, religion, employment status, geography, and citizenship are other characterizations of vulnerability. In practice, these classifications are used independently; a truly comprehensive approach to characterizing vulnerability must consider the range of factors that contribute to vulnerability.

6. Riley (2005).
7. World Health Organization (2019c).
8. Ibid.

The capability approach, developed by Nobel Prize–winning economist Amartya Sen, provides a broader framework for understanding vulnerability. The capability approach emphasizes individuals' ability to achieve the kind of lives that they value, including being in good health.[9] In this understanding, the focus is shifted from a lack of resources (e.g., income poverty) to the deprivation of the capabilities to achieve a healthy life. It involves the deprivation of a broader set of factors, such as unequal access to resources, rights, goods, and services (including health services) across economic, political, social, and cultural dimensions that operate at individual, household, community, country, and global levels.[10] As such, individuals can suffer deprivation from more than one capability (see box 7-1).

The theory of intersectionality recognizes the coexistence of multiple intersecting factors that can multiply the disadvantages that an individual or group experiences, exacerbating societal inequities and social injustice.[11] Consider the example of a hypothetical migrant in the United States. If the person is an undocumented female, she may be more vulnerable than a documented female, and both may be more vulnerable than a man in their respective situation. The interactions between their multiple vulnerabilities have a direct impact on their overall vulnerability and their ability to access services such as healthcare. However, if the same undocumented female migrant needed to access healthcare in France, she might have fewer barriers to accessing services, as France provides emergency, pediatric, and maternity care to all undocumented migrants.[12] Because a range of individual and contextual factors determine a particular individual's vulnerability, it becomes important to understand how their intersectionality affects health.

The causes of vulnerability can change. For instance, countries are exposed to frequent shocks such as natural disasters, disease outbreaks, and movements of population across borders. These shocks can both exacerbate existing vulnerabilities by disproportionally affecting those who are already worse off, and create new vulnerable populations. Thus, patterns of vulnerability are constantly changing and should be considered a dynamic phenomenon. Health systems that can prevent, reduce the impacts of, and effectively recover from these shocks are said to be resilient and are cornerstones of ensuring universal coverage of health services to vulnerable groups.[13]

9. Sen (2001).
10. Tangcharoensathien and others (2018).
11. Collins (1986).
12. Gray and van Ginneken (2012).
13. Russo and others (2017).

Box 7-1. Operationalizing a Context-Specific Definition of Vulnerability

Some countries have gone to great lengths to describe and collect data on factors that contribute to social exclusion and vulnerability. In the United Kingdom, a number of attempts have been made to define and measure the extent of individual capabilities in order to monitor policy and hold government accountable. One effort is the development of a framework to measure capabilities by the Centre for Analysis of Social Exclusion (Burchardt and Vizard, 2007). This framework considers the interaction of personal characteristics, the level and distribution of resources, and other contextual factors as they relate to ten domains of capabilities that were valued by the population of the country. These domains of capabilities were operationalized through the development of a list of forty-eight indicators that describe progress toward equality in the United Kingdom (Alkire and others, 2009). Through this initiative, research can be done to identify the most vulnerable groups in the country and systematically design and evaluate programs to increase their capabilities. Such an approach can be replicated in other settings with indicators specific to that context.

Service Coverage of Vulnerable Populations

The first component of the SDGs for achieving UHC (SDG target 3.8.1) involves ensuring that people in need of promotive, preventive, curative, rehabilitative, or palliative health services receive them at sufficient quality. The World Bank and WHO have developed a service coverage index to monitor coverage of essential health services based on sixteen indicators that denote performance across a range of health conditions. Based on this index, coverage of essential services has increased by about 20 percent from 2000 to 2015; however, at least half of the world's population still does not have full coverage of essential health services.[14] For example, the median coverage across countries of the satisfied demand for modern family planning methods was recently estimated at 48 percent.[15] Within countries, socioeconomic disparities in coverage of essential services suggest that the progress made has not been equitable.

For a subset of essential health services for maternal and child health and infectious diseases, disparities in service coverage can be explored across income, education, and geographic settings of mothers (figure 7-1). Individuals who are poor or less educated have worse coverage for every outcome, though the disparities can be small in some cases (e.g., child diarrhea treated). Other analyses have found lower coverage of maternal and child health services among the poor,

14. World Health Organization and the World Bank (2017).
15. Countdown to 2030 Collaboration (2018).

rural, and less educated women.[16, 17] When vulnerabilities such as being poor, rural residence, and low education intersect, the joint outcome is far worse than for any single vulnerability considered individually (figure 7-2). A systematic review of the impact of vulnerabilities and service coverage found that there is a direct correlation between coexisting vulnerability factors and healthcare disparities.[18] The same study reported that some types of vulnerability are frequently studied, such as poverty, being a racial/ethnic minority, having a chronic physical or mental illness, lack of insurance, and old age; however, there is a paucity of information on other factors such as migrant status or multimorbidity as aspects of vulnerability in the context of health systems.[19]

Little is known about some kinds of vulnerable populations, such as migrants.[20] Migrants—international and internal migrants, refugees, and internally displaced people (IDP)—have received little attention within UHC discussions. There were 258 million international migrants in 2017, representing 3.4 percent of the world's population[21] and 40 million IDP in the same year, according to the UNHCR.[22] The health of all migrant groups is important, though the vulnerabilities and health needs of some (e.g., economic migrants) can be different from those of refugees. Noncitizens such as unregistered refugees and immigrant populations, in particular, are more likely to be afflicted by interacting vulnerabilities emanating from poverty, religion, and ethnicity. Economic migrants present a special case. They often perform jobs that have poor work environments, which places them at higher health risk while they may not have access to care due to government policy, lack of citizenship, or lack of clarity on legal status.[23] According to International Labour Organization (ILO), there were 164 million migrant workers (64 percent of all international migrants) globally in 2017.[24] Only some destination countries extend healthcare coverage to migrant workers and their families in the home country, and offer portability of health benefits when migrant workers return home.[25]

16. Ibid.
17. Victora and others (2018).
18. Grabovschi and others (2013).
19. Grabovschi and others (2013).
20. Ibid.
21. OECD/ILO/IOM/UNHCR (2018).
22. UNHCR (2017).
23. Benach and others (2011).
24. OECD/ILO/IOM/UNHCR (2018).
25. Holzmann (2016).

Figure 7-1. Median Level of National Coverage by Wealth and Education Groups

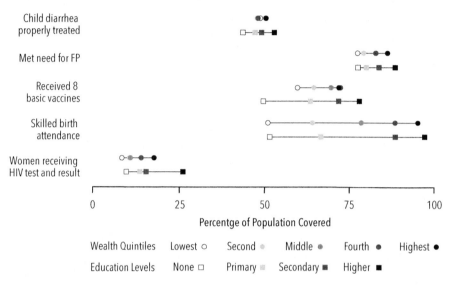

Median level of coverage of five health service indicators across wealth quintiles and education levels from the most recent Demographic Health Survey from eighty-three low- and middle-income countries (LMICs) between 1990 and 2017.

Notes: These five service indicators are, from top to bottom; (i) the percent of live births in the five (or three) years preceding the survey delivered at a health facility; (ii) the percentage of children born in the five (or three) years preceding the survey, who had diarrhea and received either oral rehydration solution or recommended home fluids; (iii) the percentage of currently married or in-union women whose stated need for family planning is met; (iv) the percentage of children from twelve to twenty-three months who had received all eight basic vaccinations; and (v) the percentage of women who had an HIV test in the twelve months preceding the interview and received their test results.

Source: ICF (2019).

Financial Protection of Vulnerable Populations

Ensuring that individuals who get needed care do not suffer undue financial hardship is the second component of the SDG indicator for monitoring progress toward UHC. When out-of-pocket payments (OOP; payments made directly to providers net of any insurance reimbursements) exceed a threshold percentage of household income or consumption expenditure (usually 10 percent), these costs are considered to be catastrophic. Overall, financial protection from high OOP appears to be worsening—the incidence of catastrophic health spending (SDG indicator 3.8.2) rose from 9.7 percent of the world's population in 2000 to

Figure 7-2. Median National Skilled Birth Attendance Coverage by Various Vulnerabilites

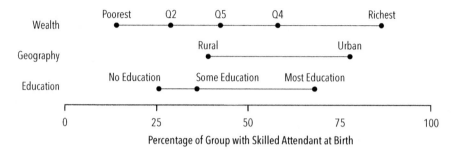

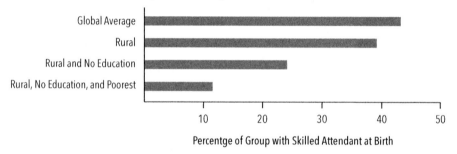

Intersectionality and Coverage of Skilled Birth Attendance

Median national percent of births occurring in a facility across wealth, geographic, and education levels within ninety-one LMICs.

Notes: Percent of births that take place in a facility is then examined through the lens of intersectionality, as coverage of facility births is examined across groups with multiple vulnerabilities (location of residence, education level, and poverty).

Source: World Health Organization (2019c).

11.7 percent (about 808 million) in 2010.[26] Such financial hardships are felt at a higher rate by vulnerable groups such as the poor, those with low socioeconomic status, the elderly, or migrants. Nationally, the median annual rate of change of catastrophic payment incidence is increasing, suggesting that despite the progress made by some countries, much work must be done to ensure adequate financial protection against catastrophic health spending.[27] Even in countries such as China and Thailand, which have well-established health financing systems that provide financial protection, there are subpopulations that continue to

26. Wagstaff and others (2018).
27. Ibid.

experience catastrophic household expenditure. One study in China found that 44.9 percent of elderly households experienced catastrophic health expenditure, compared to rates of 26.5 percent in the general public in the same province.[28] In Thailand, certain factors were associated with higher rates of catastrophic health expenditure, mainly having less education, being elderly, or having people with disabilities in the household.[29] Thus, the presence of a supposedly universal health financing system in a country does not automatically ensure that everyone, especially vulnerable populations, has financial protection.

Government policies can provide inequitable access to financial protection. In some countries with universal health insurance systems, the healthcare costs (prepayment and/or the copayment at the point of service use, sometimes indirect cost additionally) of the poor are subsidized. However, the benefits covered by such subsidized systems are often minimal, especially when compared to other basic packages within the same country. Further, systems that are based on social health insurance models through payroll deductions often exclude the informal sector from accessing the same benefits as those who are formally employed. The elderly are also vulnerable to healthcare-related financial hardship due to limited income, and greater need for health services due to their experiencing a greater burden of chronic illnesses relative to the general population.[30] A multi-country study found that the elderly were less likely to even be covered by health insurance programs in Africa.[31] This systematic exclusion of certain groups from health financing systems contributes to the increased vulnerability of such subpopulations, and is a considerable barrier to achieving financial protection.

Purposively targeting the most vulnerable populations in health financing reforms is an effective strategy to ensure that financial protection is expanding to all parts of the population. A series of reviews have examined how insurance systems in European, Asian, and Latin American countries define and treat vulnerable populations and have broadly concluded that countries must still make targeted efforts to expand payment subsidies and/or exemptions and service packages to these populations in order to continue progress toward UHC.[32, 33, 34] A core challenge in this effort is the fact that correctly targeting and subsequently reaching beneficiaries is difficult; in several Asian health insurance programs,

28. Yang and others (2016).
29. Somkotra and Lagrada (2009).
30. Lee and others (2009).
31. Parmar and others (2014).
32. Vilcu and Mathauer (2016).
33. Vilcu and others (2016).
34. Mathauer and Behrendt (2017).

only about half of the intended vulnerable target groups are currently covered.[35] This stems in large part from the difficulties in identifying such groups, but also from challenges associated with determining the appropriate mechanisms of providing financial coverage (e.g., reimbursement versus in kind). Where countries have been able to successfully identify and reach vulnerable populations with financial protection schemes, the health gains have been impressive.[36] Such strategies should be designed and implemented according to local context, government political will, and available resources.

Policy Options Available to Achieve UHC for Vulnerable and Marginalized Populations

The principle of progressive universalism is a useful guide for reaching vulnerable populations with UHC. By deliberately directing resources to the neediest in society, it advocates a bottom-up approach: first bringing benefits to those who are worst off. In this section, we argue that operationalizing this principle requires better information on vulnerable populations, health systems oriented toward primary healthcare, adequate financing for health, and the adoption of innovative technologies. It also needs an understanding of the political factors that can impede policies that favor vulnerable and politically weak groups.

Better Understanding and Information on Vulnerable Populations

Understanding the vulnerabilities that affect health in a population and having accurate and timely information on the health of vulnerable populations is critical for directing appropriate health services to these groups. Yet information on the health of vulnerable groups tends to be fragmented. A first step in producing actionable information on vulnerable populations requires understanding the sources of vulnerability in a population and how it relates to the risk of poor health or financial hardship related to use of health services. Household surveys, which are the principal means of collecting information on population health in low- and middle-income countries (LMICs), can be oriented to provide adequate representation of vulnerable populations. Well-functioning national systems of civil registration and vital statistics can provide up-to-date information on population health, including vulnerable groups. Establishing such systems, however, is an ongoing challenge for many LMICs due to, among other things, a lack of technical and financial resources and political pressures to suppress information

---

35. Vilcu and others (2016).
36. Ruiz and others (2018).

on these groups. There are other options. Some countries, like Brazil and Ethiopia, have successfully used community health workers to collect information on the health and other vital statistics of all households in communities. This "census-based" community approach offers a way of both routinely collecting information on people's health and vital events and directing health services toward vulnerable groups (see box 7-2).

Collecting information on some vulnerable groups, like migrants, requires special effort and care. Despite the high and growing levels of global migration, information systems on migrants, particularly on their health, is weak. Current data on international migration is fragmented and contextually specific. There is no agreed set of standardized migration indicators that source and destination countries collect.[37] Moreover, what data are collected are often not publicly available. Such issues limit efforts to understand the scale of global migration, to develop evidence-based policies to manage migration, and to know the extent to which migrants, particularly refugees and labor migrants, are able to access health and other services.[38, 39] In many cases, this reflects political mobilization to limit the rights of migrants. While there have been efforts to independently collect information on migrants in some countries, it is important that routine national systems for collecting information on populations (e.g., household surveys or surveillance systems) also identify and include migrant populations. Routinely collecting information on migrant populations may not be acceptable to everyone. There is every danger that governments or anti-migrant groups can use such information in ways that is detrimental to the well-being of migrants. Indeed, migrants themselves may be reluctant to participate in such processes. Better information on migrants and their health is necessary to increase their access to health services, and requires involvement of different actors (e.g., national governments) and ministries (e.g., health, labor, foreign affairs, trade and industries, NGOs). However, governments will need to also demonstrate confidence that such information will be used carefully and without prejudice to migrants' well-being.

Progressive Universalism through Primary Healthcare-Oriented Health Systems

Countries with health systems that are built on a strong primary healthcare (PHC) platform have demonstrated improvements in substantially expanding coverage of essential healthcare services, improving population health, and

---

37. Bilsborrow (2017).
38. OECD/ILO/IOM/UNHCR (2018).
39. Bilsborrow (2017).

Box 7-2. Community Health Workers and Community-Based Census

Primary healthcare programs with strong community-based services have demonstrated health gains, especially in regard to maternal, neonatal, and child health. The Census-Based Impact-Oriented approach and similar strategies aim to understand the most important health needs of a community via community outreach efforts (such as focus groups, meeting, and home visits) and epidemiologic monitoring using community censuses, surveys, and vital events reporting. Community health workers or community volunteers regularly visit all households in their jurisdiction and, depending on the context, provide a range of services from health education to collecting information on family health and providing basic curative services and commodities to the household. Such models are used in Bangladesh, Ethiopia, and Brazil, among others.

reducing disparities in access to healthcare and health.[40, 41, 42, 43] Health systems oriented around PHC offer the potential of providing vulnerable populations with essential health services and financial protection. For one, PHC puts emphasis on addressing the determinants of health—the social, economic and environmental, and individual characteristics that underpin many of the causes of vulnerability in populations (see box 7-3).[44] Community-based services, an important feature of PHC, is often also the only way to identify and reach vulnerable populations, due to their geography or other causes of vulnerability. In particular, the practice of community health workers regularly visiting all households in a community, applied in countries like Bangladesh and Brazil, offers a powerful way to reach vulnerable populations, identify those at risk of poor health, and connect them with appropriate care.[45] For example, community delivery of services is beneficial to older populations, because they may find it difficult to access fixed health services delivery points other than their residences, due to mobility issues. They are also more likely to suffer from chronic illness that requires stronger health promotion, medical treatment or surgery at higher-level facilities, and a sustained engagement over long periods of time with healthcare providers. This issue will grow in prominence as the global population aged sixty years or over, estimated to be 962 million in 2017, is projected to double by 2050, with the majority of the world's older population living in LMICs.[46]

40. Starfield and others (2005).
41. Lawn and others (2008).
42. World Health Organization (2013).
43. Macinko and others (2009).
44. World Health Organization and United Nations Children's Fund (2018).
45. Perry and others (1999).
46. Department of Economic and Social Affairs Population Division (2017).

Box 7-3. Evolution of Primary Healthcare

Primary healthcare (PHC) as an approach to improving population health was first articulated in the 1978 Alma-Ata Declaration. Its essential elements are built around three pillars; meeting people's health needs through comprehensive promotive, protective, preventive, and/or curative services; addressing the broader determinants of health; and empowering individuals, families, and communities to optimize their health. This conceptualization has been redefined repeatedly since Alma-Ata. PHC has been variously defined as the provision of ambulatory or first-contact personal healthcare services; as a set of priority health interventions for low-income populations (also called selective PHC); as basic preventive, promotive, and curative health services delivered by non-specialist health workers; as health services delivered close to communities; or as broader health strategy that focuses on the economic, social, and political aspects of health rather than simply health service provision.

Vulnerable groups, such as the poor, ethnic groups, migrants, or the socially marginalized, often live in resource-poor areas where facility-based health services are traditionally weak. Further, beliefs, stigma, education, their legal status (in the case of international migrants or refugees), financial constraints, and a lack of language proficiency can limit their ability to participate in health services proactively. By emphasizing outreach services in communities, PHC strategies can better target vulnerable groups with comprehensive essential health services. PHC-oriented health systems can reduce healthcare costs for both the government and patients. The focus on prevention and management of illness at the primary-care level avoids escalation of health issues to more complex and costly conditions; the reliance on basic infrastructure and health workers with basic training offers an affordable way of delivering services. Because out-of-pocket payments for health are primarily comprised of expenditures on outpatient visits and medicines, access to publicly funded PHC services and affordable essential medicines can substantially lower financial hardship experienced by patients.[47]

PHC as the foundation of UHC offers a progressive universalism approach to developing health systems. The advancement of health systems oriented around PHC requires action on several fronts. For one, all levels of care in the health system—primary, secondary, and tertiary—need to be well-functioning and have strong referral linkages. Second, the historical prioritization of communicable diseases and reproductive conditions has largely shaped the organization of PHC services. Important areas for action here include strengthening capacity to also manage noncommunicable diseases and emphasizing preventive and promotive healthcare. Third, primary care services in many countries are challenged by

47. World Health Organization (2010).

issues of low financing, inadequate material resources, and poor quality of care. This often results in patients bypassing primary health centers and seeking care elsewhere.[48] Investing in improving quality of care in health systems is critical to addressing this issue.[49] This can be achieved through better in-service and pre-service training, an appropriate incentive environment that promotes better quality of care by health workers, and adequate financing. Fourth, many LMICs have pluralistic health systems, where there is a large private sector (formal or informal) present. Often the vast majority of outpatient visits is catered by the private sector.[50] Strategies to suitably engage the private sector are necessary to ensure access to quality and affordable health services.

Attention to Financing Healthcare

Providing financial protection to vulnerable populations remains one of the most pressing challenges for achieving UHC. For one, countries lack adequate fiscal space to provide adequate coverage of subsidized healthcare to vulnerable populations. For governments facing fiscal constraints, there are several options, including prioritizing health by increasing the health budget or increasing health revenues by raising general or earmarked taxes in a progressive manner so the burden is on those who can afford to pay. Increasing health budgets or raising general taxes are often difficult, due to competing priorities and political acceptability. However, earmarking taxes, particularly revenue-earmarking by taxing items such as alcohol, tobacco, and sugary drinks offers an important way of raising additional revenues for health to cover vulnerable populations. Besides raising revenues for health, such earmarking also helps to reduce consumption of unhealthy products. Countries like the Philippines have had success with using "sin taxes" to increase funding for health, though the long-term sustainability of revenue streams from sin taxes is questionable.[51] With that in mind, looking for innovative ways to finance healthcare is important.

Countries can also use their available health resources more efficiently. One strategy to achieve this is by integrating packages of cost-effective promotive, preventive, and curative NCD interventions, such as those identified in the Disease Control Priorities, which can be delivered through population-based, community, health center, and hospital platforms.[52] Keeping with the spirit of progressive universalism, countries can adopt an essential set of services that

---

48. Kruk and others (2009).
49. Rao and Sheffel (2018).
50. Bhatia and Cleland (2001).
51. Kaiser, Bredenkamp, and Iglesias (2016).
52. Watkins and others (2018).

can be offered to all people, and this can be subsequently scaled up. Another strategy to use health resources more efficiently is to control the costs of healthcare. One example is Japan, where close collaboration between representatives of healthcare providers and the Ministries of Health and Finance has resulted in periodic social insurance fee schedule review, enabling the country to control overall expenditure while meeting the health needs of Japan's rapidly aging population. Further, because expenditures on drugs constitute the biggest share of out-of-pocket payments, regulating the cost of medicines or promoting the use of quality-assured generics is another important strategy to lessen the financial hardship on household. Global financing mechanisms on drug research and development, international trade agreements, and the judicious use of compulsory licensing of drugs that are respectful both of patents and of the right to healthcare, can promote greater access to affordable essential medicines. At the same time, increasing numbers of substandard and falsified medical products pose an unacceptable risk to public health. In these areas, government action at the regional and global level can help increase access to affordable medicines through the use of quality-assured generics.

Countries whose health budgets depend on donor contributions constitute an important case. While aid per capita for health more than doubled across low-income countries from US$4 to US$10 from 2000 to 2016, public spending on health increased only slightly (by about US$3 per capita).[53] Consequently, for these countries, the share of health in overall domestic public spending declined during the same period.[54] Within a decade, more than fifty countries will transit away from depending on external donors for financing healthcare.[55] The extent to which these countries can smoothly transition depends on the political choices of government leaders, as well as the nature of the transition process executed by donor agencies. It is also important to recognize that improvements in national income do not necessarily translate into improvements for all—there are likely to be sub-national regions or population groups that have not benefited from increases in average income. As such, withdrawing donor support on the basis of changes in average national income may be detrimental for many. Establishing donor coordination mechanisms is important to ensure that global health assistance contributes to the establishment of long-term, sustainable health-financing solutions.

53. World Health Organization (2018).
54. Ibid.
55. UHC 2030 (2017).

The Potential of Technological Innovations

Innovations in digital health technology can play an important role in providing vulnerable populations with increased access to healthcare. Technological innovations, such as mobile phones and portable diagnostic devices, among others, have demonstrated effectiveness in increasing the availability of basic diagnostic services in underserved geographies, enhanced the capacity of lay health workers to monitor the health of their communities, improved their ability to provide quality care, and to provide health-related messaging to their clients. Telemedicine has enabled patients in underserved geographies to access specialist care remotely.[56]

Several recent innovations in digital health technologies offer the potential of increased healthcare access to vulnerable populations. Mobile money technology, by which money can be easily transferred using mobile phones, offers the potential of users being reimbursed by insurance companies more efficiently or of directly receiving financial benefits from government programs, such as conditional cash-transfer programs in health. This can help to better target beneficiaries, improve the reputation of government programs by ensuring timely receipt of benefits, and reduce opportunities for corruption. The use of drones in Rwanda is also an example of improving service access.[57] Here, drones have been used to carry blood and life-saving supplies over long distances where supply routes are traditionally difficult to navigate. Such new technology holds enormous potential to reach vulnerable populations, particularly those living in hard-to-reach areas. The use and adaptation of such technologies, along with ensuring necessary regulatory frameworks, can help vulnerable populations overcome barriers to accessing essential health supplies and services.

Conclusion

Providing vulnerable populations with affordable, quality healthcare remains a pressing challenge even as an increasing number of countries are formalizing political commitments to UHC. This is true both of countries that have established UHC systems or have yet to do so; and whether the groups considered vulnerable are the poor, the elderly, individuals with low socioeconomic position, or individuals who live in particular geographies. This difficult task of providing coverage to vulnerable populations is constrained by several factors: understanding vulnerabilities, identifying who the vulnerable are, having adequate resources—financial, human and material—to provide affordable quality

56. Shea and others (2009).
57. Ackerman and Koziol (2019).

services, and effectively directing health resources at these groups. This chapter has attempted to highlight some potential solutions to address these challenges.

The principle of progressive universalism is a useful guide to frame UHC strategies while recognizing the importance of reaching vulnerable populations. By deliberately directing resources to the neediest in society, it advocates a bottom-up approach to first bring benefits to those who are worst off. Information on vulnerable populations is critical to understanding their health needs, as well as to empowering them and to directing services toward them. Orienting health systems to have a strong PHC foundation offers a way to reach vulnerable populations with affordable and integrated essential preventive, promotive, and curative health services. Health systems oriented toward PHC can offer important population health gains, in an affordable manner, to governments and patients. However, linkages with secondary and tertiary care levels, and quality of services, and adequate financing are necessary conditions for this. For certain neglected vulnerable groups, such as migrants, special efforts need to be made to collect information on their health. Migrant workers should be offered access to health and social security benefits in the country where they work, comparable to those of local workers.[58, 59] To reach this point, health benefits of migrant workers must be coordinated by both source and destination countries through mechanisms such as bilateral social security agreements.[60]

Efforts to provide vulnerable populations with affordable, quality healthcare need to be cognizant of the political impediments that lie along this path. These policies may not be favored by those with power in government or within society. For instance, issues like intolerance of foreigners, ethnic and racial xenophobia, and subsidizing the economically weak using public funds have become major political issues. Civil society and development partners are an important resource in advocating for and directing global health funds to vulnerable populations, and to make access to affordable, quality health services a reality for all.

References

Abubakar, I., and others, "The UCL-*Lancet* Commission on Migration and Health: The Health of a World on the Move," *Lancet*, vol. 392, no. 10164 (December 2018), 2606–54.

Ackerman, E. and M. Koziol, "The Blood Is Here: Zipline's Medical Delivery Drones Are Changing the Game in Rwanda," *Institute of Electrical and Electronics Engineers Spectrum*, vol. 56, no. 5 (May 2019), 24–31.

58. Abubakar and others (2018).
59. Zimmerman, Kiss, and Hossain (2011).
60. Benach and others (2011).

Alkire, S., and others. 2009. "Developing the Equality Measurement Framework: Selecting the Indicators." Equality and Human Rights Commission.

Bhatia, J. C. and J. Cleland, "Healthcare Seeking and Expenditure by Young Indian Mothers in the Public and Private Sectors." *Health Policy Plan*, vol. 16, no. 1 (March 2001), 55–61.

Benach, J., and others, "Migration and Low-Skilled Workers in Destination Countries," *Public Library of Science Medicine*, vol. 8, no. 6 (June 2011), e1001043.

Bilsborrow, R. 2017. "The Global Need for Better Data on International Migration and the Special Potential of Household Surveys," Grand-Saconnex, Switzerland.

Bloom, G., "Service Delivery Transformation for UHC in Asia and the Pacific," *Health Systems & Reform*, vol. 5, no. 1 (January 2019), 7–17.

Burchardt, T. and P. Vizard. 2007. "Definition of Equality and Framework for Measurement: Final Recommendations of the Equalities Review Steering Group on Measurement."

Chemor Ruiz, A., A. E. O. Ratsch, and G. A. Alamilla Martínez, "Mexico's Seguro Popular: Achievements and Challenges," *Health Systems & Reform*, vol. 4, no. 3 (July 2018), 194–202.

Collins, P. H., "Learning from the Outsider Within: The Sociological Significance of Black Feminist Thought," *Social Problems*, vol. 33, no. 6 (October 1986), S14–S32.

Countdown to 2030 Collaboration, and others, "Countdown to 2030: Tracking Progress toward Universal Coverage for Reproductive, Maternal, Newborn, and Child Health," *Lancet*, vol. 391, no. 10129 (April 2018), 1538–48.

Department of Economic and Social Affairs Population Division. 2017. "World Population Ageing 2017," New York.

Grabovschi, C., C. Loignon, and M. Fortin, "Mapping the Concept of Vulnerability Related to Healthcare Sisparities: A Scoping Review," *BMC Health Services Research*, vol. 13, no. 1 (December 2013), 94.

Gray, B. H. and E. van Ginneken. 2012. "Healthcare for Undocumented Migrants: European Approaches." Issue Brief (Commonw. Fund) 33: 1–12. December.

Hart, J. T., "The Inverse Care Law," *Lancet,* vol. 297, no. 7696 (1971), 405–41.

Holzmann, R., "Do Bilateral Social Security Agreements Deliver on the Portability of Pensions and Healthcare Benefits? A Summary Policy Paper on Four Migration Corridors between EU and Non-EU Member States," *IZA Journal of European Labor Studies*, vol. 5, no. 1 (December 2016), 17.

ICF. 2019. The DHS Program STATcompiler. Funded by USAID (www.statcompiler.com).

Kaiser, K., C. Bredenkamp, and R. Iglesias. 2016. "Sin Tax Reform in the Philippines: Transforming Public Finance, Health, and Governance for More Inclusive Development." The World Bank.

Kruk, M. E., and others. 2009. "Bypassing Primary Care Facilities for Childbirth: A Population-Based Study in Rural Tanzania," *Health Policy Plan*, vol. 24, no. 4 (July 2009), 279–88.

Lawn, J. E., and others, "Alma-Ata 30 Years On: Revolutionary, Relevant, and Time to Revitalize," *Lancet*, vol. 372, no. 9642 (September 2008), 917–27.

Lee, T.-H. J., I. Saran, and K. D. Rao, "Ageing in India: Financial Hardship from Health Expenditures," *International Journal of Health Planning and Management*, vol. 33, no. 2 (April 2018), 414–25.

Macinko, J., B. Starfield, and T. Erinosho., "The Impact of Primary Healthcare on Population Health in Low- and Middle-Income Countries," *Journal of Ambulatory Care Management*, vol. 32, no. 2 (2009), 150–71.

Mathauer, I. and T. Behrendt, "State Budget Transfers to Health Insurance to Expand Coverage to People Outside Formal Sector Work in Latin America," *BMC Health Services Research*, vol. 17, no. 1 (2017).

OECD/ILO/IOM/UNHC. 2018. "G20 International Migration and Displacement Trends Report 2018."

Ooms, G. and R. Hammonds. 2015. "Anchoring Universal Health Coverage in the Right to Health," World Health Organization.

Parmar, D., and others, "Enrollment of Older People in Social Health Protection Programs in West Africa—Does Social Exclusion Play a Part?" *Social Science & Medicine*, vol. 119 (2014), 36–44.

Perry, H., and others, "Attaining Health for All Through Community Partnerships: Principles of the Census-Based, Impact-Oriented (CBIO) Approach to Primary Healthcare Developed in Bolivia, South America," *Social Science & Medicine*, vol. 48, no. 8 (April 1999), 1053–67.

Rao, K. D. and A. Sheffel, "Quality of Clinical Care and Bypassing of Primary Health Centers in India," *Social Science & Medicine*, vol. 207 (June 2018), 80–88.

Riley, J. C., "Estimates of Regional and Global Life Expectancy, 1800–2001," *Population and Development Review*, vol. 31, no. 3 (September 2005), 537–43.

Russo, G., G. Bloom, and D. McCoy, "Universal Health Coverage, Economic Slowdown and System Resilience: Africa's Policy Dilemma," *BMJ Global Health*, vol. 2, no. 3 (August 2017), e000400.

Sen, A., *Development as Freedom* (Oxford and New York: Oxford University Press, 2001).

Shea, S., and others, "A Randomized Trial Comparing Telemedicine Case Management with Usual Care in Older, Ethnically Diverse, Medically Underserved Patients with Diabetes Mellitus: 5 Year Results of the IDEATel Study," *Journal of the American Medical Informatics Association*, vol. 16, no. 4 (July 2009), 446–56.

Somkotra, T. and L. P. Lagrada, "Which Households Are at Risk of Catastrophic Health Spending: Experience in Thailand after Universal Coverage," *Health Affairs*, vol. 28, no. 3 (May 2009), w467–w478.

Starfield, B., L. Shi, and J. Macinko, "Contribution of Primary Care to Health Systems and Health," *Milbank Quarterly*, vol. 83, no. 3 (September 2005), 457–502.

Tangcharoensathien, V., and others, "Addressing the Health of Vulnerable Populations: Social Inclusion and Universal Health Coverage," *Journal of Global Health*, vol. 8, no. 2 (2018).

UHC 2030. 2017. "Statement on Sustainability and Transition from External Funding."

UNHCR. 2017. "Global Trends: Forced Displacement in 2017."

Victora, C. G., and others, "Applying an Equity Lens to Child Health and Mortality: More of the Same Is Not Enough," *Lancet*, vol. 362, no. 9379 (July 2003), 233–41.

Vilcu, I. and I. Mathauer, "State Budget Transfers to Health Insurance Funds for Universal Health Coverage: Institutional Design Patterns and Challenges of Covering Those Outside the Formal Sector in Eastern European High-Income Countries," *International Journal for Equity in Health*, vol. 15, no. 1 (2016).

Vilcu, I., and others, "Subsidized Health Insurance Coverage of People in the Informal

Sector and Vulnerable Population Groups: Trends in Institutional Design in Asia," *International Journal for Equity in Health*, vol. 15, no. 1 (2016), 1–29.

Wagstaff, A., and others, "Progress on Catastrophic Health Spending in 133 Countries: A Retrospective Observational Study," *Lancet Global Health*, vol. 6, no. 2 (February 2018), e169–e179.

Watkins, D., and others, "Universal Health Coverage and Essential Packages of Care" in *Disease Control Priorities: Improving Health and Reducing Poverty*, 3rd ed. (Washington, D.C.: World Bank, 2017).

World Health Organization. 2010. "Health Systems Financing: The Path to Universal Coverage," WHO.

———. 2013. "The World Health Report 2008—Primary Healthcare (Now More Than Ever)," WHO.

———. 2018. "Public Spending on Health: A Closer Look at Global Trends," WHO.

———. 2019a. "What Is Universal Coverage?" (www.who.int/health_financing/universal_coverage_definition/en/).

———. 2019b. "Repository of Health Budgets" (www.who.int/health_financing/topics/budgeting-in-health/repository/en/).

———. 2019c. "Global Health Observatory (GHO) data." WHO (www.who.int/gho/en/).

World Health Organization and World Bank. 2017. "Tracking Universal Health Coverage: 2017 Global Monitoring Report." Geneva, Switzerland.

World Health Organization and United Nations Children's Fund. 2018. "A Vision for Primary Healthcare in the Twenty-First Century." Geneva, Switzerland.

Yang, T., and others, "Catastrophic Health Expenditure: A Comparative Analysis of Empty-Nest and Non-Empty-Nest Households with Seniors in Shandong, China," *BMJ Open*, vol. 6, no. 7 (July 2016), e010992.

Zimmerman, C., L. Kiss, and M. Hossain, "Migration and Health: A Framework for Twenty-First Century Policy-Making," *Public Library of Science Medicine*, vol. 8, no. 5 (May 2011): e1001034.

CHAPTER EIGHT

No Woman Left Excluded from Financial Services

Eiji Yamada, Erica Paula Sioson,
Enerelt Murakami, and Akira Murata

Access to financial services, especially formal and secured ones, is an essential part of modern life that enhances people's economic opportunity and security. However, most adults in developing countries remain financially excluded. Furthermore, more women than men have persistently been kept out of the system due to various socioeconomic reasons. In particular, the gender gap in financial inclusion, measured by the gap in ownership of an account at formal financial institutions (FIs), including digital finance, has been unchanged for the past three rounds of the Global Findex report—2011, 2014, and 2017—despite the progress in overall financial inclusion in developing countries.

Recent literature reveals that narrowing the gender gap in financial inclusion can help achieve Sustainable Development Goals (SDGs), prompting the international community to advocate for the enhancement of women's access to financial services. Since the first Global Findex report, in 2011, quantified the volume of the global gender gap, studies and advocacies on this issue have rapidly emerged.[1] The global discussion reached newer heights in the Denarau Action Plan in 2016 in a forum organized by the Alliance for Financial Inclusion (AFI), an international alliance specializing in enhancing financial inclusion.[2] Under the name of the Denarau Action Plan, financial authorities from several countries committed to closing the gender gap in financial inclusion through

1. See World Bank (2017).
2. See AFI, 2016, Denarau Action Plan.

political initiatives, peer learning, data collection, and collaboration with various stakeholders. However, the world has not yet observed a substantial shrinkage of this gap.

To deepen our understanding of how to narrow the gender gap, this chapter explores statistics recently made available from the Global Findex database and a unique dataset from Japan International Cooperation Agency – Research Institute's (JICA-RI) study in rural areas in the Philippines. The empirical description exhibits the international, intranational, and intra-community variations in financial inclusion as well as gender gaps, suggesting several policy implications that need to be considered to realize gender-equitable financial inclusion globally.

We first revisit why women's financial inclusion, especially the ownership of accounts at FIs, is important. Cross-country data from Global Findex as well as the survey data in the Philippines are then discussed to describe significant heterogeneity in the gender-equitable financial inclusion among developing countries and within a developing country. In the concluding section, we propose measures for developing countries and the international community to promote more gender-equitable financial inclusion.

Revisiting the Benefits of Gender-Equitable Financial Inclusion

How much does financial inclusion matter for the development of low- and middle-income countries? While owning a bank account or a mobile money account seems less urgent than other more fundamental SDGs—for instance, alleviating poverty and hunger, maintaining people's health, mitigating disaster, protecting the environment, and securing industrial growth—one cannot easily write off the importance of financial inclusion. Nevertheless, financial inclusion is an important first step that enables individuals to manage their finances, to save for unforeseen expenses, to invest in their education and health, and to start businesses. In other words, having a financial account pulls the unbanked and underserved into the formal economy in a way that will boost economic efficiency.

Therefore, financial inclusion has been recognized as an important driver to achieve various economic and welfare improvements, as it has been featured as targets in six of seventeen SDGs, as listed in table 8-1.[3] Access to financial services is regarded as one of the basic steps to help people secure economic stability and a healthy life. Furthermore, it plays an important role in enabling people to increase their income and expand business. Currently, Goal 1 and Goal 8 set the specific financial inclusion indicators:

3. UNSTAT (2017).

Table 8-1. Selected Goals and Targets Directly Related to Financial Inclusion in the SDGs

Goal	Target
SDG 1: Eradicate poverty.	1.4. By 2030, ensure that all men and women, in particular the poor and the vulnerable, have equal rights to economic resources, as well as access to basic services, ownership, and control over land and other forms of property, inheritance, natural resources, appropriate new technology, *and financial services, including microfinance.*
SDG 2: End hunger, achieve food security and improved nutrition, and promote sustainable agriculture.	2.3. By 2030, double the agricultural productivity and incomes of small-scale food producers, in particular women, indigenous peoples, family farmers, pastoralists, and fishers, including through secure and equal access to land, other productive resources and inputs, knowledge, *financial services,* markets, and opportunities for value addition and non-farm employment.
SDG 3: Ensure healthy lives and promote well-being for all at all ages.	3.8. Achieve universal health coverage, *including financial risk protection,* access to quality essential healthcare services, and access to safe, effective, quality, and affordable essential medicines and vaccines for all.
SDG 5: Achieve gender equality and empower all women and girls.	5.a. Undertake reforms to give women equal rights to economic resources, as well as access to ownership and control over land and other forms of property, *financial services,* inheritance, and natural resources, in accordance with national laws.
SDG 8: Promote sustained, inclusive, and sustainable economic growth, full and productive employment, and decent work for all.	8.3 Promote development-oriented policies that support productive activities, decent job creation, entrepreneurship, creativity, and innovation, and encourage the formalization and growth of micro-, small- and medium-size enterprises, including through *access to financial services.*
	8.10 *Strengthen the capacity of domestic financial institutions to encourage and expand access to banking, insurance, and financial services for all.*
SDG 9: Build resilient infrastructure, promote inclusive and sustainable industrialization, and foster innovation.	9.3 Increase the access of small-scale industrial and other enterprises, in particular in developing countries, to *financial services, including affordable credit,* and their integration into value chains and markets.

Source: Based on UNSTAT (2017).

1.4.1. Proportion of population living in households with access to basic services (including financial services)

8.10.1 (a). Number of commercial bank branches per 100,000 adults

8.10.1 (b). Number of automated teller machines (ATMs) per 100,000 adults

8.10.2. Proportion of adults (fifteen years and older) with an account at a bank or other financial institution or with a mobile-money-service provider

Why Women's Financial Inclusion Is Important

Global evidence backs up the importance of financial inclusion for both men and women in achieving the SDGs. Several studies stress the benefit of narrowing the gender gap in financial inclusion. Women's financial inclusion can enhance further inclusiveness for women and women's autonomy; allow for better use of household resources; and reduce the vulnerability of their households and businesses. In short, closing the gender gap in financial inclusion enables women to contribute more to promoting countries' economic growth, thus reducing poverty and inequality, developing employment opportunities, and building inclusive societies.[4]

In the Philippines, women who started their own savings accounts increased decisionmaking power in such a way that their households were more likely to buy a washing machine and other durable goods that might benefit women's work.[5] In Nepal, education spending increased by 20 percent when women-headed households were given access to digital savings accounts.[6] Having a formal financial account is important for women to access loans and credit and to make transactions. It is essential, also, to save money and build assets in a safe place, which can, in turn, help pull those women and their families out of poverty. Savings interventions can facilitate the growth of women's businesses as they channel earnings and personal savings to invest further.[7] Past literature on savings also show effects on women's empowerment and positive household welfare impacts.[8]

The benefit of financial inclusion may be especially important in a society

---

4. AFI (2017).

5. Ashraf, Karlan, and Yin (2010).

6. Prina (2015).

7. Boyd and Aldana (2015).

8. See Holloway and others (2017); Trivelli and de los Rios (2014); and Karlan and others (2017).

where women's participation in economic activity is culturally restricted. In Honduras, JICA has provided technical assistance to beneficiary women of a Conditional Cash Transfer (CCT) program by the "graduation approach" of the Consultative Group to Assist the Poor (CGAP) since 2015. The project provided a series of financial trainings on saving, household financial management and planning, financial services, and entrepreneurship skills. Results from the randomized controlled trial (RCT) implemented along with the project reveals that the project achieved a significant increase in the financial inclusion of women beneficiaries. For example, the trainings achieved a 17.4 percent increase in bank account holdings among rural women participants. Furthermore, the annual income from microenterprises was 1.6 times larger for the training participants. Not limited to these economic impacts, the intervention to increase women's financial inclusion has a potential to change the male dominated society, a factor pointed out as a major obstacle to shrinking the gender gap. While Honduras is known for its *machismo* (male dominance) culture, the study finds that the project contributed to improve the situation for women. Regarding household decisionmaking, the husbands of the participating women were 10 percent less likely to exclude their wives when making decisions about the household.[9]

Does Account Ownership Really Matter?

It is important to note that most of the previously mentioned benefits of financial inclusion will not materialize unless the banked women actually use the financial services. While financial inclusion is usually measured in terms of account ownership at an FI, it does not necessarily mean the holder actively uses those financial services. It is widely acknowledged that many macroeconomic, microeconomic, and social factors affect the decision to use financial services other than just simply having access to it.

Nevertheless, Global Findex data reveal that account ownership is an important step to facilitate the use of financial services. Since saving, investment, and access to credit are the key channels through which financial inclusion can deliver development impacts, let us look at the relationship between account ownership and saving/borrowing. According to the three rounds of the Global Findex data, account ownership (at an FI or at a mobile money service) is significantly positively associated with the incidence of saving at or borrowing from a formal FI, for both men and women. The regression coefficient of the share of adults who saved at a formal FI in the previous one year on the ratio of owning an account ranges around 0.3 for both men and women, across various specifications. This

9. Matsuda and others (2019).

means that if the account ownership ratio increases by 10 percentage points, the share of adults experiencing formal saving increases by 3 percentage points. Similarly, the regression analysis for borrowing experience finds that the increase of the account ownership ratio by 10 percentage points leads to a 1 to 2 percentage-point increase in borrowing from a formal financial institution.

In addition, the relationship between informal saving/borrowing and account holding reveals an interesting indication of the potential demand for formal financial access. In many countries with low financial inclusion, the share of adults who saved or borrowed informally—as measured by saving or borrowing at/from friends, relatives, and saving clubs during the past one year—exceeds the share of adults with an FI account. This means that there is a substantial size of unmet demand for formal financial services in countries with low financial inclusion. In countries where most people do not have formal accounts, the need for formal financial services is being filled by the use of informal ones. What this means is that many do not have accounts not because of a lack of need for formal accounts, but because of other constraints that lead them to utilize instead informal services. We can expect, therefore, that as formal accounts become more widely available as well as easier to use and access, they will supplant informal ones.

This relationship between account ownership and saving/borrowing is virtually the same for both men and women. Similar to the account ownership ratio, there are gender gaps in the use of financial services. What, then, does narrowing the gender gap in account ownership mean for the gender gap in saving and borrowing? The results of a similar regression suggest that narrowing the gender gap in account ownership is significantly associated with narrowing the gender gap in the use of finance. For instance, for the case of formal saving, shrinking the gender gap of account ownership by 10 percentage points will reduce the gender gap in saving by 1.7 to 2.7 percentage points. For the gender gap in borrowing, the magnitude of reduction becomes around 1.2 percentage points against a 10 percentage-point reduction in the gap in account ownership.

Given these results from the Global Findex data, in the following empirical discussions, we will focus on financial inclusion measured as formal and mobile money account ownership.

Global Trends and Variations in the Gender Gap in Financial Inclusion

Owning bank accounts is quite common in advanced countries. Adults are expected to have an account, as most daily financial transactions—such as receiving salary, payment for public services, credit card settlement, and government transfers—are designed to be made through a bank account. Having bank accounts is sometimes a precondition for purchasing or renting a house, getting loans for a business, and other asset transactions. Therefore, access to financial services is an essential part of modern life that enhances people's economic opportunity and security. However, access to affordable and useful financial services, or financial inclusion, is not universal. There exists a stark disparity between developing countries and developed countries in financial inclusion, and a large proportion of the population in developing countries has been financially excluded. According to the World Bank's Global Findex report in 2017, 1.7 billion adults do not have access to financial services; most of them live in developing countries.

While the unbanked population is still huge, recent progress is encouraging. In 2011, the ratio of adults with at least one bank or mobile money account was only 51 percent globally. By 2017, the ratio had risen to 69 percent.[10] This means that about 1 billion people have been newly financially included in the years between 2011 and 2017. Figure 8-1 plots the growth of financial inclusion in percentage-point change between 2011 and 2017 against the initial 2011 level of financial inclusion. Almost all the countries in the database have experienced an increase in financial inclusion, as is obvious from the fact that no country is located below the zero-horizontal line. Furthermore, countries with low initial inclusion rates made rapid progress. For example, countries such as Tajikistan, Senegal, Uganda, and Kyrgyz, whose 2011 level of financial inclusion were below 40 percent, observed a very impressive pace of inclusion by around 40 percentage points.

Notwithstanding this overall improvement, the expansion of financial access has sometimes left disadvantaged groups behind. One of these groups is women. In nearly all developing countries, women overrepresent the unbanked population, which means that the share of women among the unbanked is greater than the share of women in the total adult population. According to the Global Findex report in 2017, women are 7 percentage points less likely to have an account than men, globally, and the gap widens to 9 percentage points in the case of developing countries. In some countries, such as Bangladesh, Pakistan, and Turkey, the gap amounts to double-digits. This is a huge gap. To cancel the 7 percentage points global gender gap in 2017, which means increasing the global women's account holding ratio of 65 percent to the men's 72 percent, 190 million more women have to get access to an account. In addition, the gap has been persistent in recent years and seems to be hard to narrow quickly. Since the first Global Findex report was released in 2011, the gap among developing countries has not reduced as quickly, shrinking only from 10 percentage points to 9 percentage points in six years.

10. World Bank (2017).

Figure 8-1. The Global Convergence of Financial Inclusion, 2011-17

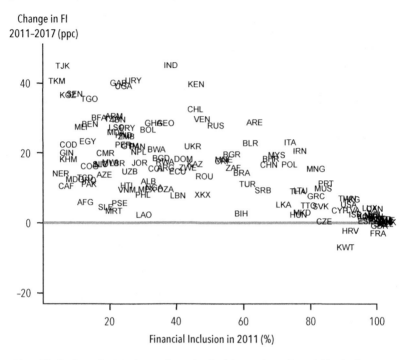

Note: The horizontal axis refers to the ratio of adults owning a financial institution account or a mobile money account, which are jointly termed here as financial inclusion. The vertical axis is for the change between 2011 and 2017 of financial inclusion at percentage point change. Placement of each three-character abbreviation of the country represents the country's location on the axis.

Source: Author's calculation using World Bank (2017).

What is behind the global persistence of the gender gap despite the overall strong progress in financial inclusion? A disaggregated analysis reveals that countries are heterogeneous in gender inclusiveness. Figure 8-2 depicts the relationship between the progress in overall financial inclusion and the change in gender gap from 2011 to 2017. The horizontal axis represents the percent increase in overall financial inclusion as measured by the share of banked adults. The vertical axis shows the 2011–17 change in gender gap, computed by subtracting women's financial inclusion from men's. A positive number means that the gender gap widened between the two periods. The size of the circle shows the size of the unbanked population in 2017. What is clear from this figure is that there is no systematic relationship between the overall progress in financial inclusion and in closing the gender gap, meaning that financial inclusion does not automatically result in improving the gender gap. Some countries, such as India, achieved both overall improvement and shrinking of the gender gap. On the contrary, many countries significantly widened the gender gap while they achieved a mild overall increase in the share of banked adults. Of seventy-seven developing countries where men were more financially included than women in 2011, forty-seven countries widened the gender gap further by 2017. It is noteworthy that countries with a large unbanked population, such as Pakistan, Nigeria, and Bangladesh, widened the gender gap by the largest magnitude between 2011 and 2017. Figure 8-2 illustrates the reason the global gender gap remained unchanged despite overall progress in financial inclusion: countries bifurcate into a group with gender-inclusive progress (such as India) or into a group where progress tended to be geared more toward improving men's access (such as Pakistan, Nigeria, and Bangladesh).

As described, recent decades evidenced an advancement in financial inclusion.

Figure 8-2. Changes in Financial Inclusion and Gender Gap, 2011–17

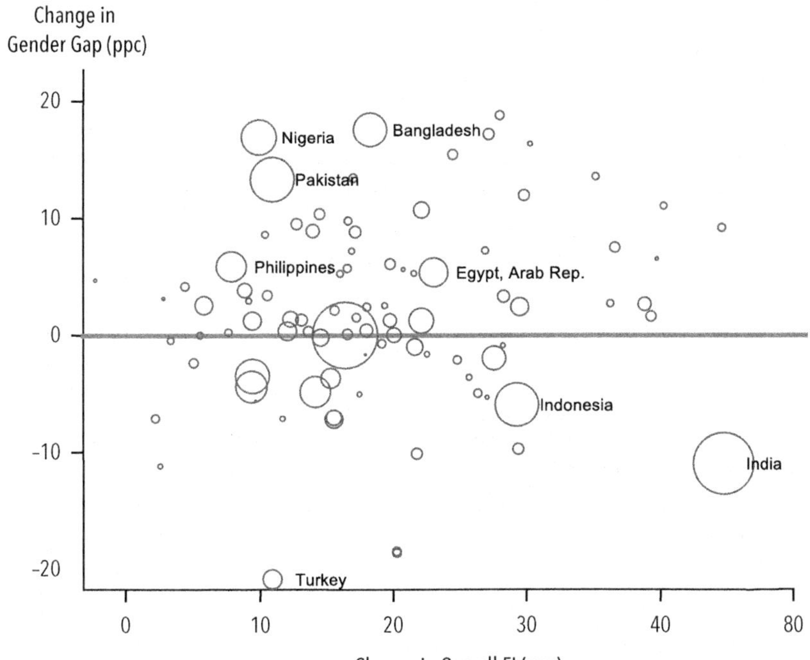

Note: The horizontal axis plots the change in overall financial inclusion, in percentage point change, between 2011 and 2017. The vertical axis represents the change in gender gap in financial inclusion between 2001 and 2017 by percentage point change, where the gender gap is given by subtracting women's financial inclusion from men's. Circle size relates to the size of the unbanked population as of 2017.

However, the progress in overall financial inclusion has not necessarily been inclusive for women. In many countries, financial inclusion in recent years tended to be geared toward improving men's access, inadvertently widening the gap between men and women. Whether the countries with low financial inclusion can catch up by 2030 crucially depends on how they can include more women who are currently excluded. Policy measures to ensure gender-equitable financial inclusion in developing countries is, thus, an urgent need. As of 2017, in most of the countries with a low level of financial inclusion (below the international average of 69 percent), financial inclusion tends to be higher for men, as figure 8-3 shows. Therefore, for the next decade, reducing the global unbanked population inevitably means to make more women banked. Furthermore, a group of countries require special attention—namely Bangladesh, Pakistan, and Nigeria—as they have widened the gender gap by a great magnitude, leaving a huge proportion of unbanked population.

Intranational and Intra-Community Variation

Countries are widely heterogeneous in terms of gender gap in financial inclusion, which raises the question of how much it varies within a given country. Unfortunately, there are a limited number of studies on the detailed intranational geography of the gender gap. As with many other economic indicators, financial inclusion and its gender gap within a country may be as diverse as those between countries. A recent unique study by JICA-RI in the Philippines reveals interesting findings in terms of intranational and intra-community variations in the gender gap in financial inclusion.

JICA-RI conducted a field survey from 2016 to 2017 in two rural communities in the Philippines. Located in northern Philippines, the municipality of Dingras in the province of Ilocos Norte had a population of around 39,000 in 2015, and is classified as a second class municipality in terms of per capita annual income. Located in southern Philippines, the municipality of Bansalan, in Davao del Sur, had a population of 60,000 in 2015 and is relatively richer than Dingras, with the status of a first class municipality.[11] Both municipalities substantially depend on overseas workers and on the remittances those workers send to their families in the villages. Four hundred households (200 remittance-receiving and 200 non-receiving) were randomly selected for interview in each of the municipalities. Since the main purpose of the survey was to understand the

---

11. In the Philippines, a municipality is first class if the annual per capita income of its residents is greater than 55 million pesos. If it is between 45 million and 55 million pesos, the municipality is called second class.

Figure 8-3. Financial Inclusion and Gender Gap, 2017

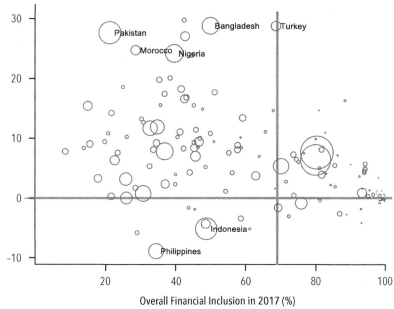

Gender Gap in Financial
Inclusion in 2017 (%)

Overall Financial Inclusion in 2017 (%)

Note: The horizontal axis refers to the overall financial inclusion measured by the ratio of adults owning an account with a financial institution or mobile money service in 2017. The vertical axis refers to the gender gap in financial inclusion in 2017 measured by subtracting women's financial inclusion from men's. The circle size represents the size of the country's unbanked population as of 2017. The vertical line in the middle-right of the graph represents 69 percent, the global average of financial inclusion.

Source: Author's calculation using World Bank (2017).

financial behavior of households receiving remittances from overseas workers, households receiving remittances were oversampled. The survey questionnaire asked for information on individual account ownership at banks, microfinance institutions, and cooperatives, the three forms of formal financial institutions in rural areas in the Philippines. Since the survey asked for the account ownership of all the individuals within a household, it provides insights on the within-household distribution of financial inclusion.

The Philippines can be considered an exceptional country in the global perspective: data from the Global Findex database for the Philippines from 2011, 2014, and 2017 show, overall, a modest but continuous increase in the rate of having bank accounts equally for both men and women.[12] While financial inclusion rates remain lower compared to neighboring countries such as Malaysia, Thailand, and Indonesia, a comparison between access to bank accounts by men and by women in the Philippines shows very interesting results. From 2011 to 2017, the Global Findex database shows a gender gap reversal, where women with bank accounts outnumber men by as much as 15 percentage points in 2011, with the difference decreasing until 2017. Not only in having accounts at formal institutions do women outperform men; in terms of having savings, data from the 2017 Financial Inclusion data of the Bangko Sentral ng Pilipinas (BSP) show that women are twice as likely to have an account than men in general.[13]

What factors contribute to this gender gap reversal? In the literature, several interconnected factors are raised. One reason is the high remittance inflow to the country. The Philippines depends highly on overseas workers and remittances, where one in ten households sends a migrant worker overseas; remittances account for 10 percent of the national GDP. Remittances, both international and domestic, make up a big proportion of person-to-person (P2P) transactions in the country. According to the survey by the BSP, 32 percent of Filipino adults had a remittance transaction in 2017. Among them, the incidence of receiving money is higher for females and situated in rural areas.

A second reason for this reversal is the strategy of expanding access points for microfinance and other more easily accessible FIs since the year 2000. The strategy encouraged the installation of access points to banks and microfinance institutions in 90 percent of the municipalities in the country.[14] According to data from the BSP, in 2017, there were 162 banks with microfinance operations serving almost 2 million borrowers, with outstanding loans amounting to 17 billion Philippine pesos.[15] The difference between women and men in microfinance account ownership is at 13.7 percentage points, suggesting that microfinance may be a more familiar and easier to access option for women.[16]

Third, the national government has been active in campaigning for better financial inclusion of both men and women. Overarching the policies to facilitate financial inclusion is the Philippine government's National Strategy for Financial Inclusion (NSFI), which spans financial literacy programs for migrants, students, professionals, and other sectors.[17] For a long time, the Filipino government has also been eager to facilitate digital finances. In 2000, the BSP formulated

12. World Bank (2017).
13. Bangko Sentral ng Pilipinas (2017a).
14. Ibid. (2017b).
15. Ibid.
16. Ibid. (2017a).
17. Ibid. (2015).

regulations to allow local FIs to offer electronic banking services. This move resulted in the emergence of GCash and Smart Money, two of the pioneering e-money services in the country.[18] Furthermore, the government has begun implementation of the Philippine Identification System (PhilSys), which aims to provide a means to establish a verifiable digital identity that will enable Filipinos to open accounts and use financial services more efficiently and to be able to participate in the digital economy.[19] In addition, the National Retail Payment System (NRPS), launched in 2015, "aims to create a safe, efficient, and reliable electronic retail payment system that is interconnected and interoperable."[20] These government initiatives might have helped overcome the physical distance to FIs that has been a major barrier to women's financial inclusion.

However, this gender gap reversal at the national level is not observed in the survey data in the two rural municipalities. The situation is quite diverse across municipalities and household remittance-receiving status. While women's financial inclusion (the ratio of adults having bank, MFI, or cooperatives accounts) is higher for remittance-receiving households, men's inclusion tends to be higher in Dingras overall (figure 8-4). In Dingras, while the gender gap is more than 13 percentage points regardless of remittance-receiving status, 10.1 percent of adult women in remittance-receiving households own a formal account, while the ratio is only 6.7 percent for non-receiving households. In Bansalan, the gender gap reverses for remittance-receiving households, with 25.0 percent of women in remittance-receiving households owning an account, compared to men at 19.8 percent. Again, for women in non-receiving households, the ratio declines to 17.3 percent.

Another observation from figure 8-4 is that women's inclusion is more volatile than men's inclusion across different regions and remittance-receiving statuses. Namely, men's financial inclusion is stable around 20 percent across all four groups, while women's varies widely. Even though the data is not nationally representative, it is noteworthy that women's financial inclusion might be more susceptible to local conditions than men's.

As seen, women's financial inclusion is quite low in general in the surveyed municipalities. However, a more detailed look at the data reveals the heterogeneous degree of financial exclusion across households: whether the household is totally or partially excluded from financial services speaks volumes about the diverse situation of unbanked women. One of the important dimensions to understand the degree of exclusion is to see whether the unbanked woman lives

18. See Lopez (2017) and Llanto and others (2018).
19. Bangko Sentral ng Pilipinas (2018).
20. Ibid.

Figure 8-4. Women's and Men's Financial Inclusion in Two Municipalities

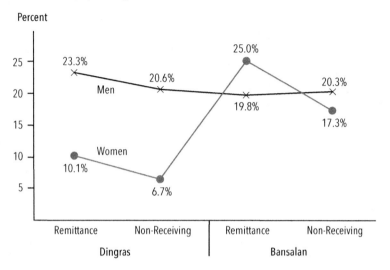

Note: Financial inclusion is measured by the ratio of adults (fifteen years or above) with at least one account either at the bank, microfinance, and cooperatives, within each category.

Source: Authors' calculation using JICA-RI's survey in the Philippines.

with a household member who owns an account. If nobody else has an account, she would be the most excluded from financial services, not having a chance to see, through her household member's experiences, how convenient and important it is to have and use a financial account. Households that are totally excluded from financial services will tend to coincide with the households that are the most economically excluded, with the lowest level of assets and income, which hinders them from accessing finance. For those unbanked women and their family members, barriers such as lack of income and assets, the cost of having an account (such as minimum deposit requirement), lack of documents and IDs, as well as geographical constraints may be binding regardless of gender.

Partially excluded unbanked women live in a different type of household. She has a household member who owns an account, either a man or a woman, or both. Compared to the unbanked woman in a totally excluded household, the degree of exclusion may be lower for her. While the cost of having an account may matter here, as well, gender-specific constraints such as social norms and intra-household bargaining can play a big role within this type of household.

Let us illustrate. Figure 8-5 categorizes unbanked women into four typologies of financial exclusion, based on the financial inclusion of other household members, in each municipality across different remittance-receiving statuses. The first type is an unbanked woman without other household members owning a financial institution account, which appears as "Nobody else banked" in the figure. The remaining are unbanked women living with at least one banked household member. The second type, "Only men banked," is an unbanked woman in a household where only men, and no other women, are banked. On the contrary, an unbanked woman is categorized "Only women banked" if there is at least one woman and no men in her household who is banked. Finally, "Both banked" is for an unbanked woman in a household with both men and women banked.

The most excluded unbanked women, "Nobody else banked," make up 40 percent of the unbanked women among the remittance-receiving households. The share is much larger among the non-receiving households, with 54.2 percent for Dingras and 53.9 percent for Bansalan. As is evident from the figure, the share of unbanked women with household-level financial exclusion does not depend on the municipality. However, the remittance-receiving status of the household may have an impact; the share of women with "Nobody else banked" is significantly higher among the non-receiving households. Note that more than 40 percent of unbanked women live with at least one banked household member regardless of region and remittance-receiving status. Except for remittance-receiving households in Bansalan, the majority of banked household members are men.

Thus, unbanked women do not belong to a homogenous group. As seen from figure 8-5, roughly half of the total unbanked women are financially excluded at the household level. Another half are excluded within the household, where at least one of her household members has an account at a financial institution but she herself does not have one. Most of these partially excluded women have a male banked member within her household, except for the case of remittance-receiving households in Bansalan.

Women in completely excluded households and those in partially excluded households face different types of problems. The former face constraints common to both men and women, rather than gender-specific issues. For the latter, the question is why she cannot or does not get an account while the men in her household can. In other words, there may be gender-specific barriers that should be further investigated.

Conclusion: Implications from the Analysis

As seen from the data, countries are widely diverse in terms of achievements in overall improvement of financial inclusion and in the shrinking of the gender gap. In recent years, almost all the countries in the world improved financial inclusion rates, increasing the share of their population that has access to financial services. While some countries have witnessed impressive progress in both

Figure 8-5. Financial Inclusion of Household
Members of an Unbanked Woman

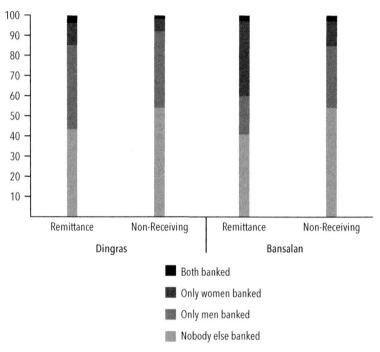

Note: Share in percent in terms of status of financial inclusion of other household members of unbanked women, by municipality and remittance-receiving status.
Source: Authors' calculation using JICA-RI's survey in the Philippines.

overall and gender-equitable financial inclusion, others have experienced a widening of the gender gap. This suggests that narrowing the gender gap is not an automatic process of development, and it should be deliberately prioritized in the next decade, especially for the countries with widening gender gaps. Figure 8-2 identifies the countries that need special attention. Some countries—such as Bangladesh, Pakistan, and Nigeria—while improving overall financial inclusion, have made progress geared toward better achievement of financial inclusion for men than women in the recent years; these form a stark contrast with a group of countries that have rapidly narrowed the gender gap, such as India, Turkey, and Iran.

There may be something to learn from those countries that have made significant achievements. Apart from India and China, the majority of unbanked women live in Bangladesh, Pakistan, and Nigeria. While there already have been several development projects addressing the gender gap in financial inclusion supported by international donors,[21] these countries should scale up their efforts given the significant size of the population of unbanked women. It is, thus, crucial for these countries to call for assistance—from knowledge sharing to technical assistance—from the international society to solve the problem.

Currently, several international initiatives, such as AFI and Women's World Banking, have emerged, and they are enthusiastically promoting the strategy of international peer learning. For example, AFI hosts various peer learning fora, inviting high-level financial authorities from developing member countries to encourage mutual learning from their experiences. The countries experiencing a widening gender gap are encouraged to use the opportunities provided by these international initiatives to learn from others and to appeal for financial and technical cooperation from donors.

Existing studies have identified a wide range of demand-side and supply-side barriers to financial inclusion for women, from material constraints—such as financial literacy and capacity, physical distance, and the cost of holding an account—to social constraints such as gender norms and intra-household bargaining power.[22] These studies address the variations of the barriers across different places and promote the designing of policies and financial products that can overcome the barriers faced by unbanked women. Recent studies tend to recommend developing products that take into account the specific needs and preferences of women, as Holloway and others state in their conclusion: "Researchers should continue to explore the role of gender norms and intra-household bargaining power in women's economic empowerment outcomes, and test product and program innovations that can directly address women's unique preferences and the challenges they may face."[23]

However, there is a dearth of knowledge on how to understand women's specific needs and preferences. As revealed through the study in the Philippines, there are substantial intranational and intra-community variations in the

21. Development agencies have made assistance available to these countries to increase female financial inclusion. For example, already, in the 1990s, JICA supported the early expansion of the Grameen Bank in Bangladesh by the ODA Loan. As observed in recent decades, the progress of female empowerment in Bangladesh, which is a specific feature of the miraculous socioeconomic development of Bangladesh, is largely attributable to the wide penetration of MFIs in the country (Mahmud and others 2018). In Pakistan, JICA has recently started a livelihood improvement project for female home-based workers in Sind Province through their financial inclusion using FinTech.

22. For material constraints, see Grohmann and others (2018). For physical distance, see Beck and others (2007). For cost of holding accounts, see Beck and others (2008). For social constraints, see Holloway and others (2017).

23. Holloway and others (2017).

situation of gender-equitable financial inclusion. Even within a single village, unbanked women are in heterogeneous degrees of financial inclusion and exclusion. Roughly half of unbanked women live in partially-banked households, suggesting that the reason they are unbanked may be different from the women in totally-unbanked households. Determining the commonly applicable needs and preferences of these different types of unbanked women can be challenging. Moreover, designing widely replicable policies and products addressing specific needs can also be quite difficult.

Data remains limited and expensive: it requires time to collect, and localized approaches take time to develop and implement. Therefore, in addition to field studies in developing countries, the world may benefit from the experiences of developed countries that achieved gender-equal financial inclusion decades ago. In developed countries, men and women use common products, and there seems to be no consensus that gender-differentiated products specifically addressing women's needs have played an important role in completing the full financial inclusion of women. Before the emergence of digital technologies, and before gender equality started to be seriously discussed, those countries had made progress in terms of achieving financial inclusion equally for both men and women. Therefore, along with deepening the understanding of women's needs and preferences in the various contexts in developing countries, it should be fruitful to also integrate the experiences of developed countries.

In addition to solutions within the reach of the financial sector, there could be nonfinancial approaches to facilitate women's financial inclusion. In this regard, some of JICA's experiences provide lessons on the potential of such approaches. For example, through the ex-post evaluation of a project aimed at facilitating the expansion of small-scale business loans and microfinance loans in Egypt, JICA found that women borrowers needed a variety of nonfinancial assistance, such as business and marketing consultation, information on other successful women entrepreneurs, and facilitation to acquire understanding and support from family members and relatives.[24]

Given the global and local diversity of the situation, realizing equal financial inclusion for men and women is important but remains challenging. Being attentive to this issue while facilitating international mutual learning of experiences from both developed and developing countries will be indispensable so as not to leave any woman behind.

---

24. Sueyoshi (2016).

References

AFI. 2016. Denarau Action Plan: The AFI Network Commitment to Gender and Women's Financial Inclusion. www.afi-global.org/sites/default/files/publications/2016-09/Denarau%20Action%20Plan.pdf.

———. 2017. Bridging the Gender Gap: Promoting Women's Financial Inclusion. www.afi-global.org/sites/default/files/publications/2017-11/AFI2017_Gender_full_AW_ISBN_digital.pdf.

Ashraf, Nava, Dean Karlan, and Wesley Yin. 2010. "Female Empowerment: Impact of a Commitment Savings Product in the Philippines." *World Development* 38, no. 3: 333–44.

Boyd, C., and U. Aldana. 2015. "The Impact of Financial Education on Conditional Cash Transfer Beneficiaries in Peru." In F. Veras and C. Robino, "Social Protection, Entrepreneurship and Labour Market Activation," *Policy in Focus* 12, no. 2. IPC-UNDP: pp. 26–27.

Bangko Sentral ng Pilipinas. 2015. National Strategy for Financial Inclusion. www.bsp.gov.ph/downloads/publications/2015/PhilippinesNSFIBooklet.pdf.

———. 2016. Financial Inclusion in the Philippines, no. 6. Series of 2016. www.bsp.gov.ph/downloads/Publications/2016/FIP_1Sem2016.pdf.

———. 2017a. Financial Inclusion Survey: Moving Towards Digital Financial Inclusion. www.bsp.gov.ph/downloads/Publications/2017/2017FISToplineReport.pdf.

———. 2017b. Report on the State of Financial Inclusion in the Philippines. www.bsp.gov.ph/downloads/Publications/2017/Financial%20Inclusion.pdf.

———. 2018. Financial Inclusion in the Philippines. Financial Inclusion Dashboard, no. 8. www.bsp.gov.ph/downloads/Publications/2018/FIP_1Sem2018.pdf.

Beck, Thorsten, Asli Demirguc-Kunt, and Maria Soledad Martinez Peria. 2007. "Reaching Out: Access to and Use of Banking Services across Countries." *Journal of Financial Economics* 85, no. 1: 234–66.

———. 2008. "Banking Services for Everyone? Barriers to Bank Access and Use around the World." *World Bank Economic Review* 22, no. 3: 397–430.

Grohmann, Antonia, Theres Kluhs, and Lukas Menkhoff. 2018. "Does Financial Literacy Improve Financial Inclusion? Cross Country Evidence." *World Development* 111: 84096.

Holloway, Kyle, Zahra Niazi, and Rebecca Rouse. 2017. "Women's Economic Empowerment Through Financial Inclusion: A Review of Existing Evidence and Remaining Knowledge Gaps." Innovations for Poverty Action. www.poverty-action.org/sites/default/files/publications/Womens-Economic-Empowerment-Through-Financial-Inclusion-Web.pdf.

Karlan, Dean, and others. 2017. "Impact of Saving Groups on the Lives of the Poor." Proceedings of the National Academy of Sciences of the United States of America. March: 201611520

Llanto, Gilberto M., Maureen Ane D. Rosellon, and Ma. Kristina P. Ortiz. 2018. Philippine Institute for Development Studies. Discussion Paper Series. 2018–2022.

Lopez, M. 2017. "E-Money Transactions Hit All-Time High in 2016." Business World Online. www.bworldonline.com/content.php?section=Finance&title=e-money-transactions-hit-all-time-high-in-2016&id=145584.

Mahmud, M., and others. 2018. "Development Transformation in Bangladesh: An Overview." In *Economic and Social Development of Bangladesh-Miracle and Challenges* edited by Y. Sawada, M. Mahmud, and N. Kitano. Cham: Palgrave Macmillan.

Matsuda, A., and others. 2019. "Financial Inclusion and Female Empowerment: Evidence from Honduras." Mimeo.

Prina, Silvia. 2015. "Banking the Poor via Savings Accounts: Evidence from a Field Experiment." *Journal of Development Economics* 115, issue C: 16–31.

Sueyoshi, Y. 2016. "FY2016 Ex-Post Evaluation of Japanese ODA Loan Project 'Micro Enterprise Assistance Project.'" www2.jica.go.jp/en/evaluation/pdf/2016_EG-P31_4.pdf.

Trivelli, C., and J. De los Ríos. 2014. In Breve 54: Creating Financial Assets: The Case for Savings Accounts as Means for Economic Independence and Empowerment for Women. Proyecto Capital.

UNSTAT. April 20, 2017. "Tier Classification for Global SDG Indicators." https://unstats.un.org/sdgs/files/Tier%20Classification%20of%20SDG%20Indicators_20%20April%202017_web.pdf.

World Bank. 2017. The Global Findex Database 2017. https://globalfindex.worldbank.org/node.

CHAPTER NINE

Leaving No One Behind
Can Tax-Funded Transfer Programs Provide Income Floors in Sub-Saharan Africa?

Nora Lustig, Jon Jellema, and Valentina Martinez Pabon

Introduction

Sub-Saharan Africa (SSA) has experienced remarkable growth since the mid-1990s. Real economic activity in the region grew 4.6 percent per year during the twenty-year period between 1996 and 2016. Several national economies in the region grew at a rate that exceeded 5 percent per year during this period. The gains from greater growth in SSA were achieved not only by resource-rich countries but also by non-resource-rich, low-income countries. However, while the share of the population living below the international poverty line of $1.90 a day declined from 55 percent in 1990 to 41 percent in 2015,[1] population growth

---

1. PovcalNet, http://iresearch.worldbank.org/PovcalNet/povDuplicateWB.aspx.

The authors are very grateful to David Coady, Homi Kharas, Landry Signé, and other participants for their invaluable comments and suggestions. We are also grateful to Stephen Arriz, Haley Renda, and Emilia Nordgren for excellent research assistantship. The empirical results presented in the section Taxes, Transfers, and Poverty under the Current Fiscal Systems of this chapter come from the background document "Fiscal Policy in Africa: Welfare Impacts and Policy Effectiveness" by Alejandro de la Fuente, Jon Jellema, and Nora Lustig (forthcoming). The authors are most grateful to the country-specific teams at the World Bank that shared data and useful inputs and for their thoughtful comments and advice. The findings, interpretations, and conclusions in this chapter are entirely those of the authors. The findings do not necessarily represent the view of the World Bank Group, its Executive Directors, or the countries they represent.

alone brought the absolute number of poor people from 280 million in 1990 to 413 million in 2015. Furthermore, Sub-Saharan Africa was the only developing region that did not attain the Millennium Development Goal 1 (MDG 1) of halving extreme poverty by 2015.

Given that economic growth alone will take a long time to substantially reduce poverty, could countries in SSA rely on tax-funded cash transfers to provide income floors in the meantime? Leaving aside the politics of tax and subsidies reforms and the administrative challenges faced by large-scale cash transfer programs, the answer depends crucially on whether the resources required to provide an adequate income floor can be raised in practice. There are two obvious sources for additional spending: foregone subsidy expenditure and increased tax collection. In countries where subsidies (especially energy subsidies) are still common, would income floors be achievable by eliminating subsidies and reallocating the resources to cash transfers? Otherwise, how much would taxes need to be increased to finance the income floor?

In this chapter, we estimate the poverty impact and the incidence of taxes of implementing alternative income floors through cash transfers in nine SSA countries: Comoros, Ghana, Ivory Coast, Namibia, South Africa, Tanzania, Togo, Uganda, and Zambia. The "income floors" are defined in two ways: using the World Bank International Poverty Line of US$1.90 a day (in 2011 PPP)[2] for all countries and using the World Bank Income Class International Poverty Lines, which vary by countries' income levels.[3] For the set of countries in this analysis, there are three income class-specific poverty lines: US$1.90 a day for low income countries (Comoros, Tanzania, Togo, and Uganda); US$3.20 a day for lower middle-income countries (Ghana, Ivory Coast, and Zambia); and, US$5.50 a day for upper middle-income countries (Namibia and South Africa).

Results vary by country but in general are not encouraging. Providing an income floor by raising domestic taxes frequently implies such large increases in additional taxes that disincentives and negative impacts on tax collection are potentially huge. Some options become infeasible when taxes are increased to such a degree that certain individuals are left with negative incomes.

The main source of information used in this chapter are the fiscal incidence analyses completed by the CEQ Institute together with the World Bank, the IMF, and the OECD; where permission has been given, these analyses are summarized in the CEQ Data Center on Fiscal Redistribution (CEQ Data Center).[4] The

---

2. This International Poverty Line is used to track progress of Goal 1, Target 1 of the Sustainable Development Goals.

3. See Jolliffe and Prydz (2016).

4. This data is available upon request except in the cases in which authors or other organizations have proprietary rights. In these cases, the request must be placed directly to the author or

household surveys used in the fiscal incidence studies were enumerated between 2010 and 2015.[5] These studies use the common methodological framework described in Nora Lustig (2018), allowing sound cross-country comparisons.[6]

The country set in this analysis is limited by data availability; nonetheless, our sample represents diversity in both macroeconomic and fiscal characteristics. According to the World Bank classification system, for example, four are low-income countries (Comoros, Tanzania, Togo, and Uganda), three lower middle-income countries (Ghana, Ivory Coast, and Zambia), and two upper middle-income ones (Namibia and South Africa). Comoros, Uganda, and Tanzania are in East Africa; Zambia, South Africa, and Namibia in Southern Africa; and Ghana, Ivory Coast, and Togo in West Africa. The nine countries also feature distinct public social welfare systems. In particular, government spending on cash transfer programs as a percent of pre-fiscal income ranges from zero or almost zero (Comoros, Ivory Coast, Togo, and Uganda); above 0.1 percent but less than 0.5 percent (Ghana, Tanzania, and Zambia); to levels of spending comparable to advanced OECD countries in Namibia and South Africa (4.3 percent and 6 percent, respectively). Except for Namibia and South Africa, subsidies (in particular, energy subsidies) represent between 70 and 100 percent of government spending in the combined category of transfers and subsidies (table 9-1).[7, 8]

organization. For information, please contact Jon Jellema: (jon.jellema@ceqinstitute.org). For a country-specific description of the fiscal systems and assumptions, please see: for Comoros, World Bank (2017); for Ghana, Younger, Osei-Assibey, and Oppong (2017); for Ivory Coast, Jellema and Tassot (forthcoming); for Namibia, Namibia Statistics Agency and World Bank (2017); for South Africa, Inchauste and others (2017); for Tanzania, Younger, Myamba, and Mdadila (2016b); for Togo, Jellema and Tassot (2018); for Uganda, Jellema and others (2018); for Zambia, de la Fuente and others (2017).

5. The household surveys are Comoros: Enquête sur L'emploi, le Secteur Informel et la Consommation des Ménages aux Comores (2014); Ghana: Living Standards Survey (2012–2013); Ivory Coast: Enquête sur le Niveau de Vie des Ménages (2015); Namibia Household Income and Expenditure Survey (2009–2010); South Africa: Income and Expenditure Survey (2010–2011); Tanzania: Household Budget Survey (2011–2012); Togo: Questionnaire des Indicateurs de Base du Bien-être (2015); Uganda: National Household Survey (2012–2013); and, Zambia: Living Conditions Monitoring Survey (2015). Except for South Africa's household survey, which reports on incomes and expenditures, the rest of the countries' surveys report consumption. Whether income or consumption, the welfare measure includes consumption of own production (except for South Africa) and imputed rent for owner's occupied housing (except for Tanzania).

6. For details, see chapters 1, 4, 6, and 8 in Lustig (2018).

7. Note that the size of taxes and transfers with respect to pre-fiscal income, shown in table 9-1, is calculated as the ratio of taxes and transfers included in the fiscal incidence analysis to the pre-fiscal incomes in the household surveys and, thus, will not equal the ratio of taxes and transfers to GDP calculated from administrative data, except by chance.

8. As explained in the text, the size of taxes and transfers come from the fiscal incidence exercise and not from the country's fiscal administrative accounts.

Table 9-1. Gross National Income per Capita, Population, and the Size of Taxes and Transfers

	Characteristics					Taxes, transfers, and subsidies as a share of pre-fiscal income (%)								
Country	Development category (2018)	Year of Survey	GNI/ capita (2011 ppp)	GNI/ capita growth (%) 2013-17	Population	Direct taxes	Indirect taxes	Total taxes	Indirect taxes as a share of total taxes	Direct transfers	Indirect subsidies	Total transfers plus subsidies	Subsidies as a share of Total Transfers	Total Transfers plus subsidies as a share of Total Taxes
Comoros	LI	2014	2,529	0.3	747,155	1.26	2.20	3.46	63.6	0.00	0.00	0.00	0	0.0
Ghana	LMI	2013	3,724	2.6	26,347,424	4.55	6.31	10.86	58.0	0.16	2.13	2.28	93	21.0
Ivory Coast	LMI	2015	3,142	5.8	23,110,501	1.08	4.22	5.30	79.6	0.00	0.48	0.48	100	9.1
Namibia	UMI	2010	8,139	1.8	2,059,840	7.74	6.73	14.47	46.5	4.29	0.85	5.15	17	35.6
South Africa	UMI	2010	11,639	0.1	50,423,022	19.54	13.70	33.23	41.2	5.94	0.91	6.84	13	20.6
Tanzania	LI	2011	2,169	3.9	42,270,137	4.33	6.69	11.03	60.7	0.42	1.08	1.50	72	13.6
Togo	LI	2015	1,520	3.4	7,008,900	0.94	12.08	13.02	92.8	0.00	0.20	0.20	100	1.5
Uganda	LI	2012	1,576	1.0	32,250,627	2.68	2.03	4.71	43.2	0.09	0.26	0.35	73	7.5
Zambia	LMI	2015	NA	NA	15,403,570	0.70	6.60	7.31	90.4	0.28	1.81	2.09	87	28.6
Average (except for population)			4,305	2.4	199,621,177	4.76	6.73	11.49	64.01	1.24	0.86	2.10	41	15.3

Note: Taxes and transfers are shown as as a share of pre-fiscal income (Market Income plus Pensions) unless otherwise noted.

Source: Comoros (Belghith and others 2017); Ghana (Younger, Osei-Assibey, and Oppong 2016); Ivory Coast (Tassot and Jellema 2019); Namibia (Sulla, Zikhali, and Jellema 2016); South Africa (Inchauste and others 2017); Tanzania (Younger, Myamba, and Mdadila 2016a); Togo (Tassot and Jellema 2018); Uganda (Jellema and others 2016); Zambia (de la Fuente, Jellema, and Rosales 2018). WDI, https://data.worldbank.org/indicator/SI.POV.NAHC.

The section that follows presents the impact on poverty of the current fiscal systems of taxes and transfers. The next section, "Poverty and Tax Burden under Alternative Policy Scenarios," presents the results of alternative simulated policy scenarios. Conclusions are presented in the last section. Additional methodological details are described in an online appendix.[9]

Taxes, Transfers, and Poverty under the Current Fiscal Systems

Measuring the Impact of Taxes and Transfers on Inequality and Poverty: Methodology

The results presented in this section are based on Alejandro de la Fuente, Jon Jellema, and Nora Lustig (forthcoming), and use as inputs the fiscal incidence analyses cited in table 9-1. Applying what is known in the literature as the accounting approach, these fiscal incidence studies estimate how the burden of taxes and the benefits of transfers and subsidies are distributed among individuals. The studies provide estimates of the impact of the fiscal system on poverty and inequality via the calculation of pre-fiscal and post-fiscal income concepts.

The pre-fiscal income concept used here is equal to earned and unearned income from wages and capital,[10] plus private transfers, plus pensions from public contributory pension systems.[11] Income from noncontributory pensions (also known as social pensions), in contrast, is treated as a government transfer. Post-fiscal income here is equivalent to the CEQ Assessment "Consumable Income" concept.[12] Starting from pre-fiscal income, consumable income is constructed by adding direct cash transfers (conditional and unconditional; pure cash or near-cash transfers) and subsidies (electricity, food, fuel, etc.), and subtracting direct taxes (payroll taxes, personal income taxes, etc.) and indirect taxes (VAT, excise taxes, sales taxes, etc.).[13] Once pre-fiscal and consumable incomes are available

9. The appendix can be found online at http://commitmentoequity.org and is also available upon request.

10. Incomes from capital tend to be grossly underreported in household surveys. In particular, they do not include undistributed profits, for example.

11. In other words, income from old-age pensions in contributory systems is considered part of pre-fiscal income (contributions are treated as a form of forced savings) and not treated as a government transfer. The rationale behind this assumption is discussed by Lustig and Higgins in chapter 1 of Lustig (2018). For some of the nine countries, the scenario with contributory pensions treated as government transfers is available upon request.

12. Note that this welfare variable is different from international databases such as the World Bank's PovCal report. The inequality and poverty indicators in international databases are (primarily) for disposable income; that is, they never include the effect of indirect taxes or subsidies on measured inequality and poverty.

13. Our analysis does not use the concept *final income* because we focus on the cash portion

for each individual, we proceed to estimate the inequality and poverty indicators and compare them.[14]

The fiscal incidence studies used here are point-in-time rather than lifecycle and do not incorporate behavioral or general equilibrium effects. That is, we do not claim that the pre-fiscal income reported here equals the true counterfactual income in the absence of taxes and transfers. It is a first-order approximation.[15] Moreover, although public spending on, for example, education, health, and infrastructure has an inherent investment element that is likely to affect long-run inequality and poverty dynamics, typical fiscal incidence analysis does not capture these dynamic effects.

The analyses here are not, however, mechanical accounting applications. We analyze the incidence of taxes by their economic rather than their statutory incidence, and take into account tax evasion. Typically, individuals who do not report being registered in the social security administration are assumed not to pay personal income and payroll taxes. In the case of consumption taxes, for purchases from informal sellers, it is assumed that no consumption taxes are paid (at least, directly at the time of purchase, although the price of the good may carry the effect of taxes on inputs). If there is no information on the place of purchase, some studies assume that households in rural areas do not pay consumption taxes. We assume that payroll taxes and contributions (both by employee and employer) in the formal sector are borne by labor and that consumption taxes (and subsidies) are fully shifted forward to consumers. This is equivalent to assuming that the supply of labor and demand for goods and services are perfectly inelastic.[16] In all but the case of Uganda, the fiscal incidence analyses incorporated the indirect effects of subsidies (and indirect taxes).[17]

of the fiscal system. Results including final income and the progressivity of education and health spending can be found in de la Fuente, Jellema, and Lustig (forthcoming).

14. In the section Poverty and Tax Burden under Alternative Policy Scenarios, we also present results for the impact on poverty under alternative simulation scenarios with the gross income concept, which equals pre-fiscal, plus cash transfers (and before any taxes).

15. In a variety of settings, a first-order approximation suffices for a reasonable impact estimate. David Coady and others, for instance, state, "The first order estimate is much easier to calculate, provides a bound on the real-income effect, and is likely to closely approximate a more sophisticated estimate. Finally, since one expects that short-run substitution elasticities are smaller than long-run elasticities, the first-order estimate will be a better approximation of the short-run welfare impact" (Coady and others 2006, p. 9).

16. The economic incidence, strictly speaking, depends on the elasticity of demand and/or supply of a factor or a good, and the ensuing general equilibrium effects. In essence, the accounting approach implicitly assumes zero demand price and labor supply elasticities, and zero elasticities of substitution among inputs, which may not be far-fetched assumptions for analyzing effects in the short run, especially when changes are small. For more details on methodological assumptions, see the appendix posted online at http://commitmentoequity.org.

17. Comoros has no subsidies. The following countries in our sample include the indirect effects:

Indirect effects may occur when the subsidized (taxed) good is used as an input in the production of other goods. For example, fuel subsidies have a direct benefit to consumers when they buy gasoline or kerosene and an indirect benefit in the form of lower transport prices.

Measuring the Impact of Taxes and Transfers on Inequality and Poverty: Results

What is the impact of the current fiscal system on poverty?[18] We examine three different indicators (or indicator sets) to answer this question. We estimate "traditional" indicators like the poverty headcount ratio or poverty gap at both pre- and post-fiscal incomes. We also estimate the extent to which the pre-fiscal poor populations end up as "net payers" to the fiscal system (rather than "net recipients") in cash terms.[19] A third indicator—Fiscal Impoverishment, proposed by Higgins and Lustig (2016)—measures the extent to which fiscal policy makes the post-fiscal poor *poorer* or contributes to the transformation of the pre-fiscal non-poor population into the post-fiscal poor population.[20]

As shown in table 9-2 panel (a), with the exception of Namibia and South Africa, the combined effect of the existing system of taxes (direct and indirect) and transfers (direct cash and near-cash transfers and subsidies) increases post-fiscal poverty or leaves it unchanged even if measured with the extreme international poverty line of US$1.90 a day.[21] Note that the increase in poverty occurs despite the fact that inequality falls, which emphasizes that inequality-reducing policies *do not necessarily* protect poor and vulnerable households. Moreover, the extent of fiscal

Ghana: indirect effects for VAT and electricity subsidies; Ivory Coast: indirect effects for indirect taxes and electricity. The subsidies are allocated to households based on their share of electricity consumption as a proportion of total consumption of electricity; Namibia: indirect effects for taxes and subsidies are estimated using the Input-Output method (Jellema and Inchauste 2018); South Africa: indirect effects for taxes and subsidies are estimated using the Input-Output method; Tanzania: indirect effects for petroleum and import duties but no indirect effects for value added tax or subsidies; Togo: indirect effects for indirect taxes and electricity subsidies. The subsidies are allocated to households based on their share of electricity consumption as a proportion of total consumption of electricity; Zambia: indirect effects for taxes and subsidies are estimated using the Input-Output method. For more details, see the appendix posted online at http://commitmento equity.org.

18. By "current" we mean the fiscal system that prevailed in the year of the household survey.

19. That is to say, without the addition of benefits provided via in-kind services.

20. As shown by Sean Higgins and Nora Lustig (2016), there are several indicators of fiscal impoverishment that fulfill the basic desirable axioms of a poverty measure. In this chapter, the proportion of impoverished (in the sense described here) as a share of the total population is used.

21. The SDG 1 uses the $1.25 per day measured in 2005 purchasing power parity international poverty line, which is equivalent to the $1.90 per day 2011 purchasing power parity international poverty line. The latter formally replaced the $1.25 poverty line in October 2015. See www.world bank.org/en/topic/poverty/brief/global-poverty-line-faq.

Table 9-2. Baseline: Fiscal Policy's Impact on Poverty and Fiscal Impoverishment

Panel (a) $1.90 a Day International Poverty Line

Country	Survey year	Baseline Market income plus pensions (pre-fiscal)			Baseline Consumable income (post-fiscal)						Fiscal Impoverishment Headcount (%)
		Headcount (%)	Squared poverty gap (%)	Gini	Headcount (%)		Squared poverty gap (%)		Gini		
Comoros	2014	13.6	1.6	0.44	14.1	+	1.7	+	0.43	–	13.8
Ghana	2013	10.5	1.4	0.44	11.9	+	1.5	+	0.42	–	9.6
Ivory Coast	2015	21.2	2.9	0.40	22.9	+	3.2	+	0.40	=	21.7
Namibia	2010	30.4	7.5	0.65	26.2	–	3.3	–	0.60	–	15.7
South Africa	2010	30.4	13.8	0.72	19.6	–	2.6	–	0.63	–	3.9
Tanzania	2011	49.6	6.6	0.38	53.5	+	7.4	+	0.35	–	50.0
Togo	2015	35.6	5.9	0.40	41.4	+	7.3	+	0.39	–	41.8
Uganda	2012	37.3	5.0	0.44	38.1	+	5.0	=	0.42	–	29.2
Zambia	2015	57.0	18.2	0.56	58.1	+	18.4	=	0.55	–	46.5

Panel (b) Country-Specific International Poverty Lines

Country	Survey year	Baseline Market income plus pensions (pre-fiscal)			Baseline Consumable income (post-fiscal)						Fiscal Impoverishment Headcount (%)
		Headcount (%)	Squared poverty gap (%)	Gini	Headcount (%)		Squared poverty gap (%)		Gini		
Comoros	2014	13.6	1.6	0.44	14.1	+	1.7	+	0.43	-	13.8
Ghana	2013	29.8	4.7	0.44	32.2	+	5.2	+	0.42	-	27.6
Ivory Coast	2015	50.6	9.4	0.40	52.7	+	10.0	+	0.40	=	50.8
Namibia	2010	68.3	27.3	0.65	70.3	+	24.0	-	0.60	-	46.1
South Africa	2010	57.9	27.6	0.72	59.9	+	18.9	-	0.63	-	19.7
Tanzania	2011	49.6	6.6	0.38	53.5	+	7.4	+	0.35	-	50.0
Togo	2015	35.6	5.9	0.40	41.4	+	7.3	+	0.39	-	41.8
Uganda	2012	37.3	5.0	0.44	38.1	+	5.0	=	0.42	-	29.2
Zambia	2015	74.5	30.8	0.56	76.1	+	31.4	+	0.55	-	63.0

Notes: For panel (b): Comoros, Tanzania, Togo, and Uganda: $1.90 a day international poverty line. Ghana, Ivory Coast, and Zambia: $3.20 a day country-specific international poverty line. Namibia and South Africa: $5.50 a day country-specific international poverty line. Fiscal impoverishment, or FI, is the number of pre-fiscal poor (nonpoor) who are made poorer (poor) at post-fiscal income by fiscal policy (i.e., the existing combination of taxes, transfers, and subsidies) measured as a share of the total population.

Source: de la Fuente, Jellema, and Lustig (forthcoming) based on Comoros (Belghith and others 2017); Ghana (Younger, Osei-Assibey, and Oppong 2016); Ivory Coast (Tassot and Jellema 2019); Namibia (Sulla, Zikhali, and Jellema 2016); South Africa (Inchauste and others 2017); Tanzania (Younger, Myamba, and Mdadila 2016a); Togo (Tassot and Jellema 2018); Uganda (Jellema and others 2016); and, Zambia (de la Fuente, Jellema, and Rosales 2018).

impoverishment exceeds 20 percent in five of the nine of countries and is above 40 percent in Tanzania, Togo, and Zambia. Even in countries where the poverty headcount rate falls, as in Namibia, fiscal impoverishment reaches more than 10 percent of the total population. As shown in panel (b) of table 9-2, with country-specific poverty lines, the post-fiscal headcount ratio is higher for all countries, and the squared poverty gap is higher for all but Namibia, South Africa, and Uganda. In no country is the fiscal impoverishment ratio lower than 10 percent, and it is higher than 40 percent in Ivory Coast, Namibia, Tanzania, Togo, and Zambia.

Another indicator of the impact of taxes and transfers on living standards is their incidence. Figure 9-1 shows the extent to which, on average, individuals in the decile specified on the horizontal axis are net receivers from or net payers to the fiscal system. Net receivers are those individuals for whom post-fiscal income is *higher* than pre-fiscal income, indicating that tax burdens are smaller (in absolute magnitude) than total benefits received from transfer and subsidy expenditures. Net payers are those individuals for whom post-fiscal income is *lower* than pre-fiscal income, indicating that tax burdens are larger (in absolute magnitude) than total benefits received from transfer and subsidy expenditures. With the exception of

Figure 9-1. Baseline: Net Payers of the Fiscal System by Decile

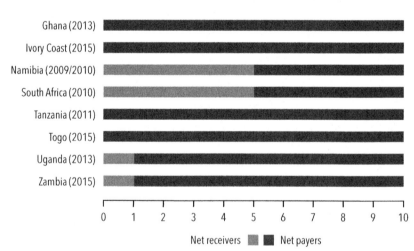

Source: de la Fuente, Jellema, and Lustig (forthcoming) based on Comoros (Belghith and others 2017); Ghana (Younger, Osei-Assibey, and Oppong 2016); Ivory Coast (Tassot and Jellema 2019); Namibia (Sulla, Zikhali, and Jellema 2016); South Africa (Inchauste and others 2017); Tanzania (Younger, Myamba, and Mdadila 2016a); Togo (Tassot and Jellema 2018); Uganda (Jellema and others 2016); and, Zambia (de la Fuente, Jellema, and Rosales 2018).

Namibia and South Africa (and to a much lesser degree, Uganda and Zambia), the entire population—including the poor—are, on average, net payers into the system.

In principle, it is desirable for the poor—especially the extreme poor—to be net receivers of fiscal resources in cash so that poor individuals can consume the minimum amounts of food and other essential goods accounted for in the estimation of poverty-line expenditure. As discussed in de la Fuente, Jellema, and Lustig (forthcoming), the proximate causes for fiscal impoverishment in our sample of countries is the reliance on indirect taxes as the main channel to collect transfers, combined with the fact that a very large portion of the resources (70 percent or more in six of our nine countries) is spent on general price subsidies (especially on energy subsidies) rather than on direct transfers (see table 9-1). Excise taxes, VAT, and other indirect taxes affect every individual—rich or poor—consuming goods or services, some of which will carry an explicit or implicit indirect tax charge.

According to de la Fuente, Jellema, and Lustig (forthcoming),

> As the ratio of consumption to income tends to be higher for poor households, indirect taxes—when measured as a share of own income—often weigh more heavily on the poor even while in absolute terms richer households bear a greater burden from indirect taxes. For households living at or near the poverty line, the reduction in purchasing power (over real goods and services) from indirect taxes can drive their real expenditure levels below the poverty line.

On the spending side, as shown by Coady, V. Flamini, and L. Sears (2015), a very large share of benefits from price subsidies in general goes to high-income households. In our sample, in seven of nine countries, the richest 10 percent of individuals capture a share of subsidy expenditures that is higher than 10 percent (figure 9-2).[22]

---

22. It is also the case that, in all countries but Namibia 80 percent or more of tax revenues are allocated to other spending categories (different from transfers or subsidies). The latter include spending on education, health, and infrastructure, as well as public goods. Leaving aside corruption, high wages for bureaucrats, and waste, this type of spending should create at least some benefits to the poor in the form of access to services and/or higher economic growth. However, the question is whether the extreme poor (especially those below the international poverty line of $1.90 a day) should have to (implicitly) pay for these benefits given that, by definition, they do not have enough money to cover their basic needs.

Figure 9-2. Baseline: Concentration Share of
Subsidies in the Richest 10 Percent

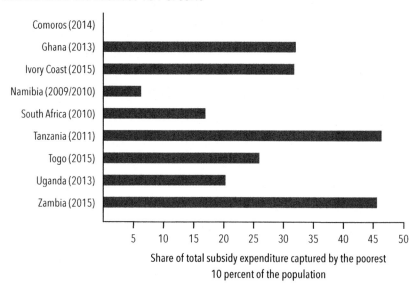

Share of total subsidy expenditure captured by the poorest
10 percent of the population

Source: de la Fuente, Jellema and Lustig (forthcoming) based on Comoros (Belghith and others 2017); Ghana (Younger, Osei-Assibey and Oppong 2016); Ivory Coast (Tassot and Jellema 2019); Namibia (Sulla, Zikhali and Jellema 2016); South Africa (Inchauste and others 2017); Tanzania (Younger, Myamba and Mdadila 2016a); Togo (Tassot and Jellema 2018); Uganda (Jellema and others 2016); and. Zambia (de la Fuente, Jellema and Rosales 2018).

Poverty and Tax Burden under Alternative Policy Scenarios

Measuring the Impact of Changing the Size, Targeting, and Coverage of Cash Transfers under Alternative Financing Scenarios: Methodology

In this section, we estimate the impact on poverty and the incidence of taxes of implementing alternative scenarios for increasing cash transfer spending in Comoros, Ghana, Ivory Coast, Namibia, South Africa, Tanzania, Togo, Uganda, and Zambia. Specifically, we simulate the first-round effects on poverty and the incidence of taxes that result from changing the existing cash transfer system (called the baseline scenario) by alternative budget-neutral "policy" scenarios in which the size, targeting, and/or coverage of the transfers is changed.[23] By

---

23. Cash transfer programs included in the baseline cover noncontributory programs only; that is, means-tested conditional and unconditional cash transfers, cash transfers based on categorical targeting (for example, people with disabilities), and noncontributory pensions. The programs included in our baseline analysis by country are described in the appendix posted online at http://commitmentoequity.org.

budget-neutral, we mean that if the scenario entails an increase in spending, we allow taxes to increase so the financing gap is closed. In all simulated scenarios, we assume that current subsidy spending is eliminated, and the saved resources are used to increase the budget available for cash transfers. In other words, we assume that the first source of financing the transfer to attain the corresponding income floor is the elimination of price subsidies.

How should one define sensible transfer magnitudes? If we wish to provide an income floor equivalent to poverty-line expenditure, should one use the same poverty line for all countries or use country-specific international poverty lines?[24] Since there are arguments in favor of both, here we produce poverty results for the baseline and the simulated scenarios using the World Bank International Poverty Line of US$1.90 a day (in 2011 PPP)[25] and the World Bank Income Class International Poverty Lines, which vary by countries' income levels since, in richer countries, higher international poverty lines are more appropriate. As described by Jolliffe and Prydz (2016), each income class-specific poverty line is chosen as the median of the national poverty lines of the countries in that income class. Specifically, there are three income class-specific poverty lines: US$1.90 a day for low income countries (Comoros, Tanzania, Togo, and Uganda); US$3.20 a day for lower middle-income countries (Ghana, Ivory Coast, and Zambia); and US$5.50 a day for upper middle-income countries (Namibia and South Africa).

Our scenarios first consider a spending-neutral[26] reallocation of current expenditures on transfers and consumption subsidies. We generate these scenarios to demonstrate how much fiscally-induced poverty reduction is diminished when spending on transfers is shifted from targeted to universal schemes. Spending-neutral scenarios are also useful to estimate how much is gained in terms of fiscally-induced poverty reduction if current spending on subsidies is reallocated to universal cash transfers. In particular, we are able to determine how much poverty remains even after such a significant shift in expenditures in countries that start out with significant resources devoted to consumption subsidies. The

24. These country-specific international poverty lines should not be confused with national extreme or moderate poverty lines.

25. Goal 1, target 1 of the Sustainable Development Goals (SDGs) specifies: "By 2030, eradicate extreme poverty for all people everywhere, currently measured as people living on less than $1.25 a day." See https://sustainabledevelopment.un.org/topics/povertyeradication. The $1.25 poverty line was calculated using the purchasing power parity conversion factors for 2005. In October 2015, however, the official international poverty line to track SDG progress was changed to $1.90 a day, which was calculated using the 2011 purchasing power parity conversion factors. See www.worldbank.org/en/topic/poverty/brief/global-poverty-line-faq.

26. In order to simplify the analysis, we have assumed current program-specific expenditures can be transformed costlessly into other program-specific expenditures.

second set of scenarios generates and allocates transfers that are (roughly) equivalent to the average poverty gap, and the third set generates and allocates transfers that are equivalent to poverty-line expenditure.

For each of the spending-neutral, poverty gap, and poverty-line scenarios, we generate two different coverage levels:

- Perfectly-targeted, in which total resources are allocated first among the poor in lexicographic order (starting from the poorest). When available resources are capped (as in the spending-neutral scenario), transfers are allocated first to the very poorest individual until her income is equivalent to the next-poorest individual; then to those two individuals until their individual incomes are equivalent to the third-poorest individual; then to those three individuals until their individual incomes are equivalent to the fourth-poorest individual; and so on until available resources are exhausted. In the targeted poverty gap scenario, each poor individual receives a transfer equivalent to her actual poverty gap[27] and in the targeted poverty line scenario, each poor individual receives a transfer equivalent to the corresponding poverty line.

- Universal, in which we divide total resources by total population and give each individual this average in the form of a universal basic income (UBI).

Whenever the spending-neutral reform does not provide enough additional expenditure for the coverage target—that is, when government spending on simulated transfers is higher than current spending on transfers and subsidies—we simulate the effect of the required increase in taxes necessary to provide funding for the additional transfer spending. We consider two types of tax increases: a proportional increase in direct taxes and a proportional increase in indirect taxes. Table 9-3 summarizes these ten scenarios and their characteristics.

Larger transfers with higher coverage levels imply greater increases in expenditure and therefore greater increases in additional taxes to fund that expenditure. The most expensive scenario—providing a poverty-line transfer to everyone (scenario 10 in table 9-3)—is clearly infeasible for most fiscal systems while implying overall burdens from taxes that are incompatible with most reasonable estimates of labor market and consumption behavior. We chose to include scenario 10 anyway, as it allows us to demonstrate the impossibility (in practical terms) of

---

27. In perfectly-targeted, spending-neutral and poverty gap scenarios, the covered population receives non-uniform transfers such that the post-transfer income in the covered population is uniform.

implementing a UBI strategy in the set of middle- and low-income countries we have analyzed here.[28]

As discussed, to capture the impact on living standards after considering the financing mechanisms, the relevant post-fiscal welfare variable is per capita consumable income. To assess whether a scenario is welfare-increasing or welfare-reducing, we calculate the change in poverty measured with consumable income vis-à-vis pre-fiscal income for each of the ten transfers-cum-financing scenarios. We then compare these changes with the analogous change in poverty observed in the baseline scenario.

In our simulations, we estimate the effect on poverty using two poverty measures: the poverty headcount and the squared poverty gap. In this chapter, we show results only for the latter, but the former are available upon request. There is a clear rationale in using these two measures: the poverty headcount is widely used in policy circles but fails to capture the impact of poverty reforms among the extreme poor. To give an example, assume that direct transfers cover the extreme poor, but fewer households whose income or consumption lies close to the poverty line (which is the case, for instance, in South Africa). As shown in Jamele Rigolini and others (forthcoming), "a spending-neutral UBI reform may show greater poverty reduction when measured with the poverty headcount index (because with the UBI all households close to the poverty line would now receive a transfer—and hence "jump" over the poverty line); but the reform would come at the expense of higher extreme poverty, because the budget would be 'taken away' from the extreme poor to be redistributed among a greater number of people. The squared poverty gap measure, by giving a greater weight to the welfare of the extreme poor, would capture such an increase in extreme poverty."

As indicated, we produce the policy simulations using the $1.90 per day international poverty line and country-specific international poverty lines that change depending on the development category assigned by the World Bank's classification system.

To recapitulate, our simulations consist of replacing the baseline spending on cash transfer programs and consumption subsidies with the ten simulated policy scenarios described above and summarized in table 9-3. These policy scenarios, however, should not be interpreted as normative country-specific proposals. Our intention is to explore the implications on poverty if existing resources were better targeted and the implications for the distribution of tax burdens if we wanted to raise more domestic resources to provide an income floor for the poor or across the board (as in a UBI program). In addition, as indicated from the start, these

---

28. See, for example, Acemoglu (2019) and references therein for a current summary of the debate surrounding UBI strategies.

Table 9-3. Policy Scenarios: A Summary

Scenario		Transfer System	Budget	Source of additional financing*	Eligibility rules	Average transfer per beneficiary	Allocation rule
1	Spending Neutral	Targeted	Total direct transfers and subsidies in current system	Not applicable	Anybody with prefiscal income below the selected poverty line (International $1.90 or International Country-specific)	Total spending on cash transfers and subsidies in baseline divided by the sum of individuals reached by the allocation rule	Allocation proceeds lexicographically as follows: starting with the poorest individual, she or he receives a transfer until her/his income equals the income of the second poorest individual; then the poorest and second poorest individuals receive transfers until their incomes are equal to the income of the third poorest individual, and so on. This procedure is repeated until resources are exhausted
2		Universal			Total population	Total spending on cash transfers and subsidies in baseline divided by the total population	Allocated to every individual
3	Poverty Gap	Targeted	Total poverty gap	Direct Taxes	Anybody with prefiscal income below the selected poverty line (International $1.90 or International Country-specific)	Average poverty gap	Allocated to individuals below the selected poverty line in the amount necessary to close each individual's poverty gap
4		Targeted		Indirect Taxes		Average poverty gap	
5		Universal	Average poverty gap times total population	Direct Taxes	Total population	Average poverty gap	Allocated to every individual
6		Universal		Indirect Taxes		Average poverty gap	

7	Poverty Line	Targeted	Selected poverty line times the number of individuals with prefiscal income below the selected poverty line	Direct Taxes	Anybody with prefiscal income below the selected poverty line (International $1.90 or International Country-specific)	Allocated to individuals below the selected poverty line
8				Indirect Taxes	International $1.90 poverty line and International Country-specific poverty line	
9		Universal	Selected poverty line times total population	Direct Taxes	Total population	Allocated to every individual
10				Indirect Taxes		

Note: The budget available in scenarios 1 and 2 is also available in scenarios 3 to 10, therefore only scenarios 3 to 10 require additional financing.

simulations contemplate first-order effects only. In particular, pre-fiscal incomes do not change in response to simulated taxes and transfers. In reality, any policy changes of the type simulated here would induce behavioral responses and general equilibria would have to be redetermined; pre-fiscal incomes would likely be different from the baseline. One of the key points of this hypothetical exercise is, in fact, to show that these non-marginal changes could potentially result in such large disincentive effects in the labor market and associated tax efficiency costs that they should not realistically be considered economically or politically feasible policy options.

Measuring the Impact of Changing the Size, Targeting, and Coverage of Cash Transfers under Alternative Financing Scenarios: Results

To start, we compare the average transfer to the poor and the coverage of the poor population under the alternative scenarios.[29] These are shown in table 9-4. As expected, if subsidies are replaced by transfers in full, under the spending-neutral scenario, when resources are targeted to the poor (in lexicographic order) until resources are exhausted, the average spending per poor person is higher than in the baseline, but the coverage is significantly lower. If instead of targeting resources, baseline spending on transfers and subsidies is divided by the entire population (a UBI), the average transfer is, of course, lower than when resources are targeted, but at the same time, the average transfer is higher than the baseline in all but Namibia and South Africa, where spending on subsidies is relatively small (compared to transfers, that is). By definition, the average transfer in the poverty gap scenario will tend to be higher than in the baseline. In the poverty line scenario, it will be higher than in the baseline and the poverty gap scenario. By construction, the average transfers under the targeted and the universal scenarios are identical. The average transfer equals the average poverty gap in the poverty gap scenario and the $1.90 per day international poverty line (panel [a]) and the country-specific international poverty lines in the poverty line scenario (panel [b]).

What is the impact of the alternative policy scenarios on poverty? Because the headcount ratio is sensitive to movements of individuals (into or out of poverty) around the poverty line, we focus on the impact on the squared poverty gap, an indicator that is more sensitive to the reduction in poverty the poorer individuals are and, thus, more in line with our concern in providing an income floor.[30] Tables 9-5 and 9-6 show the impact on the squared poverty gap for the baseline and the ten policy scenarios with the $1.90 international poverty line and the

29. Table 9-4 includes the spending scenarios only because the size and coverage of transfers are not affected by how the financing gap is funded (for example, by direct or indirect taxes).

30. Results using the headcount ratio are available upon request.

country-specific international poverty lines, respectively. In panel (a), we show the change (in percent) between the squared poverty gap measured with gross income (pre-fiscal income plus transfers) and the squared poverty gap measured with pre-fiscal income. By definition, results in panel (a) do not include the effect of the additional taxes needed to make the proposed change budget neutral. Panels (b) and (c) show the change between the squared poverty gap measured with consumable income (which includes the impact of direct and indirect taxes) and the squared poverty gap measured with pre-fiscal income. The results shown in panel (b) are calculated assuming the financing gap is fully funded with a proportional increase in direct taxes: that is, everyone's direct taxes are increased in the same proportion. The results shown in panel (c) are calculated assuming the financing gap is fully funded with a proportional increase in indirect taxes: that is, everyone's indirect taxes are increased in the same proportion.

As shown in panel (a) in tables 9-5 and 9-6, before considering the required increase in taxes, poverty would be eliminated in full or almost in full if transfers are made equal to the average poverty gap (columns 4 and 5) or the poverty line (last two columns). Incorporating the effect of higher taxes, however, changes the conclusions significantly. When taking into account the required increase in taxes, some of the population's consumable income becomes negative, and there is extreme reranking (in some countries, the pre-fiscal top incomes end up with negative incomes after taxes and, thus, move from being the pre-fiscal richest to the poorest of the population).[31] These scenarios are infeasible because some individuals would have to pay more in taxes than they earn and receive in transfers. As observed in tables 9-5 and 9-6, a universal basic income equal to the poverty line (either the $1.90 a day or the country-specific line) and funded with a proportional increase in direct taxes is never feasible. With country-specific poverty lines, not even the targeted poverty line scenario funded with an increase in direct taxes is feasible (with the exception of Comoros). A more or less general result is that scenarios tend to be feasible whenever the required additional funding is financed by a proportional increase in indirect taxes. Unsurprisingly, of all the scenarios requiring additional revenues from taxes, the one that is almost always feasible is the poverty gap scenario with perfect targeting.

In short, the scenario that is systematically feasible[32] is the one in which each individual's poverty gap is closed (perfect targeting) and the required additional resources are paid for with a proportional increase in indirect taxes. Under this

31. A scenario is defined as "not feasible" whenever the proportion of individuals with negative consumable income is higher than 0.1 percent and there is extreme reranking. Even in the absence of extreme reranking, reranking could be large enough so that groups switch position in the ranking with post-fiscal income. For more details, see Jellema, Lustig, and Martinez (forthcoming).

32. The only case in which it is not feasible is Zambia when the poverty gap is estimated with its country-specific poverty line.

Table 9-4. Average Transfer and Coverage of the Poor under the Six Alternative Spending Scenarios

Panel (a) $1.90 a Day International Poverty Line

| Country | Spending Neutral | | | | | Poverty Gap ($) | | Poverty Line ($) | |
| | Baseline | | Perfect targeting | | Universal | Perfect targeting | Universal | Targeted | Universal |
	Per poor person ($)	Coverage of the poor (%)	Per beneficiary ($)	Coverage of the poor (%)	Per capita ($)	Average per poor person	Per capita	Per poor person	Per capita
Comoros	-	-	-	-	-	0.55	0.55	1.90	1.90
Ghana	0.05	65	0.56	100	0.16	0.56	0.56	1.90	1.90
Ivory Coast	0.01	36	0.37	26	0.02	0.58	0.58	1.90	1.90
Namibia	0.67	83	0.78	100	0.40	0.78	0.78	1.90	1.90
South Africa	1.55	98	1.12	100	0.97	1.12	1.12	1.90	1.90
Tanzania	0.02	78	0.29	27	0.04	0.60	0.60	1.90	1.90
Togo	0.00	45	0.27	7	0.01	0.64	0.64	1.90	1.90
Uganda	0.01	52	0.27	12	0.01	0.58	0.58	1.90	1.90
Zambia	0.03	10	0.29	38	0.06	0.96	0.96	1.90	1.90

Panel (b) Country-Specific International Poverty Lines

Country	Baseline		Spending Neutral			Poverty Gap ($)		Poverty Line ($)	
			Perfect targeting		Universal	Perfect targeting	Universal	Targeted	Universal
	Per poor person ($)	Coverage of the poor (%)	Per Beneficiary ($)	Coverage of the poor (%)	Per capita ($)	Average per poor person	Per capita	Per poor person	Per capita
Comoros	–	–	–	–	–	0.55	0.55	1.90	1.90
Ghana	0.06	68	0.90	59	0.16	1.07	1.07	3.20	3.20
Ivory Coast	0.01	44	0.37	11	0.02	1.18	1.18	3.20	3.20
Namibia	0.47	75	1.05	55	0.40	3.21	3.21	5.50	5.50
South Africa	1.25	96	2.13	79	0.97	3.46	3.46	5.50	5.50
Tanzania	0.02	78	0.29	27	0.04	0.60	0.60	1.90	1.90
Togo	0.00	45	0.27	7	0.01	0.64	0.64	1.90	1.90
Uganda	0.01	52	0.27	12	0.01	0.58	0.58	1.90	1.90
Zambia	0.04	100	0.29	29	0.06	1.90	1.90	3.20	3.20

Notes: In the perfect targeting spending neutral scenario, total spending is distributed among the poor, starting with the poorest until resources are exhausted. In the perfect targeting poverty gap scenario, each poor person receives in transfers enough to close her/his poverty gap. Comoros does not have transfers or subsidies and, hence, average transfer per poor person and coverage of the poor are zero in the baseline. For panel (b): Comoros, Tanzania, Togo and Uganda: $1.90 a day international poverty line. Ghana, Ivory Coast and Zambia: $3.20 a day country-specific international poverty line. Namibia and South Africa: $5.50 a day country-specific international poverty line.

Sources: Authors' calculations based on Comoros (Belghith and others 2017); Ghana (Younger, Osei-Assibey, and Oppong 2016); Ivory Coast (Tassot and Jellema 2019); Namibia (Sulla, Zikhali, and Jellema 2016); South Africa (Inchauste and others 2017); Tanzania (Younger, Myamba, and Mdadila 2016b); Togo (Tassot and Jellema 2018); Uganda (Jellema and others 2016); and, Zambia (de la Fuente, Jellema, and Rosales 2018).

Table 9-5. Change in Pre-Fiscal to Post-Fiscal Squared Poverty Gap for Alternative Policy Scenarios ($1.90 a Day International Poverty Line)

Country	Baseline (%)	Spending Neutral (%)		Poverty Gap (%)		Poverty Line (%)	
		Perfect targeting	Universal	Perfect targeting	Universal	Targeted	Universal
Panel (a): Gross Income							
Comoros	-	-	-	-100	-84	-100	-100
Ghana	-7	-100	-33	-100	-81	-100	-100
Ivory Coast	0	-39	-5	-100	-81	-100	-100
Namibia	-62	-100	-53	-100	-81	-100	-100
South Africa	-91	-100	-83	-100	-88	-100	-100
Tanzania	-2	-31	-9	-100	-86	-100	-100
Togo	0	-9	-1	-100	-83	-100	-100
Uganda	-2	-16	-3	-100	-83	-100	-100
Zambia	-2	-25	-10	-100	-91	-100	-100
Panel (b): Consumable Income and with financing gap funded with direct taxes							
Comoros	3	3	3	-100	NF	-100	NF
Ghana	8	-96	-19	-96	NF	-98	NF
Ivory Coast	8	-31	4	-98	NF	NF	NF
Namibia	-56	-97	NF	-97	-77	-100	NF
South Africa	-81	-90	-67	-94	-81	-98	NF
Tanzania	12	-16	5	NF	NF	NF	NF
Togo	23	17	24	NF	NF	NF	NF
Uganda	1	-12	1	-98	NF	NF	NF
Zambia	1	-20	-4	-99	-89	NF	NF

| Country | Baseline (%) | Spending Neutral (%) | | Poverty Gap (%) | | Poverty Line (%) | |
		Perfect targeting	Universal	Perfect targeting	Universal	Targeted	Universal
Panel (c) Consumable Income and with financing gap funded with indirect taxes							
Comoros	3	3	3	-99	NF	-80	NF
Ghana	8	-96	-19	-96	-68	-99	-96
Ivory Coast	8	-31	4	-98	-69	-98	NF
Namibia	-56	-97	NF	-98	-72	-99	-97
South Africa	-81	-90	-67	-97	-81	-99	-98
Tanzania	12	-16	5	-88	-62	-46	NF
Togo	23	17	24	-86	-58	-90	-77
Uganda	1	-12	1	-97	-69	-80	NF
Zambia	1	-20	-4	-94	-82	NF	NF

Notes: NF = not feasible. In these scenarios, taxes would have to be increased by so much that consumable income turns out negative for a share of the population and there is extreme reranking. Comoros does not have transfers or subsidies and, hence, the spending neutral scenario does not apply.

Sources: Authors' calculations based on Comoros (Belghith and others 2017); Ghana (Younger, Osei-Assibey, and Oppong 2016); Ivory Coast (Tassot and Jellema 2019); Namibia (Sulla, Zikhali and Jellema, 2016); South Africa (Inchauste and others 2017); Tanzania (Younger, Myamba, and Mdadila 2016b); Togo (Tassot and Jellema 2018); Uganda (Jellema and others 2016); and, Zambia (de la Fuente, Jellema, and Rosales 2018).

Table 9-6. Change in Pre-Fiscal to Post-Fiscal Squared Poverty Gap for
Alternative Policy Scenarios (Country-Specific International Poverty Lines)

Country	Baseline (%)	Spending Neutral (%)		Poverty Gap (%)		Poverty Line (%)	
		Perfect targeting	Universal	Perfect targeting	Universal	Targeted	Universal
Panel (a): Gross Income							
Comoros	–	–	–	-100	-84	-100	-100
Ghana	-3	-79	-19	-100	-83	-100	-100
Ivory Coast	0	-10	-3	-100	-86	-100	-100
Namibia	-19	-37	-20	-100	-94	-100	-100
South Africa	-47	-76	-40	-100	-93	-100	-100
Tanzania	-2	-31	-9	-100	-86	-100	-100
Togo	0	-9	-1	-100	-83	-100	-100
Uganda	-2	-16	-3	-100	-83	-100	-100
Zambia	-1	-10	-5	-100	-94	-100	-100
Panel (b): Consumable Income and with financing gap funded with direct taxes							
Comoros	3	3	3	-100	NF	-100	NF
Ghana	10	-67	-4	-94	NF	NF	NF
Ivory Coast	7	-2	5	NF	NF	NF	NF
Namibia	-12	-28	NF	NF	NF	NF	NF
South Africa	-32	-61	-24	NF	NF	NF	NF
Tanzania	12	-16	5	NF	NF	NF	NF
Togo	23	17	24	NF	NF	NF	NF
Uganda	1	-12	1	-98	NF	NF	NF
Zambia	2	-6	-1	NF	NF	NF	NF

Country	Baseline (%)	Spending Neutral (%)		Poverty Gap (%)		Poverty Line (%)	
		Perfect targeting	Universal	Perfect targeting	Universal	Targeted	Universal
Panel (c): Consumable Income and with financing gap funded with indirect taxes							
Comoros	3	3	3	-99	NF	-80	NF
Ghana	10	-67	-4	-94	-66	-97	-96
Ivory Coast	7	-2	5	-89	NF	NF	NF
Namibia	-12	-28	NF	-86	-76	-88	NF
South Africa	-32	-61	-24	-89	-79	-96	-96
Tanzania	12	-16	5	-88	-62	-46	NF
Togo	23	17	24	-86	-58	-90	-77
Uganda	1	-12	1	-97	-69	-80	NF
Zambia	2	-6	-1	NF	NF	NF	NF

Notes: Comoros, Tanzania, Togo, and Uganda: $1.90 a day international poverty line. Ghana, Ivory Coast, and Zambia: $3.20 a day country-specific international poverty line. Namibia and South Africa: $5.50 a day country-specific international poverty line. NF = not feasible. In these scenarios, taxes would have to be increased by so much that consumable income turns out negative for a share of the population and there is extreme reranking. Comoros does not have transfers or subsidies and, hence, the spending neutral scenario does not apply.

Sources: Authors' calculations based on Comoros (Belghith and others 2017); Ghana (Younger, Osei-Assibey, and Oppong 2016); Ivory Coast (Tassot and Jellema 2019); Namibia (Sulla, Zikhali, and Jellema 2016); South Africa (Inchauste and others 2017); Tanzania (Younger, Myamba, and Mdadila 2016b); Togo (Tassot and Jellema 2018); Uganda (Jellema and others 2016); and, Zambia (de la Fuente, Jellema, and Rosales 2018).

scenario, post-fiscal poverty is always lower than the baseline. And, although the change in poverty is not the highest among the scenarios considered here, it is always among the highest, as shown in figure 9-3. Panels (a) and (b) of figure 9-3 show the change in the pre-fiscal to post-fiscal squared poverty gap for the baseline, the spending-neutral scenario (targeted and universal) and the poverty gap and poverty line scenarios (targeted and universal) with the financing gap funded by a proportional increase in indirect taxes for, respectively, the $1.90 a day international poverty line and the country-specific international poverty lines.

However, even though the poverty gap scenario funded with indirect taxes is frequently feasible and requires the smallest increase in taxes, it does not mean that the required marginal tax increase is economically feasible. To assess this, we look at the incidence of taxes by decile for this scenario and compare it to the baseline incidence.[33] This is shown in table 9-7 using the $1.90 a day international poverty line in panel (a) and the country-specific international poverty lines in panel (b). The additional tax burden (the difference between the incidence under the policy scenario and the baseline) with the $1.90 a day international poverty line is very high for Tanzania, Togo, Uganda, and Zambia. In contrast, the tax burden would actually be lower for all deciles in South Africa and for some deciles in Ghana and Namibia. When using the country-specific international poverty lines, the increase in the tax burden by decile (and, thus, the implied increase in marginal taxes) is very high for all but Comoros.

What does the additional tax burden look like in specific countries? In South Africa, the richest and most unequal country, the baseline headcount ratio with the country-specific international poverty line of US$5.50 is 60 percent (table 9-2). Thus, the burden of the higher indirect taxes required to finance the targeted poverty gap scenario would appear larger (when measured relative to post-fiscal incomes) for the top 40 percent, since that group would not be receiving any transfers. The increase in the tax burden (the difference between the baseline incidence and the scenarios) for the top 40 percent is 5 to 6 percentage points of pre-fiscal income, which is perhaps feasible economically (if not politically). South Africa is a country where the universal poverty line scenario using the US$1.90 a day poverty line. Under this universal basic income scenario, extreme poverty would be eradicated (table 9-5). However, the change in tax burden for the nonpoor (about 80 percent of the population has incomes above US$1.90 a day, based on table 9-2) is quite steep. The middle deciles (3 to 6) would have to forego between 19 to 10 percentage points of their pre-fiscal income in additional taxes, respectively. In Tanzania, a low-income country, the

---

33. The incidence here is measured as the ratio of the fiscal intervention of interest (e.g., transfers, direct taxes, and so on) to pre-fiscal income.

baseline poverty headcount ratio with the $1.90 a day poverty line equals 53 percent (table 9-2). Thus, the burden of the higher indirect taxes required to finance the targeted poverty gap scenario would appear larger (when measured relative to post-fiscal incomes) for the top 50 percent, since they would not be receiving any transfers. The increase in the tax burden for the top 50 percent is 8 to 10 percentage points of pre-fiscal income (roughly double compared to baseline), which, in principle, seems utterly high.

Conclusions

We have shown that, using the lowest World Bank International Poverty Line of $1.90 a day, the existing combination of taxes and transfers increases post-fiscal poverty (the headcount ratio and the squared poverty gap) in all countries in our sample, except upper middle-income Namibia and South Africa. With income class international poverty lines for lower middle-income and upper middle-income countries, there are no exceptions. This undesirable result is broadly due to the fact that the poor pay consumption taxes but receive very little in the form of cash transfers and only a small share of total subsidies. We call this phenomenon fiscal impoverishment.

One way to get rid of fiscal impoverishment is by eliminating subsidies and using those resources to increase cash transfers targeted to the poor. This targeted spending-neutral scenario would reduce the post-fiscal squared poverty gap in all countries but Comoros and Togo, where it would still be higher than the pre-fiscal one (in Togo, to a lesser extent than in the baseline).[34] Even though real-locating resources from general price subsidies to targeted transfers would yield better poverty outcomes in most countries, we would still be far from providing an income floor close to the country-specific international poverty lines. Also, under this scenario, a portion of the not-so-poor poor would receive no transfers.

What happens if we increase the size of transfers to equal the poverty line or the average poverty gap? Under both scenarios, by definition, poverty would be eradicated, but the first one is more expensive. For either policy to be budget neutral, taxes would need to increase. Here we consider two options: financing the fiscal gap with direct taxes and financing it with indirect taxes. How much taxes need to be increased depends on whether transfers are universal or targeted to the poor with perfect targeting. These can be seen as upper and lower bounds of the cost of eradicating poverty.

---

34. In Togo, the increase in the post-fiscal squared poverty gap is smaller than the baseline increase in the post-fiscal squared poverty gap. Results are the same for the $1.90 a day and the country-specific international poverty lines.

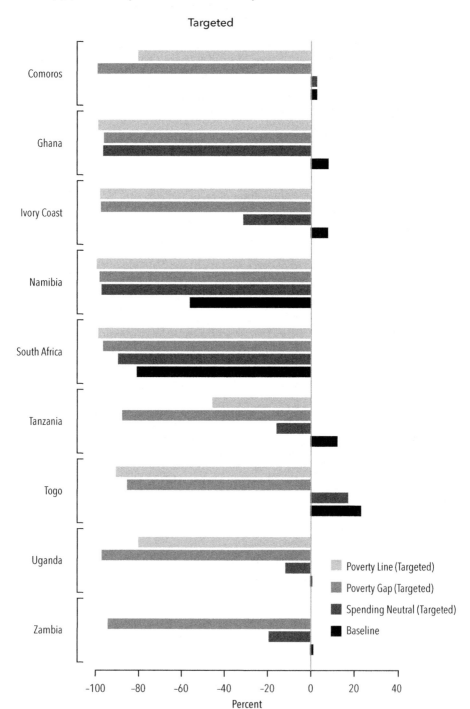

Figure 9-3. Change in Squared Poverty Gaps under Alternative Policy Scenarios and Poverty Lines

Panel (a) $1.90 a Day International Poverty Line

Targeted

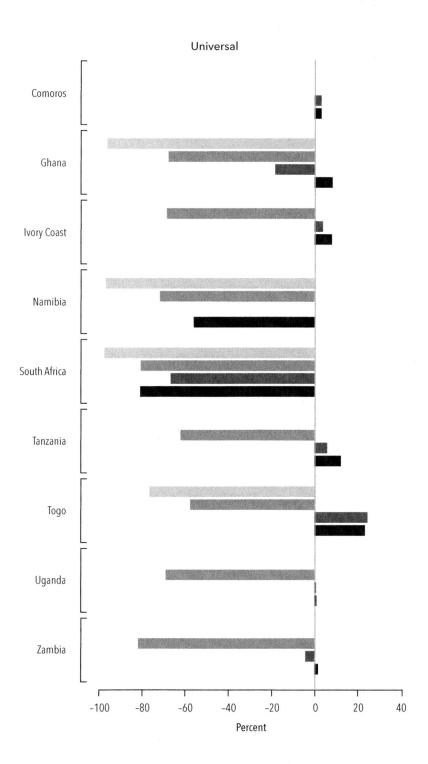

Universal

Panel (b) Country-Specific International Poverty Lines

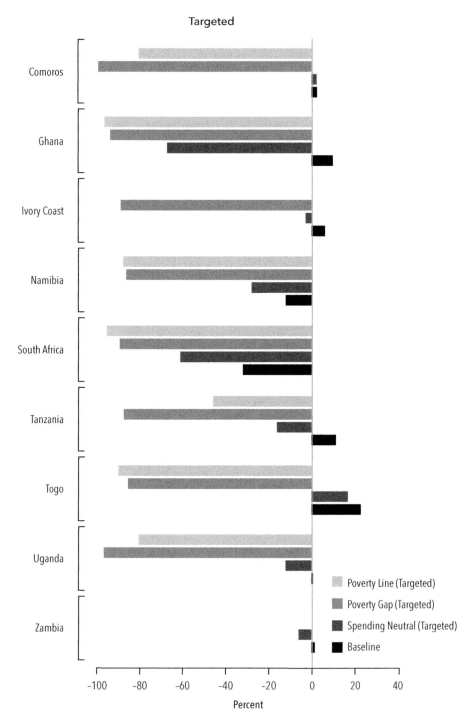

Targeted

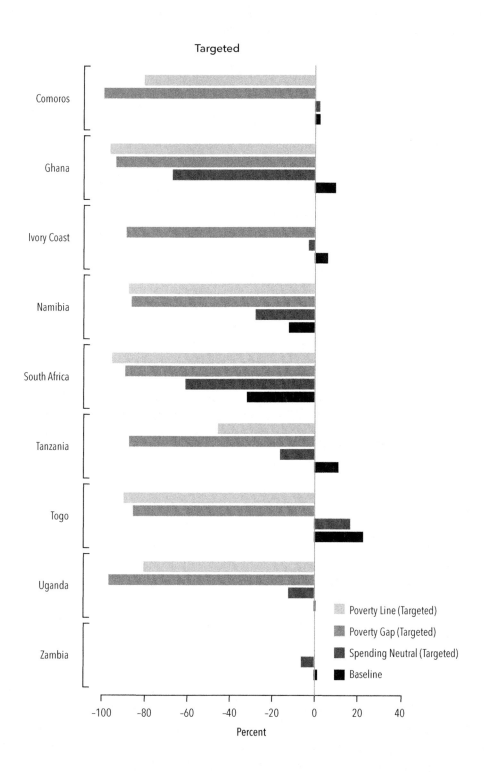

Targeted

Poverty Line (Targeted)	
Poverty Gap (Targeted)	
Spending Neutral (Targeted)	
Baseline	

Percent

Notes: For panel (b): Comoros, Tanzania, Togo, and Uganda: $1.90 a day international poverty line. Ghana, Ivory Coast, and Zambia: $3.20 a day country-specific international poverty line. Namibia and South Africa: $5.50 a day country-specific international poverty line. Not feasible scenarios are not shown. In the not feasible scenarios, taxes would have to be increased by so much that consumable income turns out negative for a share of the population and there is extreme reranking. Comoros does not have transfers or subsidies and, hence, the spending neutral scenario does not apply.

Sources: Authors' calculations based on Comoros (Belghith and others 2017); Ghana (Younger, Osei-Assibey, and Oppong 2016); Ivory Coast (Tassot and Jellema 2019); Namibia (Sulla, Zikhali, and Jellema 2016); South Africa (Inchauste and others 2017); Tanzania (Younger, Myamba, and Mdadila 2016b); Togo (Tassot and Jellema 2018); Uganda (Jellema and others 2016); and, Zambia (de la Fuente, Jellema, and Rosales 2018).

Our results show that setting income floors equal to the country-specific poverty lines and financed with an increase in direct taxes—even in the least expensive scenario when resources are perfectly targeted to the poor—is either outright not feasible because there would be extreme reranking of individuals and negative post-fiscal incomes or economically not feasible because the tax burden on the non-poor would be significantly higher (table 9-6, panel b). This is true even in South Africa (the richest country of the group).

If income floors are financed with indirect taxes (table 9-6, panel c), there are a number of countries in which closing the poverty gaps with perfect targeting becomes feasible (in the sense that there is no extreme reranking or post-fiscal negative incomes). The increase in indirect taxes paid by the non-poor, however, could still be steep (table 9-7). The required increase in indirect taxes are either economically inefficient or politically unrealistic. This is so even for upper middle-income countries such as Namibia and South Africa. The lack of feasibility, of course, gets exacerbated for the most costly scenario where everybody in the population receives a transfer equal to the country-specific poverty line (a UBI).

Although we present results for the perfect targeting scenario, this is for the purpose of showing how difficult setting budget-neutral income floors could be even in the least costly case. We are aware that a perfectly targeted transfer would never be feasible in practice. As discussed by Caitlin Brown, Martin Ravallion, and Dominique van de Walle (2016), identifying precisely who is and is not poor remains complicated due to unreliable data, weak information systems, and a lack of administrative capacity in poor countries. Moreover, as discussed by Raj M. Desai and Homi Kharas (2017), targeting may not be politically feasible, either. On top of infeasibility on the revenue collection side, the ability to implement a reasonably well-targeted transfer program (high coverage of the poor and low leakages to the nonpoor) could be low to nonexistent except in more advanced countries, such as Namibia and South Africa.

The results presented here do not take into account all domestic revenue sources that could be used to fund direct transfers. For example, when survey data does not adequately reflect top incomes, total subsidies and total direct and indirect tax revenue allocated in the incidence exercises tends to be below the administrative or budgetary totals. One would like to investigate how the resource envelope—including the marginal revenues necessary for increased transfer spending—would change if administrative totals are used instead of survey-based ones. Jellema, Lustig, and Martinez Pabon (forthcoming), explore the implications of assuming these additional resources are made available to fund the income floors.

In addition, as indicated by Mick Moore, Wilson Prichard, and Odd-Helge

Table 9-7. Incidence of Total Taxes (Direct and Indirect) by Decile for the Targeted Poverty Gap Scenario Financed by Indirect Taxes (%) (Scenario 4 in table 9-3)

Decile	Comoros		Ghana		Ivory Coast		Namibia		South Africa		Tanzania		Togo		Uganda		Zambia	
	Baseline	Poverty Gap (Targeted)	Baseline	Poverty Gap (Targeted)	Baseline	Poverty Gap (Targeted)	Baseline	Poverty Gap (Targeted)	Baseline	Poverty Gap (Targeted)	Baseline	Poverty Gap (Targeted)	Baseline	Poverty Gap (Targeted)	Baseline	Poverty Gap (Targeted)	Baseline	Poverty Gap (Targeted)
Panel (a) $1.90 a Day International Poverty Line																		
1	1	2	7	8	3	8	21	21	502	313	5	18	10	32	1	7	5	40
2	1	2	7	6	3	6	10	10	40	29	5	16	11	23	1	6	5	27
3	2	3	7	6	4	6	9	6	26	14	5	15	11	19	1	6	5	23
4	2	3	7	6	4	6	9	6	23	11	5	14	11	17	2	6	5	21
5	2	3	8	6	4	6	9	6	21	12	6	14	11	17	2	6	5	19
6	2	3	8	7	4	6	9	7	21	14	6	14	12	17	2	7	6	19
7	3	4	9	8	5	7	10	8	22	16	7	16	12	18	2	7	6	20
8	3	5	10	8	5	7	12	10	24	19	8	18	12	18	3	8	7	22
9	3	4	11	9	6	8	15	13	29	25	9	20	12	19	3	9	7	23
10	5	7	15	13	7	10	17	15	38	35	20	31	16	22	9	16	9	26
Total	3	5	11	9	5	8	14	12	33	29	11	21	13	20	5	11	7	24

Decile	Comoros		Ghana		Ivory Coast		Namibia		South Africa		Tanzania		Togo		Uganda		Zambia	
	Baseline	Poverty Gap (Targeted)	Baseline	Poverty Gap (Targeted)	Baseline	Poverty Gap (Targeted)	Baseline	Poverty Gap (Targeted)	Baseline	Poverty Gap (Targeted)	Baseline	Poverty Gap (Targeted)	Baseline	Poverty Gap (Targeted)	Baseline	Poverty Gap (Targeted)	Baseline	Poverty Gap (Targeted)
																	Panel (b) Country-Specific International Poverty Lines	
1	1	2	7	18	3	21	21	146	502	1526	5	18	10	32	1	7	N/A	N/A
2	1	2	7	12	3	17	10	68	40	132	5	16	11	23	1	6	N/A	N/A
3	2	3	7	10	4	16	9	54	26	71	5	15	11	19	1	6	N/A	N/A
4	2	3	7	9	4	16	9	48	23	50	5	14	11	17	2	6	N/A	N/A
5	2	3	8	10	4	16	9	44	21	37	6	14	11	17	2	6	N/A	N/A
6	2	3	8	10	4	15	9	39	21	28	6	14	12	17	2	7	N/A	N/A
7	3	4	9	11	5	16	10	33	22	27	7	16	12	18	2	7	N/A	N/A
8	3	5	10	12	5	17	12	34	24	30	8	18	12	18	3	8	N/A	N/A
9	3	4	11	13	6	18	15	35	29	35	9	20	12	19	3	9	N/A	N/A
10	5	7	15	17	7	23	17	36	38	43	20	31	16	22	9	16	N/A	N/A
Total	3	5	11	13	5	19	14	38	33	41	11	21	13	20	5	11	N/A	N/A

Notes: Comoros does not have transfers or subsidies and, hence, the spending neutral scenario does not apply. For panel (b): Comoros, Tanzania, Togo, and Uganda: $1.90 a day international poverty line. Ghana, Ivory Coast, and Zambia: $3.20 a day country-specific international poverty line. Namibia and South Africa: $5.50 a day country-specific international poverty line. N/A = Not applicable. In Zambia, based on table 9-6, the scenario in panel (b) would not be feasible.

Sources: Authors' calculations based on Comoros (Belghith and others 2017); Ghana (Younger, Osei-Assibey, and Oppong 2016); Ivory Coast (Tassot and Jellema 2019); Namibia (Sulla, Zikhali, and Jellema 2016); South Africa (Inchauste and others 2017); Tanzania (Younger, Myamba, and Mdadila 2016b); Togo (Tassot and Jellema 2018); Uganda (Jellema and others 2016); and, Zambia (de la Fuente, Jellema, and Rosales 2018).

Fjeldstad (2018), there are potentially a whole series of additional revenues that could be tapped by adequately taxing the personal incomes of wealthy people or their property ownership; reducing excessive and unjustified tax exemptions to investors; curbing corruption in tax collection; proper taxing of mining; increasing excise taxes on tobacco and alcohol; reducing "leaks" in VAT collection; and introducing gross turnover or excise taxes to compensate for taxes lost as a result of transnational companies shifting profits overseas.

While there are no country-specific estimates for the countries analyzed in this chapter, according to these authors, revenue lost due to base erosion and profit shifting in developing countries can range between 1 and 2 percent of GDP. While revenues from these other sources could potentially increase the domestic resources available for providing an adequate income floor, in general, they would still not be enough to reach these floors at reasonable marginal tax rates for the middle-classes and the rich in most of the countries. Resources coming from other countries or multilateral organizations will need to come into play as well.

References

Acemoglu, Daron. 2019. "Why Universal Basic Income Is a Bad Idea." Project Syndicate, June 7, https://www.project-syndicate.org/commentary/why-universal-basic-income-is-a-bad-idea-by-daron-acemoglu-2019-06.

Belghith, Nadia Belhaj Hassine, Jon Jellema, and Shireen Mahdi. 2017. "CEQ Master Workbook: Comoros (2014)." CEQ Data Center on Fiscal Redistribution, CEQ Institute, Tulane University, and the World Bank.

Brown, Caitlin, Martin Ravallion, and Dominique van de Walle. 2016. "A Poor Means Test? Econometric Targeting in Africa." NBER Working Paper 22919. National Bureau of Economic Research.

Coady, David. 2006. "The Distributional Impacts of Indirect Tax and Public Pricing Reforms." In *Analyzing the Distributional Impact of Reforms*, edited by Aline Coudouel and Stefano Paternostro. World Bank.

Coady, D., V. Flamini, and L. Sears. 2015. "The Unequal Benefits of Fuel Subsidies Revisited: Evidence for Developing Countries." In *Inequality and Fiscal Policy*, edited by B. Clements, R. de Mooij, S. Gupta, and M. Keen. International Monetary Fund.

Coady, David, and others. 2006. "The Magnitude and Distribution of Fuel Subsidies: Evidence from Bolivia, Ghana, Jordan, Mali, and Sri Lanka." Working Paper 06/247. International Monetary Fund.

de la Fuente, Alejandro, Jon Jellema, and Nora Lustig. (Forthcoming). "Fiscal Policy in Africa: Welfare Impacts and Policy Effectiveness." World Bank Policy Research Working Paper, World Bank.

de la Fuente, Alejandro, Jon Jellema, and Manuel Rosales. 2018. "CEQ Master Workbook: Zambia (2015)." CEQ Data Center on Fiscal Redistribution. CEQ Institute, Tulane University, the World Bank, and the International Monetary Fund.

de la Fuente, Alejandro, Manuel Rosales, and Jon Jellema. 2017. "The Impact of Fiscal Policy on Inequality and Poverty in Zambia." World Bank Policy Research Working Paper 8246 (November). World Bank.

Desai, Raj M., and Homi Kharas. 2017. "Is a Growing Middle-class Good for the Poor? Social Policy in a Time of Globalization." Global Policy and Development Working Paper 105 (July). Brookings Institution.

Higgins, Sean, and Nora Lustig. 2016. "Can a Poverty-Reducing and Progressive Tax and Transfer System Hurt the Poor?" *Journal of Development Economics* 122: 63–75.

Inchauste, Gabriela, and others. 2017. "The Distributional Impact of Fiscal Policy in South Africa." In *The Distributional Impact of Taxes and Transfers. Evidence from Eight Low-and Middle-Income Countries*, edited by Gabriela Inchauste and Nora Lustig. World Bank.

Inchauste, Gabriela, and others. 2016. "CEQ Master Workbook: South Africa (2010–2011)." CEQ Data Center on Fiscal Redistribution (March 6). CEQ Institute, Tulane University, and the World Bank.

Jellema, Jon. 2017. "Fiscal Incidence Analysis." In Comoros Poverty Assessment (English). World Bank. World Bank Group.

Jellema, Jon, and others. 2016. "CEQ Master Workbook: Uganda (2012–2013)." CEQ Data Center on Fiscal Redistribution (July 28). CEQ Institute, Tulane University, and International Growth Center.

———. 2018. "Uganda: The Impact of Taxes, Transfers, and Subsidies on Inequality and Poverty." Chapter 19 in *Commitment to Equity Handbook: Estimating the Impact of Fiscal Policy on Inequality and Poverty*, edited by Nora Lustig. Brookings Institution Press and CEQ Institute, Tulane University. Free online version available at www.commitmentoequity.org.

Jellema, Jon, and Gabriela Inchauste. 2018. "Constructing Consumable Income: Including the Direct and Indirect Effects of Indirect Taxes and Subsidies." Chapter 7 in *Commitment to Equity Handbook: Estimating the Impact of Fiscal Policy on Inequality and Poverty*, edited by Nora Lustig. Brookings Institution Press and CEQ Institute, Tulane University. www.commitmentoequity.org.

Jellema, Jon, Nora Lustig, and Valentina Martinez Pabon (forthcoming). "Can Tax-funded Transfer Programs Provide Income Floors in Sub-Saharan Africa? Fiscal Incidence Analysis of Alternative Policy Simulations" CEQ Working Paper 86, CEQ Institute, Tulane University.

Jellema, Jon, and Caroline Tassot. 2018. "Analysis of the Impact of Tax and Social Protection Policies on Inequality and Poverty in Togo." OECD Development Policy Papers 12. OECD.

Jellema, Jon, and Caroline Tassot. Forthcoming. "Analyse de l'impact des politiques fiscales et de protection sociale sur les inégalités et la pauvreté au Côte d'Ivoire." OECD Development Policy Papers. OECD.

Jolliffe, Dean, and Espen Beer Prydz. 2016. "Estimating International Poverty Lines from Comparable National Thresholds" (English). Policy Research Working Paper WPS 7606. This paper was funded by the Knowledge for Change Program (KCP). World Bank Group. http://documents.worldbank.org/curated/en/837051468184454513/Estimating-international-poverty-lines-from-comparable-national-thresholds.

Lustig, Nora (ed.). 2018. *Commitment to Equity Handbook: Estimating the Impact of Fiscal Policy on Inequality and Poverty.* Brookings Institution Press and CEQ Institute, Tulane University. Free online version available at www.commitmentoequity.org.

Moore, Mick, Wilson Prichard, and Odd-Helge Fjeldstad. 2018. *Taxing Africa. Coercion, Reform and Development.* London: Zed Books and International African Institute.

Namibia Statistics Agency and World Bank. 2017. "Does Fiscal Policy Benefit the Poor and Reduce Inequality in Namibia? The Distributional Impact of Fiscal Policy in Namibia" (June). World Bank.

Rigolini, Jamele, and others. Forthcoming. "From Theory to Facts: Incidence and Costs of Universal Basic Income Programs." World Bank.

Sulla, Victor, Precious Zikhali, and Jon Jellema. 2016. "CEQ Master Workbook: Namibia (2010)," CEQ Data Center on Fiscal Redistribution. CEQ Institute, Tulane University, and the World Bank.

Tassot, Caroline, and Jon Jellema. 2018. "CEQ Master Workbook: Togo (2015)." CEQ Data Center on Fiscal Redistribution. CEQ Institute, Tulane University, and the Organization for Economic Cooperation and Development.

———. 2019. "CEQ Master Workbook: Ivory Coast (2015)." CEQ Data Center on Fiscal Redistribution. CEQ Institute, Tulane University, and the Organization for Economic Cooperation and Development.

World Bank. 2017. "Comoros Poverty Assessment" (English). World Bank Group.

Younger, Stephen, Flora Myamba, and Kenneth Mdadila. 2016a. "CEQ Master Workbook: Tanzania (2011–2012)." CEQ Data Center on Fiscal Redistribution. (April 3, 2018). CEQ Institute, Tulane University.

———. 2016b. "Fiscal Incidence in Tanzania." *African Development Review* 28, no. 3: 264–76.

Younger, Stephen, Eric Osei-Assibey, and Felix Oppong. 2016. "CEQ Master Workbook: Ghana (2012–2013)." CEQ Data Center on Fiscal Redistribution. (February 10). CEQ Institute, Tulane University.

———. 2017. "Fiscal Incidence in Ghana." *Review of Development Economics* 21, issue 4, https://doi.org/10.1111/rode.12299.

PART III
Places

CHAPTER TEN

Spatial Targeting of Poverty Hotspots

Jennifer L. Cohen, Raj M. Desai, and Homi Kharas

Introduction

The opportunities available to any child depend on many factors; the level of education, health and early nutrition, parental income, and social class all are factors that have been well documented.[1] But the dominant determinant is geography: where a child is born.[2] This geography, in turn, has many dimensions: in which country the child is born, whether in an urban or rural environment, and whether in a fast-developing or a lagging region.

The stickiest poverty over time is associated with people born in rural, lagging regions in low- and lower middle-income countries. These regions have characteristics that make development difficult. They are places where there may be some combination of conflict, ethnic fragmentation, malaria prevalence, high risk of natural disasters, and fragile ecosystems that have low soil resilience subject to significant degradation. They are places that are distant from high-density urban areas where jobs and a range of social and infrastructure services provide

---

1. For parental income, see Mayer (2002) and Dahl and Lochner (2012); for education, see Psacharopoulos and Patrinos (2018) and Isaacs and Roessel (2008); for health and nutrition, see Holding and Kitsao-Wekulo (2004), Liu and Raine (2016); and for social class, see Narayan and others (2018).

2. See World Bank Group (2009).

We would like to thank Lorenz Noe for his excellent research support, as well as Brad Parks and Tarek Ghani for their invaluable guidance on the chapter.

opportunities. They are places with substantial concentrations of poverty. These are the places we identify as "poverty hotspots."

In this chapter, we ask two basic questions: (i) where are these poverty hotspots, and (ii) how many people live in them? This is a prelude to a policy discussion on spatial targeting—the deliberate focusing of policy interventions in a specific area. We believe a greater focus on spatial targeting is indispensable for taking seriously the idea of "leave no one behind."

We start with a thought experiment. What would a global map of the world look like with shaded areas for all poverty hotspots, defined as subnational regions (districts or provinces within a country) that are on track to have a per capita GDP of $4,900 or less in 2011 PPP terms in 2030?[3]

We find 840 poverty hotspots globally, from a universe of 3,609 districts, states, and provinces. They are in 102 countries. All of the thirty-four current low-income countries have at least one hotspot (even if more than half of these also have one or more prosperous regions). Similarly, thirty-nine of forty-six lower middle-income countries have at least one poverty hotspot, along with eighteen of fifty-two upper middle-income countries assessed. Eight of the sixty-nine high-income countries assessed have poverty hotspots by our measure (three countries are not classified by the World Bank).

These broad facts support our contention that there is considerable uneven-ness in economic development within countries, and that subnational spatial tar-geting may be necessary to reduce these disparities. Country targeting, the tool most commonly used by aid agencies, is too blunt to deal with the unevenness of progress within countries.

What can be done? Broadly speaking, there are two types of solutions to address poverty hotspots. Let people move, or develop the places faster. Both are inherently difficult. Migration, even within a country, can have high personal costs, and, in theory, the impact on those left behind is ambiguous. Those who remain can benefit from remittances and, potentially, from less population pres-sure on limited natural resources. On the other hand, they can suffer if migrants are more dynamic, entrepreneurial, and hard-working. If migrants leave, taking scarce capital from their families with them, they can depress their source areas even more.

The reality is that migration is a complex decision, dependent on many fac-tors. As shown later in the chapter, we estimate that more than 1 billion people

---

3. The threshold of $4,900 is chosen by triangulating macroeconomic and microeconomic rea-soning. At the macro level, it corresponds to the income level below which the extreme poverty headcount rate typically remains above 20 percent. At the micro level, it roughly corresponds to a level of daily household expenditure where the probability of falling below the national poverty line in a middle-income country is less than 10 percent (Lopez-Calva and Ortiz-Juarez 2015).

live in poverty hotspots, and the population in these areas has been growing and is expected to continue to grow for the next couple of decades, reaching 1.7 billion people in 2030. This increase reflects the fact that fertility rates are high among poor families. Natural population growth outweighs out-migration in most poor places. So out-migration, while in theory a very long-run potential solution, is not the answer for poverty hotspots in the timeframe of Agenda 2030.

The alternative is to accelerate the economic growth of poverty hotspots, but this is difficult to do in an economically efficient way. In most countries, growth is most efficient when it builds on market forces of agglomeration, specialization, and trade. These conditions favor urban centers. Market forces, if left unattended, can, therefore, result in persistent disparities across regions, which is why we find hotspots in the first place. While there is sound analytical evidence for conditional spatial convergence (the idea that poorer places grow faster than richer places, all other things being equal), in practice, many things are not equal. Infrastructure, human capital, urbanization, institutional factors, and exposure to shocks and disease all play a role in concentrating economic activity and human settlements in some places at the expense of others.

What is the right policy response to this? Some countries have experimented with targeting physical infrastructure and improving connectivity of lagging regions, others with investing in human capital. Spatial subsidies for production in lagging regions have also commonly been used.[4] Special economic zones relax infrastructure and regulatory burdens in specific places. But these interventions tend to be expensive and may not reflect an efficient use of public funds.

It is fair to say that there is no single blueprint, but a range of interventions might help accelerate growth in specific places. Luckily, subnational spatial analysis offers more opportunity to identify the correlates of growth than do cross-country regressions. The subnational analysis in this chapter has more than 3,600 data points in a cross-section. With cross-country analysis, a typical data set would be under 150 data points.

The data suggest that poverty hotspots have characteristics that distinguish them from other places. First, the level of initial human capital—health and probably education—is low and seems to be correlated with subsequent low rates of income growth. We say "probably" for education because, unfortunately, the data on subnational educational attainment is very spotty—some countries have it, others do not—and it is not easily comparable across countries. Second, several indicators of physical infrastructure and market connectivity, like accessibility to a nearby city or the distance to the capital, are poor in hotspots and this has

4. The European Union is perhaps the best example: see European Committee of the Regions (2018).

a significant impact on growth. Third, hotspots display an inability to reduce the incidence or impact of shocks, such as conflict-related deaths, or improving resilience to weather-related shocks, like droughts. Finally, although our focus here is on subnational spatial targeting, many hotspots are in countries that themselves are growing slowly. These national growth drivers (including institutional and governance quality) clearly have an important bearing on what can be achieved at the subnational level.

Each poverty hotspot can be associated with one or more of these types of growth constraints. In this chapter, we do not pretend to reach any definitive conclusions, but rather aim to illustrate how a geospatial approach can suggest new and better insights for policymaking. Further refinement of the methodology and data will, undoubtedly, yield additional insights. Our conclusion, however, is that there is already enough evidence to support a far better data-driven approach to spatial targeting than is currently in use. We illustrate the benefits of taking a spatial approach with some examples of what is now being done, but our main conclusion is that more spatial targeting is needed. In fact, we conclude with the observation that aid, at least in the case of the World Bank, which is one of the few major aid agencies that has geocoded its projects, is allocated roughly evenly to poverty hotspots and non-poverty hotspots. If the hotspots are, indeed, revealing of where the major problems really lie, then a reallocation of aid to focus more on poverty hotspots could be a powerful tool to ensure no one is left behind.

Why Do Some Places Develop while Others Do Not?

Economic activity is unevenly distributed across space. Even as national incomes converge, many pockets within and across countries show widening disparities. What explains persistent stagnation in some places and such rapid development in others?

Macroeconomists have long grappled with this question. Some claim that poor countries will inevitably catch up with their rich counterparts over time.[5] Others stress that it is endogenous factors—policies, institutions, and country specifics—that put certain areas on the fast-track to economic growth.[6] Separate strands of thought emphasize the deep geographic roots of growth, considering that variables such as climate type, temperature, precipitation, and soil suitability play a role in agricultural productivity and trade.[7]

Building on this debate, Vollrath (2019) offers a perspective on the uneven

---

5. See absolute convergence theory.
6. See conditional and club convergence theory.
7. Henderson and others (2018).

distribution of nightlights across the globe.[8, 9] Drawing on the work of Michaels and Rauch (2013), Vollrath asks a simple question: Is the world more like France or more like Britain? French patterns of urbanization, Vollrath explains, are likely the vestiges of Julius Caesar's city planning in 46 B.C. Modern-day French urban centers rest on the foundations of old Roman towns and forts, hinting at the role that historical events or institutions play in global development. By comparison, British cities are more likely to be organized around areas with navigable waterways. Following the collapse of the Western Roman Empire, medieval towns across modern-day Britain were abandoned and fell into decay. When the British economy revived, activity became concentrated in trade-suitable geographies that were quite different from those that existed in Roman times. The key insight of this work is that economic growth across the world depends on both historical and geographic factors.

Henderson and others (2018) find that geography predicts nearly half of the distribution of economic activity across the world, in keeping with the British model.[10] They conclude that variables associated with agricultural productivity hold the greatest explanatory power, although trade-related characteristics such as proximity to the coast and navigable waterways are significant as well. Other scholars have also documented the link between geography and economic growth: Gallup, Sachs, and Mellinger (1999), Gallup and Sachs (2001), and Sachs and Malaney (2002) argue for the direct effects of geography on income growth via channels such as agricultural productivity, disease burden, and transport costs; Myrdal (1968), Kamarck (1976), and Masters and McMillan (2001) document high correlations between income per capita and climate and temperature; Sachs and Warner (2001) reaffirm the curse of natural resources; and the UN Millennium Project (2005) notes the effect of adverse agronomic conditions, transport risk, and malaria ecology.

Henderson and others' research emphasizes the role institutions play in promoting or hindering economic growth: North (1990) famously made the argument for institutional determinants of growth; Hall and Jones (1999) illustrate the effects of differing government policies and institutions on output per worker; and Acemoglu, Johnson, and Robinson (2001) argue that colonization patterns explain large differences in income per capita across countries, citing on the one hand "extractive" European powers, and on the other hand "Neo-Europes" that replicated European institutions by ensuring property rights and checks on power.

---

8. Nightlights are commonly used as a proxy for human economic activity.

9. Vollrath (2019).

10. Henderson and others (2018) quoted in Vollrath (2019).

Despite fissures in the literature, most would concede that uneven economic development is the product of two forces: geography and institutions. In this chapter, we operate on this premise: disparities across regions are likely due to environmental and sociopolitical differences that directly or indirectly affect human and physical capital accumulation, exposure to human and natural shocks, and rule of law. Although geographic determinants of poverty are difficult to overcome with available policy levers, the literature provides hope that spatially targeted policy interventions can set countries, communities, and people on track to greater economic prosperity and well-being.

Subnational Poverty Hotspots

It is well known that subnational areas within countries exhibit substantial inequality in wealth and development across a number of dimensions.[11] Most of these dimensions, including the multidimensional aspects of poverty, are correlated with per capita income levels and so, as a shorthand, we try to identify those areas in the world trending toward the lowest GDP per capita in 2030. These areas, by definition, start today as very poor areas and have low recent growth rates, a feature that in our baseline scenario we assume to continue to 2030, partly because of the low underlying trend growth in each hotspot's respective national economy. We look at all subnational units in the world, with boundaries given by the first-level disaggregation in the Database of Global Administrative Areas (GADM-1). In other words, we look at all administrative units just below the national level, consisting of 3,609 subnational cantons, districts, governorates, prefectures, provinces, and states, in all countries in the world.

We start our identification of poverty hotspots by looking at initial levels of GDP per capita in subnational areas. These data are taken from Ghosh and others (2010) and reproduced by AidData in an online database of subnational variables.[12] Ghosh and others obtain subnational GDP per capita data by allocating national GDP to subnational areas based on luminosity from nighttime lights, adjusted to take into account caps on urban centers that are present in the most common, merged stable lights source available from the National Oceanic and Atmospheric Administration (NOAA). They also factor in estimates for the informal economy made by Schneider (2009a, 2009b) and use a separate method for assigning agricultural output across subnational areas. Combining these estimates with spatial estimates of population through the LandScan™

11. See, for example, Gennaioli and others (2014).
12. See Goodman and others (2019).

Global Population Database allows for the calculation of an annual figure for subnational GDP per capita.

Unfortunately, AidData published subnational GDP per capita for only a single year: 2006. To bring this up to date, and to make forecasts, we turn to an alternative openly-available data set that looks at subnational growth rates, provided by Kummu and others (2018). They provide data for subnational incomes for each year between 1990 and 2015, based on a compilation of other research. We take the Kummu growth rate of each subnational unit from 2006 to 2015 to update our base year to 2015.

The second step is to derive a forecast of subnational growth from 2015 to 2030. We do this by establishing a relationship between subnational and national growth rates and then taking forecasts for national growth from the International Monetary Fund (IMF). Using the Kummu data, we obtain a relationship between subnational income growth in each country and the national growth rate and assume it stays constant over time. In other words, if subnational region "a" in country "j" grows faster (or slower) than the national average during 2006 to 2015, we assume it will grow faster (or slower) than the national average by the same amount during the period 2015 to 2030. In this way, we link subnational growth to national growth.

National growth forecasts out to 2024 are taken from the IMF World Economic Outlook April 2019 database. We assume countries will grow at the same rate between 2024 and 2030 as forecast by the IMF for the six-year period from 2018 to 2024. Equipped with national growth rates for the period 2015 to 2030, a GDP per capita baseline value in 2015 and a relationship between subnational growth and national growth, we project subnational GDP per capita to 2030.[13]

We define "poverty hotspot" income areas as those with annual GDP per capita of less than $4,900 in 2011 PPP dollars in 2030. This threshold approximately doubles the current threshold definition used by the World Bank to designate countries as "low income," when adjusted to convert from the Atlas Method of national income actually used by the World Bank to 2011 purchasing power parities.

The map in figure 10-1 shows subnational hotspots within national boundaries. We note four "clusters" of 2030 hotspots.

- *Tropical Africa:* The largest cluster extends from the Sahel to northern Angola, and the southern borders of Zambia, Zimbabwe, and Mozambique.

---

13. Further details are provided in the appendix to this chapter.

- *Tropical Latin America:* This range is a scattering of areas including parts of Central America (including all of Nicaragua), Haiti, the Caribbean coast of Venezuela and most of its central and southern regions, part of Ecuador and Colombia, Suriname and French Guiana, and northeastern Brazil.

- *Central-South Asia:* This includes subnational areas stretching from Tajikistan and Kyrgyzstan to most of Afghanistan, northwestern Pakistan, Kashmir on both sides of the line of control, much of Nepal, the Indian states of Bihar and Manipur, and parts of Bangladesh and Myanmar.

- *Southeast Asia-Western Oceania:* This area includes sections of Cambodia, Vietnam, the Philippines, Indonesia (Aceh and Bengkulu provinces of Sumatra, some of the Lesser Sunda and Molucca Islands, and Timor), East Timor, much of Papua New Guinea, and the Solomon Islands.

In addition to these areas, there are other more scattered zones: Syria, Mongolia, Russia's Altai Republic, North Korea, and most of western Yemen. OECD countries and China do not display any hotspot regions.

The map shows 840 poverty hotspots globally, of a universe of 3,609 districts, states, and provinces (for 157 districts, there are no available data). Around 1.2 billion people live in these hotspots. Although we have not attempted to construct poverty estimates for subnational regions (this would require some estimate of income distribution within each region), we feel confident that most households in extreme poverty in 2030 will be found in these places.

One hundred and two countries, about half the number in the world, have at least one region with an income level at or below $4,900, but in seventy-eight of these countries at least one other region also has a higher income. In other words, in a majority of developing countries, there are likely to be both "poverty hotspots" and prosperous areas in 2030. Even among today's low-income countries, our forecasts suggest that over half the countries will have some prosperous regions, above the $4,900 threshold. Similarly, thirty-eight of forty-six lower middle-income countries could have at least one region that qualifies as a poverty hotspot, along with eighteen of fifty-two upper middle-income countries. Eight high-income economies have at least one hotspot.

The Correlates of Poverty Hotspots

Poverty hotspots have a number of characteristics that distinguish them from other places. Table 10-1 shows how poverty hotspots compare to other places in developing countries. The hotspots are poor, with average per capita income levels of less than $2,000, compared to $11,000 in other developing country regions. They have far slower per capita income growth (0.8 percent in 2006–15

Figure 10-1: Subnational Poverty Hotspots, 2030

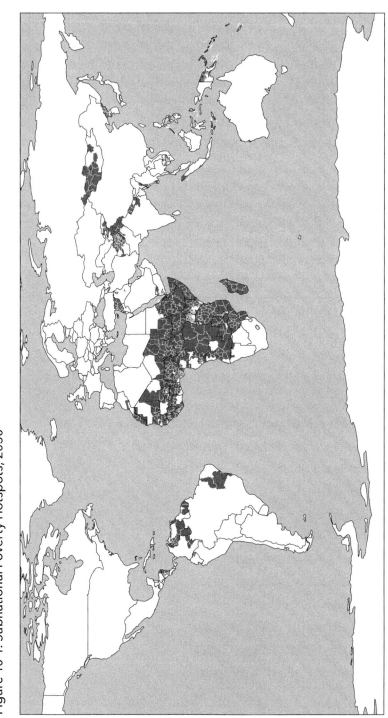

compared to 4.9 percent in non-hotspot places). They have lower human development scores and far poorer infrastructure. They have substantially higher deaths from civil conflict, although violence has lessened since the 1990s at about the same rate as other places. They have less exposure to drought but, as we will show, the impact of drought is likely to be severe (table 10-1).

Policy Issues for Spatial Targeting of Poverty Hotspots

Any discussion of spatial targeting of policy interventions has to start with an understanding of what factors are likely to influence income growth levels in specific places. We use the annualized change in nighttime luminosity per capita

Table 10-1. Characteristics of Poverty Hotspots and
Other Regions within Developing Countries

	Hotspot	Other
Mean GDP per capita 2006, 2011 PPP ($)	1,858	7,317
Mean GDP per capita 2015, 2011 PPP ($)	2,005	11,238
Growth rate 2006–15, Annual (%)	0.8	4.9
Mean World Bank Aid commitments per capita (1989–2014 total) ($)	129.1	103.7
Mean HDI	0.47	0.66
Mean number of battle deaths 1989–2000 per 100K population	160	80
Mean number of battle deaths 2013–17 per 100K population	23	8
Growth rate in deaths (%)	-85	-91
Soil quality index	4.9	4.6
Mean drought events	0.5	1.0
Mean distance to roads (m)	11,709	7,122
Mean travel time to cities (minutes)	549	314
Total population, 2015 (billions)	1.2	4.7
Total population, 2030 (billions)	1.7	5.5
Population growth rate, annual 2015–30 (%)	2.4	1.0
Mean air temp 1980–2014 (degrees Celsius)	23	18
Mean annual precipitation 1980–2014 (mm)	100	90

Source: Author's calculations. See appendix for data sources.

over the period 2003 to 2013 as a proxy for GDP per capita growth and regress this on a number of subnational variables. We chose to base the analysis on subnational administrative units, which vary considerably in size, rather than grid cells that have a fixed spatial area, because much of the data are more easily accessible for administrative units, and, in the final analysis, the policy choices to be made will likely be implemented through administrative units. As a robustness check, we do the regressions separately using the entire sample of countries and for developing countries only, and with and without country fixed effects. The results, and the data sources, are summarized in the appendix to this chapter.

There seems to be strong empirical evidence that while certain places indisputably face geographic constraints—such as extreme temperatures, inhospitable soil, and proximity to the national border—other variables within the purview of policymaking also hold significant explanatory power. Human capital, infrastructure and connectivity, shock-readiness, and governance all impact the extent to which a region develops or lags, suggesting that public officials have at their disposal a powerful antidote to poverty: inclusive policies and institutions.

Most of the variables in the regression have the expected signs. Consistent with other studies, the initial level of GDP per capita is negatively related to growth. Our best point estimate of this conditional convergence is that for every doubling of initial GDP per capita, the expected subsequent annual growth rate in the region falls by between 0.9 percentage points (a coefficient of -0.013) and 1.4 percentage points (a coefficient of -0.02). Other significant variables include the rule of law, an index of soil suitability, various measures of infrastructure adequacy, malaria ecology, a broader measure of human development, exposure to drought or flood, and the change in conflict-related deaths. Some of these variables are linked to each other so coefficients must be carefully interpreted; the human development index contains elements of both health and income, which are, in turn, proxied by other variables in the regression. Access to a major city is closely but inversely correlated with distance to a road. Exposure to floods has a positive sign—most floods occur around river banks and replenish good alluvial soil, so they can carry a benefit.[14] The only surprise in the data is that being close to the coast does not seem to matter in a significant way.

Our purpose in doing these regressions is not to craft precise point estimates in the correlations or to identify specific policy interventions but, rather, to gain insight into the type of intervention that could potentially be expected to yield

14. Indeed, a robustness check in the regression interacting soils and floods shows this positive relationship between the two.

positive results. In our mind, the regression analysis shows that four classes of intervention could be important: (i) human development; (ii) infrastructure and connectivity; (iii) resilience to shocks; and (iv) governance and institutions. In each of these cases, we highlight actual examples of where governments have used geo-referenced spatial data to assist efforts to alleviate subnational constraints to development.

Human Capital

Human capital, defined as the "productive wealth embodied in labor, skills, and knowledge," is central to accelerating development in lagging places.[15] Aid organizations and governments alike tend to focus on improving access to education and ensuring the population has adequate health and nutrition services.

In our regressions, we use the initial year value of the Human Development Index (HDI) from the United Nations Development Program (UNDP), calculated from gridded data at five arc-minute resolution, averaged at the subnational level.[16] Additionally, we control for malaria as a proxy for disease burdens. Malaria ecologies are commonly associated with low-growth areas due to effects on the poverty, productivity, and health of the population. Malaria and other diseases affect the economy through adverse consequences for childhood development and the quality of human capital for decades.[17] We use a malaria "temperature suitability" score rather than the actual prevalence of malaria, so as to avoid endogeneity. The regression results suggest there is strong evidence that the initial level of human capital is important in ensuing regional growth.

Several governments have used high-quality, granular data on education and health to improve human capital. Providing evidence from two experiments on information exposure at the village-level in India, Pandey and others (2007, 2009) report that access to information has positive effects on human capital. The experimental studies randomly assigned exposure to information regarding citizen responsibilities and rights having to do with education, health, and governance services. Pandey and others conclude that the exposure resulted in greater participation in school management, better child health outcomes, improved student learning outcomes, and more frequent village council meetings.[18]

---

15. United Nations (1997).

16. Kummu and others (2018). The HDI includes the level of GDP per capita, which is separately included as an independent variable in the regressions. Unfortunately, the data do not permit us to identify the education and health components individually, so there is multicollinearity between the HDI variable and the level of GDP per capita variable. This does not bias the coefficients or the predictions of the model, but requires caution in interpretation.

17. Holding and Kitsao-Wekulo (2004).

18. BenYishay and Parks (2019).

Another example comes from Papua New Guinea. There, the rainy climate, limited infrastructure, and isolated geography create a fertile ground for the spread of malaria. However, the World Health Organization reports that malaria incidence halved between 2004 and 2017 as a result of increased funding for diagnosis and treatment of the infection, as well as near-universal distribution of long-lasting insecticidal nets.[19] High-quality and timely surveillance aided planners in determining where the most vulnerable populations reside and how best to target bed net distribution. One particular m-health initiative was instrumental in strengthening malaria surveillance across provinces. The mobile application provides a secure online platform for healthcare professionals that maps in real-time the outbreak of malaria at a village level, as well as the availability of treatment and diagnostics in nearby health facilities. The cases are geocoded and uploaded on average nine days from the date of testing. Rosewell and others (2017) conclude that using these mobile and geospatial technologies has strengthened the National Health Information System (NHIS) in Papua New Guinea through greater integration and accessibility of subnational data.

In Ethiopia, one problem has been how to decide where to build schools. Despite heavy government investments in the education sector, the overall level of education in Ethiopia remains low, with illiteracy rates for women in rural areas at over 50 percent, compared to 16 percent in urban centers.[20] The gender disparity is high: over half of Ethiopian women, defined as ten-years-old and above, were illiterate in 2013 as compared with 32 percent of men. In collaboration with the U.S. Department of Labor, the International Rescue Committee (IRC) began an initiative to build schools and train teachers to increase access to, and improve the quality of, schooling. The project required that implementers locate schools within walking distance of children out-of-school, near other networks of formal primary schools, and in close proximity to main roads.[21] IRC Ethiopia built a geographic database of demographic data and primary school location, among other variables, to map the construction of schools. Highly disaggregated data permitted a nuanced understanding of where schools could be built to reach the highest number of out-of-school children. Similar school mapping projects are underway globally, including one led by UNICEF Innovation.[22]

Each of these examples suggests that using geospatial data to allocate resources to reach those furthest behind can be a successful strategy for building human development. We would simply add that such efforts should not be considered

19. World Health Organization (2017).
20. United Nations Development Programme (2018).
21. ESRI (2009).
22. See UNICEF, "School Mapping," www.unicef.org/innovation/school-mapping.

just sector-by-sector, but perhaps also should involve a coordinated push across a range of interventions in the most disadvantaged places.

Infrastructure and Connectivity

In their seminal report *Reshaping Economic Geography* (2009), the World Bank argues that distance—or the time and cost required to connect economic production hubs—is a critically important correlate of growth. The better the infrastructure and connectivity, the greater the mobility of labor and goods.

We use several spatial measures of infrastructure to account for the impact of connectivity on subnational development. We use data on the distance to a road (a proxy for road density) at the beginning of the period, the distance to the national border (areas close to the border can be far from the heart of the national economy), the distance to a coastline (coastlines can offer opportunities to engage in international trade), the travel time in minutes to a city of at least 50,000 people, and the travel time to the capital city. All these variables, except distance to the coast, are significant in our empirical results. There are many other variables associated with connectivity, including access to broadband, financial inclusion, and access to non-transport infrastructure like power and telecommunications. We have not yet found suitable spatial proxies, on a global scale, to include these variables, but would guess that they, too, would prove to be important.

What are the implications for policy? In general, it is easier to anticipate higher benefits when initial access is limited. If a region has a very low density of roads, it is easier to double the existing access than if the region starts off with a high road density. But our analysis reveals only information on the benefits of greater connectivity; it does not include a consideration of cost. For example, building a road in a far-flung region with low population density might be expensive in a cost-benefit calculus. Detailed analysis is required for any given project, but, nevertheless, it is heartening to realize that, on average, investment in connectivity could raise regional growth.

Satellite and luminosity data are making it easier to see and analyze the connective linkages in a region, as well as their proximity to villages and major transport hubs. In this way, planners can identify and evaluate the impact of road projects. A good example of this technique comes from an analysis of new transportation infrastructure in the Palestinian territories. There, Israeli checkpoints and roadblocks result in heavy traffic and delays along major roads, costing Palestinians an estimated US$185 million per year due to extra time and mileage.[23] Protracted conflict also produces routine damage to bridges and roads; during

---

23. Isaac and Rishmawi (2015), Khalil and others (2015) quoted in Ives and others (2017).

the 2008–09 Israel-Gaza conflict, an estimated 167 kilometers of paved and unpaved roads sustained damage.[24] Several infrastructure projects are underway, including USAID's $900 million investment in the Infrastructure Needs Program (INP) II. To date, the project has funded the construction or rehabilitation of fifty-nine rural road segments in the West Bank.[25] AidData and USAID teamed up to evaluate the effect of road improvements on economic development in the Palestinian territories. Using luminosity as a proxy for economic activity, the team found a statistically significant increase in nighttime lights due to INP II road projects. In communities where multiple road segments were improved, the economic impact was even larger. Their findings suggest that improving roads in rural areas with multiple access points to larger road networks and in more urban, densely-populated areas is an important policy priority.[26]

Exposure to Environmental and Violent Political Shocks

Climate and environmental change pose an increasing risk to the global community: concentrations of CO_2 and other long-lived greenhouse gases continue to increase; biodiversity is declining; tropical reefs and oceanic habitats are facing profound losses; and 25 percent of all land is degraded.[27] Addressing environmental shocks is central to accelerating development and ensuring that places are not left further behind. At the same time, and often in interrelated ways, environmental shocks can precipitate political shocks that result in conflict-related deaths.[28]

While short-term fixes are unlikely, policies can support shock-readiness and resilience. Climate resistant architecture[29] and drought technology,[30] for example, can aid communities and individuals facing extreme climates. Land registration and transparency can reduce the risk of conflict.

The severity, duration, and frequency of various shocks affect the resilience of subnational areas and their developmental trajectories. We look at human and natural shocks in the form of political conflict and drought, respectively. Both factors have been associated with persistent underdevelopment and poverty at the national level, with some analyses showing that the two are related—that drought can increase the likelihood of conflict over resources.[31]

24. OCHA (2016) quoted in Ives and others 2017.
25. BenYishay and others (2018).
26. Ibid. (2019).
27. UNEP (2019).
28. Smith in Chandy, Kato, and Kharas (2015).
29. OECD (2018).
30. UN Permanent Missions (2018).
31. Miguel, Satyanath, and Sergenti (2004).

The measurement of conflict is empirically tricky. Violence is decreasing worldwide although the number of civil conflicts is on the rise.[32] According to the OECD, political violence has spread across more than fifty countries in the past decade and a half.[33] But previous conflict is not a good predictor of future conflict. If past conflict has been resolved, then growth can rebound rapidly. On the other hand, if past conflict simply breeds a new round of conflict going forward, then growth can be impeded. What seems to be important is whether the political situation is stabilizing or not. Accordingly, we use the change in the average number of deaths (per 100,000 population) from war, armed conflict, and political violence in a base period (1989 to 2000) compared to a more recent period (2013 to 2017) as an indicator of the "shock" associated with conflict. For natural hazard shocks, we use a measure of the number of drought events from 1981 to 2001. We also add a measure of exposure to floods, although we expect this could be a benefit to growth in areas where land suitability is high for agricultural crop production. Our empirical approach suggests that shocks affect growth. The implication is that policy interventions should try to anticipate and mitigate these effects.

A good example is the use in Mozambique of recreational drones to monitor crop yields. Agriculture is at the fore of economic activity in Mozambique, employing over 80 percent of the labor force.[34] The majority of those in agricultural occupations are smallholder farmers who are highly susceptible to climate shocks and natural disasters, which are not infrequent on Mozambique's arable land. Many of these farmers lack access to actionable information on best use of limited resources (for example, fertilizer, water, and seeds). In response, the Third Eye project has set up a network of recreational drones to increase the provision of highly granular data on crop yield.[35] Sensors on the drones measure the reflection of near-infrared light and visible red light that, when combined, provide a Normalized Difference Vegetation Index (NDVI). By indicating whether vegetation is healthy or under stress, NDVI values show where crops may lack fertilizer or water, or face other constraints. Early data suggests that crop production in Mozambique has increased by 41 percent and water productivity by 55 percent as a result of this information.[36]

New geospatial technologies also could help inform policy interventions in conflict-affected regions. In the Democratic Republic of the Congo (DRC),

32. Blattman and Miguel (2010).

33. OECD. 2016. *States of Fragility: Understanding Violence*. OECD Publishing: p. 20.

34. USAID, "Agriculture and Food Security," www.usaid.gov/mozambique/agriculture-and-food-security.

35. See Third Eye, www.thirdeyewater.com/.

36. African Union & The New Partnership for Africa's Development (NEPAD 2018).

ineffective land management has contributed to violence and protracted conflict that may have had its origins in the late nineteenth century, when Belgian colonial powers introduced new policies on land and forest tenure that superseded the authority of traditional leadership. Competing systems of land management, further complicated by 1970 land use legislation, led to rising tension that produced violence, human rights abuses, and destruction of property. Sharing the Land, an initiative run by Christian Bilingual University of Congo students, sought to address heightened conflict by coupling community organizing principles with geospatial technologies.[37] Using data from satellites, household surveys, and government records, the group compiled, mapped, and publicized land ownership claims in a northern region of the DRC. A USAID blog credits the group with promoting transparent and equitable land ownership practices.[38]

Governance and Institutions

Good governance is a primary driver of economic development and, as discussed earlier, there are limits to what can be achieved at the subnational level if national policies are inadequate. As one proxy for national governance and institutions, we use the rule of law indicator for the year 2000, from the World Bank's Worldwide Governance Indicators database. As a robustness check, we also run the regressions with country fixed effects, a technique that captures, in a summary fashion, a wide range of governance and institutional differences between countries. Unfortunately, we do not have comparable global indicators of subnational governance quality, although these would be helpful in understanding how local level governance can mitigate national shortcomings. We find that the rule of law is highly significant, but in a nonlinear way. Initial small improvements in the rule of law are linked to little difference to growth, and can even be harmful. But further improvements have an exponential, positive association with growth.

Can spatial analysis help improve governance? We believe so. Consider the example of how geo-coded polling in Nigeria is helping build trust in elections. Since Nigeria's transition to democracy in 1999, violence has erupted among political party supporters around the national elections. Violence reached a peak in the span of three days after the 2011 election, when 800 people died in election-related clashes. Building public confidence in Nigeria's Independent National Electoral Commission (INEC) is central to ensuring a credible and

37. See Center on Conflict and Development, "DRC: Sharing the Land," Texas A&M University, https://condevcenter.org/sharing-the-land/.
38. Lobo (2016).

peaceful election cycle.[39] The International Foundation for Electoral Systems (IFES) partnered with INEC to address one dimension of the election process: polling stations. For decades, Nigeria has offered just under 120,000 polling stations despite rapid urbanization and a growing population. To better manage voting points, an IFES GIS and data management specialist devised a database of polling stations that inventories and spatially locates all places reporting election results. This and related data provides electoral stakeholders with a trusted hub of information and informs efforts to roll out additional polling units in congested areas.[40] Though the 2019 Nigerian election was not without logistical hurdles and political violence, use of a single geospatial database of all polling locations, trusted by all stakeholders, likely mitigated tensions in the preparations ahead of elections and in the resolution of disputes in the aftermath.

Accelerating Development in Poverty Hotspots

Using a simple, stochastic simulation method (see appendix for details), we can simulate what might happen to the growth in GDP per capita if policy interventions were to change some of the underlying correlates of growth.

Figure 10-2 summarizes the marginal effects of several variables. For example, doubling road network density within a subnational area will add just over 1 percentage point to annual growth rates. Mitigating the impact of droughts by half adds another percent. An additional percent increase in growth may be achieved by raising the HDI score by 10 percent (at the country level, this would be the equivalent of Rwanda raising its HDI score to that of Angola, Iraq raising its score to that of Thailand, or South Africa raising its score to that of Brazil). Doubling a country's Rule of Law score adds 0.75 percent. Cutting the rate of conflict deaths by half increases growth by an additional 0.5 percent. Finally, increasing the accessibility of urban areas adds about 0.4 percent to growth. These six reforms, therefore, would add 4.5 percent to a subnational region's annual growth over the next ten years. Cumulated over a decade, this is enough to add over 50 percent to a region's GDP per capita.

We have given examples of how policy reforms can use geospatial information to achieve greater impact on lagging areas. We also believe the potential for greater use of spatial targeting in allocating public spending is high. While we do not have geo-coded data on domestic public spending, AidData has published geo-located information on World Bank projects.[41] They show that between

39. Verjee and others (2018).
40. International Foundation for Electoral Systems (2015).
41. AidData (2017).

Figure 10-2. Marginal Effects of Changes at
the Subnational Level on Growth

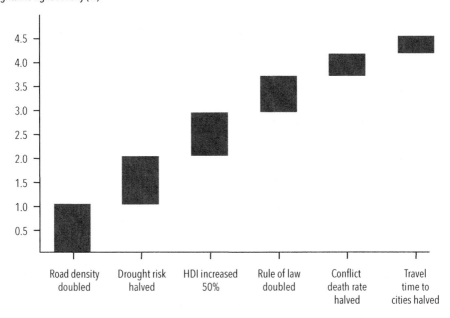

Notes: Estimated effects are generated via stochastic simulation of the specification in
column 1, Table A2 (Appendix), each of which represents the effect of changes to each of the
explanatory variables along the horizontal axis, while setting all other control variables at their
sample means.

1989 to 2014, the World Bank committed aid worth $129 per person in poverty
hotspot areas and $104 in other developing country areas. This is a small dif-
ference compared to the difference in needs; a far greater share of aid should be
going to hotspot areas if extreme poverty is to be eradicated by 2030.

Conclusion

By 2030, perhaps 1.7 billion people will still live in places where the average
income level leaves them close to being in, or falling into, extreme poverty. A new
toolkit of advanced geospatial technologies now permits an ever-more granular
understanding of where the most vulnerable reside and what can be done to get

them back on track. It is a fallacy to believe that natural migration will move people from poor areas to places that offer more opportunity. At least for the time being, higher fertility rates associated with being poor are pushing population growth rates in poor places above those in more prosperous places, even within each country.

BenYishay and Parks (2019) suggest that the availability and provision of location-specific data can (i) highlight underserved areas, (ii) encourage public officials to allocate resources to areas identified as underserved, and (iii) provide citizens with accountability mechanisms that help ensure that resource allocation is more responsive to local needs. In this chapter, we have taken a first step at identifying the most underserved places in the world, although we freely acknowledge that further work is needed to make this into an actionable tool. We also provide suggestive evidence that aid, from at least one major multilateral donor whose projects have been geo-coded, does not historically have a sufficient bias toward poverty hotspots. Finally, we are encouraged by the proliferation of subnational data that now exists and that could, and should, be more widely disseminated to help citizens benchmark themselves against their neighbors.

Our central takeaway: Spatial targeting offers considerable promise in ensuring that geography will not become destiny for large numbers of people in developing countries.

Appendix

Stochastic Simulation Procedure

Much can be learned about the distributional properties of a random variable by sampling from the underlying probability distribution that generated that variable. We rely on the "Clarify" procedure developed by King, Tomz, and Wittenberg (2000), which uses Monte Carlo simulation of parameter distributions to estimate predicted outcome values. For each coefficient to be estimated in a regression model, 1,000 out-of-sample observations are simulated using the known properties of each independent variable (including mean and standard deviation). The result is a series of randomly generated parameters with the same distributional characteristics as each of the variables in the model—in effect, multiple observations on the initial coefficients. Using these out-of-sample observations, we then generate predicted values of our dependent variable by setting any particular regressor at a particular value, while setting all other regressors at their sample means.

Table 10 A-1. Variable Descriptions and Sources

Variable	Measurement	Source
Nighttime light density	Natural-log mean nightlight luminosity in 30 arc-second resolution averaged within each GADM-1 in 2003 and 2013 polygon divided by GADM-1 population.	DMSP-OLS Nighttime Lights, version 4, NOAA's National Geophysical Data Center.
GDP per capita	2006 GDP data based on nighttime luminosity, converted to 2006 PPP dollars apportioned by population based on LandScan data; 30 arc-second resolution averaged within each GADM-1 polygon in natural logs. Divided by summed population for each GADM-1 polygon using Gridded Population of the World (GPW), v4	Ghosh and others (2010) and Gridded Population of the World (GPW), v4 (SEDAC, CIESIN)
Population density	2005 population count at 15 arc-minute resolution summed within each GADM-1 polygon divided by polygon area	Gridded Population of the World (version 4), NASA's Socioeconomic Data and Applications Center (SEDAC)
Rule of law	2000 rule of law index from Worldwide Governance Indicators	Worldwide Governance Indicators
Normalized difference vegetation index	Difference between near-infrared (which vegetation strongly reflects) and red light (which vegetation absorbs), at 30 arc-second resolution averaged within each GADM-1 polygon	Pedelty and others (2007)
Road density	Mean distance (m) to roads between 1980 and 2010 (depending on the country) at 0.5 × 0.5 degree resolution, averaged within each GADM-1 polygon	Global Roads Open Access Data Set, Version 1 (gROADSv1)
Distance to borders	Distance (m) from GADM-1 centroid to nearest international border	Global Administrative Areas (GADM)
Travel time to cities	Travel time (mins.) to the nearest city of 50,000 using land (road/off road) or water (navigable river, lake and ocean) based travel at 5 km × 5 km resolution, averaged within GADM-1 polygons, in natural logs; accessibility is computed using a cost-distance algorithm for travelling between two locations on a regular raster grid	Nelson (2008)
Travel time to capital	Value of average estimated travel time (mins.) to capital city at 5 km × 5 km resolution, averaged within GADM-1 polygons	European Commission

Variable	Description	Source
Drought events	Count of area where monthly precipitation is lower than 50% of the median value calculated for the period 1961–90 during at least three consecutive months, summed within each GADM-1 polygon	Global Risk Data Platform
Flood risk	Global risk induced by flood hazard from 1 (low) to 5 (extreme), at 30 arc-second resolution, averaged within GADM-1 polygons	Global Risk Data Platform
Distance to coastline	Haversine distance (m) from GADM-1 centroid to nearest coastline	World Vector Shorelines from A Global Self-Consistent, Hierarchical, High-Resolution Geography Database
Malaria suitability	Temperature suitability index for P. falciparum transmission, 2010, at 5 km × 5 km resolution, averaged within GADM-1 polygons	The Malaria Atlas Project
Conflict deaths	Sum of deaths attributable to war and political conflict georeferenced by incident between 1989 and 2000, summed within GADM-1 polygons, divided by 100,000 GADM-1 population	Uppsala Conflict Data Program
Human Development Index	2005 HDI score in 30 arc-second resolution, averaged within each GADM-1 polygon.	Kummu, Taka, and Guillaume (2018)
World Bank project value per capita	Aid data from World Bank Donor System, geocoded and published by AidData. Covers projects from 1995 to 2014. Version 1.4.2.	AidData GeoQuery (2018)
Mean annual precipitation	Average precipitation per year. Created using UDel Precipitation dataset (v4.01). 1980–2014	UDel Precipitation dataset via GeoQuery (2018)
Mean annual temperature	Average air temperature per year. Created using UDel Precipitation dataset (v4.01). 1980–2014	UDel Precipitation dataset via GeoQuery (2018)

Note: For all variables x with zero values, natural logs are calculated as Ln(1 + x).

Table 10 A-2. Change in Subnational Economic Activity Per Capita, 2003 to 2013

	(1)	(2)	(3)	(4)
	All countries	Developing countries	All countries	Developing countries
GDP per capita (Ln, 2006)	-0.013***	-0.014***	-0.018***	-0.020***
	(0.002)	(0.002)	(0.004)	(0.005)
Population density (Ln, 2005)	-0.009***	-0.010***	-0.005**	-0.005**
	(0.001)	(0.001)	(0.002)	(0.002)
Human Capital:				
Human Development Index (2005)	0.036**	0.053***	0.020	0.018
	(0.015)	(0.018)	(0.018)	(0.021)
Malaria suitability (Ln)	-0.001	-0.003***	-0.002*	-0.002
	(0.001)	(0.001)	(0.001)	(0.001)
Infrastructure and Connectivity:				
Distance to roads (m, Ln)	-0.005***	-0.009***	-0.003	-0.008**
	(0.002)	(0.002)	(0.002)	(0.004)
Distance to country border (m, Ln)	0.007***	0.009***	0.003*	0.005**
	(0.001)	(0.002)	(0.002)	(0.002)
Distance to coastline (m, Ln)	-0.000	0.000	0.002	0.001
	(0.001)	(0.001)	(0.002)	(0.003)
Travel time to cities (mins., Ln)	0.004**	0.006**	0.005**	0.008**
	(0.002)	(0.003)	(0.002)	(0.003)
Travel time to capital (mins., Ln)	-0.002***	-0.002***	-0.001**	-0.001**
	(0.000)	(0.000)	(0.001)	(0.001)
Exposure to Shocks:				
Difference in conflict deaths, 1989–2000 vs. 2013-2017 (per 100,000, Ln)	-0.003***	-0.003***	0.002	0.002
	(0.001)	(0.001)	(0.001)	(0.001)
Drought exposure (Ln)	-0.004**	-0.005**	-0.001	-0.001
	(0.002)	(0.002)	(0.001)	(0.002)
Flood risk (Ln)	0.023***	0.033***	0.001	0.002
	(0.004)	(0.005)	(0.005)	(0.006)
Normalized difference vegetation index (Ln)	0.007***	0.010***	0.004	0.006
	(0.002)	(0.003)	(0.005)	(0.006)

	(1)	(2)	(3)	(4)
	All countries	Developing countries	All countries	Developing countries
Governance:				
Rule of law (2000)	-0.006***	0.017***		
	(0.002)	(0.004)		
Rule of law^2 (2000)	0.002*	0.019***		
	(0.001)	(0.003)		
N	3,054	2,260	3,054	2,260
n	189	130	189	130
Adjusted/Overall R^2	0.178	0.146	0.143	0.085
$p < F$	0.000	0.000	0.000	0.000
Country-fixed effects	No	No	Yes	Yes

Notes: Dependent variable is log-difference in nighttime luminosity per capita between 2003 and 2013 in annual terms. Estimation is by ordinary least squares (OLS) with standard errors (columns 1 and 2) and errors clustered by *n* countries (columns 3 and 4). Intercepts (all columns) and fixed effects for *n* countries (columns 3 and 4) are estimated but not reported. Developing countries are those with GNI per capita (current dollars, Atlas method) less than $12,055 in 2017.
    *** $p < 0.01$, ** $p < 0.05$, * $p < 0.1$

References

Acemoglu, Daron, Simon Johnson, and James A. Robinson. 2001. "The Colonial Origins of Comparative Development: An Empirical Investigation." *American Economic Review* 91, no. 5: 1369–401.

African Union & The New Partnership for Africa's Development (NEPAD). 2018. "Drones on the Horizon: Transforming Africa's Agriculture." www.nepad.org/publication/drones-horizon-transforming-africas-agriculture.

AidData. 2017. WorldBank_GeocodedResearchRelease_Level1_v1.4.2 geocoded dataset. Williamsburg, VA, and Washington, DC: AidData. http://aiddata.org/research-datasets.

BenYishay, Ariel, and Brad Parks. 2019. "Can Providing Local Data on Aid and Population Needs Improve Development Decision-Making? A Review of Recent Experimental Evidence." AidData at William & Mary.

BenYishay, Ariel, and others. 2018. "A Quiet Revolution in Impact Evaluation at USAID." Future Development. The Brookings Institution. www.brookings.edu/blog/future-development/2018/10/08/a-quiet-revolution-in-impact-evaluation-at-usaid/.

———. 2019. "Evaluation of the Infrastructure Needs Program II." AidData, William & Mary. https://www.aiddata.org/publications/evaluation-of-usaid-west-bank-gaza-infrastructure-needs-program.

Blattman, Chris, and Edward Miguel. 2010. "Civil War." *Journal of Economic Literature* 48, no. 1: 3–57.

Center on Conflict and Development. "DRC: Sharing the Land." Texas A&M University. https://condevcenter.org/sharing-the-land/.

Dahl, Gordon B., and Lance Lochner. 2012. "The Impact of Family Income on Child Achievement." *American Economic Review* 102, no. 5: 1927–56.

ESRI. 2009. "GIS Best Practices: GIS in Africa." www.esri.com/~/media/Files/Pdfs/library/bestpractices/gis-in-africa.pdf.

European Committee of the Regions. 2018. "Spatial Planning and Governance within EU Policies and Legislation and Their Relevance to the New Urban Agenda." European Union.

Gallup, John Luke, and Jeffrey D. Sachs. 2001. "The Economic Burden of Malaria: The Intolerable Burden of Malaria: A New Look at the Numbers." *American Journal of Tropical Medicine and Hygiene* Suppl 64, no. 1: 85–96.

Gallup, John Luke, Jeffrey D. Sachs, and Andrew D. Mellinger. 1999. "Geography and Economic Development." *International Regional Science Review.* https://doi.org/10.1177%2F016001799761012334.

Gennaioli, Nicola, and others. 2014. "Growth in Regions." *Journal of Economic Growth* 19, no. 3: 259–309.

Ghosh, Tilottama, and others. 2010. "Shedding Light on the Global Distribution of Economic Activity." *Open Geography Journal* 3, no. 1: 148–61.

Goodman, Seth, and others. 2019. "GeoQuery: Integrating HPC Systems and Public Web-Based Geospatial Data Tools." *Computers and Geosciences* 122: 103–12.

Hall, Robert E., and Charles I. Jones. 1999. "Why Do Some Countries Produce So Much More Output Per Worker Than Others?" *Quarterly Journal of Economics* 114, no. 1: 83–116.

Henderson, J. Vernon, and others. 2018. "The Global Spatial Distribution of Economic Activity: Nature, History, and the Role of Trade." *Quarterly Journal of Economics* 133, no. 1: 357–406. https://doi.org/10.1093/qje/qjx030.

Holding, Penny A., and Patricia K. Kitsao-Wekulo. 2004. "Describing the Burden of Malaria on Child Development: What Should We Be Measuring and How Should We Be Measuring It?" *American Journal of Tropical Medicine and Hygiene* 71, no. 2: 71–79.

International Foundation for Electoral Systems. 2015. "IFES and INEC Partners to Build Trust in Nigeria's Elections." www.ifes.org/news/ifes-and-inec-partner-build-trust-nigerias-elections.

Isaac, Jad, and Khaldoun Rishmawi. 2015. "Status of the Environment in the State of Palestine 2015." Applied Research Institute – Jerusalem. ARIJ. www.arij.org/files/arijadmin/2016/Final_SOER_2015_opt_r.pdf.

Isaacs, Julia B., and Emily Roessel. "Impacts of Early Childhood Programs." The Brookings Institution. www.brookings.edu/research/impacts-of-early-childhood-programs/.

Ives, Matthew C., and others. 2018. "A Fast Track Analysis of Infrastructure Provision in Palestine: Outcomes from the ITRC/UNOPS Collaboration." ITRC and UNOPS. www.itrc.org.uk/wp-content/PDFs/PalestineFTA_online.pdf.

Kamarck, Andrew M. 1976. "The Tropics and Economic Development: A Provocative Inquiry into the Poverty of Nations." International Bank for Reconstruction and Development.

King, Gary, Michael Tomz, and Jason Wittenberg. 2000. "Making the Most of Statistical Analyses: Improving Interpretation and Presentation." *American Journal of Political Science* 44, no. 2: 341–55.

Kummu, Matti, Maija Taka, and Joseph H. Guillaume. 2018. "Gridded Global Datasets for Gross Domestic Product and Human Development Index over 1990–2015." *Scientific Data* 5: 180004.

Liu, Jianghong, and Adrian Raine. 2016. "Nutritional Status and Social Behavior in Preschool Children: The Mediating Effects of Neurocognitive Functioning." *Maternal and Child Nutrition* 13, no. 2.

Lobo, Archip. 2016. "Sharing the Land: Using Mapping Technology to Resolve Disputes." USAID. https://blog.usaid.gov/2016/02/sharing-the-land-using-mapping-technology-to-resolve-disputes/.

Mankiw, N. Gregory, David Romer, and David N. Weil. 1992. "A Contribution to the Empirics of Economic Growth." *Quarterly Journal of Economics* 107, no. 2: 407–37.

Masters, William, and Margaret S. McMillan. 2001. "Climate and Scale in Economic Growth." *Journal of Economic Growth* 6, no. 3: 167–86.

Mayer, Susan E. 2002. *The Influence of Parental Income on Children's Outcomes.* Wellington: Knowledge Management Group, New Zealand Ministry of Social Development.

Michaels, Guy, and Ferdinand Rauch. 2013. "Resetting the Urban Network: 117–2012." CEPR Discussion Papers 9760.

Miguel, Edward, Shanker Satyanath, and Ernest Sergenti. 2004. "Economic Shocks and Civil Conflict: An Instrumental Variables Approach." *Journal of Political Economy* 112, no. 4: 725–53.

Myrdal, Gunnar. 1968. *Asian Drama: An Inquiry into the Poverty of Nations.* Three volumes. New York: Pantheon.

Narayan, Ambar Narayan, and others. 2018. "Fair Progress? Economic Mobility across Generations around the World." World Bank Group.

Nelson, A. 2008. "Estimated Travel Time to the Nearest City of 50,000 or More People in Year 2000." Global Environment Monitoring Unit – Joint Research Centre of the European Commission, Ispra Italy. http://forobs.jrc.ec.europa.eu/products/gam/

North, Douglass C. 1990. *Institutions, Institutional Change, and Economic Performance.* Cambridge University Press.

OCHA. 2016. "Humanitarian Bulletin: Occupied Palestinian Territory, United Nations, Office for the Coordination of Humanitarian Affairs." www.ochaopt.org/documents/ocha_opt_the_humanitarian_monitor_2016_01_05_english.pdf.

OECD. 2016. *States of Fragility 2016: Understanding Violence.* Paris: OECD Publishing. https://dx.doi.org/10.1787/9789264267213-en.

———. 2018. "Climate-Resilient Infrastructure." OECD Environment Policy Paper 14. www.oecd.org/environment/cc/policy-perspectives-climate-resilient-infrastructure.pdf.

Pandey, Priyanka, Sangeeta Goyal, and Venkatesh Sundararaman. 2009. "Community Participation in Public Schools: Impact of Information Campaigns in Three Indian States." *Education Economics* 17, no. 3: 355–75.

Pandey, Priyanka, and others. 2007. "Informing Resource Poor Populations and the Delivery of Entitled Health and Social Services in Rural India. A Cluster Randomized Controlled Trial." *Journal of American Medical Association* 298, no. 16: 1867–75.

Pedelty, Jeffrey, and others. 2007. "Generating a Long-Term Land Data Record from the AVHRR and MODIS Instruments." IEEE International Geoscience and Remote Sensing Symposium, July 23: 1021–25.

Psacharopoulos, George, and Henry Anthony Patrinos. 2018. "Returns to Investment in Education: A Decennial Review of the Global Literature." *Education Economics* 26, no. 5: 445–58.

Rosewell, Alexander, and others. 2017. "Health Information System Strengthening and Malaria Elimination in Papua New Guinea." *Malaria Journal* 16, no. 278. https://doi.org/10.1186/s12936-017-1910-0.

Sachs, Jeffrey D., and Pia Malaney. 2002. "The Economic and Social Burden of Malaria." *Nature* 415, no. 6872: 680–85.

Sachs, Jeffrey D., and Andrew M. Warner. 2001. "The Curse of Natural Resources." *European Economic Review* 45: 827–38.

Schneider, Friedrich. 2009a. "The Size of the Shadow Economy in 21 OECD Countries (in % of 'Official' GDP) Using the MIMIC and Currency Demand Approach: from 1989/90 to 2009." Johannes Kepler Universitat Linz, Austria.

Schneider, Friedrich. 2009b. "The Size of the Shadow Economy for 25 Transition Countries over 1999/00 to 2006/07: What Do We Know?" Johannes Kepler Universitat Linz, Austria.

Smith, Stephen C. 2015. "The Two Fragilities: Vulnerability to Conflict. Environmental Stress, and Their Interactions as Challenges to Ending Poverty." In *The Last Mile in Ending Extreme Poverty* by Chandy, L., H. Kato, and H. Kharas. Brookings Press: 328–68.

Third Eye. www.thirdeyewater.com/.

United Nations. 1997. "Glossary of Environment Statistics, Studies in Methods." Series F: 67.

United Nations Development Programme. 2018. "Ethiopia National Human Development Report 2018: Industrialization with a Human Face." UNDP Ethiopia: 26. http://hdr.undp.org/sites/default/files/ethiopia_national_human_development_report_2018.pdf.

UNEP. 2019. *Global Environmental Outlook GEO-6: Health Planet, Healthy People.* Cambridge University Press.

UNICEF. "School Mapping." https://www.unicef.org/innovation/school-mapping.

UN Millennium Project. 2005. "Investing in Development: A Practical Plan to Achieve the Millennium Development Goals." United Nations Development Programme.

UN Permanent Missions. 2018. "Using Technology to Find Water in Drought-Stricken Somalia." www.un.int/news/using-technology-find-water-drought-stricken-somalia.

USAID. "Agriculture and Food Security." www.usaid.gov/mozambique/agriculture-and-food-security.

Verjee, Aly, Chris Kwaja, and Oge Onubogu. 2018. "Nigeria's 2019 Elections: Change, Continuity, and the Risks to Peace." *United States Institute of Peace.* www.usip.org/publications/2018/09/nigerias-2019-elections-change-continuity-and-risks-peace.

Vollrath, Dietrich. 2019. "The Deep Roots of Development – Part 5." Growth Economics. https://growthecon.com/blog/Deep-Roots-5/.

World Bank Group. 2009. "Reshaping Economic Geography." World Development Report 43738.

World Health Organization. 2017. "Despite Overwhelming Challenges, Papua New Guinea has Made Major Strides against Malaria." www.who.int/news-room/feature-stories/detail/despite-overwhelming-challenges-papua-new-guinea-has-made-major-strides-against-malaria.

CHAPTER ELEVEN

Leaving No Fragile State and No One Behind in a Prosperous World: A New Approach

Landry Signé

H undreds of millions of people are left behind in fragile states despite the efforts of the international community to make progress on development and alleviate conflict. People in fragile states are victim to persistent poverty,[1] enduring violence, poor public facilities, deteriorating infrastructure,[2] limited civil and political liberties,[3] deteriorating social conditions,[4] minimal to nonexistent economic growth,[5] and, often, humanitarian crises.[6] Research and policies on state fragility build on concepts of limited state capacity, legitimacy, insecurity, stability and socioeconomic, demographic, human development, environmental, humanitarian, and gender contexts to determine states' apparent effectiveness or ineffectiveness in fulfilling the role of the state. Within this context, fragility has become a catch-all concept encompassing fragile states, weak states, failed states, collapsing or decaying states, conflict-affected countries, post-conflict countries, brittle states, and states with limited legitimacy, authority, capacity, governance, security, and socioeconomic and human development.

1. Collier (2007).
2. Rotberg (2011).
3. Bah (2012).
4. Van de Walle (2004).
5. Brainard and Chollet (2007).
6. Nwozor (2018).

The author would like to express his sincere appreciation to Payce Madden, Genevieve Jesse, and Elise El Nouchi, who contributed to the research, data analysis, fact-checking, and visual elements of this chapter.

When used without conceptual clarification and contextual consideration, as is often the case, the concept of fragility lacks usefulness for policymakers, as the various types, drivers, scopes, levels, and contexts of fragility require different responses. Neglecting to consider the complexity and multidimensionality of fragility and failing to tailor solutions to individual contexts undermines the effectiveness of the global fight to leave no fragile state behind in a prosperous world and to leave no one behind in fragile countries. For simplicity, "fragility" in this chapter will broadly refer to states' capacity to "manage conflict, make and implement public policy, and deliver essential services."[7] Building on this definition, this chapter brings nuance to the concept of fragility and systematizes policy solutions based on political conflicts and policy ambiguities through the introduction of a framework for a new approach to fragility.

Too many fragile states remain left behind in this prosperous world,[8] constituting a serious risk to global stability and prosperity. Fragility as a concept has been addressed in practice through the diplomatic, political, economic, development, humanitarian, and security fields; each of these fields often implementing distinct solutions to achieve specific goals over the past two decades. Despite the implementation of numerous solutions, and some notable success stories, the international community has not succeeded in eliminating fragility, and many countries have remained "trapped" in fragility for decades. While the misalignment of resources, including aid, investment, and technical assistance, has contributed to the persistence of fragility, many attempts to address fragility have failed even when given sufficient resources. To face the complexity, a new approach that focuses on the political economy of policy implementation and service delivery is needed to more effectively implement policies designed to target the root causes of fragility and leave no one and no country behind. Such an approach should also align resources to the needs and capacities of countries and consider the individual contexts of countries, including their level of policy ambiguity, conflict, decentralization, and private sector support.

The application of sufficient, targeted resources—including aid, foreign direct investment, and tax revenue—is critical to fight fragility. In fact, some fragile countries are also among the lowest recipients of aid per capita: among the bottom twenty recipients of aid per capita, nine are classified as having moderate or serious fragility, and one is classified as having high or extreme fragility.[9] As stated by Landry Signé (2018), studying how institutions shape development

---

7. Marshall, Monty G., and Gabrielle Elzinga-Marshall (2016). State Fragility Index and Matrix 2016. Center for Systemic Peace. http://www.systemicpeace.org/inscr/SFImatrix2016c.pdf.

8. World Bank (2019a, 2019b); OECD (2018).

9. The countries with moderate or serious fragility among the bottom twenty recipients of aid per capita are Egypt, Indonesia, the Philippines, Iran, India, Venezuela, Kazakhstan, Algeria, and Equatorial Guinea. Angola is the only country with high or extreme fragility in the bottom twenty.

strategies, economic growth, regional integration, and structural transformation in Africa,[10] this chapter also illustrates that:

> key arguments against aid from Dambisa Moyo's *Dead Aid* (2009) or William Easterly's *White Man's Burden* (2006) are partially wrong, while Paul Collier's *Bottom Billion* (2007), Jeffrey Sachs's *End of Poverty* (2005), Nicolas van de Walle's *Overcoming Stagnation in Aid Dependent Countries* (2005), and Steven Radelet's *Primer on Foreign Aid* (2006) critical but favorable perspectives about aid are mostly right. Of course, indigenous and entrepreneurial solutions with "searchers" (Easterly 2006), private investment, trade, and entrepreneurship (Moyo 2009) are of critical importance and should not be substituted by foreign interventions. However, despite many failures and "horror stories about aid bureaucracy" (Collier 2007), if aid is appropriately structured with better policies and accountability (Radelet 2006; van de Walle 2005), the world's poor [and fragile states] require more aid, not less (Sachs 2005). Rightly done, "aid makes private investment more attractive and so helps to keep capital in the countries." Aid is therefore "part of the solutions rather than part of the problem. The challenge is to complement it with other actions" (Collier 2007). A well-targeted, tailored, and structured aid program is good for both the poorest and for business, especially when integrated in a broader pro-growth, pro-business, pro-poor agenda with accountable and effective governance with responsible and competent political leadership.

This is particularly relevant for fragile states, understood to be natural recipients of aid.

This chapter systematically studies fragility, and the critical importance of assisting people left behind in fragile countries, while providing solutions to leave no state behind in a prosperous world. The originality of this new, synthesized approach to studying state fragility lies in streamlining the solutions at the development-security-humanitarian nexus with a novel implementation framework. This chapter builds on the existing literature on state fragility, which arose in the 1990s and defined the role of the state for its citizens and the general characteristics of state failure. It then uses both case studies and descriptive statistics to explain why some countries have remained trapped in fragility while others have exited it, and moves on to propose strategies that can be used to eradicate both fragility and poverty in those countries.

Using data from the previous twenty years, this chapter undertakes a quantitative analysis of fragile indicators' prevalence in State Fragility Index-classified

10. Signé (2018).

states. The chapter expands the State Fragility Index (SFI) classifications and advances the discussion on fragile states and populations being left behind by using qualitative data—including historical research, content analysis of political structuring, and examples of institutional success—and quantitative data—including data indicating economic development (tax revenue, foreign aid, foreign direct investment [FDI], and poverty headcount), human development (education and youth, life expectancy, gender gap, refugees, and internally displaced people), and the prevalence of conflict.

The chapter concludes with new solutions to state fragility that harmonize the roles of the domestic and international private and public sectors for the initial benefit of the population and then the overall benefit of the state. The chapter also provides a new implementation framework to bridge the gap between the policy intentions and the implementation outcomes aiming at fixing fragility and people left behind in fragility, and provides options to operationalize policies that take into consideration the levels of policy ambiguity and political conflict within countries. This overview and analysis of the numerous indicators of fragility brings nuance to the discussion on why defining fragility has been thus far inconclusive and inadequate in inspiring solutions to fragility in all contexts.

Fragile States Left Behind in a Prosperous World

Fragile states are consistently left behind despite myriad policies attempting to address fragility. According to the OECD (2018), 1.8 billion people, or 24 percent of the global population, continue to live in fragile contexts in 2018. By 2030, people living in fragile contexts will total 2.3 billion and by 2050, 3.3 billion people. These numbers indicate the pressing challenge to address fragility in the short and long term.

Implementing effective solutions to fragility is one of the most difficult tasks for policymakers due to the cyclical nature of the causes and drivers of fragile states (table 11-1), evidenced by the consistency of fragile state rankings (figure 11-1). The political economy of policy implementation and service delivery[11, 12] and access to resources have consistently hindered the international community's efforts to improve the economic performance and resilience process in fragile states in general, and in Africa in particular.[13] According to the World Bank, in 2017, excluding Ethiopia, Kenya, and Nigeria, just 3.2 percent of all FDI in Sub-Saharan Africa reached fragile states, showing that outside of a few major

---

11. This includes the level of political conflict and complexity in a given state, and the clarity or ambiguity of the relevant policy options.
12. Signé (2015, 2016a, 2016b, 2017b, 2017c, 2017d).
13. Signé (2017a, 2018).

Table 11-1. Drivers of Fragility

Political	Social	Conflict	Economic	External	Geography and climate
Weak institutions (Jackson 1982; Kaplan 2008; Rotberg 2002, 2003)	Limited rights	Civil war (Rotberg 2003; Lindemann 2008; Ross 2004)	Limited growth (Marshall 2008)	Intra-state conflict (Ayoob 1996)	"Bad neighbours syndrome" and urbanization (McLoughlin 2012)
Low participation (Ghani 2009); Mass electoral politics (Mansfield 2008)	Ethnic tensions (Brown 2012; Rotberg 2003)	Enduring light conflict (Rotberg 2011)	Low income and economic decline (McLoughlin 2012; Marshall 2008)	Transnational instability (Ayoob 1996)	Environmental risks (Vallings and Moreno Torres 2005)
Patronage systems (Brown 2012)	Gender oppression	Escalating ethnic conflicts (Goldstone 2008)	Global economic shocks (McLoughlin 2012)	Regional guerillas (Goldstone 2008)	Landlocked infrastructure (Collier 2007)
Leadership mistakes (Rotberg 2003)	Lack of social contract between incumbent elite groups and constituent ethnic communities (Douma 2006)	Revolutionary wars, ethnic wars, genocide and politicide (Esty and others 1998)	Weak infrastructures (Rotberg 2002)	Highly politicized international political economy policies (McLoughlin 2012)	Natural resources (Collier 2007; Mc Loughlin 2012; Vallings and Moreno-Torres 2005; Rotberg 2003; Ross 2004)
Structural flaws (Rotberg 2003)	Group grievances (Christensen 2017)		Increased income inequalities (Sachs 2003)		
"Political capacity": organizational age and legitimacy (Jackmann 1993)	Severe identity fragmentation (McLoughlin 2012)		Lack of competence in economic governance (Brainard and Chollet 2007)		
Repressed political competition (Goldstone 2008)	Horizontal inequalities and poverty (McLoughlin 2012; Hinds 2015)				
Limited resources offered to politicians (Bates 2008)					

Figure 11-1. Persistence of Fragility

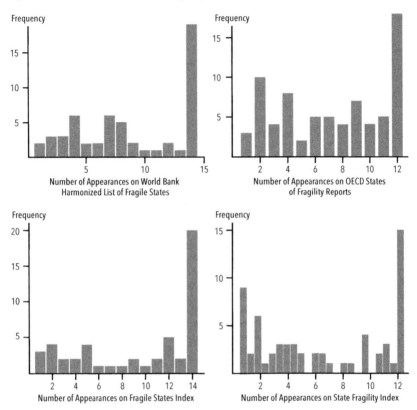

Source: State Fragility Index and World Bank Group.

countries, little FDI reaches fragile African countries. The inconsistent and incomplete application of aid and FDI to fragile states traps states within perpetual cycles of fragility.

Fragile contexts are characterized as "off track" and, thus, very unlikely to independently improve government effectiveness, build the private sector, reduce conflict and violence, respond adequately and quickly to natural hazards, and minimize environmental risks. Low education levels and health challenges characterize fragile states and reinforce future fragility. State failure relates to state fragility in that it is considered a "continuum of experiences" afflicting states with weak institutions and the characterization of "a cycle of failed government, persistent poverty, and civil war."[14]

14. Chandra and Ramesh (2005); Collier (2007).

People Left Behind in Fragile States

Within fragile states, it is vital to ensure that the needs of the population are met and that no one is left behind. The premise of "leaving no one behind" lies in addressing the interrelated concerns of poverty, inequality, humanitarian crises, and rights abuses. Globally, people are left behind as a result of social marginalization, economic disparity, political ineffectiveness, environmental challenges, and structural challenges. As of 2015, the percentage of people living at or below the international poverty line of US$1.90 per day was 35.9 percent in thirty-five fragile and conflict-affected situations.[15] This represents a decrease of over 20 percent since 1990, but an increase from 138 million people to 166 million during the same period.[16] Figure 11-2 shows the frequency and trend of extreme poverty among SFI-designated fragile, trapped, and not fragile states.[17]

Estimates that half of the world's poor will live in fragile countries by 2030 often do not factor in the compounding effect of violence on creating instability and poverty. People caught in crises are at higher risk of being left behind, and reactionary policies to violence in fragile states without contextualizing policy solutions prevent long-term improvement. Figure 11-3 demonstrates the relationship of political violence and state fragility; however, further interdisciplinary research is needed to understand the causal linkages between fragility and economic or social motivations for unrest.

Large-scale conflict and low-level violence also have contributed to the recent dramatic increase in refugees and displaced persons throughout the world. Displaced persons totaled an estimated 68.5 million globally in 2017, with the refugee population totaling 16.2 million of all displaced persons.[18] Half of all refugees are children, and refugees generally remain refugees or exiled persons for ten years on average.[19] Refugee-hosting countries also face the threat of fragility; twelve of the top fifteen refugee-hosting countries are considered fragile, and thirteen are classified as low- or middle-income.[20]

Fragile states also share the challenge of widespread gender inequality. Across

15. World Bank (2018b).
16. Ibid.
17. The SFI scores countries from 0 (no fragility) to 25 (extreme fragility) are based on the country's effectiveness and legitimacy in the areas of security, politics, economics, and social or human capital. Countries with a score of 16 or higher are classified as having high or extreme fragility, while countries with a score between 8 and 15 have moderate or serious fragility. In 2018, twenty-three countries were classified as highly or extremely fragile: the Democratic Republic of the Congo (DRC), South Sudan, the Central African Republic, Sudan, Afghanistan, Yemen, Burundi, Somalia, Ethiopia, Chad, Iraq, Myanmar, Niger, Nigeria, Guinea, Côte d'Ivoire, Zimbabwe, Angola, Cameroon, Guinea-Bissau, Mauritania, Pakistan, and Rwanda.
18. Samman and others (2018).
19. Ibid.
20. Ibid.

Figure 11-2. Poverty Headcount and Fragility

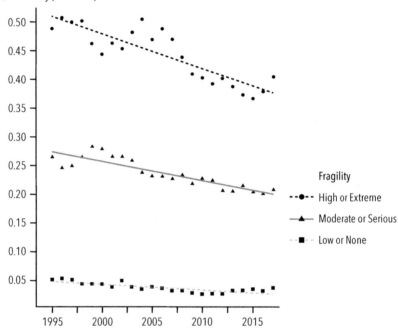

Average Poverty Headcount
Ratio at $1.90 a Day (2011 PPP)

Fragility

- - ● - - High or Extreme

——▲—— Moderate or Serious

- - ■ - - Low or None

Data sourced from State Fragility Index and World Bank Group

Figure 11-3. Conflict and Fragility

Average Magnitude of Societal
and Interstate Major Episodes
of Political Violence

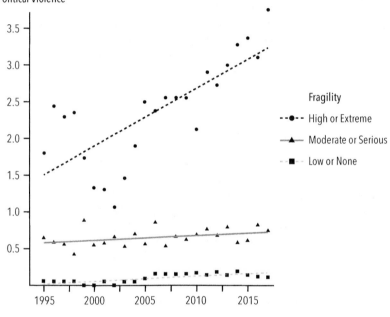

Data sourced from State Fragility Index and Center for Systemic Peace

all low- and middle-income countries, 50 percent of women who marry before the age of eighteen, thus reducing their access to education and other opportunities, are in fragile and conflict-affected states.[21] By 2030, this number is projected to reach 70 percent, or approximately 3.2 million young women.[22]

Primary school enrollment is also lower in fragile states, indicating the reinforcing effects of fragility on long-term sustainable development. Figure 11-4 shows that while the most fragile states have made some progress to improve the educational future of youth, they still have the lowest levels of primary school enrollment when compared to less fragile states.

While progress has been made in primary education, there remains a gender gap in education access within fragile countries, particularly at the secondary and higher levels (figure 11-5). This is indicative of a wider issue of gender equality in fragile states, where women are less likely to have educational, economic, and other opportunities and more likely to marry early and be subjected to gender discrimination.

Two of the final important measurements of human development in fragile states compared to the rest of the world are the health and life expectancy of individuals. Life expectancy measures indicate a state's capacity to ensure the physical well-being of its citizens through agricultural and food programs; affordable, accessible, and high-quality healthcare; and security from violence. Figure 11-6 shows the average life expectancy of people living in fragile states at different levels of severity. While average life expectancy has increased in all categories of states over the past decades, those living in extremely fragile states continue to have much lower average life expectancies than those in less fragile or stable states.

Two Decades of Focus on Fragility

The focus on state fragility has not been isolated within the highest echelons of international development or security communities. States and international organizations have all contributed their shaping ideas toward defining and fixing "fragile" states. The early 1990s saw the rise of "fragility" both as a concept and a reality that development organizations first addressed using broad donations targeted toward state building and capacity strengthening as the foundational problems of "fragile," "failing," and "decaying" states. Weak institutions and political inefficiencies drove the debate on pulling fragile states out of the known reinforcing factors of recent (or ongoing) conflict, poor economic performance,

21. Ibid.
22. Ibid.

Figure 11-4. Primary School Enrollment and Fragility

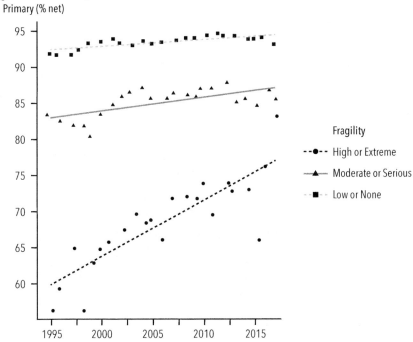

Average School Enrollment,
Primary (% net)

Fragility
--●-- High or Extreme
—▲— Moderate or Serious
-■- Low or None

Data sourced from State Fragility Index and World Bank Group

Figure 11-5. Gender Gap in Education Access and Fragility

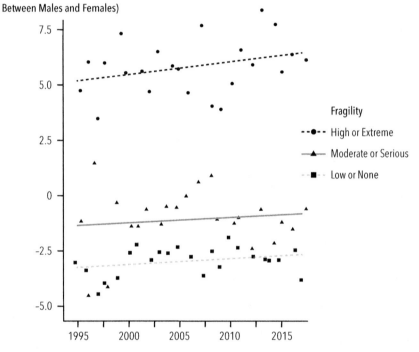

Average Gap in Secondary School
Enrollment (Difference in % Net Enrollment
Between Males and Females)

Data sourced from State Fragility Index and World Bank Group

Figure 11-6. Life Expectancy and Fragility

Average Life Expectancy at
Birth, Total (Years)

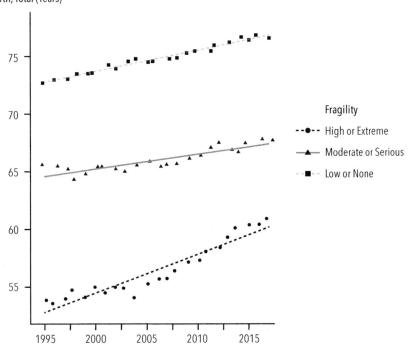

Data sourced from State Fragility Index and World Bank Group

low institutional quality, and inadequate enforcement of government contracts or rule of law.[23] These conclusions were reinforced by a general belief in "structural reform" for poverty-stricken, conflict-affected countries and accompanying policies to draft donor agreements with strict policy adherence to accountable governance and market liberalization.

The World Bank and the OECD have contributed to conceptualize and disseminate the concept of "fragile states," setting a global agenda on aid prioritization and policy solutions to fix fragility. The World Bank institutionalized the donor-driven agenda against fragility under its "low-income countries under stress" (LICUS) approach, launched in 2002.[24] "Severe," "core," and "marginal" LICUS countries were determined according to their per capita income within the International Development Association eligibility, the Country Policy and Institutional Assessment's (CPIA) overall performance, and its specific ratings for public sector management and institutions.[25] These criteria now determine "fragile states" according to the changed lexicon, but the fundamental understanding of fragile states remains located within prior efforts to secure conflict-affected states, strengthen post-conflict countries, address weak institutions, and develop critically underdeveloped nations, helping them transition to self-reliance.

The OECD also has played a major role in the creation and diffusion of donor interests in regard to fragile states. Starting with the Learning and Advisory Process on Difficult Partnership, headed by the United Kingdom in 2003, international experts and organizations were brought together at the OECD to tackle governance and post-conflict reconstruction issues. This process became the Fragile States Group, which leads data collection on countries that fail to implement development aid and works to incorporate "fragility" as an independent focus for the OECD.[26]

The agenda on fragility has been influenced through key convenings, including the Rome Declaration (2003),[27] aimed at coordinating and harmonizing aid, and the Marrakech Action Plan (2004),[28] focusing on managing development

23. Deléchat and others (2015).
24. Carvalho (2006).
25. Nay (2014).
26. Ibid.
27. The Rome Declaration was the result of the first High Level Forum on Aid Effectiveness, which outlined the principles driving donor commitments. Some principles included accounting for "partner country" priorities, harmonizing missions and reporting, cooperating with other donors, and supporting government leadership and ownership of development results. For the full declaration, see: OECD, "HLF1: The First High Level Forum on Aid Effectiveness," Rome (2019), www.oecd.org/dac/effectiveness/hlf-1thefirsthighlevelforumonaideffectivenessrome.htm.
28. The Marrakech Action Plan came out of a 2002 roundtable on measurement, monitoring, and managing results and the 2003 Development Committee's intent to create an action plan focused on improving statistical capacity. The action plan suggests an interdependent approach

results. Although these events were not specifically organized to address state fragility (as they were related to the developing world in general), they have since been recognized as foundational to coordinating aid in fragile contexts. In 2005, world leaders approved the Paris Declaration on Aid Effectiveness,[29] committing their countries and donors to improve the impact quality of aid on development.[30] The Paris Declaration, more straightforwardly, acknowledged the need to adapt aid delivery in fragile states, to align national development strategies with donor policies and procedures, and to enhance accountability and transparency in implementation.

The follow-up to the Paris Declaration, the Accra Agenda for Action,[31] adopted in 2008, solidified the global focus on fragile states through a development lens. This resolution emphasized the authority and responsibility of developing countries to manage the development process through local institutions and partnerships with donors, civil society organizations, and the private sector. The Principles for Good International Engagement in Fragile States (2007) put state-building first in its list of principles for addressing states emerging from conflict or facing severe poverty and development challenges. These international strategies were accompanied by regional and national efforts to streamline development assistance—private and public—toward specific fragility-related issues, including conflict, violence, poverty, gender inequality, and low human development. These early attempts to institutionalize strategies to address fragile states recognized the interconnected aspects of fragility but failed to prevent or solve many cases of modern fragile states. A lack of consensus about fragility as a "syndrome" or a "symptom" has led scholars to question the validity of state-building as the primary approach to solving fragility. Whereas most development

between national and international partners to create a more effective international system better suited to support development efforts. For the full report, see: Willem de Vries, Sylvester Young, Trevor Croft, Antoine Simonpietri, Charles Lufumpa, Brian Hammond, Robert Johnston, Jan Vandemoortele, and Roger Edmunds, *The Marrakech Action Plan for Statistics: Better Data for Better Results—An Action Plan for Improving Development Statistics* (English) (World Bank Group, 2004), http://documents.worldbank.org/curated/en/493571468279866267/The-Marrakech-action-plan-for-statistics-better-data-for-better-results-an-action-plan-for-improving-development-statistics.

29. The Paris Declaration resulted from the second High Level Forum on Aid Effectiveness, focusing on five pillars: ownership, alignment, harmonization, managing for results, and mutual accountability. The main contribution of this document lies in its specific implementation measures and the establishment of a monitoring system to assess progress. For the full declaration, see: OECD, "Paris Declaration and Accra Agenda for Action," www.oecd.org/development/effectiveness/parisdeclarationandaccraagendaforaction.htm.

30. OECD (2018).

31. The Accra Agenda for Action recommitted states to the Paris Declaration's five pillars and proposed improvement in ownership, inclusive partnerships, delivering results, and capacity development. For the full declaration, see: OECD, "Paris Declaration and Accra Agenda for Action."

practitioners advocate for institution-building over strict security assistance, especially in fragile or conflict situations, some scholars[32] problematize the role of local elite actors in corrupting state-building initiatives.

In more recent years, strategies developed at the World Bank, African Development Bank, and U.S. Congress showcase efforts to revitalize the fight against fragility with contextualized, targeted solutions. Building on the momentum of the Paris Declaration (2005), Accra Agenda (2008), Dili Declaration (2010–11),[33] Busan Partnership for Effective Development Cooperation (2011),[34] Monrovia Roadmap (2011),[35] and New Deal (2011),[36] global institutions recognize fragile states as the main obstacles to achieving the Sustainable Development Goals (SDGs).[37]

The World Bank has consistently focused on providing aid to mitigate the

---

32. Lamb (2015).

33. The International Dialogue on Peacebuilding and Statebuilding in 2010 led to a declaration of the four priority challenges to effective cooperation in conflict-affected and fragile states. This dialogue and declaration specifically mentioned capacity development, aid instruments, planning processes, and political dialogue. For the full declaration, see: PBS Dialogue, 2011, "Dili Declaration: A New Vision for Peacebuilding and Statebuilding," International Dialogue on Peacebuilding and Statebuilding, www.oecd.org/dac/gender-development/45250308.pdf.

34. In 2011, government, civil society, private sector, and other actors met at the fourth High Level Forum on Aid Effectiveness to reach a consensus on enhancing development cooperation. The Busan Partnership Agreement supports four main principles: 1) ownership of development priorities by developing countries, 2) a focus on results, 3), partnerships for development, and 4) transparency and shared responsibility. For the full agreement, see: OECD, "Busan Partnership for Effective Development Co-operation," Fourth High Level Forum on Aid Effectiveness (July 2012), www.oecd.org/dac/effectiveness/49650173.pdf.

35. The Monrovia Roadmap resulted from the Second International Dialogue on Peacebuilding and Statebuilding in June 2011. The Roadmap set out five objectives to "reduce and prevent conflict and human suffering and to reach the [Millennium Development Goals] MDGs in situations of fragility and conflict." The five objectives included: 1) legitimate politics, 2) security, 3) justice, 4) economic foundations, and 5) revenues and services. For the complete report, see: International Dialogue on Peacebuilding and Statebuilding, "The Monrovia Roadmap on Peacebuilding and Statebuilding" (July 2011), www.icnl.org/research/library/files/Transnational/monrovia.pdf.

36. The New Deal resulted from the same forum as the Busan Partnership and furthers partnerships among fragile and conflict-affected states, development actors, and civil society to improve development policy and practice. The New Deal narrowed the Busan Partnership's priorities for stakeholders toward achieving the Peacebuilding and Statebuilding Goals (PSGs), using the FOCUS outline for assessment and engagement and the TRUST model in implementation and monitoring. For the full deal, see: International Dialogue on Peacebuilding and Statebuilding, "A New Deal for Engagement in Fragile States," www.pbsbdialogue.org/media/filer_public/07/69/07692de0-3557-494e-918e-18df00e9ef73/the_new_deal.pdf.

37. The seventeen Sustainable Development Goals are part of the 2030 Agenda for Sustainable Development, adopted in 2015 by all United Nations Member States. These goals provide a framework and call to action for all countries to enhance efforts toward ending poverty, hunger, and fifteen other deprivations. For more data on the SDGs, see: "Sustainable Development Goals," United Nations, 2019, https://sustainabledevelopment.un.org/?menu=1300.

impact of fragility, conflict, and violence, a strategy echoed by the LSE-Oxford Commission in its recent report on escaping fragility and consequent extreme poverty, mass migration, terrorism, illicit trafficking, and violence.[38] The World Bank outlined a highly-targeted approach in 2018 to address the specific challenges of fragile states by doubling the financing allocated to solving the root causes of fragility, and considers youth unemployment, low job creation, gender inequality, and a lack of government services as the primary root causes of fragility that can be addressed from the development perspective. Thus far, the World Bank has allocated $2 billion for countries hosting large numbers of refugees, and has supported the development of the Kakuma Refugee Camp's entrepreneurial programs, a cash-for-work program in the Central African Republic, and the Regional Sahel Pastoralism Support Project.[39] These programs all support a state-building approach to solving fragility, emphasizing the power of development-focused resources.

The U.S. Institute of Peace (USIP) defines the specific role of the United States in building resilience against violent extremism—one of the compounding factors that can propagate the fragility trap. This strategy follows the World Bank's turn toward prevention, prioritizing those partnerships with civil society and governments that can create inclusive governance processes and community consultations against violent extremists' attempts to undermine resilient states. USIP outlines responsibilities for each branch of the U.S. government to ensure these partnerships receive adequate funding, national attention, and technical support from U.S. agencies with expertise in security and intelligence.

The African Development Bank (AfDB) (2015), in its 2014–19 strategy to address fragility and build resilience in Africa, also focused heavily on the political economy and conflict aspects of fragile states. The AfDB prescribes a regional approach to fragility—specifically including non-state actors, women, and the private sector—to build resilience and combat the spillover effects that jeopardize the development of entire regions that host fragile contexts. The AfDB lists five drivers of fragility on the African continent, including poverty and exclusion, the youth bulge, urbanization and spreading informality, extractive industries and climate disruption, and resources. These drivers inspire the AfDB's funding decisions, which focus on inclusive politics, citizen security, justice, and traditional human and development needs.

These strategies represent the shift over the last two decades from a strict focus on institution- and capacity-building to greater attention on foreign aid and investment. But although aid has supplemented the provision of public goods,

38. World Bank (2019b).
39. Thornton (2018).

it has also become a replacement for tax revenues and resilient fiscal policies that can more sustainably and reliably respond to changes in aid levels or external economic shocks. Figure 11-7 shows the consistently low levels of domestic resource mobilization (DRM) among fragile states over the past forty years. Such a low level of DRM means that the support of the international community is necessary to address fragility, as most fragile countries have, thus far, not been able to mobilize sufficient domestic resources to finance their political, social, economic, and institutional development and exit fragility.

Some Successes, but Not Winning the Battle

The adoption of the Millennium Development Goals (MDGs) in 2000 and the SDGs in 2015 has facilitated the mobilization of the international community to comprehensively address issues related to poverty, inequality, insecurity, and other global development challenges. In turn, and as a result of domestic prioritization and increased levels of aid, improvements have been seen in the health and education sectors. In general, aid to fragile countries has increased as a result of greater attention to the unique challenges faced in fragile states and the potential effects of fragility on hindering other states' development and success. Figure 11-8 shows the levels of aid to fragile states over the past two decades. When looking at the aggregated data, the group of countries with high or extreme levels of fragility has, overall, received more aid than others, both in real terms and as a percent of GDP. However, on a per capita basis, fragile and non-fragile countries receive similar amounts of aid. This is indicative of a wider issue, where resources—financial or otherwise—are not provided to those states or regions that are the most in need or could use them most effectively. Among the top ten recipients of aid per capita in 2017, only one country was classified as having high or extreme fragility and two as having moderate or serious fragility.[40] Despite the coordination of the international communities in pursuit of the SDGs, there remain issues regarding the misalignment of resources.

It also is important to note the disparity between aid to countries that are highly or extremely fragile compared to those that have only moderate or serious fragility. While countries in the high or extreme stages of fragility certainly should be prioritized, countries in the moderate or serious stage are susceptible to becoming more fragile without the necessary resources to counter growing threats to stability. In some moderately or seriously fragile countries, particularly

---

40. The top ten recipients of aid per capita in 2017 were, in order: Syria, the Solomon Islands, Jordan, Mongolia, Serbia, Cape Verde, Lebanon, Montenegro, Timor Leste, and South Sudan. Of these, South Sudan is classified as having high or extreme fragility, and Syria and the Solomon Islands are classified as having moderate or serious fragility.

Figure 11-7. Tax Revenue and Fragility

Average Tax Revenue (% of GDP)

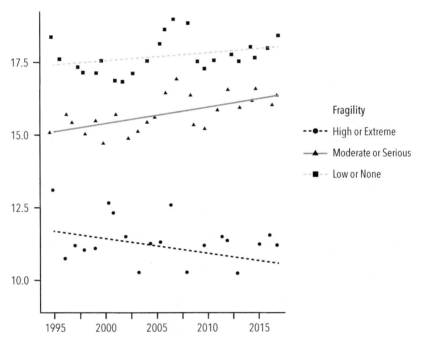

Figure 11-8. Aid and Fragility

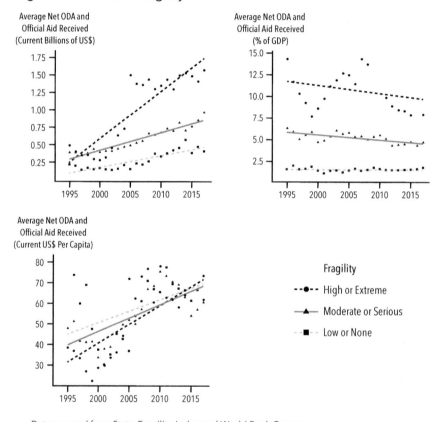

Data sourced from State Fragility Index and World Bank Group

those still in the process of exiting fragility, there may be more scope for support with official development assistance.

New strategies for addressing fragility have increased the focus on FDI and business-first engagements in fragile states, although this focus has yet to translate to significant increases in FDI to fragile states: as figure 11-9 shows, highly or extremely fragile states still receive, on average, little FDI in real terms and as a percent of GDP, although FDI has increased on average in moderately and seriously fragile states. Joe Huxley (2019) found that only 3.23 percent of all foreign direct investment in Sub-Saharan Africa reached fragile states in 2017.

Though the current paradigm of addressing fragility encourages a focus on economic growth and the building of self-reliant economies, FDI and other development assistance funds and projects are often not coordinated enough or subject to the same levels of domestic accountability. Corruption and resource mismanagement on the part of international and domestic actors continue to undermine the work of development and investment stakeholders and keep states in intense need during crises and poor growth during "stable" periods. Furthermore, approaches to fragility are heavily reliant on a humanitarian-development discourse that prioritizes the requirements and interests of donors over the entrepreneurial potential of individuals and firms in fragile states. This, and the generally high perceptions of risk to investing in fragile states, explains the very low levels of FDI in highly-fragile states and indicates the challenges that remain to overcome risk perceptions and incorporate fragile states into the global push for entrepreneurship and domestic growth.

Other drivers of growth and fragility reduction are expansionary, adaptable fiscal policies that can accommodate low demand and domestic consumption. One successful example of poverty reduction and economic growth occurred in the Kyrgyz Republic. Since the end of the Soviet Union, the Kyrgyz Republic has faced poor growth due to challenges of structural transformation, weak governance, poor connectivity, and a limited industrial base.[41] Growth began in the early 2000s when remittances from exported migrant labor began fueling domestic consumption and the provision of services. Strong fiscal policies allowed for the transition from low-productivity agriculture to more informal urban employment. This transition encouraged growth, while import-export bazaar trade sustained growth and contributed to significant poverty reduction between 2005 and 2009. Still, the country risks falling back into sustained fragility and low growth due to high remaining levels of poverty and vulnerability to shocks. Numerous fragile states have experienced similar trajectories of limited gains and threats to return to poverty and fragility.

41. World Bank Group (2018b).

Figure 11-9. FDI and Fragility

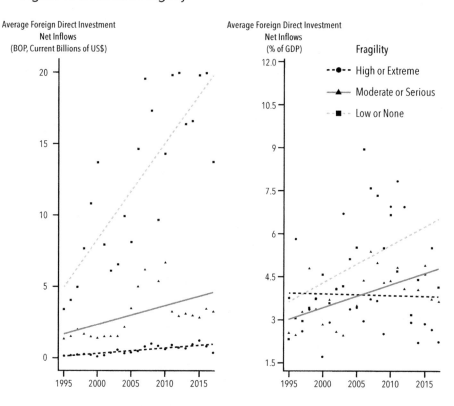

Data sourced from State Fragility Index and World Bank Group

New Approaches to Addressing Fragility

A new approach to addressing fragility is necessary to fill the theoretical, methodological, and policy gaps of previous and current policies. Table 11-2 outlines current policy options that can be carried out by internal and external stakeholders, with some policies requiring the support of both groups. Current policies, however, have too often failed to effectively address the cyclical nature of the drivers of fragility, thus leaving people behind. This doesn't mean that such policies are technically irrelevant in all cases, but that the political economy of implementation in fragile contexts is not sufficiently taken into consideration, as further elaborated in the next section.

A comprehensive approach to state fragility must be based on the intent to build state resilience and ensure that all aspects of fragility are addressed simultaneously and contextually. State resilience requires a long-term agenda and the establishment of sufficient political will and social cohesion within the populace to maintain the state in the short- and long-term. The focus on resilience will require policymakers to structure state investment so that it does not increase the vulnerability of the state or the population, preventing leaders from putting the short-term accumulation of power over the long-term need of breaking the cycle of fragility. Special attention must also be given to women, girls, and youth, as they are often the most likely to be left behind.

Many organizations and stakeholders are now beginning to develop new strategies for fragility, including the World Bank, the EU, and France.[42] Donors are also seeking to "harmonize" aid, which will necessarily lead to a change in levels of contributed aid, either overall or by specific donor agencies. This change in aid levels should lean toward an increase in humanitarian assistance where extremely fragile situations call for extra funding and international mechanisms of accountability. Furthermore, in fragile states with prominent civil society and private sectors, foreign aid should consider transitioning toward rebuilding commercial and economic sectors for the overall growth of the state. Two approaches that are currently underutilized and still being developed include private sector solutions and city-based approaches. These solutions account for context, the role of the private sector, and local actors within the security-development nexus of fragility interventions and can, thus, help lift states from fragility and ensure no one is left behind within fragile states.

The private sector and business community have the resources and

---

42. These strategies include the World Bank's future strategy for fragility, conflict, and violence (consultations currently ongoing); the EU's *New Deal for Engagement in Fragile States* (reaffirmed in 2016) focusing on peacebuilding, state-building, and improving international cooperation with fragile states; and France's *Prevention, Resilience and Sustainable Peace* strategy (2018) focusing on prevention, inclusive governance and the social contract, and improved coordination of French actions.

Table 11-2. Current Approaches to Fragility

Internal	External
Decentralization of decisionmaking, implementation, and mobilization of resources (Von Haldenwang 2016; Prah 2004)	**Private investment** focused on job creation and decreasing infrastructure gaps (LSE-Oxford Commission on State Fragility, Growth and Development 2018; François and Sud 2006)
Inclusive resource mobilization in rural and urban areas (OECD Report 2018)	**Partnerships** with civil society organizations (CSOs) (OECD Report 2018)
Economic diversification of exports and domestic production (OECD Report 2018; EU 2011)	**Technical assistance** to improve core service delivery (security, water, education) (McLoughlin 2012; Chauvet and Collier 2005)
Domestic security strategy adapted from the international security strategy (LSE-Oxford Commission on State Fragility, Growth and Development 2018; USIP 2019)	**Peace and conflict mediation** (Vallings and Moreno-Torres 2005; Diamond 2006; Kimenyi, Mbaku, and Moyo 2010; EU 2011)
Institutional reform and strengthening at the national and local level and provision of inclusive institutions (Vallings and Moreno-Torres 2005; Hout 2010; CICID 2018)	**Facilitated aid,** both monetary and technical, particularly to generate turnaround in post-conflict situations (McLoughlin 2012; Chauvet and Collier 2005; Rajan and Subramanian 2005; Diamond 2006; EU 2011)
Political settlements that expand institutional representation (Kimenyi and others. 2010)	**Regional partnerships and cooperation** (Vallings and Moreno-Torres 2005)
Formal (social) recognition of group identities and creation of shared national identity (Kaplan 2008; LSE-Oxford Commission on State Fragility, Growth and Development 2018)	**Debt relief** (LSE-Oxford Commission on State Fragility, Growth and Development 2018)
Power-sharing and political settlement particularly for the resolution of conflicts (LSE-Oxford Commission on State Fragility, Growth and Development 2018; Yoo 2011; Jones, Elgin-Cossart, and Esberg 2012)	**Engagement with local groups and leaders** to help build coalitions for reform (USIP 2019)

Macroeconomic policy reform to achieve stability and accelerate growth (World Bank 2018; Rajan and Subramanian 2005; EU 2011)

Strengthening rule of law by increasing checks, accountability, and transparency (World Bank 2019a, Baker 2007)

Improved domestic resource mobilization to finance higher levels of public investment and enhanced social services (World Bank 2019a; EU 2011)

Regeneration of legitimate power (Diamond 2006)

Cooperation between military and law enforcement (Dempsey 2006)

Recognition and use of traditional institutions for conflict resolution and governance (Prah 2004; Kaplan 2010)

Re-establishment of security through disarmament, demobilization, peacekeeping, and security sector reform (Brinkerhoff 2005; EU 2011)

Labor market and entrepreneurship programs (Blattman and Ralston 2015)

Inclusive education programs (Chauvet and Collier 2004; Ghani and Lockhart 2009)

Gender inclusive/specific programs and policies (Baranyi and Powell 2005, OECD Report 2018)

Improvement of health systems (Newbrander, Waldman, and Shepherd-Banigan 2011)

Improving legal capacity for justice and regulation (LSE-Oxford Commission on State Fragility, Growth and Development 2018; EU 2011)

Supporting international accountability efforts through funding of assessment, monitoring, and evaluation programs and increased transparency (USIP 2019; EU 2011)

Political assistance to support democracy and facilitate political transitions (Rajan and Subramanian 2005; Diamond 2006; Kimenyi, Mbaku, and Moyo 2010)

Humanitarian and relief efforts, including refugee support, containment of diseases and famine (Baker 2007)

Long-term approach (Rocha Menocal 2011)

Coordination across institutions and actors (Zoellick 2008; CICID 2018; EU 2011)

management potential to contribute to conflict resolution; unlock growth and development; and finance specific initiatives, including for dialogue among conflicting parties, national conflict resolution and prevention programs, local negotiations for services, and programs to reduce grievances both locally and nationally.[43] Other short-term measures include creating jobs, particularly those that can employ demobilized military and security forces; building business opportunities in immediate service delivery for relief from conflict and fragility; designing training programs to accommodate infrastructure and regulatory challenges; increasing access to domestic capital flows, including microfinancing and remittances; and strengthening national and local institutions to prioritize domestically-driven businesses and industrial development.[44]

In the long term, the private sector should take the lead in facilitating the entry of new enterprises to local, national, and regional markets. Encouraging regional investment in new post-conflict or post-fragility private sector enterprises will increase capital flows and instill confidence in international investors to promote long-term business and stability. Additionally, ventures in telecommunications and mobile services, such as telemedicine and mobile banking, can thwart residual institutional corruption and fill gaps in service delivery.[45] Finally, the private sector, which is often by necessity inclusive in its actions, can play a crucial role in mitigating social exclusion. The private sector infiltrates different socioeconomic strata further than the public sector,[46] and its relationship with citizens can bring stability by creating a feeling of inclusion throughout all of society, preventing the emergence of violence related to exclusion.[47]

The private sector's contribution to state stability can be enhanced through its partnership with the public sector at the local level. Indeed, strong local government institutions foster development by encouraging private sector investment: when institutions are solid, the private sector benefits from transparent and accountable business dealings with the local government, which improves processes such as resource governance.[48] To respect local contexts, the private sector can also apply conflict-sensitive business practices. These consist of proactive efforts from companies not to interfere with the host country through its operations to minimize the impact those operations could potentially have on enhancing violence or corruption.[49]

---

43. Peschka and Emery (2011).
44. Ibid.
45. Ibid.
46. Ibid.
47. Ingram and Papoulidis (2017).
48. Besada (2013).
49. Ballentine (2005).

FDI also must be specifically targeted toward economic development priorities that address underlying dimensions of conflict and corruption, such as unemployment, service supply constraints, and unvaried domestic production.[50] It is important to acknowledge that FDI in the private sector and large-scale business operations, such as in extractive resource industries in Central Africa or mining operations in the Dominican Republic, has increased fragility in some countries.[51] Investing and generating economic opportunity on the back of political, ethnic, religious, or social tensions will only further reduce stability and peace within already fragile states. Still, FDI in local industries has the unique advantage, compared to nation- or donor-led stabilization policies, of removing the economic conditions that contribute to groups' grievances, poverty, hunger, and political rivalry—creating short-term and long-term avenues for exiting stages of fragility.[52]

Current approaches tend to favor private sector involvement through mandatory, internationally set regulations in conflict-driven countries. The main justification for this approach is that it is extremely difficult for national governments to act as regulators of the private sector in weak states because of their poor institutional capacities (figure 11-10), which creates a need for the international community to oversee the process of mandatory regulation. This approach can be efficient, particularly when it combines domestic legislation and monitoring actions of international governance. For example, in the case of the Kimberley Certification Scheme, penalties were applied for noncompliance with domestic legislation, altering the balance of incentives and resulting in efficient regulation.[53] Overall, such regulatory partnerships are expected to be efficient solutions to state fragility issues by providing strong regulation frameworks that strengthen states' legitimacy and allowing for private sector participation in state-building processes.

Although addressing fragility requires the coordinated involvement of actors at many levels, including through the private sector and at the local, rural, urban, regional, national, continental, and international levels, subnational and, in particular, city-based approaches are currently underutilized. Approaches to state fragility often overlook the impact of fragile cities on causing, perpetuating, and solving fragility. Developing appropriate solutions for cities such as Lagos in Nigeria or Kinshasa in the DRC will have a substantial impact on poverty and fragility reduction; 90 percent of future population growth throughout the

50. Ganson and Wennmann (2018).
51. Ibid.
52. Ibid.
53. Ballentine (2005).

Figure 11-10. Government Effectiveness and Fragility

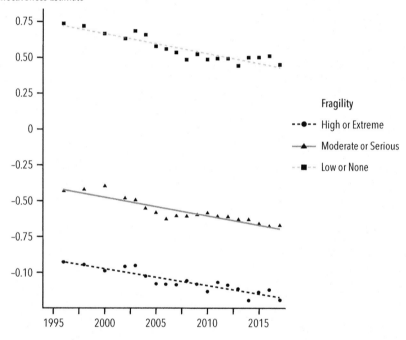

Average Governmental
Effectiveness Estimate

Data sourced from State Fragility Index and World Bank Group

world is projected to occur in the developing world's cities and their surrounding communities.[54] Rapid urbanization and changing demographic dynamics can often drive national grievances.

A decentralized approach to addressing fragility by considering the impact of cities and their local governing institutions can provide necessary insight on solutions to general state fragility. As the social contract that exists between citizens and the federal government on the basis of security and service provision also exists at the urban municipal level and rural subregional level, the purview of local governments to provide contextualized services, welfare, representation, and security to urban citizens should be prioritized as an avenue for stabilization, growth, and development.[55]

Foreign assistance and stabilization policies are still largely targeted toward the centralized state system[56] and specific rural areas, which are often afflicted with the most severe consequences of conflict, hunger, poverty, and disaster. However, the economic and social strata of urban areas also can experience these devastating effects and are likely to undermine humanitarian efforts to fix state fragility at the rural level. New practices in humanitarian relief have begun to focus on the regional and local levels, including cities, as sites requiring the same level of attention within the security and development nexus.[57] This new focus is bringing increasing attention to the vulnerability of cities within development, emergency, and environmental action discourse. Urban violence, for example, was acknowledged as one of the most pressing challenges in the 2007 conference on the Red Cross pilot project in Rio de Janeiro,[58] and increasing emphasis is being put on the study of humanitarian implications in cities where levels of violence are on par with Abidjan or Mogadishu, such as Medellin or Ciudad Juarez.

While fragile cities have been identified as a new challenge within humanitarian discourse, it is less clear how their characteristics and dimensions are to be defined. Some strong links between city and state fragility exist, including the rupture of social contracts binding citizens with the government, the weakness of governance systems,[59] and the inability of public authorities to deliver basic public services. The notion of urban conflict is also strongly identified as a defining element of fragile states, and the study of urban violence often relies on the same frameworks used in studies of state fragility. For example, a report issued in 2010 by the London School of Economics argued that analysis of fragile cities

54. Muggah (2015).
55. Ibid.
56. Muggah (2013).
57. Nogueira (2014).
58. Ibid.
59. Muggah (2013).

must be based on the typical analysis applied to fragile states. The notions are clearly intertwined.[60] On the other hand, fragile cities have many characteristics that distinguish them from fragile states, and many new concepts are emerging that are linked to fragile cities but disconnected from state fragility. For example, the emergence of the concept of "military urbanism" focuses on cities as the first site of warfare in the twenty-first century, and consequently reshapes the approach to fragility with a special focus on a new paradigm of urban settings.[61] The implications of this new focus are the attribution of violence to the speed of urbanization, which differs from the approach taken to study state fragility.[62]

The unique characteristics of fragile cities complicate typical solutions to state fragility and engender a need for decentralized rather than top-down approaches. Cities are highly complex environments with various levels of governing arrangements, and their management relies on their relationship with national governments. As cities are not sovereign and do not have full autonomy over their resources and laws, implementation of solutions is particularly difficult.[63] One method of implementing solutions to address fragility in both rural and urban areas is to build systems in which transparency and accountability are central elements. Often, the divide between local government elites, international actors, and the local population prevents the implementation of effective governing bodies. Building solutions that promote effective governance reconstruction—a core parameter for stability—requires filling the gaps of legitimacy, security, and effectiveness, and can be done only through transparency and accountability.[64]

Framework for a New Approach to Fragility

These solutions, as well as the current approaches to fragility detailed in table 11-2, can be successful only when paired with effective and contextualized implementation strategies, given the critical role of the political economy of implementation in successful delivery.[65] Fragile cities, in particular, present new challenges for solution implementation. One means to improve the design and implementation of interventions into fragile states is to contextualize implementation strategies based on the prevalence of political conflict or complexity. This method is based on policy implementation theories that examine reasons why critical differences occur between the initial intent of a policy and the outputs

60. Nogueira (2014).
61. Muggah (2013).
62. Nogueira (2014).
63. Selby (2018).
64. Brinkerhoff (2007).
65. Signé (2015, 2016a, 2016b, 2017b, 2017c, 2017d).

of that policy after the final stages of implementation and methods to improve the success of policy implementation. Working from an adaptation of Matland's conflict-ambiguity model (table 11-3), policymakers can determine a relative level of political conflict or violence and the clarity of policy goals or means within a country to determine the primary tools that should be used to address fragility. Framing approaches within this matrix can help establish comprehensive policies that restore security with the long-term goal of building institutional resilience and domestic capacity to grow. It can also help better align the provision of financial and technical resources to states that are most able to use them to eliminate fragility and improve the lives of their residents.

This matrix also can provide a useful framework for operationalizing the wide range of solutions available to policymakers and development organizations.

Approaches for Low Ambiguity/Low Conflict

When levels of both conflict and ambiguity are low, implementation is likely to succeed if the necessary resources are available and implementation is mostly administrative in nature. Overall, states with low ambiguity and low conflict have clearly-defined goals and a set of well-understood procedural steps to accomplish policy goals. Rwanda typifies this category due to the country's clear and generally accepted development policy goals. In Rwanda, there is low conflict, due to consensus among government officials and the country's relatively high levels of stability, and low ambiguity, due to the clarity of policy goals and processes. Rwanda now requires additional financial resources, including FDI, aid, and tax revenue, as well as reinforcement of current administrative capacity to foster development and implementation of various solutions. Liberia and Sierra Leone provide other examples of countries that, in recent years, have had low ambiguity and low conflict.

This scenario of fragility has the highest initial potential of exiting fragility. Without focused resources and international, regional, and local support for the state, though, fragility can become ingrained. International and domestic actors should focus on the mobilization of domestic resources for investment, infrastructure, and growth prospects and the provision of aid for technical services. The stabilization of the economic and social sectors of the state will ensure institutional resources are allocated for low-level securitization and political expediency and can lead to a smooth transition out of low-level conflict and into resiliency.

Table 11-3. Political Conflict/Policy Ambiguity Matrix

	Low Conflict	High Conflict
Low Ambiguity	*Type of implementation:* Administrative – clear goals and strategies exist but labor, capital, or technological resources are needed	*Type of implementation:* Political – clear goals and strategy exist but conflict makes implementation difficult
	Factors needed for success: Resources, motivation, learning, competency, processes	*Factors needed for success:* Power, autonomy, governance, leadership
	Potential internal strategies: Public-private partnerships, encouragement of entrepreneurial and moderate-risk ventures, employment support, and training programs	*Potential internal strategies:* Domestic security sector reform, inclusive political participation, inclusive resource mobilization, inclusive education and gender programs
	Potential external strategies: Private investment focused on resource-building, partnerships with civil society organizations, technical assistance	*Potential external strategies:* Peace and conflict mediation, facilitated aid with donor accountability, regional partnerships and cooperation
	Illustrative case: Rwanda	*Illustrative case:* South Sudan

High Ambiguity		
	Type of implementation: Contextual – overarching goals may exist but strategies are vague or disagreed upon and consensus is needed	*Type of implementation:* Symbolic – overarching goals may exist but strategies are unclear and conflict further complicates implementation
	Factors needed for success: Vary based on contextual conditions, institutional factors, organizational structures, and culture	*Factors needed for success:* Coalition strength, incentives and constraints, network management, communication, conflict reduction
	Potential internal strategies: Institutional reform, decentralization of decisionmaking, and implementation	*Potential internal strategies:* Domestic security sector reform, inclusive political settlements, formal recognition of group identities
	Potential external strategies: Partnership with civil society organizations, regional partnerships and cooperation	*Potential external strategies:* Peace and conflict mediation, facilitated aid with donor accountability, regional partnerships and cooperation for security and stabilization
	Illustrative case: Equatorial Guinea	*Illustrative case:* Democratic Republic of Congo

Approaches for Low Ambiguity/High Conflict

In the scenario of high conflict and low ambiguity, power is the prime determinant of successful policy implementation, as successful implementation depends on the ability of the government to ensure the compliance of other actors. Low ambiguity and high conflict countries include Mali and South Sudan. In South Sudan, for example, the establishment of the country in 2011 represented a clear policy response to fragility in Sudan. Conflict now exists between the country's political parties, but both major groups have clear leadership and political strategies. The primary challenge for the country, then, is not to refine policy strategies but to resolve conflict and provide an inclusive base for graduation from fragility.

With high conflict and violence but solidified political parties or institutions, the state will also be challenged to recognize all the identities and groups within its boundaries. Thus, these situations must have strict accountability for inclusive political participation in security operations, reform, and transitions out of conflict, as the formal recognition of all groups' identities will build the foundation for long-term resilience. These situations will also require a focus on the disparities between urban-rural areas to ensure full implementation of security and governance solutions. Solidified political will has high potential to encourage foreign direct investment and private sector revitalization during the securitization process. Political leaders should, therefore, facilitate labor market and entrepreneurship programs to address economic and social grievances before these grievances reinforce conflict and overall fragility.

Approaches for High Ambiguity/Low Conflict

This scenario typically represents state fragility fueled by a variety of domestic grievances that permeate the local political arena and create tension among local actors. These states can often be "trapped" in fragility, with political disagreements and constant transitions preventing total reform. Implementation in this scenario is highly dependent on contextual conditions, as policy and implementation strategies are rarely clearly defined or substantial. Often, broad goals may be widely accepted, but there may be a lack of clarity in how these goals should be met. Equatorial Guinea provides an example of a high-ambiguity, low-conflict fragile context. While little conflict exists in the country, specific international policies and implementation strategies to successfully remove the country from fragility are unclear. Intersecting issues of governance, natural resource capture, inequality, and low human development further complicate the development of effective policy strategies and increase ambiguity. In recent years, Haiti has become a high-ambiguity, low-conflict country.

The first area of opportunity for international and domestic actors in this scenario is to implement institutional reform at the national and local level that can pave the way for future inclusive political reforms. International actors should especially prioritize partnerships with neutral civil society organizations to avoid introducing political preferences into the domestic scenario. Domestic actors can coordinate with regional and international actors to introduce dispute resolution processes designed to anticipate and resolve political disputes in the short- and long-term that might undermine efforts to build resiliency.

Approaches for High Ambiguity/High Conflict

High-ambiguity, high-conflict situations are those most likely to produce and sustain fragility; success in these scenarios relies on the strength of the implementing coalition. High-ambiguity, high-conflict situations are common in fragile contexts. Iraq, Afghanistan, Yemen, and the DRC, for example, all fit in this category. Somalia provides another illustrative example: the extent of internal violence and inadequate government structures in the country continually demand immediate action, while state illegitimacy, lack of formal enterprise, and a severe proneness to internal shocks prevent resolutions in the short- and long-term. Somalia's fragility is reinforced by its limits to establishing central institutions as well as the nature and scope of its lawlessness and the dynamics of its armed conflicts. Approaches to addressing fragility in Somalia should focus on the security sector and regional cooperation as well as inclusive political settlements.

In situations where states face high levels of conflict and uncertainty about the strength of incumbent institutions or political leaders, international and domestic actors with the intent of addressing short- and long-term fragility need to focus on reinforcing, stabilizing, and strengthening authority. Research acknowledges that high-conflict situations need security and stabilization in the immediate period of intervention, but securitization of conflict should be coordinated with the potential to become a long-term national security strategy. In high-conflict scenarios, the coordination among international, continental, and regional actors is imperative to ensure broad-scale support for solutions and long-term support of the programs implemented during conflict. International actors can ultimately encourage the decentralization of decisionmaking and the mobilization of resources, but political and security strategies also must account for the domestic context, including the inherent capacity of local security forces and the specific shortcomings to establishing security in said state. Foreign aid may be invited by the host country, but invitations for aid and mandates for its extent and role should be determined before aid enters a fragile context.

Conclusion

The ongoing, dynamic study of state fragility demonstrates the complexity of why states become and remain fragile and the need to leave no one behind within fragile states. One of the primary methods of addressing fragility used by the international community and domestic actors for decades is to develop strategies that seek to prevent worsening fragility and the devolution of states from "stable," and to continuously encourage resiliency against shocks that may induce long-term fragility. This approach has made some progress but has not accomplished the ever-challenging task of pulling states out of the fragility trap and into a process of sustainable recovery. By better considering the political economy of successful implementation[66] and aligning resources to the individual contexts of countries through the use of an ambiguity-conflict framework, the efficacy of approaches to fragility can be improved and fewer people left behind. This approach can also help to better align the use of resources, including aid, foreign direct investment, and tax revenue, for the countries and people who need them most.

The process of implementing solutions requires input from all internal and external stakeholders, with the assurance that marginalized and underrepresented groups have their opinions heard at the decisionmaking level. Incorporating the private sector can be an effective means of implementing solutions due to its ability to both contribute to and exacerbate state fragility. The decentralized approach also necessitates an analysis of city fragility, which complicates typical solutions to state fragility and engenders a need for decentralized rather than top-down approaches. These approaches, in addition to other current solutions, can be more effectively implemented when framed within the context of a country's levels of policy ambiguity and political conflict. Using this framework, policymakers can determine the relative level of conflict and the clarity of policy approaches within a country to determine the primary tools that should be used to address fragility and the resources that are needed to support graduation from fragility. Overall, the method of defining and categorizing state fragility in this report adds to the extensive research already done on the subject and contributes new ideas about how to adapt solutions to the context and specific needs of fragile states and populations.

---

66. Signé (2015, 2016a, 2016b, 2017b, 2017c, 2017d).

References

"Sustainable Development Goals." 2019. United Nations. sustainabledevelopment. un.org/?menu=1300.

"The Monrovia Roadmap on Peacebuilding and Statebuilding." 2011. International Dialogue on Peacebuilding and Statebuilding. www.icnl.org/research/library/files/ Transnational/monrovia.pdf.

AfDB. 2015. "African Development Bank Strategy for Addressing Fragility and Building Resilience in Africa – The AfDB Group Strategy 2014–2019." https:// www.afdb.org/en/documents/document/addressing-fragility-and-building-resilience-in-africa-the-afdb-group-strategy-2014-2019-48812.

AU. 2019. "High-Level Side Event on 'Migration and Displacement in Africa: Addressing the Underlying Causes through Innovative Risk Financing Mechanisms." Addis Ababa, Ethiopia: African Union.

Bah, Abu Bakarr. 2012. "State Decay: A Conceptual Frame of Failing and Failed States in West Africa." *International Journal of Politics, Culture, and Society* 25, no. 1-3: 71–89.

Ballentine, Karen, and Heiko Nitzschke. 2005. *Profiting from Peace: Managing the Resource Dimension of Civil War*. Boulder, CO: Lynne Rienner.

Baker, Pauline H. 2007. "Fixing Failing States: The New Security Agenda." *Whitehead J. Dipl. & Int'l Rel.* 8: 85.

Baranyi, Stephen, and Kristiana Powell. 2005. "Fragile States, Gender Equality and Aid Effectiveness: A Review of Donor Perspectives."
http://www.nsi-ins.ca/wp-content/uploads/2012/10/2005-Fragile-States-Gender-Equality-and-Aid-Effectiveness-A-Review-of-Donor-Perspectives.pdf.

Bates, Robert H. 2008. "State Failure." *Annual Review of Political Science* 11. https://doi. org/10.1146/annurev.polisci.11.060606.132017.

Bates, Robert H. 2015. *When Things Fell Apart*. Cambridge University Press.

Besada, Hany. 2013. "Doing Business in Fragile States: The Private Sector, Natural Resources and Conflict in Africa." Background Research Paper submitted to the High Level Panel on the Post-2015 Development Agenda, 2013. https://www. post2015hlp.org/wp-content/uploads/docs/Doing-Business-in-Fragile-States-The-Private-Sector-Natural-Resources-and-Conflict-in-Africa-FINAL-May-25-2013.pdf.

Blattman, Christopher, and Laura Ralston. 2015. "Generating Employment in Poor and Fragile States: Evidence from Labor Market and Entrepreneurship Programs." http:// dx.doi.org/10.2139/ssrn.2622220

Brainard, Lael, and Derek Chollet, eds. 2007. *Too Poor for Peace?: Global Poverty, Conflict, and Security in the 21st Century*. Brookings Institution Press.

Brinkerhoff, Derick W., ed. 2007. *Governance in Post-Conflict Societies: Rebuilding Fragile States*. Routledge.

Brinkerhoff, Derick W. 2005. "Rebuilding Governance in Failed States and Post-Conflict Societies: Core Concepts and Cross-Cutting Themes." *Public Administration and Development* 25, no. 1: 3–14. https://doi.org/10.1002/pad.352.

Brown, Seyom, and Vanda Felbab-Brown. 2012. "Nepal, on the Brink of Collapse." *New York Times* 5.

Carvalho, Soniya. 2006. "Engaging with Fragile States: An IEG Review of World Bank Support to Low-Income Countries Under Stress." World Bank Group, Independent Evaluation Group.

Chandra, Simon Chesterman, and Michael Ignatieff Ramesh. 2005. *Making States Work: State Failure and the Crisis of Governance*. United Nations University Press.

Chauvet, Lisa, and Paul Collier. 2004. "Development Effectiveness in Fragile States: Spillovers and Turnarounds." *Centre for the Study of African Economies, Department of Economics, Oxford University.*

———. 2005. "Policy Turnarounds in Failing States." Centre for the Study of African Economies, Department of Economics, Oxford University.

CICID. 2018. *Prevention, Resilience, and Sustainable Peace Strategy.* www.diplomatie.gouv.fr/en/french-foreign-policy/governance/building-a-lasting-peace-and-combatting-fragilities.

———. 2007. *The Bottom Billion: Why the Poorest Countries are Failing and What Can Be Done About It.* Oxford University Press.

Christensen, Jason. 2017. "Dimensions of State Fragility: Determinants of Violent Group Grievance, Political Legitimacy, and Economic Capacity." University of Central Florida Electronic Theses and Dissertations. https://stars.library.ucf.edu/etd/5587/.

Collier, Paul. 2007. *The Bottom Billion: Why the Poorest Countries Are Failing and What Can Be Done About It.* Oxford: Oxford University Press.

Deléchat, Corinne, and others. 2015. "Exiting from Fragility in Sub-Saharan Africa: The Role of Fiscal Policies and Fiscal Institutions." IMF Working Paper (December).

Dempsey, Thomas. 2006. *Counterterrorism in African Failed States: Challenges and Potential Solutions.* Diane Publishing.

Diamond, Larry. 2006. "Promoting Democracy in Post-Conflict and Failed States." *Taiwan Journal of Democracy* 2, no. 2: 93–116.

Douma, Pyt. 2006. "Poverty, Relative Deprivation and Political Exclusion as Drivers of Violent Conflict in Sub-Saharan Africa." *Journal on Science and World Affairs* 2, no. 2: 59–69. https://gsdrc.org/document-library/poverty-relative-deprivation-and-political-exclusion-as-drivers-of-violent-conflict-in-sub-saharan-africa/.

Easterly, William. 2006. *The White Man's Burden: Why the West's Efforts to Aid the Rest Have Done So Much Ill and So Little Good.* New York: Penguin.

Esty, Daniel, and others. 1998. "Failed States and International Security: Causes, Prospects, and Consequences." The State Failure Project: Early Warning Research for U.S. Foreign Policy Planning. http://mstohl.faculty.comm.ucsb.edu/failed_states/1998/papers/gurr.html.

European Union. 2011. *New Deal for Engagement in Fragile States.* www.newdeal4peace.org/new-deal-snapshot.

François, Monika, and Inder Sud. 2006. "Promoting Stability and Development in Fragile and Failed States." *Development Policy Review* 24, no. 2: 141–60.

Ganson, Brian, and Achim Wennmann. 2018. *Business and Conflict in Fragile States: The Case for Pragmatic Solutions.* London: Routledge.

Ghani, Ashraf, and Clare Lockhart. 2009. *Fixing Failed States: A Framework for Rebuilding a Fractured World.* Oxford University Press.

Goldstone, Jack A. 2008. "Pathways to State Failure." *Conflict Management and Peace Science* 24, no. 4: 285–96. https://doi.org/10.1080%2F07388940802397343.

Hinds, Roisin. 2015. "Economic Growth and Fragility." *GSDRC Helpdesk Research Report* 1214: 1–9.

Hout, Wil. 2010. "Between Development and Security: The European Union, Governance and Fragile States." *Third World Quarterly* 31, no. 1: 141–57.

Huxley, Joe. 2019. "Financing the Frontier: Risk, Reward, and Reality in Africa's Fragile States." The Brookings Institution – Foresight Africa: 91–93.

Ingram, George, and Jonathan Papoulidis. 2017. "Rethinking How to Reduce State Fragility." The Brookings Institution. www.brookings.edu/blog/up-front/2017/03/29/rethinking-how-to-reduce-state-fragility.

Jackman, Robert, W. 1993. "Power without Force: The Political Capacity of Nation-States." Ann Arbor: University of Michigan Press.

Jackson, Robert H., and Carl G. Rosberg. 1982. "Why Africa's Weak States Persist: The Empirical and the Juridical in Statehood." World Politics 35, no. 1: 1–24.

Jones, Bruce, Molly Elgin-Cossart, and Jane Esberg. 2012. "Pathways Out of Fragility: The Case for a Research Agenda on Inclusive Political Settlements in Fragile States." New York: CIC.

Kaplan, Seth D. 2008. Fixing Fragile States: A New Paradigm for Development. ABC-CLIO.

———. 2010. "Rethinking State-Building in a Failed State." Washington Quarterly 33, no. 1: 81–97.

Kimenyi, Mwangi S., John Mukum Mbaku, and Nelipher Moyo. 2010. "Reconstituting Africa's Failed States: The Case of Somalia." Social Research 77, no. 4: 1339–66.

Lamb, Robert. 2015. "Fragile States Cannot Be Fixed with State-Building." Center for Strategic and International Studies. https://www.csis.org/analysis/fragile-states-cannot-be-fixed-state-building.

Lindemann, Stefan. 2008. "Do Inclusive Elite Bargains Matter? A Research Framework for Understanding the Causes of Civil War in Sub-Saharan Africa." Crisis States Discussion Papers. http://citeseerx.ist.psu.edu/viewdoc/download?doi=10.1.1.856.3611&rep=rep1&type=pdf.

LSE-Oxford Commission on State Fragility, Growth and Development. 2018. "Escaping the Fragility Trap." International Growth Centre.

Mansfield, Edward, D., and Jack Synder. 2008. "Exchange: The Sequencing 'Fallacy'." Journal of Democracy 18, no. 3: 5–9. http://doi.org/10.1353/jod.2007.0047.

Marshall, Monty G., and Benjamin R. Cole. 2008. "Global Report on Conflict, Governance and State Fragility." Foreign Policy Bulletin 18, no. 1: 3–21. https://doi.org/10.1017/S1052703608000014.

Marshall, Monty G., and Gabrielle Elzinga-Marshall. State Fragility Index and Matrix 2016. Center for Systemic Peace. http://www.systemicpeace.org/inscr/SFImatrix2016c.pdf.

McLoughlin, Claire, and Richard J. Batley. 2012. "The Politics of What Works in Service Delivery: An Evidence-Based Review." Effective States and Inclusive Development Research Centre Working Paper 06. https://dx.doi.org/10.2139/ssrn.2141852.

Moyo, Dambisa. 2009. Dead Aid: Why Aid Is Not Working and How There Is a Better Way for Africa. New York: Farrar, Straus, and Giroux.

———. 2014. "International Organizations and the Production of Hegemonic Knowledge: How the World Bank and the OECD Helped Invent the Fragile State Concept." Third World Quarterly 35, no. 2: 210–31.

Muggah, Robert. 2015. "Fixing Fragile Cities: Solutions for Urban Violence and Poverty." Foreign Affairs. https://www.foreignaffairs.com/articles/africa/2015-01-15/fixing-fragile-cities.

Muggah, Robert. 2013. "Fragile Cities Rising." IPI Global Observatory. https://theglobalobservatory.org/2013/07/fragile-cities-rising/.

Newbrander, William, Ronald Waldman, and Megan Shepherd-Banigan. 2011. "Rebuilding and Strengthening Health Systems and Providing Basic Health Services in Fragile States." *Disasters* 35, no. 4: 639–60.

Nogueira, Joao P. 2014. "From Fragile States to Fragile Cities: Redefining Spaces of Humanitarian Practices." Humanitarian Action in Situations Other Than War, Discussion Paper 12. https://igarape.org.br/wp-content/uploads/2016/04/From-Fragile-States-to-Fragile-Cities.pdf.

Nwozor, Agaptus. 2018. "African Union, State-Building and the Challenges of State Fragility in Africa." *AUSTRAL: Brazilian Journal of Strategy & International Relations* 7, no. 13.

Organization for Economic Cooperation and Development (OECD). 2007. "Principles for Good International Engagement in Fragile States and Situations."

———. 2008. "The Paris Declaration on Aid Effectiveness and the Accra Agenda for Action."

———. 2012. "Busan Partnership for Effective Development Co-operation." Fourth High Level Forum on Aid Effectiveness. Busan, Republic of Korea. www.oecd.org/dac/effectiveness/49650173.pdf.

———. 2018. "States of Fragility 2018."

———. 2019. "Rome Declaration," First High Level Forum on Aid Effectiveness. Rome, Italy. www.oecd.org/dac/effectiveness/hlf-1thefirsthighlevelforumonaideffectivenessrome.htm.

Peschka, Mary P., and James J. Emery. 2011. "The Role of the Private Sector in Fragile and Conflict-Affected States." World Development Report 2011 Background Papers, World Bank. http://hdl.handle.net/10986/27316.

Prah, Kwesi Kwaa. 2004. "African Wars and Ethnic Conflicts: Rebuilding Failed States." Human Development Report 2004.

Radelet, Steven. 2006. "A Primer on Foreign Aid." Center for Global Development Working Paper 92. www.cgdev.org/publication/primer-foreign-aid-working-paper-92.

Rajan, Raghuram G., and Arvind Subramanian. 2005. "What Undermines Aid's Impact on Growth?" IMF Working Paper. International Monetary Fund.

Rocha Menocal, Alina. 2011. "State Building for Peace: A New Paradigm for International Engagement in Post-Conflict Fragile States?" *Third World Quarterly* 32, no. 10: 1715–36.

Ross, Michael, L. 2004. "What Do We Know about Natural Resources and Civil War?" *Journal of Peace Research* vol. 41, no. 3. https://doi.org/10.1177%2F0022343304043773.

Rotberg, Robert I., ed. 2003. *When States Fail: Causes and Consequences.* Princeton: Princeton University Press.

Rotberg, Robert I. 2002. "Failed States in a World of Terror." *Foreign Affairs* 81, no. 4: 127–40. www.jstor.org/stable/20033245.

———. 2007. "The Failure and Collapse of Nation States." *Staatszerfall und Governance.* Nomos Verlagsgesellschaft mbH & Co. KG.

———. 2011. "Failed States, Collapsed States, Weak States: Causes and Indicators." In *State Failure and State Weakness in a Time of Terror.* Brookings Institution Press, World Peace Foundation.

Sachs, Jeffrey. 2005. *The End of Poverty: How We Can Make It Happen in Our Lifetime.* New York: Penguin.

Sachs, Jeffrey. 2003. "Institutions Don't Rule: Direct Rule of Geography on Per Capita Income." NBER Working Paper No, 9490. https://doi.org/10.3386/w9490.

Samman, Emma, and others. 2018. "SDG Progress: Fragility, Crisis, and Leaving No One Behind." The Overseas Development Institute. https://www.odi.org/sites/odi.org.uk/files/resource-documents/12424.pdf.

Selby, J. David, and Kevin Desouza. 2018. "Fragile Cities in the Developed World: A Conceptual Framework." Forthcoming in *Cities*. https://ssrn.com/abstract=3291665.

Signé, Landry. 2015. "Mobilizing Resources for Africa: Financing and Capacity-Building Strategies for Effective Delivery of the Sustainable Development Goals." Brussels / Washington: German Marshall Fund of the United States. www.gmfus.org/publications/mobilizing-resources-africa.

———. 2016a. "How to Implement Domestic Resource Mobilization (DRM) Successfully for Effective Delivery of SDGs in Africa? Part 1 – An Innovative Policy Delivery Model." OCP Policy Center. www.ocppc.ma/sites/default/files/OCPPC-PB1623.pdf.

———. 2016b. "How to Implement Domestic Resource Mobilization (DRM) Successfully for Effective Delivery of SDGs in Africa? Part 2 – Illustrative Actionable Solutions for Policy Leaders." OCP Policy Center. www.ocppc.ma/sites/default/files/OCPPC-PB1624.pdf.

———. 2017a. *Innovating Development Strategies in Africa: International, Regional and National Actors*. Cambridge University Press.

———. 2017b. "Public Service Delivery – What Matters for Successful Implementation and What Can Policy Leaders Do?" Policy Paper PP-17/04. OCP Policy Center. www.ocppc.ma/sites/default/files/OCPPC-PP1704.pdf.

———. 2017c. "Policy Implementation – A Synthesis of the Study of Policy Implementation and the Causes of Policy Failure." Policy Paper PP-17/03. OCP Policy Center. www.ocppc.ma/sites/default/files/OCPPC-PP1703.pdf.

———. 2017d. "Why Do Development Policies Often Fail in Africa? Perspectives on the World Development Report 2017." africaupclose.wilsoncenter.org/why-do-development-policies-often-fail-in-africaperspectives-

———. 2018. *African Transformation, African Development: How Institutions Shape Development Strategy*. Cambridge University Press.

Thornton, Phil. 2018. "Fragile State: World Bank Poverty Target Rests on Weakest Economies." Global Capital. www.globalcapital.com/article/b1bblfkl9wdp19/fragile-state-world-bank-poverty-target-rests-on-weakest-economies.

USAID, US. 2004. "Foreign Aid: Meeting the Challenges of the Twenty-First Century." White Paper. U.S. Agency for International Development.

USIP. (2019). "Preventing Extremism in Fragile States: A New Approach."

Vallings, Claire, and Magüi Moreno Torres. 2005. "Drivers of Fragility: What Makes States Fragile?" PRDE Working Papers 12824, Department for International Development (DFID), United Kingdom.

Vallings, Claire, and Magui Moreno-Torres. April 2005. "Drivers of Fragility: What Makes States Fragile?" PRDE Working Paper No. 7, Department for International Development. http://comminit.com/fragile-contexts/content/drivers-fragility-what-makes-states-fragile.

Van de Walle, Nicolas. 2004. "The Economic Correlates of State Failure: Taxes, Foreign Aid, and Policies." In *When States Fail: Causes and Consequences,* edited by Robert Rotberg. 2010: 94-115.

————. 2005. *Overcoming Stagnation in Aid-Dependent Countries.* Center for Global Development.

Von Haldenwang, Christian, and Jorn Gravingholt. 2016. "The Promotion of Decentralization and Local Governance in Fragile Contexts." German Development Institute Discussion Paper 20. https://doi.org/10.13140/RG.2.2.19927.88480.

World Bank. 2018a. Poverty and Shared Prosperity 2018: Piecing Together the Poverty Puzzle. Washington D.C.: World Bank Group.

World Bank. 2018b. "From Vulnerability to Prosperity: A Systematic Country Diagnosis the Kyrgyz Republic." World Bank Group. documents.worldbank.org/curated/en/516141537548690118/pdf/Kyrgyz-Republic-SCD-English-Final-August-31-2018-09182018.pdf.

————. 2019. Poverty and Equity Data Portal. http://povertydata.worldbank.org/poverty/home/

————. 2019a. "Africa's Pulse: An Analysis of Issues Shaping Africa's Economic Future." World Bank Group, 19. hdl.handle.net/10986/31499.

————. 2019b. "World Bank Group Strategy for Fragility, Conflict and Violence 2020–2025: Concept Note." World Bank Group.

Yoo, John. 2011. "Fixing Failed States." *California Law Review*: 95–150.

Zoellick, Robert B. 2008. "Fragile States: Securing Development." *Survival* 50, no. 6: 67–84.

CHAPTER TWELVE

The Importance of City Leadership in Leaving No One Behind

Tony Pipa and Caroline Conroy

T o transform our world, we must transform its cities," emphasized UN Secretary-General Ban Ki Moon in 2016, the year the UN's member states embarked on implementation of the Sustainable Development Goals (SDGs). The inclusion of a separate goal—SDG 11—calling for "inclusive, safe, resilient, and sustainable" cities marked a major shift from the Millennium Development Goals (MDGs), where urban areas received limited attention. The subsequent launch of the New Urban Agenda, adopted in 2016 at Habitat III,[1] saw countries reaffirm their commitment to sustainable urbanization and set a new global standard for urban development.

Together, these two global governance frameworks recognize and elevate the importance of cities to sustainable development. National governments increasingly acknowledge the need for place-based policies and investments, and recognize that success on the SDGs means getting urbanization right.

SDG 11 was a breakthrough, clearly establishing the significance of cities to the 2030 Agenda. A dedicated goal, however, risks limiting the perspective of national governments and other stakeholders. Current implementation is struggling to avoid the pitfalls. Cities matter far beyond the confines of SDG 11, both because of the interdependencies between that goal and other SDGs and because cities are places where the agenda's lofty aspirations must

---

1. United Nations Conference on Housing and Sustainable Urban Development in Quito, Ecuador, on October 20, 2016.

be translated into progress felt by real people living in real communities. Cities often form much of the frontlines but have too little of the mandate to advance overall SDG progress.

In particular, urbanization will have essential implications for achieving one of the most revolutionary and challenging aspects of the 2030 Agenda: the imperative to "leave no one behind." Already home to more than half the world's population, cities will grow by 2.5 billion people by 2050. Almost all that increase will take place in developing countries in Africa and Asia. While overall poverty has declined in the world, the urban share of overall poverty has increased,[2] which means that as the world urbanizes, the world's poor also are urbanizing. Successfully leaving no one behind will require attention to this dynamic. This chapter grapples with two major questions to inform this discourse.

To What Extent Are the Left Behind in Cities?

Urbanization in developing countries has accelerated in recent decades. The least developed parts of the world sustained the highest urban growth rates between 1995 and 2015, with Africa urbanizing the fastest.[3] The trends show no sign of slowing down. Between 2014 and 2025, the global number of megacities[4] is projected to grow from nineteen to twenty-seven, of which twenty-one will be in developing countries.[5]

Urbanization and Poverty

Historically, increases in urbanization have been linked to economic growth and increased development, marked by economic shifts from agriculture to more productive sectors. The experience of the United States and Europe made it natural to expect increases in city populations as industrialization produced growth.[6]

Today, the link between national income and urbanization has weakened. There is general acknowledgement, for example, that urban and industrial development in Africa are disconnected.[7] The policy shifts that accompanied industrialization in Western developed economies—which resulted in worker benefits and protections, investments in human capital and infrastructure, and greater productivity—are largely absent in many of Africa's growing cities, which are

2. World Bank and IMF (2013).
3. UN-Habitat (2016).
4. The United Nations Department of Economic and Social Affairs defines mega-cities as urban agglomerations having over 10 million inhabitants.
5. Ball and Linn (2014).
6. Glaeser (2014).
7. UNECA (2017).

dominated by informality and severe gaps and disparities in connectivity and mobility.[8]

This growth in urban populations also raises concerns about the intersection of poverty with environmental considerations. In general, increasing population density within geographically compact cities can be beneficial, particularly in reducing traffic-related pollution and increasing energy efficiency. However, if handled poorly, rapid urbanization, accompanied by urban sprawl, could be a recipe for expansive slums and environmental degradation. As migration due to climate shifts gains momentum, cities may have to absorb from 20 to 200 million more people. Yet while the urban population in the developing world is projected to double in size by 2030, the land area covered by cities will triple.[9]

More broadly, up to 70 percent of urban residents in the Global South may be underserved, lacking access to basic services such as housing, water, waste management, and transportation.[10] The cities in the Global South expected to grow the fastest have the least financial resources per capita to manage the growth.[11]

Two of Africa's most populous countries, Nigeria and the Democratic Republic of Congo (DRC), currently have the largest numbers of extremely poor people in the world, and are projected to retain those rankings in 2030.[12] Half of Nigeria's population lives in cities, as does more than 40 percent of the population of the DRC. Exactly how many of the relevant poor people in these two countries live in urban areas is unclear, but in 2016, the UN estimated that 55 percent of Africa's urban population lived in slums. This gives an indication of the extent of the problem.[13]

Two cities illustrate the pace of change. In 1960, Lagos, Nigeria, had a population of 200,000 people. Today, while the specific number is debated, some estimates put the population of its metro area at almost 20 million. This is a 100-fold increase in just sixty years. Kinshasa, the capital city of the DRC, grew at an average annual rate of 5.1 percent between 1984 and 2010.[14] With a current estimated population of 12 million, it is expected to become the largest city in Africa by 2030, home to 21 million.

These trends signal that attention must be paid to the shifting relationship between urbanization and poverty. "To reach the furthest behind first,"[15] countries must clarify not only who those people are but where they live.

8. Lall and others (2017).
9. Angel and others (2010).
10. Beard and others (2016).
11. UN DESA (2014).
12. Kharas and others (2019).
13. United Nations (2016).
14. IBRD and World Bank (2018).
15. UNGA (2015).

Too Little Data

The urban challenge of people being left behind is complicated by the fear that urban poverty in the Global South is poorly measured and may be significantly underestimated.[16] Household surveys such as the Demographic and Health Surveys (DHS), which have been conducted for decades, provide policymakers with an attractive standard for comparison across countries and time, two key dimensions for benchmarking progress on the SDGs. But DHS surveys are conducted at the national level and often have sample sizes too small to disaggregate geographically.[17]

For example, one recent study used DHS data to analyze the progress of cities on reaching the SDGs.[18] Because of the limited scope of DHS data, just eight targets and ten indicators could be measured, and only twenty cities[19] met the criteria for periodicity. When narrowing to just the targets and indicators for SDG 11, three developing country cities[20] had data available for only half the indicators, and even those had challenges of comparability and quality.

The other traditional measurement option, and a more common source, is census data. While availability is more widespread, many national governments do not provide detailed data to local authorities. Moreover, the typical ten-year gap in data collection limits its usefulness for measuring progress.[21] While researchers often attempt to extrapolate trends from national data, it is difficult to create a holistic picture of urban environments. Lack of a globally accepted definition of "urban" complicates the exercise.

The pervasive informality of many economic relationships in urban areas in developing countries poses additional challenges. A recent study compared independent estimates and official census figures of the number of people living in Nairobi's Kibera slum, and found discrepancies that ranged from 18 to 59 percent.[22] Such differences are likely not unusual.

Household surveys and census data are not the only sources or means to

---

16. Mitlin and Satterthwaite (2013).
17. Levy and others (2015).
18. Lucci and others (2016).
19. Cities selected for analysis by the ODI that met their criteria include: Abidjan, Côte d'Ivoire; Accra, Ghana; Addis Ababa, Ethiopia; Bamako, Mali; Bogota, Colombia; Brazzaville, Republic of Congo; Conakry, Guinea; Dar es Salaam, Tanzania; Harare, Zimbabwe; Jakarta, Indonesia; Kigali, Rwanda; Kinshasa, DRC; Lima, Peru; Lusaka, Zambia; Manila, Philippines; Maputo, Mozambique; Mumbai, India; Nairobi, Kenya; Ouagadougou, Burkina Faso; and Phnom Penh, Cambodia.
20. These cities were: Bogota, Colombia; Mumbai, India; and Nairobi, Kenya.
21. Levy and others (2015).
22. Lucci and others (2017).

measure the realities of urban life. Government ministries, civil society organizations, and local governments all have useful and relevant data. Much of it is not public, and often it is siloed and fragmented. Collecting and curating it is a challenge. Making it useful will require a concerted effort and innovative approaches.

Too Little Attention

While challenges with data accessibility, quality, and definition at the local level may seem like a technical problem, these issues go to the heart of the global commitment to reach the most difficult first. The case can be made that when it comes to rapidly growing places, especially in developing countries, national and global leaders are not adequately equipped to understand just how many people are being left behind. As urban growth rates accelerate, this situation is likely to worsen. The risk is that the poor will become increasingly invisible, at least in a statistical sense. Not just left behind, they may be left out altogether.

To the extent that countries have provided specific data on vulnerable populations in their Voluntary National Reviews (VNRs) presented at the UN, they have focused almost exclusively on distinctive personal characteristics, such as sex, age, disability, and race. In 2018, no country's VNR combined the data from their "leave no one behind" analysis with an examination of the physical location of those populations and/or locally-led efforts to reach them.[23]

National governments must urgently begin to clarify, through their VNRs and data systems, exactly where people are getting left behind, especially in their main urban corridors. Greater investment and increased capacity in government statistical offices, both national and local, to collect and analyze city-level data are critical and must be encouraged. The expense and time necessary to conduct household surveys, however, necessitates a call to action to leapfrog beyond business-as-usual approaches.

Launching a global partnership for local development data would help mobilize political attention and investment at a scale and speed consistent with the pace of growing urban populations. Such a partnership could provide a platform for stakeholders from national governments, municipal governments, technology companies and start-ups, investors, civil society, and academia to combine their expertise; uncover and analyze local data focused on the poorest and most vulnerable; and assess its national and global implications.

A partnership can steer the resources and expertise of such initiatives to cities most in need, targeting initiatives to urban areas experiencing the fastest growth rates in low-income countries. A key first step might also include creating a data

---

23. Kindornay (2019).

floor for cities, building the capacity to track a small set of people-centered metrics relevant to poverty, nutrition, education, water and waste, accessibility, pollution, jobs, and violence, as well as equity. This could help drive necessary data investments, facilitate identification of the geographic location of gaps in progress, and highlight potential policy interventions.

More broadly, a number of emerging data initiatives could be linked to help deliver higher quality urban-level poverty data at a faster rate. A new poverty mapping initiative with leadership from the World Bank and several data research institutes seeks to maximize the use of satellite, mobile phone, and social media data while respecting privacy boundaries. The World Council on City Data (WCCD) is implementing ISO 37120 certification for sustainable development of communities, and has mapped its indicators against the SDGs. Other indices, such as the Social Progress Index and the city-level indices being created by the Sustainable Development Solutions Network (SDSN), are also engaging with cities to provide additional insights.

Is SDG 11 Enough for Cities?

SDG 11 is the primary entry point for cities into the 2030 Agenda, inserting them into the discourse of a global agreement among nation-states and helping integrate commitments from the New Urban Agenda, the Sendai Framework for Disaster Risk Reduction, and the Paris climate accord into their local plans. This is a welcome development, given the evolutions in local and multi-level governance that will be necessary if countries are to make substantial progress on these global agendas.

The targets within SDG 11 are especially attentive to the spatial characteristics of a healthy city, calling for adequate housing, accessible transport and green space, resilience to disasters, and participatory planning. It provides a basis for clarifying and focusing attention on the balance of power, responsibility, and accountability among national and other levels of government.

National Governments Need to Leave No City Behind

As national governments follow through on the commitment in the UN declaration to "work closely on implementation with regional and local authorities," that engagement should closely examine the potential for empowering local and municipal governments to address the inefficiencies or ineffective delivery of services that constrain progress.[24] In this respect, SDG 11 commits national governments to leave no city behind.

24. Abraham and Hingorani (2018).

The UN declaration never explicitly assigns specific responsibilities to local governments. (Local authorities, after all, are not signatories to the agreement.) At the same time, the implicit understanding of their necessary participation has given rise to "localization." The term has been used to mean different things in different contexts. For some people, it refers to the ownership of city governments in achieving Goal 11. Other definitions refer to the disaggregation of data to measure inequality below the national level, or to the discrete responsibilities of local governments within the agenda based on the services over which they have primary jurisdiction.[25]

For example, estimates suggest 65 percent of the SDG agenda is dependent upon subnational leadership and investment.[26] This framing implies parceling out pieces of the agenda owned by local governments and assigning them partial accountability for those portions.

Yet the most common use of localization emanates from UN consultations prior to the agreement, where "'localizing' is the process of taking into account subnational contexts in the achievement of the 2030 Agenda, from the setting of goals and targets, to determining the means of implementation and using indicators to measure and monitor progress."[27] Yet even this leaves unsaid who is doing the work and what the concrete steps are, while implying bottom-up and top-down actions.

Some national governments are working with their municipal governments to localize in this way. Both Germany and Japan, for example, have singled out local adoption of the SDGs as key to their national SDG strategies, and are providing financial support or technical assistance to cities. Local planning and budgeting for Accra is based on guidelines incorporating the SDGs created by Ghana's national development planning commission.

Yet these countries remain the exception. Most national governments have struggled to fit a robust role for city and subnational levels of government into their SDG implementation. An analysis of three years of the VNRs reported by countries to the United Nations, detailing their plans and progress on the SDGs, found that local and regional governments had been directly consulted less than 50 percent of the time.[28] Relatively few countries include examples of SDG implementation at the local level or local assessments of progress in their VNRs.

25. UCLG (2014); Lucci (2014).
26. Cities Alliance (2015).
27. Fernández de Losada (2014).
28. UCLG (2018).

City Governments: Leaving No Goal Behind

Around the world, it is emerging as common practice that mayors, city managers, and municipal officials are adapting and applying the complete SDG agenda to their local realities.

From the perspective of these leaders, SDG 11 is narrow. They see, and their citizens experience, the immediate effects of policy related to the many aspects of the 2030 Agenda, from poverty, health, and education to housing, safety, sanitation, and air pollution. The effects of climate change, environmental degradation, injustice, and lack of democratic participation are not just national or global; they are also local concerns.

While previously lacking the terminology of the SDGs, local leaders have targeted various aspects of the goals for decades. As urban areas have grown, increasing both in physical size and power, their leaders are increasingly expected to take on the full range of issues. The SDGs provide a globally accepted and vetted framework to tie together their work across these different dimensions.

At one level, the movement by city leaders to apply the SDGs can be seen as a reflection of a shift in power from the national to the local, a pattern becoming known as the "new localism."[29] In an era where national governments are struggling with political divisions and service delivery, today's local leaders are earning reputations as the ones to tackle and make progress on social problems by being pragmatic, solutions-oriented, and adept at aligning the interests of local stakeholders to a common purpose.

In one view, city leadership on the SDGs is another manifestation of this shift. The move by cities to use the SDGs as a local blueprint for development has, in many instances, occurred organically. Their leadership has found value in the framework reflecting the strategies and vision they have set out, and in linking their local actions to a movement for global progress.

But in almost all cases, city governments lack authority or agency over key parts of the SDG agenda. This varies considerably from country to country, depending on decentralization of revenue-generating and regulatory power and on types of governance structures. Even in the United States, where city governments enjoy a high level of autonomy, the full range of SDGs are generally not under their managerial control. Los Angeles city government, for example, does not have jurisdiction over the local public health or education systems.

29. Katz and Nowack (2018).

From Seventeen to Three

Although governance structures differ by country, only the largest municipal governments tend to have a bureaucracy analogous to national governments, which generally have enough ministries to divide the seventeen goals and cover the entire landscape. In many national governments, multiple ministries may be implicated in joint work to advance a single SDG. In most municipal governments, the opposite is likely to be true: one office or division would have leadership responsibility on multiple SDGs.

While city leaders may not own or have capacity to cover all parts of the agenda, their citizens still view them as responsible for its many parts. That was the message from fourteen cities in the vanguard of localizing the SDGs recently convened by the Brookings Institution at the Rockefeller Bellagio Center. Municipal leadership can outline an inclusive and comprehensive vision that provides the basis for building political will and attracting attention, investments, and partnerships, giving it a sense of power and urgency because of the direct effect on local lives. The SDGs offer the promise of a common language to engage their constituents, as well as other stakeholders and levels of government, in a holistic vision of community well-being with a common purpose and common measures of progress.

For the cities that met in Bellagio, the key to adapting the SDGs is the three-way focus on human and social development; equitable economic growth; and environmental protection and action on climate change. Rather than perfect fidelity to the seventeen goals, 169 targets, and 232 indicators measured at the national and global level, they view the critical imperative as simultaneous progress on social, economic, and environmental dimensions. The SDGs are integrative, uniting existing city plans and strategies so progress on one dimension is not made at the expense of another.

This tripartite lens forces cities to seek policy solutions and initiatives that link considerations of vulnerability and marginalization to infrastructure, jobs, environmental degradation, safety, justice, and climate adaptation. At the local level, the interdependence of the SDGs comes to life: ending homelessness or reducing slums, for example, entails addressing issues related to poverty, shelter, mobility and accessibility, jobs, education, physical and mental health, and environmental justice.

Cities are well-positioned to play an essential role in actualizing policies and initiatives that grapple with this interdependence, one of the most challenging aspects of the SDGs. They can be laboratories for developing and implementing innovations to solve multiple problems at once, an approach becoming known as "multi-solving,"[30] which benefits from starting small and experimenting in a defined setting.

30. Sawin (2018).

Documenting and Elevating Local Leadership

Cities interested in using the SDGs typically start by aligning their city strategies, plans, and priorities against the goals, testing the national SDG targets for
relevance to their local realities, and calibrating them to local development aspirations. They then identify indicators and sources of data to measure their performance and progress. There is variability and flexibility across cities' approaches.
No officially determined or universally accepted SDG targets for local purposes
exist. There is also no formal set of indicators, nor an official forum, for reporting
on local SDG progress.

In 2018, New York City pioneered the first-ever Voluntary Local Review (VLR).
Structuring the report in the format of the VNRs submitted by member states to
the UN, it provided a credible link to the official follow-up and review parameters
outlined in the UN declaration. The idea of a common city-level reporting tem-
plate, at once flexible for local needs yet consistent with the official reporting process, has found broad appeal and is sparking a burgeoning movement worldwide.
Cities as diverse as Helsinki, Kitakyshu, Rio de Janeiro, Buenos Aires, Los Angeles,
Pittsburgh, Medellin, and Durban are now undertaking or considering a VLR.

There is no definitive accounting of the number of cities attempting to localize
the SDGs. At scale, localization efforts could have significant impact, especially
on accessing the most vulnerable and hardest to reach. Cities are self-propagating
their own localization efforts through peer-to-peer relationships, exhibiting a
high degree of innovation and flexibility as they take on the agenda. This deserves
more attention and support from national governments, international organizations, and the official architecture of SDG follow-up and review.

Several actions can build upon recent momentum. A first step would be for
member states to offer some type of official standing to the VLRs, incorporating them into formal UN processes at the annual High-Level Political Forum
(HLPF). This would provide additional incentives to scale up city-specific reporting on the SDGs. VLRs might be integrated into a country's VNR, for example.

The capacity and standing of Local 2030, an initiative launched under the
purview of the UN Deputy Secretary-General, should also be strengthened and
formalized to stand as the unequivocal focal point for leveraging UN development system efforts to strengthen delivery by city and local governments on the
SDGs. The breadth and scale of city activity on the SDGs will resist centralized
approaches to manage and aggregate it, so Local 2030's strategy of building out
a network of local hubs is a welcome approach to enable scaling. It could usefully
organize the regional commissions and appropriate offices within UN agencies to
identify opportunities for cities to benefit from data and analytical support and
SDG-linked financing opportunities.

The Global Taskforce for Local and Regional Governments, led by United

Cities and Local Governments (UCLG), provides a critical complement by spearheading diplomatic efforts to ensure city participation and voice within the UN and other global governance processes. This representation is important on global policy issues that overlap with local government interests. The power of their collective representation should provide a basis for building partnerships with member states and donors willing to champion the local SDG agenda. Such collaborations could be strengthened by launching a broader alliance with member states and UN agencies, resulting in stronger connections to the official UN SDG architecture, or by creating a high-level commission that can elevate the business case and value proposition for city-specific and local implementation of the "leave no one behind" agenda.

The Global Taskforce can also help integrate the SDGs into city-to-city networks such as C40 Climate Cities, ICLEI (Local Governments for Sustainability),[31] and the Global Covenant of Mayors. This city-to-city diplomacy will be critical to helping more cities integrate the SDGs into their local planning.

Conclusion

Leading the level of government closest to their citizens, mayors and city officials have natural incentives to be concerned about their most vulnerable and marginalized residents. They hear directly from constituents about improvements or regressions in their community. The proximity turns issues like homelessness and slums, for example, from statistical abstractions into tangible and visible realities that offer a painfully regular reminder of the indignity of deprivation.

Within individual cities, those deprivations exist side-by-side with prosperity. Cities are places where the rich and poor physically intermingle, sometimes in adjacent neighborhoods, bound together by place and economic and social relationships. Inequality takes on a visible human face.

In that context, it is no surprise that mayors are increasingly vocal about an agenda that promotes fairness, inclusion, and equity, encouraging systemic changes that extend beyond services that simply enable the most marginalized to escape deprivation. Their collective agendas bear this out. For example, while the participants of the OECD's Champion Mayors initiative have set priorities that include delivery of education, health, and housing for the most vulnerable, they also include increased and inclusive opportunities for jobs and other labor issues; accessible infrastructure with greater climate resilience for all; and planning and investment targeted specifically to disadvantaged areas. In 2018, the leaders' statement of the Urban 20, a group of mayors from G20 countries using their combined voice to influence the G20 agenda, emphasized delivering

---

31. Founded in 1990 as the International Council for Local Environmental Initiatives (ICLEI).

"opportunities, safety and equality for all," and highlighted issues such as gender equity as a key concern.

Local leaders often define success as weaving together diverse groups and neighborhoods into a cohesive social fabric that promotes equality of opportunity. Their instincts are supported by evidence that social cohesion promotes resilience. This takes on added importance as cities become the destination for 60 percent of refugees and 80 percent of internally displaced people.[32]

The admonition to "reach the furthest behind first" in the UN declaration generally puts poverty, often extreme poverty, at the center of the "leave no one behind" debate. Most analytical approaches still build out an MDG-plus accounting, using basic indicators of human dignity to track it. City leaders are pushing to widen that aperture in the broader context of the SDGs, insisting on including the imperative to address inequality. As they pursue the 2030 Agenda, they will need support from above and below. Cities frame the global frontier in the fight for fairness.

References

Abraham, Reuben, and Pritika Hingorami. 2018. "Rescaling Government for an Urban Future." In *Summits to Solutions*, edited by Raj Desai, Hiroshi Kato, Homi Kharas, and John McArthur. Brookings Press: 219–38.

Angel, Shlomo, and others. 2010. "A Planet of Cities: Urban Land Cover Estimates and Projections for All Countries, 2000–2050." Working Paper. Lincoln Institute of Land Policy.

Ball, Roy W., and Johannes F. Linn. 2014. "Governing and Financing Cities in the Developing World." Lincoln Institute of Land Policy.

Beard, Victoria A., Anjali Mahendra, and Michael I. Westphal. 2016. "Towards a More Equal City: Framing the Challenges and Opportunities." Working Paper. World Resources Institute.

Cities Alliance. 2015. "Sustainable Development Goals and Habitat III: Opportunities for a Successful New Urban Agenda." Discussion Paper 3.

Fernández de Losada, Agustí. 2014. "Localizing the Post-2015 Development Agenda." United Nations Development Group.

Glaeser, Edward L. 2014. "A World of Cities: The Causes and Consequences of Urbanization in Poorer Countries." *Journal of the European Economic Association* 12, no. 5: 1154–99.

Global Parliament of Mayors. 2018. "Empowering Cities as Drivers of Change." https://www.mottmac.com/download/file?id=36551&isPreview=True.

International Bank for Reconstruction and Development (IBRD) and the World Bank. 2018. "Democratic Republic of Congo Urbanization Review." https://openknowledge.worldbank.org/bitstream/handle/10986/28931/9781464812033.pdf.

Katz, Bruce, and Jeremy Nowak. 2018. *The New Localism*. Brookings Institution.

Kharas, Homi, Kristofer Hamel, and Martin Hofer. 2019. "Rethinking Global

---

32. Global Parliament of Mayors (2018).

Poverty Reduction in 2019." Brookings Future Development (December 13). https://www.brookings.edu/blog/future-development/2018/12/13/rethinking-global-poverty-reduction-in-2019/.

Kindornay, Shannon. 2019. "Progressing National SDG Implementation: An Independent Assessment of the Voluntary National Review Reports Submitted to the United Nations High-Level Political Forum in 2018." Ottawa: Canadian Council for International Cooperation.

Lall, Somik Vinay, Vernon J. Henderson, and Anthony Venables. 2017. *Africa's Cities: Opening Doors to the World*. World Bank.

Levy, Caren, Colin Marx, and David Satterthwaite. 2015. "Urbanisation and Urban Poverty Reduction in Low- and Middle-income Countries." In *Thinking Beyond Sectors for Sustainable Development*, edited by Jeff Waage and Christopher Yap. London: Ubiquity Press: 19–28.

Lucci, Paula. 2014. "An Urban Dimension in a New Set of Development Goals." Working Paper. London: Overseas Development Institute.

Lucci, Paula, Tanvi Bhatkal, and Amina Khan. 2017. "Are We Underestimating Urban Poverty?" *World Development* 103. Elsevier: 297–310.

Lucci, Paula, and others. 2016. "Projecting Progress: Are Cities on Track to Achieve the SDGs by 2030?" Overseas Development Institute.

Mitlin, Diana, and David Satterthwaite. 2013. *Urban Poverty in the Global South: Scale and Nature*. New York: Routledge.

Sawin, Elizabeth. 2018. "The Magic of "Multi-Solving." *Stanford Social Innovation Review*. Stanford University, and Stanford Center on Philanthropy and Civil Society. https://ssir.org/articles/entry/the_magic_of_multisolving.

United Cities and Local Governments (UCLG). 2014. "How to Localize Targets and Indicators." www.global-taskforce.org/sites/default/files/2017-06/localization_targets_indicator_web.pdf.

———. 2018. "Towards the Localization of the SDGs." www.gold.uclg.org/sites/default/files/Towards_the_Localization_of_the_SDGs.pdf.

United Nations. 2016. "The Sustainable Development Goals Report 2016." https://unstats.un.org/sdgs/report/2016/.

United Nations Department of Economic and Social Affairs (UN DESA). 2014. "World Urbanization Prospects: The 2014 Revision, Highlights." https://esa.un.org/unpd/wup/publications/files/wup2014-highlights.pdf.

United Nations Economic Commission for Africa (UNECA). 2017. "Economic Report on Africa 2017: Urbanization and Industrialization for Africa's Transformation." https://www.uneca.org/publications/economic-report-africa-2017.

United Nations General Assembly (UNGA). 2015. Resolution 70/1, *Transforming our World: The 2030 Agenda for Sustainable Development*. A/RES/70/1. September 25. https://www.un.org/ga/search/view_doc.asp?symbol=A/RES/70/1&Lang=E.

United Nations Human Settlements Programme (UN-Habitat). 2016. "World Cities Report 2016." http://wcr.unhabitat.org/wp-content/uploads/2017/02/WCR-2016-Full-Report.pdf.

World Bank and the International Monetary Fund (IMF). 2013. "Global Monitoring Report 2013: Rural-Urban Dynamics and the Millennium Development Goals." https://openknowledge.worldbank.org/handle/10986/13330.

CHAPTER THIRTEEN

Left Behind or Pushed Behind?
Redistributing Power Over the Sustainable Development Goals

Paul O'Brien

"People are not 'left behind,' they are 'pushed behind.'
It's not like we all went on a nice picnic and someone
went to sleep and got forgotten."[1]

In late 2017, I went back to Korogocho, in Nairobi, where I got my start in international social justice work in the nineties.[2] The word *korogocho* means "shoulder to shoulder" in Kiswahili. There were few permanent structures, and most buildings were made of mud and sticks. The better huts had corrugated iron roofs, and the stench of open sewers was everywhere. Two hundred thousand people were crammed into a square mile of land beside Dandora, a mountain of trash.

In the middle of this slum, I saw a bright new building, one with clean floors

---

1. See https://twitter.com/fp2p/status/1071069799491518466?lang=en.
2. My first "rights and development" job was in 1993, working with a Kenyan human rights education group that was applying the work of Brazilian educators Paulo Friere (*Pedagogy of the Oppressed*), and Augusto Boal (*Theatre of the Oppressed*) to use participatory pedagogy and theatre to challenge norms around sexual and gender-based violence in Korogocho.

In looking to feminist leadership to find a way forward in navigating the language of power (a core theme in this chapter), I received constructive critique and support from Oxfam colleagues; so much so that I risk breaking a key feminist principle "nothing about us without us." I would like to think I meet this principle simply by being on my own feminist journey, but that's not enough. I can only say this would have been a significantly worse piece without guidance, debate, and discussion with the following Oxfam colleagues, all of whom I think of as feminists: Barbara Durr, Aria Grabowski, Duncan Green, Gawain Kripke, Abby Maxman, Steve Price-Thomas, Rebecca Rewald, Jo Rowlands, and Sarah Tuckey. I am deeply grateful to each of them, particularly for their challenges to my thinking. I doubt any of them agree with this entire piece. Beyond Oxfam, I am grateful to Emily Bove, Kath Campbell, Raj Desai, and Shanta Devarajan, who read segments or earlier drafts of this chapter and helped me clarify my thinking. The misstatements and weaker ideas in this piece are my own. Nothing in this piece reflects Oxfam policy.

and painted walls. It was a health clinic, the only two-story building I could see. It had a room for pregnant mothers, and one for kids with typhoid or HIV. They did not have much modern medical equipment—the records were all on news-sheet on the walls—but what they had was clean and useful.

I was sitting in that clinic with two women, Rose Ngatia and Beatrice Okoth, from the National Taxpayers Association, a local group in Kenya. I told them, "I never thought I would see a building like this in Korogocho. How did it happen?"

Okoth looked at me with her steely eyes and said:

> You know there is a Bwana Mkubwa in Korogocho ["a big man"]. The government gives him money for our place. It is tax money so it's our money. But it was not coming here. So, we decided to teach this man the right way to lead. We went to the Nairobi council and found out all the projects that were supposed to happen in Korogocho with this tax money. Then we went to this big man, and we showed him the list and we asked, "Where are our projects?"

A few nights later, the Bwana Mkubwa's thugs came to Okoth's house and knocked on her door. They told her to stop agitating. They said the next time there would not just be a threat.

Beatrice Okoth and Rose Ngatia had grown up with this. They knew these men. They knew the threat was real. One of the men threatening them was a local policeman. And the two women talked to each other that morning and decided that, this time, they would not back off.

In the days that followed, they put on their T-shirts from the National Tax-payers Association, and their badges, and they went out to more people and told them they had been threatened, but that these were the basic rights of the community and now they needed people to demand that their money be spent on schools, on health clinics, and on sewage. They went back to the Nairobi City Council, and they wrote to their MP.

A few days later, they went to the Bwana Mkubwa and showed him the petitions and told him all this, and they said they knew he was a good man, and they said they wanted to work with him to get these projects built. He looked at the petitions and told them to go away. That night, they waited for the thugs to come again. But they never came.

A few days later, bulldozers show up at the site for one of those projects to begin the work. And the Bwana Mkubwa started to release funding for each of the projects listed. [3]

---

3. Some of the funding for this health clinic came from international donors. It is a good example of aid and domestic resource mobilization coming together well.

At the end of her story, Okoth pointed her finger at me and said, "You didn't think Korogocho could have this clinic. Let me tell you: All I need is a uniform and a badge and I can get many more things built here."

Okoth's tale is not just another development story about a courageous activist. It is a story about power.

This chapter suggests that development professionals might need a different way to think about power if we are to be useful to the Okoths of this world. It starts with a brief history of thinking about power, both in philosophy and development literature. It then proposes that we need some different language and ideas to talk about power if we are to achieve the Sustainable Development Goals (SDGs), and then it applies that frame to two of the largest barriers to SDG realization: growing authoritarianism and extreme economic inequality. It closes by suggesting that the way forward in thinking about power may come from feminist leadership.

My aims in writing this chapter are two-fold: that the reader will join me in asking, first, whether people are being left behind or pushed behind and, second, who is doing the pushing. I also hope the reader finds it useful to test assumptions about how we need to think about power if we are to be useful to the Okoths of this world and achieve the SDGs.

A Brief History and Typology of Power

Through the latter part of the last millennium, influential thinkers debated the importance, exercise, and typologies of power, but they essentially agreed on one core characteristic of power: that it was a like a currency—if power was held by some, it could not be held by others.

A largely male, largely Northern cast of philosophers sought unifying theories of power to explain the world. Thomas Hobbes (1588–1679) brought us "state power," embodied in the *Leviathan*. Max Weber (1864–1920) believed state power consisted in a "monopoly of the legitimate use of physical force." Friedrich Nietzsche (1844–1900) took the debate beyond the state to include "the will to power" that lies in each of us and explains our every action. Stephen Lukes (born in 1941)[4] agreed that power can be held personally, but

4. Decisionmaking power occurs when A makes a decision that exercises power over B against B's interests; nondecisionmaking power allows A to use agenda-setting to bias what can get decided by B, and ideological power exists when A uses persuasion or false consciousness, rather than coercion or conflict, to change what B actually wants. In a sense, I wrote this chapter because I believe that Agenda 2030 exercises a form of nondecisionmaking power to shape how the development community engages on the SDGs and determines which issues are acceptable for discussion in "legitimate" public forums. My argument is that a certain species of power—zero sum redistributable and choice driven power—has become the ugly duckling of the SDGs and that Agenda 2030 regards it as illegitimate to debate.

distinguished between three dimensions of power: decisional, nondecisional, and ideological.[5]

All these thinkers agreed on one thing: They conceived of power as a zero-sum currency—essentially the ability to control or influence the resources, actions, and even the innermost thoughts of oneself or others. They debated who had power, who should have it, and how to distribute it, but they assumed (and, therefore, did not debate) that power is a currency that, if held by some, cannot be owned by others.

Then, along came Michel Foucault (1926–1984). Together with other postmodernists, Foucault sought new ways of thinking about language, ideas, identity, and ourselves. Foucault had watched the work of the philosophers of language of his time (including his own *Words and Things*) lose relevance and energy in the search for grand, unifying ideas to explain everything by limiting our thinking to "their" lens on life. He witnessed in *Discipline and Punish* and *The History of Sexuality* how the oppression of nations, prisoners, colonized peoples, and even our bodies can be better understood by opening up our thinking to different theories, types, and definitions of power realized in action.[6]

Of course, it was not just Foucault who helped shape modern thinking about power. Postmodernism did not just reveal the Northern white male heterosexual hegemony over intellectual life. For the last thirty years, the identities and voices that shape the power debate have changed. Feminists from both the North[7] and South,[8] advocates for

5. Lukes realized late in life that the zero-sum power he talked about in *Power: A Radical View* was only one "species" of power, and that power as an ability that is non-zero sum is equally important. In a sense, he presaged the argument made in this chapter—that the people in poverty need to harness both types of power (generative and zero sum) if the SDGs are to succeed.

6. That said, Foucault always "presupposes that power is a kind of power-over." See https://plato.stanford.edu/entries/feminist-power/#DefPow. He puts it this way: "if we speak of the structures or the mechanisms of power, it is only insofar as we suppose that certain persons exercise power over others" in the afterword of "The Subject and Power," in Hubert Dreyfus and Paul Rabinow, *Michel Foucault: Beyond Structuralism and Hermeneutics*, 2nd ed. (Chicago: University of Chicago Press, 1983), p. 779.

7. The best overview I've found of feminist theory on development is by Elaine Hartwick in "*Theories of Development*" 3rd ed. (2015). See chapter seven, which interrogates five strands of feminist theory (Women in Development, Women and Development, Gender and Development, Women, Environment and Development, and Postmodernism and Development).

8. Writing in 1984, the year of Foucault's death, Chandra Mohanty used Foucault's work on power to deconstruct how Western white-led voices were beginning to assert their own colonial hegemony over feminist approaches to "humanism"—the forebearer of the SDGs. She was one of the early thinkers exploring how Southern women of color were defined as "Others" or peripheral to these debates. See Chandra Mohanty, "Under Western Eyes: Feminist Scholarship and Colonial Discourses," *On Humanism and the University I: The Discourse of Humanism* 12, no. 3: 333–58.

racial justice,[9] class justice,[10] sexual and reproductive rights,[11] movement builders,[12] and those insisting on a better global balance of voices have transformed our understanding of power. The last section of this paper argues that these leaders, and particularly feminists, offer a way forward for a more honest and profound conversation about power and about who gets left behind by whom.

Power Diversion?

The word *power* has two core meanings in English, French, and German: one is an ability (I feel "powerful" today), and the other is a relationship (when you exercise your power over me). Until the late twentieth century and the postmodernist era, most discussions of power concerned relational power, of the state over citizens, the rich over the poor, men over women, and between identity groups, classes, races, and nations. It was the language of the privileged.[13]

In the late twentieth century, the intellectual and development communities rejected the language of privilege and embraced power as "ability." Particularly influential in that space were philosophers like Peter Morriss, feminist philosophers (e.g., Raewyn Connell, Nancy Hartsock), and development thinkers like Jo Rowlands,[14] Duncan Green,[15] and John Gaventa.[16]

9. One of the most interesting groups thinking about power and racial justice in the United States is Change Elemental, whose tag line demonstrates that they have taken power debates beyond zero-sum thinking: "Co-creating Power for Love, Dignity and Justice." See www.changeelemental. org.

10. One of the most influential voices for the development community is John Gaventa, whose work *Power and Powerlessness: Quiescence and Rebellion in an Appalachian Valley* (1980) applied Lukes' three dimensions to examine why those on the wrong end of economic and political power equations do not rise in rebellion.

11. Reproductive rights groups have been at the forefront of challenging attempts by states to assert power over the sexual health and reproductive rights of women. Two of the groups leading those efforts in the United States are the Center for Health and Gender Equity (www.genderhealth. org) and Planned Parenthood Federation of America (www.plannedparenthood.com).

12. Jeremy Heimans and Henry Timms wrote a fascinating book called *New Power*. I would argue, however, that it is less the "power" that is new in their book than the ways in which power moves through the world—less like a currency held by a few elites and more like a current that is "open, participatory, and peer driven."

13. In defining power in this way, men essentially were exercising a form of what Stephen Lukes called "nondecisional power," the power to determine what gets on the agenda to be decided. As Lukes said, "how we think about power may serve to reproduce and reinforce power structures and relations, or alternatively it may challenge and subvert them" (Lukes [2005] at p. 35).

14. See Jo Rowlands, "Empowerment Examined," *Development in Practice* 5, no. 2, 1995.

15. His two books on power, *From Poverty to Power: How Active Citizens and Effective States Can Change the World* (2008) and *How Change Happens* (2016), have been deeply influential in Oxfam and the development community in embracing power as a legitimate currency for development activism.

16. See John Gaventa, *Power and Powerlessness: Quiescence and Rebellion in an Appalachian Valley* (1980). He also provided the intellectual energy behind the Powercube, which differentiated

In *Power: A Philosophical Analysis,* Morriss first distinguished power as "ability" and "relational," and then argued that power as ability is all we need. He concludes that we actually do not need to debate "power over" to understand the conflictual dimensions of power. He wrote, "we can easily look at someone's power to kick others around, or their power to win conflicts. Everything that needs to be said about power can be said in terms of the capacity to effect outcomes."[17]

At around the same time, feminist thinkers in the third wave, both Northern and Southern, were exposing how zero-sum relational "power over" had been exercised largely by "hegemonic masculinity"[18] to subjugate others through history. A crucial element of rebalancing power was to rethink how we thought about power itself. Nancy Hartsock, for example, contrasted an "obedience" definition of power with what she called an "energy and competence" understanding of power, which does not involve domination but is generative: "the power some people have of stimulating activity and raising their morale."[19]

Rowlands, an Oxfam colleague and gender justice leader, unpacked power as ability when she mapped out four forms of power.[20] First, she demarcated "power over" and observed the following:

> If power is defined as "power over," a gender analysis shows that power is wielded predominantly by men over other men, and by men over women. Extending this analysis to other forms of social differentiation, power is exercised by dominant social, political, economic, or cultural groups over those who are marginalized. Power, in this sense, is in finite supply; if some people have more, others have less. This is a crucial issue. When

three types of power (visible, hidden, and invisible) on two other planes—places and spaces. See his presentation: www.powercube.net/wp-content/uploads/2009/12/Powercube-powerpoint-2007.ppt.

17. Peter Morriss, *Power: A Philosophical Analysis* (Manchester University Press, 1987).

18. "Hegemonic masculinity" is a term created by the feminist R. W. Connell to describe practices that legitimize men's dominant position in society and justify the subordination of the common male population and women, and other marginalized ways of being a man. See R. W. Connell, James Messerschmidt, "Hegemonic Masculinity: Rethinking the Concept." See https://doi.org/10.1177/0891243205278639.

19. Nancy Hartsock, *Money, Sex and Power: Towards a Feminist Historical Materialism* (Northeastern University Press, 1983): 244. See also *Feminist Perspectives on Power* at https://plato.stanford.edu/entries/feminist-power/. In taking on this non-redistributive and expansive understanding of power, Hartsock was essentially offering another view of feminism than was being offered by thinkers like Gita Sen, who saw the struggle as fundamentally redistributive and based on "class exploitation and gender subordination." See Lourdes Benaria and Gita Sen, 1982, "Class and Gender Inequalities and Women's Role in Economic Development–Theoretical and Practical Implications," *Feminist Studies* 8, no. 1 (Spring 1982): 157–76.

20. Jo Rowlands, "Questioning Empowerment, Working with Women in Honduras" (UK and Ireland: Oxfam, 1997).

power is defined as "power over," then if women gain power it will be at men's expense. It is easy to see why the notion of women becoming empowered is seen as inherently threatening, the assumption being that there will be some kind of reversal of relationships, and men will not only lose power but also face the possibility of having power wielded over them by women. Men's fear of losing control is an obstacle to women's empowerment. *But is it necessarily an outcome of women's empowerment that men should lose power; and, further, should a loss of power be something to fear?*[21] [emphasis is mine]

Rowlands does not answer her last question in that book, but her searing analysis of "power over" contributed, along with the work of Connell, Hartsock, Just Associates,[22] and other feminists and post-modernists, to changing the way development thinkers and activists talked about power. Not only was "power over" identified as exclusively patriarchal and problematic, but finite zero-sum power generally was set aside as the domain of oppressive action.

What the development community did take up from Rowlands were the three other types of power that were not so patriarchal in their roots, zero sum, or fraught with tension: "Power within," which can grow in a person as they gain self-belief and an understanding of their rights; "power with"—when collectives come together to exercise joint action and solidarity; and "power to"—the ability to decide actions and carry them out.

Armed with these three new power currencies,[23] the development and social justice community now had a new language of empowerment that did not require losers or conflict; power "within," "with," and "to" could be grown without men, the state, or corporate powerholders losing out, at least explicitly. And so we organized communities and movements and called it "power with." We deepened individuals' understanding and belief in rights and called it "power within." We mobilized groups to take action and celebrated their "power to."

---

21. Ibid., p. 11.

22. Just Associates is one of the leading groups in the United States helping social justice organizations use this four-power typology. See www.justassoicates.org. Their book, *A New Weave of People, Power and Politics*, by Lisa VeneKlasan and Valerie Miller, has become a much-sourced resource for how to apply the four powers. See the chapter titled Power and Empowerment: https://justassociates.org/sites/justassociates.org/files/07chap3_power_final.pdf.

23. Some would argue that this is exactly what Foucault intended—to expand how we imagine and define power. I would argue that Foucault never meant to go this far. Even though his two great works on power examined how power works to control our innermost thoughts, behaviors, and actions, I see nothing in his work to suggest that he sees power as something that is not relative—something that can be grown inside one person without diminishing "power over" being exercised by another person or institution.

Power as ability became a central theme of one of Oxfam's most influential thought leadership books, *From Poverty to Power*, by Green. His subtitle is telling in itself: *How Active Citizens and Effective States can Change the World*. Essentially, Green argues that the best framed task of development is to increase the power (understood as ability) of both citizens (to exercise agency) and states (to govern effectively). He has little interest in zero-sum thinking or taking away the power of states as the task of development. In his subsequent book, *How Change Happens*, he dived even deeper into the three forms of non-patriarchal power as critical to "how change happens." Like Rowlands, he situated "power over" as a toxic form of power that belongs exclusively to elites and to powerful institutions like the police and courts.[24]

John Gaventa authored a remarkable study of power in one of the poorest parts of the United States, embracing both power as ability—he documented the sense of powerlessness of miners in a remote mining valley—*and* relational power—their inability to take back political and economic power from the government or a London-based corporate mine owner. Gaventa explains why most thinkers now view "power over" as negative and the powers with, within, and to as more positive.[25]

I have come to believe that my Oxfam colleagues Rowlands, Green, and Gaventa, and some feminist thinkers have engaged in an overcorrection. While they were right to identify "power over" as the traditional domain of patriarchal societies generally, they were wrong to suggest that those fighting the injustice of poverty have no business explicitly trying to seek "power over" others as a legitimate objective of development. My instinct is that three particular types of "power over" can be usefully differentiated by the motivation behind them (visible or hidden) and their development outcomes (positive or harmful):

First, of course, Rowlands, Green, Gaventa, and others are right to name a toxic form of "power over" that has characterized colonialism, authoritarianism, racism, sexism, and most other harmful forms of exercising power.

I believe there is second, more developmentally ambiguous form of "power over" worth naming, motivated by benign intentions but often with malignant consequences. This is a problem clearly apparent in philanthropy generally ("power over" resources intended to do good but that actually do harm)[26] and even in the Millennium Development Goals (MDG).

Finally, I believe there is a developmentally positive form of "power over,"

---

24. See *How Change Happens*, p. 36.

25. See www.powercube.net/other-forms-of-power/expressions-of-power/.

26. Anand Giridharadas in *Winners Take All* (2018) offers an unflinching analysis of how the "win-win" tropes of economic and political elites and the philanthropic mindset starves development conversation of the honesty and reflection required to ask the tougher questions.

where people who do not have enough power take specific actions that redistribute zero-sum power away from those who have too much, by using their power within, with, and to. They take back the control of resources, thoughts, and actions from others. This kind of "power over" is distinctive from power as ability (with, to, and within), because it is zero sum, relational, and choice driven. It can be understood only in terms of winners and losers.[27] I do not know what to call this form of power over, but I believe it will be the secret sauce for achieving Agenda 2030.[28]

Let us return to our story from Korogocho to explain this. Beatrice Okoth certainly had "power within" by Jo's Rowland's definition. When the National Taxpayers Association gave her a badge and a T-shirt and some training, they helped Okoth believe she could stand up to the Bwana Mkubwa. In joining with Ruth and other mothers in Korogocho, she built "power with," and by confronting the Bwana Mkubwa, she clearly had the "power to" act. By most development standards, Okoth was "powerful."

Usually, the development conversation stops here, because frankly, it is rare that the people we aim to serve actually take power away from the Bwana Mkubwa's of this world. But that is exactly what happened in this story. She did not just assert a right to influence those expenditures; she took power over those expenditures and away from the Bwana Mkubwa. He no longer could spend or withhold spending with impunity. He had to listen to her.[29]

Something happened in that moment where Okoth went from asserting to exercising power, which was not just generative but finite and redistributive. In that moment, the Bwana Mkubwa had less power. As Foucault might have said, it was action power because there was a moment of action where power was redistributed, and that's what turned potency or ability into actual power.

---

27. This kind of power is what Steve Biko cared about when he wrote "the essence of politics is to direct oneself to the group which wields power," in *White Racism and Black Consciousness* (1972), an edited volume of his writings, *Steve Biko, I Write What I Like* (1978), p. 68.

28. The closest thing I've found, in a deeply moving book called *Power Under* by Steven Wineman, is "constructive rage" which is, essentially powerless rage translated into a personal force for liberation. It is not exactly what I am talking about, however, because it is essentially a way of thinking about power as ability, not about taking control from others. It is not revolutionary enough.

29. Rowlands recognized how power within and to can lead to power over when she wrote: "From a feminist perspective, interpreting 'power over' entails understanding the dynamics of oppression and internalised oppression. Since these affect the ability of less powerful groups to participate in formal and informal decisionmaking, and to exert influence, they also affect the way that individuals or groups perceive themselves and their ability to act and influence the world around them. Empowerment is thus more than simply opening up access to decisionmaking; it must also include the processes that lead people to perceive themselves as able and entitled to occupy that decisionmaking space, and so overlaps with the other categories of 'power to' and 'power from within.'" (Rowlands [1997] at p. 87).

That kind of power is what Abraham Lincoln envisioned with "government of the people, by the people, for the people," and what Thomas Jefferson understood when he told John Adams "the first principle of a good government is certainly a distribution of its powers into executive, judiciary, and legislative. . . ."

It is worth asking whether the redistribution of economic power and opportunity from those who have too much to those who do not have enough is essential to the delivery of the SDGs. My instinct is that the development community is not in agreement about whether any forms of power are finite and need to be redistributed. When a colleague of mine (who has influenced me deeply on this issue) wrote a blog in 2015 describing himself as a "power hawk" because he sees real power as finite, almost every comment on his blog post took issue with his definition of power.[30] I've had the same experience myself in conversation and found myself wondering why zero-sum relational power meets with such resistance among development thinkers and leaders. I concluded that power hawks are an endangered species in development because of history, relevance, and utility. Let me briefly explain each.

The most obvious form of zero-sum relational power—"power over"—has a toxic history. It sits comfortably with the old-fashioned patriarchal, misogynist, racist, and colonial mindset. It is brutish and exclusive. It is the language of the "haves," not the have nots. Who wants to use a currency so closely hoarded by elites when there is a new way of talking about power in which we can all see ourselves every day? Why not find a new language that is less the product and servant of the very power structures we want to change? The legacy of postmodernism is in part to seek more inclusive, less binary and zero-sum concepts.[31]

Second, more inclusive definitions of non-finite power, like power with, within, and to, are far more relevant for the vast majority of work to be done to advance the SDGs. Enhancing these types of power is something that can be done measurably and consistently within reasonable timeframes. Even more important, they matter to people facing injustice and poverty. After all, redistributing power is not the stated purpose of the SDGs—improving "well-being" or human "development" is the purpose, and it is at least arguable that well-being can be increased for the greater common good without taking anyone's power away. To put it in the language of power as ability, the world is a better place when more people have greater agency and power within, with, and to.

Third, using a more inclusive definition of power is strategically and pragmatically smart. Zero-sum realities are by their nature confrontational, and

---

30. Gawain Kripke, "Is Power a Zero Sum Game? Does Women's Empowerment Lead to Increased Domestic Violence?" (August 27, 2015), https://oxfamblogs.org/fp2p/is-power-a-zero-sum-game-does-womens-empowerment-lead-to-increased-domestic-violence/.

31. See Gaventa, *Power and Empowerment*, p. 44, www.powercube.net/wp-content/uploads/2009/11/newweave_chapter3.pdf.

confrontation usually works out in favor of those with more power to start with—not the people we serve with the SDGs. Confrontation as a strategic approach, when one starts with less power, has little utility when one wants to get things done. It is no wonder development programs that work on "empowerment" are loathe to admit that, for their programs to succeed, some powerful actor has to lose out.[32] If our goal is take power away from elites, it is rarely smart to declare that up front. My concern, however, is this: If we do not even know that taking away their power and redistributing it to people facing poverty and injustice is sometimes both necessary and right, then are we not at risk of fooling ourselves, too?

Here is my point: These concerns around history, relevance, and utility have so dominated development discourse on power that we are no longer having conversations about finite power redistribution, and that is becoming a real challenge for achieving the SDGs.[33]

Redistributable Power

To leave no one behind by 2030 will require a different development approach. We may need a new way of thinking about power that has less historic baggage than power over. I'm not sure what it should be called. For now, let us simply refer to it as "redistributable power."

Here's the point: To deliver on the SDGs, we need to broaden our focus beyond those who do not have enough power—which is the focus of "empowerment" work—to focus on those who have too much power. And we need to engage in ideas that redistribute power from the haves to the have nots. To do that, we need to think about redistributable power as more than a misfit that sits exclusively with states, with men who dominate women, or with powerful groups who use their power to dominate and exclude others. For too long, we have treated redistributable power as the ugly duckling of development—marginalizing it as unattractive and unnecessary to the "win-win" we must find to improve our world.[34] But there is real beauty in power that is finite and can be redistributed. If we want the SDGs to take flight, we should consider that.

Beatrice Okoth and Rose Ngatia redistributed power when, through courage

---

32. That's why Green argues, in *How Change Happens*, that usually "good change strategies pursue something more subtle than outright confrontation (which often plays into the hands of the powerful)," p. 37.

33. To borrow Stephen Lukes' language in *Power: A Radical View*, this chapter is an exploration of "nondecisionmaking power"—which sets the agenda in debates and makes certain issues unacceptable for discussion in "legitimate" public forums. This chapter argues that "power over" has become the ugly duckling of development—cast out as illegitimate.

34. Giridharadas, in *Winners Take All*, offers an unflinching analysis of how the "win-win" tropes of economic and political elites starves development conversation of the honesty and reflection required to ask the tougher questions.

and strategy, they held a Big Man in Korogocho to account.[35] In doing so, they exercised a form of power that may not have a good name but clearly has three discrete characteristics.

First, redistributable power is finite. It applies only to currencies of economic, political, or cultural exchange that are zero sum. A currency that is infinite, like love, hate, or dignity, cannot be controlled in this way. It is what distinguishes it from power with, within, and to. In that sense, it is like power over: either one person controls it or another does.

Second, it is exercised through human choice. Redistributable power may feel like it is a force beyond choice or control and that it can sit only in institutions or with elites, but that is not true. When we situate immense power in state institutions, corporations, or market forces, that power may seem beyond any collectivity of intention, but it is not so. We give institutions power and, collectively, we can choose to remove or redistribute that power. This is important; if power is not redistributable through human choice then there is no point asking who has been left behind in terms of power because not much can be done about it. The essence of social justice movement building is to aggregate enough power to take some back from unaccountable elites.

Third, it is relational. The measurement of redistributable power is only significant in relation to others. If on the proverbial desert island with two people, one holds a $100, which is 100 percent of the currency on the island, then she holds all the economic power. If, however, on that island, she has $100 but the other person has $9,900, then the first person does not have much economic power. This relational dimension may be the single most important contribution of rethinking the SDG challenge in terms of power.

Why does it make a difference to talk about the SDGs through the lens of redistributable power? Because we can better understand how and why people are left behind and then do something about it. As the South Korean Economist Ha Joon recently said: "People are not 'left behind,' they are 'pushed behind.' It's not like we all went on a nice picnic and someone went to sleep and got forgotten."[36]

---

35. It is important to note that this does not mean Korogocho's big man was worse off as a consequence. Power is not the same as well-being. He may actually have gained more respect and a different kind of more legitimate power from providing services, but his impunity and ability to control the resources, actions, and innermost thoughts of Okoth and Rose Ngatia was profoundly redistributed.

36. See https://twitter.com/fp2p/status/1071069799491518466?lang=en.

Those Leaving and Those Left Behind

It is time to apply redistributable power to concrete challenges facing our community. In the remainder of this chapter, I draw three conclusions: First, we should honor the spirit of "leave no one behind" by not abandoning our courageous comrades on the frontlines of political power battles against authoritarians; second, we should embrace a more honest conversation about the winners and losers of global economics and the development sector, and finally, we need a new vocabulary to speak about how power works, and we should look to feminist leaders to help us in that journey.

Those Who Defend the Political Power of Others

The SDGs cannot be met through charitable wealth transfers or official development assistance. As a rights based international activist, I believe they will be realized because public (state) and private institutions create the conditions for people to work together to meet the SDGs collectively. Why will those powerful institutions choose to create those conditions? Because it will be in their political and economic interest to do so. In short, the destiny of the SDGs depends profoundly on powerful institutions living by a set of rules and incentives that make them accountable to the citizens and consumers they serve, mediated often by domestic and international civic life.

In other words, the fulfillment of the SDGs depends on a massive power transfer, both economically (hence Goal 10, the inequality goal) and politically (hence Goal 16, the governance goal), to the people who will ensure their realization.

Why would all governments agree to this deeply liberal internationalist project? Why would authoritarian governments in China, Russia, and Hungary adopt the SDGs if success depends on a redistribution of power to their own citizens? I can envision three possible motivations for doing so.

First, they may be playing the win-win game of "philanthrocapitalism"[37]: they believe they can achieve the material benefits in most of the SDG targets and indicators without actually redistributing economic or power away from current beneficiaries in their own societies. Second, they may believe that no one is going to challenge them on power redistribution in the SDG process, despite the SDG targets: They have no intention of "developing effective accountable and transparent institutions" or ensuring "inclusive participatory and representative

---

37. Matthew Bishop and Michael Green, *"Philanthrocapitalism: How the Rich Can Save the World"* (2008), cited at length in Anand Giridharadas' book *Winners Take All*: 46.

decisionmaking at all levels."[38] Or third, they are effectively using nondecisional power (agenda setting power) to ensure that Agenda 2030 will permit them to stifle any hints of rights-based internationalism or political power redistribution through the SDG process.

Through the MDG years, autocrats and civil society embraced an awkward power game. Autocrats permitted organized civic life, both domestic and international, if it did not threaten their key interests. Civic institutions mostly played by autocrats' rules, filling service delivery gaps, "empowering" marginalized communities, giving "voice" to civilians and "building capacity" of communities. This dance lasted as long as the autocrats allowed development institutions to fulfill their missions and development actors remembered their place—which was not to be too explicit about "redistributing," "democratizing," or "politicizing" power.

As civic institutions began to recognize this game for what it was, they began to be more assertive and explicit about the need for a real power shift, and by some accounts they were succeeding. In 1997, Jessica Mathews documented in her article "Power Shift" that nation states and corporations were losing power to international institutions and civic organizations,[39] and as late at 2013, Moises Naim argued in *The End of Power*[40] that corporations and states now face so much scrutiny and engagement that they have lost their old fashioned power over customers and citizens.

My own view is that, around 2007 the rise in democratic freedoms abruptly halted, and political rights and freedoms started to decline.[41] Around the same time (and not coincidently), more civic organizations realized they needed to stop putting Band-Aids on the symptoms of poverty and get more serious about addressing root causes, which took them into the terrain of redistributing power over.[42]

For many rights-based activists, the SDGs were meant to be the last chapter in a story that distributed power to citizens in economic and political forms through

---

38. See https://sustainabledevelopment.un.org/sdg16.

39. Jessica Mathews, "Power Shift," *Foreign Affairs* (January-February, 1997): 50–66.

40. In a brilliant but terribly titled book (he does not actually argue that power *ended* but that it was distributed away from traditional sources), Moses Naim, *The End of Power: From Boardrooms to Battlefields and Churches to States, Why Being in Charge Isn't What It Used To Be*, (New York, Basic Books, Perseus Books Group, 2014).

41. When Hungarian prime minister Viktor Orban celebrated the "illiberal state" a few years ago, he claimed he was responding only to the "great redistribution of global financial, economic, commercial, political and military power that became obvious in 2008." See www.kormany.hu/en/the-prime-minister/the-prime-minister-s-speeches/prime-minister-viktor-orban-s-speech-at-the-25th-balvanyos-summer-free-university-and-student-camp. Robert Kagan argues that liberal democrats never really understood this power shift to autocracy and away from ordinary people, and still have no idea how to fight it in a *Washington Post* article, March 2019.

42. Most embraced the SDGs because they married development outcomes with more clear-eyed commitments to address relative discrepancies of economic power (Goal 10), political power (Goal 16), and gender justice (Goal 5).

ever more transparent and accountable state and private institutions.[43] They were conceived and born during a seismic power shift from 2007 to 2015.[44] That period witnessed technology, new data and social media democratizing institutions, politics, business, and, ultimately, life for the better, but also saw power being captured in public and private spaces by data acquisitive corporations, a new class of extremely wealthy plutocrats, and political autocrats, nationalists, populists, and other anti-liberal democratic forces around the world.[45] As the conflict over political power redistribution became more overt in both developing countries and developed countries, it created an existential crisis for domestic civic life and their international supporters and partners.

If we accept that the SDG realization depends on powerful institutions (both private and public) being held accountable, then what must we do to defend those who are now on the front lines of a hostile battle field? The destiny of the SDGs may depend on those frontline defenders:[46] the individuals and activists like Okoth and Ngatia who directly confront powerful institutions and "big men." As a development community, too often we distance ourselves from their struggles as a battle for power "over" and beyond our remit.

It is not an easy choice to make. If we defend civic life in increasingly political conflicts, we may lose the space ourselves to work in authoritarian regimes. But if we do not, we may leave the most courageous and necessary advocates for the SDGs stranded without support and ultimately sell out the communities who need us most, just to seek our own survival. If our only understanding of power

---

43. Champions of the liberal internationalism at the heart of the SDGs have begun to doubt their own theory of change. They still believe people want more political and economic power, realized through accountable institutions and redistributive economies. But they now recognize that people may want other things even more than these liberal ideals. As Kagan argued in *The Strongmen Are Back,* (Washington Post March 2019) "Humans do not yearn only for freedom. They also seek security; not only physical security against attack but also the security that comes from family, tribe, race and culture. Often, people welcome a strong, charismatic leader who can provide that kind of protection." Similarly, Jonathan Haidt argued in *The Righteous Mind* that liberalism is losing ground because it only appeals to three triggers of political energy—compassion, fairness and inequality, and freedom from power abuse—and does not appreciate the more conservative values of sanctity, loyalty, and respect for authority.

44. Some saw this shift earlier than others. Jessica Mathews documented in "Power Shift" in 1997 that nation states and corporations were losing power to international institutions and civic organizations. See www.foreignaffairs.com/articles/1997-01-01/power-shift.

45. These two trends were well captured in Naim's *"The End of Power."* Naim looks at how corporations and states now face levels of scrutiny and engagement that essentially diminishes their old fashioned "power over" customers and citizens.

46. See www.frontlinedefenders.org, who note in their strategic plan that "SDG indicator 16.10 (protection of fundamental freedoms) offers the opportunity to generate stronger global empirical evidence to highlight the extreme abuses against human rights advocates, journalists, and others, such as killings and enforced disappearance." See www.frontlinedefenders.org/sites/default/files/2019-2022_strategic_plan.pdf, p. 9.

refuses to acknowledge the finite, relational, and choice-driven nature of redistributable power, we risk leaving behind those who are courageously confronting the powerful. Borrowing from the historical and military roots of "leave no one behind,"[47] I would argue that they should be first in our thoughts when it comes time to leave no one behind. If real commitment means the choices we make when options are inconvenient, then the test of our commitment to the SDGs lies in how we protect the frontline defenders of the SDGs when their political voice is threatened.

What does this mean in terms of specific ways forward? Surely it will mean putting backbone into SDG 16's commitment to "provide justice for all, and build effective, accountable and inclusive institutions at all levels." In a remarkable act of nondecisional power, the SDG 16 targets and indicators fail to offer any protection for those who openly challenge governments on their SDG 16 progress. Technically, a government can restrict debate on SDG accountability and inclusion and lock up anyone who challenges that power over and still meet every target and indicator in SDG 16. How did this happen? Because the SDGs fail to acknowledge that the redistribution of political power over government is essential to sustainable development.

Biting the Hand That Feeds Us

On Saturday, March 9, 2019, the day after International Women's Day, I found myself in Paris in the middle of a peaceful march by the Yellow Jackets. French police blocked their access to government buildings, but the march was peaceful and powerful, and women led the march. This gathering in the wealthiest part of Paris was no accident. They were there to protest an economic system that was leaving them behind. The signs called for decent jobs, fair wages, and better healthcare; they were fighting against unfair taxes on them and not enough taxes on the rich. It was a march about growing inequality.

Since 2015, from the Brexit voters to the Yellow Jackets to America's increasingly polarized supporters for Trump and Alexandra Ocasio-Cortez, the call is clear: ordinary people in wealthy nations question whether today's institutions are working for them. They do not want just resource redistribution. They are calling for power redistribution away from institutions that no longer serve their interests. Populist politicians, both progressive and right-wing, who understand

47. Homi Kharas, who first articulated the SDG phrase "leave no one behind," does not claim to have borrowed from military history, but in the United States at least, the term "leave no man behind" is well known as a military value, first formally captured in the Rangers Creed: "I will never leave a fallen comrade to fall into the hands of the enemy." See www.army.mil/values/ranger.html.

this currency are gaining traction by pointing to relational disparities. No technocratic solution that ignores the underlying concerns around power has captured these groups' imagination.

These dynamics are not happening just in rich nations. While extreme poverty continues to fall globally from 1.9 billion people in 1920 to 736 million in 2015, this is too slow a rate and trends are not going well for the poorest half of humanity, (3.8 billion people), who lost 11 percent of their wealth last year.[48]

Determining who has too much redistributable power over economic resources is potentially uncomfortable for Agenda 2030. Some think it is irrelevant:[49] Why is extreme wealth a problem if new forms of finance, charitable aid, and economic growth can lift people from poverty? If Bill Gates and George Soros give most of their wealth away, then surely they are not the reason people are being left behind, so do not focus on the wealthy—focus on the poor. The rising tide will lift all boats, no matter how opulent those boats are.

In 2011, Oxfam challenged that assumption. We researched not just the "facts" of growing inequality but the causal "relationship" between extreme wealth and poverty.[50] By asking each year at the annual Davos gathering how many of the world's richest people had the same wealth as the poorest half of the planet, Oxfam hit a nerve (in 2018, it was twenty-six billionaires).[51][52]

Oxfam's research and advocacy resonated, but not primarily because people are offended by wasteful opulence—although that helps us tell our story. It struck home because people recognized that money is power, and our world grows unhealthier when power over resources resides in fewer and fewer hands. As the number of billionaires doubled globally in the last ten years, power has become ever more concentrated. It is not just morally problematic that 1 percent of Jeff Bezos' wealth is more than the whole annual health budget for Ethiopia; it is actually dangerous for our world, because it skews the playing field for all the SDGs. The reason global wealth is taxed only at 4 percent and that average

48. See https://oxfamilibrary.openrepository.com/bitstream/handle/10546/620599/tb-public-good-or-private-wealth-methodology-note-210119-en.pdf?sequence=15&isAllowed=y.

49. See this exchange between the former CFO of Yahoo and Winnie Byanyima in Davos is a good representation of the debate: https://womensagenda.com.au/latest/watch-winnie-byanyima-take-down-a-former-yahoo-cfo-at-davos/. There are many who believe it does not serve the fight against poverty to focus on limiting the economic power of the super wealthy through more progressive taxation.

50. For a good thread on Oxfam's inequality work since 2013, with accompanying links, see https://twitter.com/BenGroCo/status/1088559078333444098.

51. See www.oxfamamerica.org/static/media/files/bp-public-good-or-private-wealth-210119-en.pdf.

52. This "superfact" and the research behind it has been Oxfam's most famous global moment each year for almost a decade now, and has, we like to think, helped to shift the terms of global debate on extreme inequality.

top income tax rates, globally, fell from 62 percent in 1970 to 38 percent in 2013 is not about popular support for trickle-down economics but because extreme wealth buys extreme power and political capture.[53] As U.S. Supreme Court Justice Louis Brandeis famously said, "We may have democracy, or we may have wealth concentrated in the hands of the few, but we cannot have both."[54]

One could argue that Goal 10 (the inequality goal) of the SDGs confronts the problem of inequality. But Goal 10 is weak, in large part because it does not engage inequality as a redistributable power problem and, instead, verges on redefining "the poor" as the "unequal poor." Consider Target 10.1: "Progressively achieve and sustain income growth of the bottom 40 percent of the population at a rate higher than the national average."

If redistributable power is finite, relational, and choice driven, then confronting inequality is not just about re-describing the poor as those on the wrong end of inequality. It must lead to us explicitly holding accountable those who have too much power and money, and on this front Goal 10 and the SDGs do not do well. Not once do they name the extreme wealthy, those who have too much economic power, or even refer to "taxes," the oldest and arguably best form of economic power redistribution.[55] As one UN paper observed:

> Leave No One Behind [LNOB] frames the inequality agenda as a problem of inclusion to be addressed by relief to the poor. As such it was a successful exercise of framing on the part of those who opposed the inequality agenda. As implementation gets underway, LNOB can be seen as a coup *against* equality.[56]

Perhaps this is because the SDGs themselves embody the major economic truth of their era: they rely too heavily on a neo-liberal growth driven model of capitalism that shuns zero-sum choice making and redistributive economics over a misplaced confidence that we can continue to smash through planetary boundaries indefinitely. New economic models increasingly interrogate that assumption by recognizing the finite truth of resource depletion,[57] and by unpacking the zero-sum power dynamics behind the SDGs.

53. See https://oxfamilibrary.openrepository.com/bitstream/handle/10546/311312/bp-working -for-few-political-capture-economic-inequality-200114-en.pdf;jsessionid=656587EF12BFA95 C45B70F2DA2CC91B2?sequence=19.

54. As quoted by Raymond Lonergan in *Mr. Justice Brandeis, Great American* (1941), p. 42.

55. For a cogent argument on the way to make our world better, "stop talking about philanthropy and start talking about "taxes" and how to stop tax avoidance." See Rutgar Bregman and Winnie Byanyima at Davos: www.youtube.com/watch?v=goFzOBk9-sY.

56. Sakiko Fukuda-Parr and Thea Smaavik Hegstad, "Leaving No One Behind' as a Site of Contestation and Reinterpretation," CDP Background Paper 47, ST/ESA/2018/CDP/47.

57. Kate Raworth, *Doughnut Economics* (2017) makes this case in a cogent and engaging way.

One feminist thinker, lamenting the failure of the SDGs to really tackle power, suggests this was not an accident:

> The SDGs/2030 Agenda] understands power as a given, not as social rela-
> tions at both the macro and micro level that "leverage specific actors, pol-
> icies and practices and ultimately privilege a particular rationality in the
> governance of social order" over others . . . Powerful actors shaping the
> course of world development—including big countries, inter-government
> institutions (particularly those dealing with trade and finances), transna-
> tional corporations, and even some huge foundations and international
> non-government organizations with budgets of billions of dollars—could
> not have failed to mould Agenda 2030, contributing to emphasize certain
> aspects and marginalize others.[58]

To engage this problem more robustly, development thinkers and anti-poverty movements are going to have to confront the elite individuals and institutions who have an outsized role in determining who gets left behind.

To put it more bluntly, we may have to take some of the attention we have been putting toward better understanding those being "left behind," and marshal our efforts to ask "being left behind by whom?" Recognizing their power over economic resources may help us know the hand that feeds us and ask whether, one day, we may have to bite it.

The Leaving and Those Left Behind:
Can a Feminist Journey Bring Us Back Together?

This chapter argues that the greatest threat to those being left behind is a grow-ing hostility toward power redistribution from economic elites and populists, authoritarians, nationalists, and extremists on gender, race, and religion. Those toxic protagonists are working from a zero-sum power lens and see little benefit in giving up their own economic or political power to citizens who can then hold them accountable. If the SDGs are going to help reverse the growing political and economic power of those who have too much, new tools are needed that allow us to name redistributable power where it increasingly sits and wrest it back into the hands of ordinary people.

The language and frames of feminism may be a powerful—perhaps the most powerful—lens for development thinkers and practitioners to help redistribute

---

58. Esquivel, "Power and the Sustainable Development Goals: A Feminist Analysis," p. 12.

power from those leaving to those being left behind. I come to this conclusion after being part of a difficult journey in the organization for which I work.[59]

Last year, the Oxfam Confederation found itself in a crisis of our own making. In February 2018, investigative journalists from British newspapers published that, seven years prior, Oxfam leadership in Haiti, there to help earthquake victims rebuild their lives, had hosted sex parties and engaged sex workers from local communities. Oxfam Great Britain had done an investigation at that time, fired some staff, and allowed others to resign. In the following years, while changing our safeguarding policies, Oxfam did not do enough to expose what had happened in Haiti in 2011. The press and public condemnation were unequivocal.[60]

Those events in Haiti not only hurt Haitians and Oxfam; they harmed all those organizations working in places like Haiti and claiming to fight for justice and rights. Humanitarians come into the worst of contexts with all the power that precious resources bring. In Haiti, some Oxfam staff abused that power.[61]

Perhaps it was inevitable that, after Haiti, Oxfam would seek a deeper understanding and more honesty around how power works to impact the most vulnerable. In recommitting to embrace feminist principles in everything we do, both inside and outside the organization, we are seeking to become the change we want to see in the world in terms of holding the powerful accountable.[62]

The embrace of feminist principles[63] has helped us examine the currency of power more deeply, and revealed some fascinating pathways forward that should help make Oxfam stronger as an organization and provide crucial insights toward

59. I would like to think my feminist journey has been underway most of my professional life. I got my professional start working on domestic violence in Nairobi's slums in the 1990s and continue on that journey. Today, I am proud to work in an organization alongside and for strong feminist leaders from whom I am still learning every day.

60. The Haiti scandal was covered on the front pages of major British newspapers for thirteen consecutive days. A few stories of Oxfam staff misconduct from other contexts fueled concerns that the crisis was not a once-off.

61. Since then, Oxfam has taken significant steps to atone for what happened in Haiti and to rebuild the trust of communities, staff, donors, and partners. We formed an independent commission and committed to root out every instance of past sexual harassment abuse, assault, and misconduct and hold the perpetrators accountable. We developed safeguarding principles and protocols that every Oxfam office and staff member must adhere to, and are committed across the confederation to embracing feminist principles in everything we do.

62. Oxfam has been committed to gender justice work and feminism for decades. Since 1993, Oxfam has published the only journal focused on gender and development. See www.genderanddevelopment.org/.

63. Oxfam has worked from feminist principles for a long time. We are currently looking to publish an updated set, which will be public by the time this chapter is published. If you cannot find them online, please feel free to reach out to me for a copy. Among the likely final set of principles are (1) the personal is political, (2) nothing about us without us, (3) intersectionality, (4) men are welcomed, (5) feminism is a worldwide movement, (6) power sharing, (7) safety, (8) we care—to address unpaid care work, (9) collective care and self-care, and (10) there is no economic, social and environmental justice without gender justice.

how working on the SDGs can help redistribute power from those leaving people behind to those who are left behind.

First, feminism gives us a useful language for analyzing power in both its meanings—as ability (the power with, within, and to) and as a relationship (when one person or institution has power over another). Feminist thinkers, for example, helped us understand women's economic empowerment as generative,[64] heterogenous,[65] non-binary, and creative,[66] not zero sum.[67] By challenging power-over and zero-sum power[68] as the only way to think about power, they opened up our thinking to challenge power other than that used by dominant patriarchy and oppressive institutions.

At the same time, other feminist thinkers, particularly in the fields of economics,[69] democracy,[70] gender justice,[71] and reproductive rights[72] have deepened

64. Hannah Arendt, *The Human Condition* (Chicago University Press, 1958) saw power as "the human ability not just to act but to act in concert," p. 44.

65. More than thirty years ago, southern feminists like Chandra Mohanty and black feminists like bell hooks argued that too much feminist thinking addressed "the issues that divide women." bell hooks, *Feminist Theory from Margin to Center* (Boston: South End Press, 1984).

66. In a seminal piece in 1984, (the year of Foucault's death), Chandra Mohanty in "*Under Western Eyes: Feminist Scholarship and Colonial Discourses*," argued that Western feminists were too comfortable with a binary frame that sees only a "source of power and a cumulative reaction to power," usually with men as power holders and women as powerless. She went further in challenging this kind of humanist hegemony by exposing arguments that tend to homogenize southern women as "oppressed," leaving Western feminists as the "subjects" of this counter-history. *boundary 2*, 12, no. 3, *On Humanism and the University I: The Discourse of Humanism* (Spring-Autumn 1984): 333–58.

67. I concede this with trepidation. The development sector is too quick to coopt terms that legitimate our engagement with power without actually tackling it. As one feminist thinker has argued: "Although genuine empowerment always involves changing unequal power relations, donors and investors tend to favour an apolitical use of the term, in which power relations may actually remain wholly or virtually untouched. When used in this way, the notion of empowerment 'risks becoming a signifier of righteousness – part of the process of mystification of dominant group interests.' In other words, it becomes 'empowerment without power'." Esquivel, "Power and the Sustainable Development Goals: A Feminist Analysis," p. 14.

68. See Just Associates, "Making Change Happen," https://justassociates.org/sites/justassociates.org/files/mch3_2011_final.pdf.

69. For example, Benaria and Sen, Class and Gender Inequalities and Women's Role in Economic Development—Theoretical and Practical Implications, *Feminist Studies* 8, no 1 (Spring 1982): 157–76.

70. Jane Mansbridge, Feminism and Democracy, *The American Prospect* (Spring 1990).

71. For example, in *Justice, Gender, and the Family*, Susan Moller Okin argues that the contemporary gender-structured family unjustly distributes the benefits and burdens of familial life among husbands and wives. "Here, Okin seems to presuppose that power is a resource that is unequally and unjustly distributed between men and women; hence, one of the goals of feminism would be to redistribute this resource in more equitable ways." https://plato.stanford.edu/entries/feminist-power/#DefPow

72. For an interesting study of how a woman's legal power over her reproductive rights and body can lead to measurable increases in other forms of political and economic power, see Roger Clark, 2006, "Three Faces of Women's Power and their Reproductive Health: A Cross National Study," *International Review of Modern Sociology* 32, no. 1 (2006): 35–52, www.jstor.org/stable/41421224.

our understanding of power as a zero-sum relationship—when should the state have power over our bodies or our gender identity? Today, feminist voices are once again pushing new power debates, essentially asking whether it is time for a more radical discussion around power distribution that translates empowerment as ability into redistributed power over institutions, laws, bodies, and lives.

In *Good and Mad: The Revolutionary Power of Women's Anger,* written in the aftermath of the Trump election, Rebecca Traister is unapologetic that women's anger is going to be essential to take back power from institutions and individuals whose sexist, racist, and misogynist efforts to hold on to power cannot be diminished without confronting it head on and taking it away. A feminist approach can take us beyond the false choice between these two understandings of power and make us more fluent in moving between them, according to the opportunity and challenge.[73]

Second, feminism helps us unpack intersectionality—the interlocking systems of power that impact those left behind in terms of gender, race, economic class, sexual orientation, disability, religion, and age. When Kimberlé Crenshaw coined the term *intersectionality* thirty years ago,[74] she was focused on a U.S. court system that was too quick to view women and people of color as facing mutually exclusive harms and too slow to realize that black women, particularly, faced unique challenges that the law needed to acknowledge. Her analyses, and that by the feminist leaders who took up intersectionality, have changed social activism not just for gender and race politics but for other intersectional realities as well. Over time, the SDGs will benefit greatly from deeper intersectional approaches, not only to better understand groups that sit at the nexus of vulnerabilities because they face multiple forms of power marginalization but also to recognize which groups sit at the nexus of power over, with all the accountability that position demands.

Third, feminism asks us to consider how power works in the most private and intimate relationships and spaces. Because it sees the body and sexuality as sites of power, it demands that deeply personal transformation and social transformation go hand-in-hand. To recognize that the "personal is political" is not just a slogan. A feminist lens on the SDGs demands that we show up in a very different way, not just in terms of our analysis of who is left behind and why but also in our personal engagement to support power redistribution from those

See also www.genderhealth.org for U.S. civil society efforts to protect women's power over their sexual health and reproductive rights around the world.

73. For a useful overview of development debates by feminists, see Hartwick's "Feminist Theories of Development," in Richard Peet and Elaine Hartwick, *Theories of Development: Contentions, Arguments Alternatives*, 3rd ed. (Guildford Press, 2015).

74. See https://chicagounbound.uchicago.edu/cgi/viewcontent.cgi?referer=&httpsredir=1&article=1052&context=uclf.

who have too much to those who do not have enough power. To recognize that as a white, Northern, middle class, heterosexual, Christian male I start from a different place vis-à-vis the vast majority of intended beneficiaries, allies, and social justice peers is not self-flagellation or some form of post-patriarchy stress disorder. It is simply to recognize that the legacies that accompany my identity inform (but, hopefully, do not dictate) my relevance to power redistribution in a fast-changing world.

Perhaps because they've been thinking harder about intersectionality than most, feminist thinkers have, in my opinion, done more in the last thirty years to advance a discussion around using power differently to achieve solidarity across class, race, geography, religion, and gender to redistribute power from the haves to the have nots. Sixteen years after publishing *Under Western Eyes,* which challenged white Northern feminists to be more thoughtful in speaking for all women, Chandra Mohanty argued in 2003 that it was time for "feminist solidarity" to work together take power back from neo-liberal capitalists. She now views feminism as far more better balanced with women from "two thirds" of the world working together with one-third feminists to decolonize discussions of power and work in solidarity to rescue our planet from the direction in which it is heading.[75] Similarly, Hartwick, after surveying feminist leadership in development over the last few decades, concludes that a truly globally balanced feminism needs to overcome its "failure of nerve" to step up and "speak on behalf of poor women everywhere." Drawing from her own socialist leanings, Elaine Hartwick calls for feminists to lead a more "transformative politics" that challenges systems of economic and political power in the world.[76] I believe they will.

I've come to believe that becoming a feminist is like committing to redistributing power. For me, there are journeys, not destinations, both personal and in the world. There will never be a point where I or, for that matter, Oxfam or any development professional or organization will be free of the risk of power abuse in our organizations or in the communities where we work. What I want to strive for is humility, vigilance, honesty, and the energy to keep redistributing power in the right direction. When Oxfam called for an independent inquiry following the Haiti crisis, and that inquiry found power abuse to be a pattern in some offices, I was proud that we embraced the commission's challenge and recommitted to the journey. I am proud that we are also asking other organizations to join us on the journey to make safer our workplaces and the communities where we have the privilege to work.

75. Chandra Mohanty, "Under Western Eyes Revisited: Feminist Solidarity through Anticapitalist Struggles," in *Feminism Without Borders: Decolonizing Theory, Practicing Solidarity* (Duke University Press, 2003).

76. Peet and Hartwick, *Theories of Development,* p. 305.

In the same way, I believe that if the SDGs are to be realized, each of us must champion the redistribution of power as a journey and look to Agenda 2030 as simply a milestone along the way.

Concluding Thoughts

I started this chapter frustrated that too much SDG attention was going toward those being left behind, as if fixing their behavior and capacity was the new development challenge. I wanted the reader to ask the question: Who is pushing them behind? To answer that question, I needed to interrogate power and how it really works. But then as I went back to the philosophical and feminist roots of power analysis, I came up against a paradox. By seeking to name those who have too much power (either political or economic) as the villains of development, I risked making the story all about them and trotting out a very stale development story that puts hegemonic masculinity and old style power over at the center of the discussion (just when postmodernist social justice thinking was condemning the old, dominant narratives to a more suitable place on the periphery of development thinking).

My way to unravel that paradox was to explore the different ways feminists have talked about power. The contribution I hope this chapter makes is to go back to the question that Jo Rowlands asked more than twenty years ago: "Should a loss of power be something to fear?"

I do not believe so if people like Beatrice Okoth and Rose Ngatia can translate power with, within, and to into relational power over resources and politics. In other words, the world will be a much better place and the SDGs will have a chance of succeeding only when relational power is redistributed away from those who have too much and into the hands of those who do not have enough.

This will mean redistributing political power from the unaccountable to citizens and activists. Whether the SDGs themselves (hamstrung by the dubious ideological agnosticism of the United Nations) proclaim a political philosophy or not, the very act of asking states to publicly declare and document progress against coherent transnationally relevant long-term development goals for public accountability is profoundly political. It threatens the short-term transactional mindset of the current U.S. administration and the secretive pathologies of authoritarian states like Russia, Hungary, and China. It asks citizens and civic institutions all around the world to pay attention, to hold powerful institutions accountable, and, in so doing, to redistribute power to themselves, even in the face of increasing threats.

My hope is that some of those reading this chapter not only agree that the redistribution of political power is essential to the SDGs success but become more motivated to protect the bravest fighters in this political battlefield: those frontline defenders who risk their lives to hold governments and powerful corporations accountable. Above all, we must not leave them behind.

We also need a different economic conversation about inequality than the SDGs have offered us so far. To date, the United Nations and those participating in formulating the goals have used nondecisional (agenda setting) power to ensure the SDGs do not threaten those who have too much economic power. The most basic form of redistributing power over resources—progressive taxation—does not get a mention. Nor is there a body to which citizens can turn to seek redress for corporate tax avoidance, regressive public fiscal policies, or threats to our global fiscal system like the 7+ trillion dollars in wealth that sits in tax havens doing nothing for anyone. We need the UN to be a different kind of protagonist that is more explicit about redistributing economic power.

Finally, we need to get beyond the false choices in power debates between generative and zero-sum power. Both have their place in development practice and strategy. Feminism has given us a powerful language for generative power—the powers with, within, and to—and has helped us better understand the dangers of ignoring zero sum power when it is used as power over, either by others or by ourselves, as Oxfam did in Haiti.

In the end of the day, Oxfam's main task, and perhaps the task of other organizations too, is to stop fearing the loss of zero-sum power, to think more about helping those left behind take actual power over their futures and away from those who have too much, and finally, to embrace a journey where others have ever more control over their own destiny, identity, and future, as we challenge others to take that journey with us.

References

Arendt, Hannah. 1958. *The Human Condition*. University of Chicago Press: 44.

Benaria, Lourdes, and Gita Sen. 1982. "Class and Gender Inequalities and Women's Role in Economic Development—Theoretical and Practical Implications," *Feminist Studies* 8, no. 1: 157–76.

Bishop, Matthew, and Michael Green. 2008. *Philanthrocapitalism: How the Rich Can Save the World*. New York: Bloomsbury Press.

Boal, Augusto. 1985. *Theatre of the Oppressed*. Theatre Communications Group.

Clark, Roger. 2006. "Three Faces of Women's Power and Their Reproductive Health: A Cross National Study." *International Review of Modern Sociology* 32, no. 1: 35–52.

Connell, R. W., and James W. Messerschmidt. 2005. "Hegemonic Masculinity: Rethinking the Concept." *Gender & Society* 19(6), 829–859.

Crenshaw, Kimberlé. 1989. "Demarginalizing the Intersection of Race and Sex: A Black Feminist Critique of Antidiscrimination Doctrine, Feminist Theory and Antiracist Politics." *University of Chicago Legal Forum* 1, no. 8: 139–67.

Esquivel, Valeria. 2016. "Power and the Sustainable Development Goals: A Feminist Analysis." *Gender and Development* 24, no. 1: *9–23*.

Freire, Paulo, 1970. *Pedagogy of the Oppressed*. (30th Anniversary Ed. 2000) New York: Bloomsbury.

Foucault, Michel. 1983. "Afterward: The Subject and Power." In Hubert Dreyfus and Paul Rabinow, *Michel Foucault: Beyond Structuralism and Hermeneutics*, 2nd ed. University of Chicago Press.

Fukada-Parr, Sakiko, and Thea Smaavik Hegstad. 2018. "'Leaving No One Behind' as a Site of Contestation and Reinterpretation." CDP Background Paper 47.

Gaventa, John. 1980. "Power and Powerlessness: Quiescence and Rebellion in an Appalachian Valley." American Political Science Association.

Giridharadas, Anand. 2018 *Winners Take All: The Elite Charade of Changing the World*. New York: Penguin Random House, Alfred A. Knopf.

Green, Duncan. 2008 *From Poverty to Power: How Active Citizens and Effective States Can Change the World*. Oxfam International.

———. 2016. *How Change Happens*. Oxford University Press.

Haidt, Jonathon. 2012. *The Righteous Mind: Why Good People are Divided by Politics and Religion*. New York: Pantheon Books.

Hartsock, Nancy. 1983. *Money, Sex and Power: Towards a Feminist Historical Materialism*. Northeastern University Press: 244.

Heimans, Jeremy, and Henry Timms. 2018. *New Power: How Power Works in Our Hyperconnected World – And How to Make It Work for You*. New York: Penguin Random House.

hooks, bell. *1984. Feminist Theory from Margin to Center*. Boston: South End Press.

Kagan, Robert. 2019. "The Strongmen are Back." Democracy and Disorder. The Brookings Institution.

Kripke, Gawain. 2015. "Is Power a Zero Sum Game? Does Women's Empowerment Lead to Increased Domestic Violence?" Oxfam. https://oxfamblogs.org/fp2p/is-power-a-zero-sum-game-does-womens-empowerment-lead-to-increased-domestic-violence/.

Lukes, Stephen, 2005. *Power, A Radical View,* Red Globe Press (2nd. Edition).

Mansbridge, Jane. 1990. "Feminism and Democracy." *The American Prospect*. https://prospect.org/article/feminism-and-democracy.

Mathews, Jessica T. 1997. "Power Shift." *Foreign Affairs*. https://www.foreignaffairs.com/articles/1997-01-01/power-shift.

Mohanty, Chandra. 1984. "Under Western Eyes: Feminist Scholarship and Colonial Discourses." *On Humanism and the University I: The Discourse of Humanism* 12, no. 3: 333–58.

———. 2003. "Under Western Eyes Revisited: Feminist Solidarity through Anticapitalist Struggles," in *Feminism Without Borders: Decolonizing Theory, Practicing Solidarity* (Duke University Press).

Moller Okin, Susan. 1989. *Justice, Gender, and the Family*. United States: Basic Books, Inc.

Morriss, Peter. 1987. *Power: A Philosophical Analysis*. Manchester University Press.

Naím, Moisés. 2014. *The End of Power: From Boardrooms to Battlefields and Churches to States, Why Being in Charge Isn't What It Used to Be*. New York: Basic Books, Perseus Books Group.

Oxfam. 2014. "Working for the Few: Political Capture and Economic Inequality." https://oxfamilibrary.openrepository.com/bitstream/handle/10546/311312/ bp-working-for-few-political-capture-economic-inequality-200114-en. pdf;jsessionid=656587EF12BFA95C45B70F2DA2CC91B2?sequence=19.

———. 2019. "Public Good or Private Wealth?" (https://www.oxfamamerica.org/static/ media/files/bp-public-good-or-private-wealth-210119-en.pdf).

Peet, Richard, and Elaine Hartwick. 2015. *Theories of Development* (3rd edition). New York City: Guilford Press.

Raworth, Kate (2017) *Doughnut Economics: Seven Ways to Think Like a 21*st *Century Economist*. Chelsea Green Publishing.

Rowlands, Jo. 1995. "Empowerment Examined." *Development in Practice* 5, no. 2: 101–07.

———. 1997. "Questioning Empowerment, Working with Women in Honduras." UK and Ireland: Oxfam.

VeneKlasen, Lisa, and Valerie Miller. 2007. *A New Weave of People, Power and Politics*. United States: Stylus Publishing.

Wineman, Steven. 2003. *Power-Under: Trauma and Nonviolent Social Change*. http:// www.traumaandnonviolence.com/

Contributors

DANY BAHAR is a David M. Rubenstein fellow in the Global Economy and Development program at the Brookings Institution.

GERALD BLOOM is a physician and health economist at the Institute of Development Studies.

LINDSAY COATES is managing director of the Ultra Poor Graduation Initiative for BRAC.

JENNIFER COHEN is a project coordinator and assistant to the research vice president and director in the Global Economy and Development program at the Brookings Institution.

CAROLINE CONROY is a senior research analyst in the Global Economy and Development program at the Brookings Institution.

RAJ M. DESAI is a nonresident senior fellow in the Global Economy and Development program at the Brookings Institution, and associate professor of international development in the Edmund A. Walsh School of Foreign Service at Georgetown University.

MEAGAN DOOLEY is a research analyst in the Global Economy and Development program at the Brookings Institution.

JON JELLEMA is deputy director for the Commitment to Equity Institute (CEQ) Project at the Global Development Network (GDN).

YASUSHI KATSUMA is a professor at Waseda University's Graduate School of Asia-Pacific Studies and a director of global health affairs and governance at the Institute for Global Health Policy Research in Japan's National Center for Global Health and Medicine.

HOMI KHARAS is interim vice president and director of the Global Economy and Development program at the Brookings Institution.

GABRIEL M. LEUNG is dean of medicine and Zimmern Professor in Population Health at the University of Hong Kong.

NORA LUSTIG is Samuel Z. Stone Professor of Latin American Economics and director of the Commitment to Equity Institute (CEQ) at Tulane University. She is also a nonresident senior fellow at the Center for Global Development, the Inter-American Dialogue, and the Brookings Institution.

SCOTT MACMILLAN is a senior advisor for learning and innovation for BRAC USA.

SAEDA MAKIMOTO is executive senior research fellow at the Japan International Cooperation Agency Research Institute.

VALENTINA MARTINEZ PABON is a Ph.D. student in the Department of Economics at Tulane University.

HILARY MATHEWS is senior director of Gender Justice at CARE USA.

JOHN W. MCARTHUR is a senior fellow in the Global Economy and Development program at the Brookings Institution and senior advisor on sustainable development to the United Nations Foundation.

ENERELT MURAKAMI is a research fellow at the Japan International Cooperation Agency Research Institute.

AKIRA MURATA is a visiting fellow at the Japan International Cooperation Agency Research Institute and a lecturer at Chiba Keizai University.

JANE NELSON is director of the Corporate Responsibility Initiative at Harvard Kennedy School, and a nonresident senior fellow in the Global Economy and Development program at the Brookings Institution.

MICHELLE NUNN is president and CEO of CARE USA.

PAUL O'BRIEN is vice president for policy and advocacy at Oxfam America.

IZUMI OHNO is director of Japan International Cooperation Agency Research Institute.

MICHAEL A. PETERS is a research associate at the Johns Hopkins Bloomberg School of Public Health and a consultant at the Asian Development Bank.

TONY PIPA is a senior fellow in the Global Economy and Development program at the Brookings Institution.

KRISHNA D. RAO is an associate professor at the Johns Hopkins Bloomberg School of Public Health.

LANDRY SIGNÉ is a David M. Rubenstein fellow in the Global Economy and Development program at the Brookings Institution.

ERICA PAULA SIOSON is a research associate at the Asian Development Bank Institute.

REBECCA WINTHROP is a senior fellow and director of the Center for Universal Education at the Brookings Institution.

EIJI YAMADA is a research fellow at the Japan International Cooperation Agency Research Institute.

LAUREN ZIEGLER is a project director in the Center for Universal Education at the Brookings Institution.

Index

Page locators in italics refer to boxes, figures, and tables.

327